The
PLA Reader
for
Public Library
Directors
and
Managers

Edited by
Kathleen M. Hughes
for the
Public Library Association

Neal-Schuman Publishers, Inc.
New York   London

Published by Neal-Schuman Publishers, Inc.
100 William St., Suite 2004
New York, NY 10038

Printed and bound in the United States of America.

The paper used in this publication meets the minimum requirements of American National Standard for Information Sciences—Permanence of Paper for Printed Library Materials, ANSI Z39.48-1992.

Library of Congress Cataloging-in-Publication Data
The PLA reader for public library directors and managers / edited by Kathleen M. Hughes for the Public Library Association.
    p. cm.
  Includes bibliographical references and index.
  ISBN 978-1-55570-684-5 (alk. paper)
  1. Public libraries—United States—Administration. I. Hughes, Kathleen M. II. Public Library Association.

Z678.P55 2009
025.1'974—dc22

                                                                    2009019823

Contents

Introduction

Welcome to the *Public Library Association (PLA) Reader for Public Library Directors and Managers*, the first in a new series that is designed specifically for busy public library professionals. PLA staff and PLA committee members worked together to choose these key articles, culled from the pages of *Public Libraries* and from chapters of bestselling PLA books. For the original sources of the selections, please refer to the References list at the end of the book.

In an era of ever-encroaching budget cuts, many library directors and managers find themselves stretched increasingly thin. From working with a board of directors to making library policy recommendations, overseeing strategic plans, preparing budgets, supervising personnel, evaluating services, administering facility maintenance, overseeing materials selection, and more, it is tough for directors and managers to find time to read professional materials. In light of the often frantic pace that library managers and directors must keep in order to simply do their job, the book was designed specifically for those with a minimum of time. The collected writings in this book aim to provide accessible insight into some of the library world's most important and complex topics.

Each chapter tackles one of the prevalent topics faced by today's public libraries. They address issues such as advocacy basics, tips for retaining and motivating high-performing employees, learning more about library communications, a discussion of intellectual freedom matters, the latest topics in reference, and brief entries on technology. Each brief treatment of these important library subjects will provide knowledge crucial to becoming an outstanding library leader. By offering practical and applicable solutions to these problems, *The PLA Reader for Public Library Directors and Managers* aims to provide the best information to help public library managers and directors more effectively and successfully lead their libraries.

Carol Sheffer
PLA President, 2008–2009

Part I

The Public Library Landscape

At times the issues facing a library director seem overwhelming and ever-changing. This chapter offers clear-sighted accounts of the chief issues that dot the public library landscape. These selections not only unravel the often complex nature of these problems, but also offer ways savvy library directors can navigate them.

PLA Executive Director Greta Southard outlines the history of public library standards and explains PLA's current stand on the issue in "Public Library Standards and PLA Planning Models." Many library directors are already familiar with The Public Library Data Service, which has provided invaluable statistical information about public library trends for twenty years. "Characteristics and Trends of Public Libraries in Public Library Data Service" provides a thorough analysis of the data compiled in the 2007 Public Library Data Service, focusing on finances, library resources, annual use figures, and technology. "No Easy Targets" examines how six public libraries are coping with the economic recession, shrinking budgets, and increasing usage. Finally, the author of "Forming and Funding Public Library Foundations" lays out the steps necessary to establish a foundation for your library and also provides fundraising tips for once it is up and running.

Chapter 1

Public Library Standards and PLA Planning Models

Greta Southard

In 1962 the Public Library Association (PLA), a division of the American Library Association, published a document entitled "Interim Standards for Small Public Libraries: Guidelines Toward Achieving the Goals of Public Library Service." The "Interim Standards" were updated in 1966 in "Minimum Standards for Public Library Systems." Neither of these documents has been formally withdrawn; however, PLA began to move away from the promulgation of library standards, after the PLA Standards Committee, in 1971, decided "Minimum Standards for Public Library Systems" did not meet the needs of modern libraries.

In 1977 the U.S. Department of Education, Office of Education funded the study "The Process of Standards Development for Community Library Service." That study, which led to the development of the book, "A Planning Process for Public Libraries," was based on two assumptions:

1. The proper arena for planning and evaluating public library services is the library's own community. Since public libraries serve very diverse communities and are primarily funded by local taxes, it is appropriate that they be diverse institutions, planned by local people to meet local needs;
2. The appropriate role for the Public Library Association is to support the development of tools for public library planning and evaluation, and to make these tools readily available to library boards, administrators, and staff.

To that end, PLA has published a series of books "The PLA Results Series," which trace the development, and evolution of library planning, the most recent being, "Implementing for Results" released in 2009 and authored by Sandra Nelson for the Public Library Association. There are a number of titles in this series that are useful to library planners and managers.

Another tool in the planning portfolio is "Managing for Results: Effective Resource Allocation for Public Libraries," published in 2000. Library planners are encouraged to use community norms and to assess local conditions and needs to ensure that libraries have the tools and resources they need to provide outstanding library service.

PLA does produce an annual statistical report, "Public Library Data Service Statistical Report," which many librarians use as a benchmarking tool to look at their library as compared to other libraries with similar size of service population.

About the Author

Greta Southard is Executive Director, Public Library Association, a division of the American Library Association, Chicago, Illinois.

Characteristics and Trends of Public Libraries in the Public Library Data Service Statistical Report

Mijung Yoon and Lauren Teffeau

The Public Library Data Service (PLDS) Statistical Report, a project of the PLA, is designed to meet the needs of public library administrators and others for timely and effective library–specific data that illuminates and supports a wide variety of management decisions. The PLDS has been providing such data to the library community since 1988. PLDS is an annual survey conducted on behalf of the Public Library Association where more than 800 public libraries in the United States and Canada provide information on finances, library resources, annual use figures, and technology. An additional section asks questions on rotating topics; in 2007, the section focused on young adult library services. The information generated by PLDS is designed to meet the needs of public library administrators and others who need to make a variety of administrative decisions.

In this chapter, we provide an overview of public libraries with respect to the population of legal service area, library expenditures, and longitudinal trends. Specifically, this chapter presents: (1) the profile of public libraries that participated in PLDS 2007, (2) the influence of population size on financial and output measures, (3) outputs per expenditure and their association with other library characteristics, and (4) six-year trends for per capita statistics and other relevant measures.

Profile of Public Libraries in PLDS 2007
In 2007, 904 of 1,672 libraries responded to an invitation to participate in the survey, a response rate of 54%. The libraries ranged in size, from serving 404 to 3,976,071 people in their legal service areas. Figure 2-1 presents the distribution of participating libraries by population of legal service area.

Overall Service
In 2007, PLDS libraries served 177,284,576 patrons in the United States and Canada. When considering the U.S. alone, PLDS libraries served 55% of

5

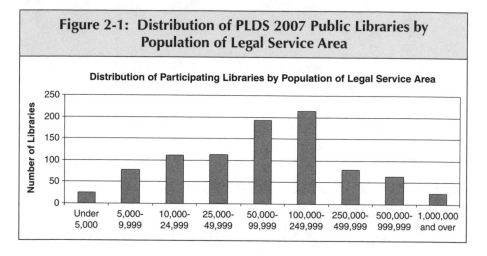

Figure 2-1: Distribution of PLDS 2007 Public Libraries by Population of Legal Service Area

Americans based on Census Bureau estimates.[1] PLDS libraries fielded a combined total of 207,413,965 reference transactions (n = 831). In 2007, PLDS libraries also provided programs to 41,366,421 total patrons (n = 868) and circulated 1,352,125,212 items (n = 882). PLDS libraries in the U.S. alone circulated 1,222,017,695 items (n = 861), that is 8.2 library items circulated per citizen in a PLDS 2007 library in legal service area and 4.5 library items per citizen in the entire U.S.[2] Table 2-1 provides a statistical summary of the characteristics of PLDS libraries for 2007.

Technology

Technology is increasingly becoming a major component of public libraries' services as demands for and availability of information technology increase. The PLDS 2007 included an undated technology section to reflect the rapidly changing technology use in public libraries.[3]

The majority of PLDS libraries reported the following features available through their library Web sites: OPAC (93%), online database (84%), personalized patron account (72%), and online reference services (71%). Regarding the content of their Web sites, 97% of libraries have a section for the library information, 94% have a calendar of events, 81% provide community links, 77% offer children and young adult pages, 66% have staff-created pages, and 64% acknowledge library friends.

Libraries are increasingly recognizing the importance of expanding technology service provision. Accordingly, 79% of libraries surveyed offer Wi-Fi inside their libraries, 40% provide access to locally produced digitized collections, and 69% used Internet filters on library computers. The libraries also reported on modes of virtual reference services. The majority of libraries (58%) offer reference via e-mail (58%), followed by online chat (30%) and instant message (17%). Details of the technology services are presented in Table 2-2.[4]

Table 2-1: Descriptive Statistics of Participating PLDS 2007 Public Libraries

	Number of Reporting Libraries	Minimum	Maximum	Total	Mean	Std. Deviation
Circulation	882	3,099	30,412,490	1,352,125,212	1,533,022	2,856,619
In-library Use of Materials	336	116	8,267,605	161,866,601	481,746	1,023,688
Population of Legal Service Area	904	404	3,976,071	177,284,576	196,111	367,822
Legal Service Area	766	1	4,162,612	4,954,370	6,468	150,505
Reference Transactions	831	33	9,904,137	207,413,965	249,596	664,508
Library Visits	823	35	17,117,800	778,636,471	946,095	1,682,366
Interlibrary Loan to Other Libraries	818	1	659,808	13,110,564	16,028	46,738
Interlibrary Loan from Other Libraries	872	5	789,640	12,432,505	14,257	46,624
Program Attendance	868	30	1,299,802	41,366,421	47,657	91,988
Holdings	887	7,500	15,686,902	479,606,496	540,706	1,070,389
Bookmobiles	264	1	10	386	1.462121	1.01
Total Public Service Hours per Month	890	10	5,230	271,580	305	509

Table 2-2: Frequency of the Libraries with Selected Technology Features

	Number of Libraries	Percent Libraries
Library with a library Web site	878	97.1
Web site features		
OPAC/on-line catalogue	843	93.3
On-line reference services	645	71.3
Library purchased on-line database	759	84.0
Personalized patron account	651	72.0
Web site content		
Basic library information (hours, etc.)	877	97.0
Programming information/events calendar	845	93.5
Children/young adult pages	694	76.8
Community links	736	81.4
Library friends' page(s)	576	63.7
Library staff created content (booklists, etc.)	596	65.9
Wireless Internet access	711	78.7
Access to locally produced digitized collections	365	40.4
Virtual reference services		
E-mail/Web form	521	57.6
Chat	267	29.5
Instant messaging	154	17.0
Computers with filtered Internet access	626	69.2
Total Number of Libraries	904	100

Young Adult Services

Few attempts have succeeded in capturing young adult library data at the national level,[5] except the survey on young adult services in public libraries by the National Center for Education Statistics (NCES) in 1994 and the similar survey with the 50 largest public libraries conducted by the Young Adult Library Services Association (YALSA) in 1998. The 2007 PLDS provides valuable information on the young adult services in North America.

The number of visits by young adults in 2007 varied from 35 to 3,500,000 visits across 194 reporting libraries, with an average of 43,112 young adult visits for each library. The number of young adult materials circulated, according to 478 reporting libraries, was 82,079 on average. The details are presented in Table 2-3.[6]

Selected Library Services by Population

The population by legal service area of individual libraries influenced the following financial and output per capita measures and other relevant output measures: library visits per capita, circulation per capita, holdings per capita, income per capita, expenditure per capita, in-library use of materials per capita, registrations per capita, and collection turnover.[7] The population group of the library did not influence program attendance per capita, circulation per borrower, or reference transactions per capita. The relationships between the population group and the financial and output measures did not show a systematic pattern.

Library visits per capita was highest (7.4 visits) for the group of libraries with populations between 5,000–9,999 and lowest (3.8 visits) for the libraries with service populations of 1,000,000 and over (Figure 2-2).

Circulation per capita and holdings per capita were highest (10.8 circulated materials and 9.3 holdings) for populations under 5,000 and lowest (5.6 circulated materials and 2.1 holdings) for populations of 1,000,000 and over (Figure 2-3).

The patterns by population of legal service area, however, differed between circulation per capita and holdings per capita. Holdings per capita

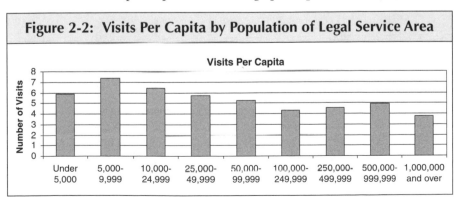

Figure 2-2: Visits Per Capita by Population of Legal Service Area

Visits Per Capita

Number of Visits

| Under 5,000 | 5,000- 9,999 | 10,000- 24,999 | 25,000- 49,999 | 50,000- 99,999 | 100,000- 249,999 | 250,000- 499,999 | 500,000- 999,999 | 1,000,000 and over |

Table 2-3: Descriptive Statistics of Young Adult Services

	Number of Libraries	Minimum	Maximum	Total	Average	Standard Deviation
Number of Young Adult Visits	194	35	3,500,000	8,363,717	43,112	260,652
Young Adult Circulation	478	135	1,496,071	39,233,847	82,079	156,248
Expenditures on Young Adult Materials Current Year	388	143	1,610,615	21,319,447	54,947	130,039
Expenditures on Young Adult Materials Past Year	384	0	1,402,572	22,296,187	58,063	149,274
Number of Young Adult Volunteers	609	0	2,488	53,741	88	224
Number of Programs for Young Adults	626	0	10,453	102,193	163	637
Number of Young Adult Program Attendance	588	0	415,245	2,130,035	3,623	18,831
FTE Young Adult Service Librarians	681	0	934	2,537	3.73	36
FTE Young Adult Service paraprofessionals	602	0	106	958	1.59	6

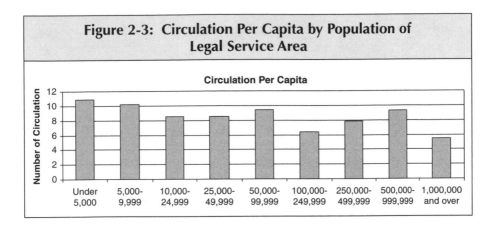

Figure 2-3: Circulation Per Capita by Population of Legal Service Area

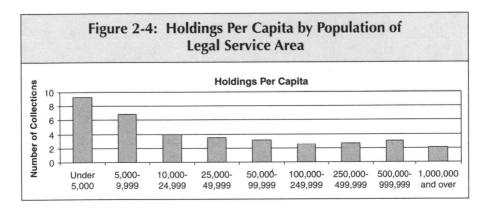

Figure 2-4: Holdings Per Capita by Population of Legal Service Area

decreased substantially as the population group size increased up to the 10,000–24,999 population range, and then showed only minor differences among the rest of the population ranges (Figure 2-4).

Income per capita and expenditures per capita were highest ($61.01 and $58.02) for the population range 5,000–9,999 and lowest ($26.80 and $26.20) for the population range under 5,000 (Figure 2-5 and 2-6).

In-library use of materials per capita was highest (6.3 materials) for populations under 5,000 and lowest (1.5 materials) for the population range 100,000–249,000 (Figure 2-7).

Percent registrations of population was highest (73%) for two smallest population groups (under 5,000 and 5,000–9,000) and lowest (44%) for two largest population groups (500,000–999,999 and 1,000,000 and over) (Figure 2-8).

Collection turnover was highest (3.4 turnovers) for the group of libraries with populations between 500,000–999,999 and lowest (1.0 turnover) for the group of libraries with service populations under 5,000 (Figure 2-9).[7]

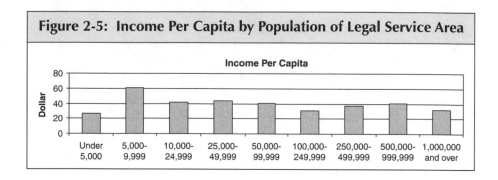

Figure 2-5: Income Per Capita by Population of Legal Service Area

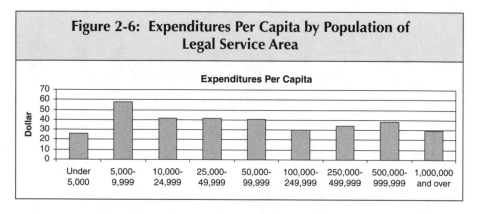

Figure 2-6: Expenditures Per Capita by Population of Legal Service Area

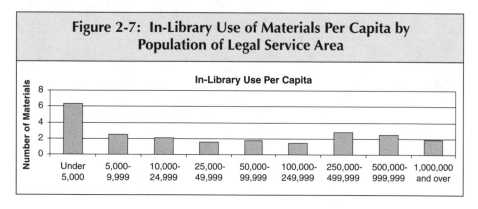

Figure 2-7: In-Library Use of Materials Per Capita by Population of Legal Service Area

Library Outputs in Relation to Expenditure

Libraries must constantly justify budgets to stakeholders, compete for ever-shrinking grant money, and stay abreast of new technologies in order to stay relevant in an increasingly digital society. In 2007, for each $1,000 of library expenditure, libraries on average generated 162 library visits, circulated 248 items, had 9 patrons attend programs, fielded 62 reference questions, and registered 11 new patrons (Table 2-4).

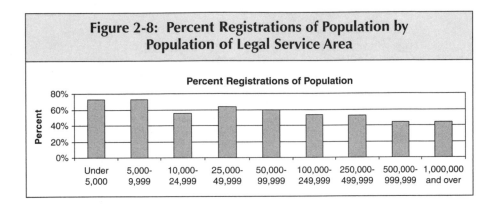

Figure 2-8: Percent Registrations of Population by Population of Legal Service Area

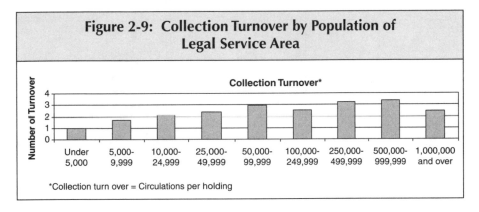

Figure 2-9: Collection Turnover by Population of Legal Service Area

Financial and Output Measure Longitudinal Trends

While the 2007 PLDS provides the most recent information about public libraries, a longitudinal trend can provide an additional valuable dimension to the information: changes over time. Only 300 libraries have consistently reported on the selected measures for all of the six years used for analysis: income, expenditures, library visits, circulation, holdings, and program attendance. As shown in Table 2-5, the libraries included in this trend analysis tended to have larger legal service areas than the other libraries as those libraries consistently participated in the PLDS since 2002.

Income and expenditure per capita steadily increased during the six-year period among reporting libraries. As shown in Figure 2-10, the pattern of increase was consistent between the library income and expenditures. The library income increased from $35.75 in 2002 to $44.42 in 2007 and the library expenditures increased from $33.33 in 2002 to $41.79 in 2007, resulting in $8.66 (income) and $8.46 (expenditures) increase per capita between 2002 and 2007.

All output measures show gradual increases during the six-year period. For circulation, the increase was steeper in 2002–2003 (0.5 materials increase

Table 2-4: PLDS 2007 Library Output Characteristics Per $1,000 of Expenditures					
	Number of Reporting Libraries	Minimum	Maximum	Average	Standard Deviation
Library Visits Per Dollar Expenditure	820	0.02	1134.61	161.85	87.39
Circulation Per Dollar Expenditure	879	18.74	1150.12	247.52	125.13
Program Attendance Per Dollar Expenditure	865	0.04	246.82	9.58	12.34
Reference Transaction Per Dollar Expenditure	828	0.43	1174.98	34.19	61.92
In-Library Use of Materials Per Dollar Expenditure	335	0.23	860.43	61.88	83.71
Library Registrations Per Dollar Expenditure	776	0.33	83.59	19.05	10.93

during the period per capita) and 2003–2004 (0.4 materials increase per capita), and then the increase became gradual (0.1 or less than 0.1 materials increase). Library visits per capita and holdings per capita show steady increases: increases were 0.0–0.2 visits per capita and 0.0–0.1 holdings per capita. Changes in collection turnover show steeper increases during 2002–2003 (0.2 turnover increase per capita) and 2003–2004 (0.1 turnover increase per capita), and then showed almost no change (less than 0.1 turnover increase per capita) during the subsequent period between 2004 and 2007. Program attendance per capita shows a unique trend in which a steep increase in 2002–2003 (0.2 attendance increase per capita) was followed by a steep decrease (0.2 attendance decrease per capita) in 2003–2004, and then

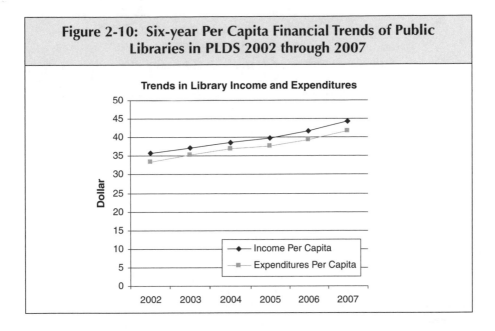

Figure 2-10: Six-year Per Capita Financial Trends of Public Libraries in PLDS 2002 through 2007

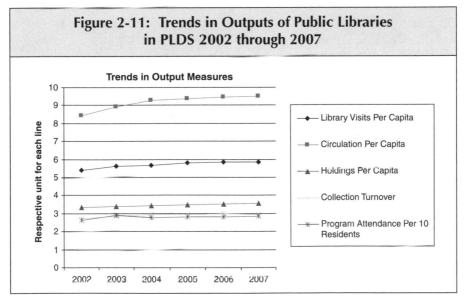

Figure 2-11: Trends in Outputs of Public Libraries in PLDS 2002 through 2007

gradually increased (less than 0.1 attendance increase per year) during the four year period between 2004 and 2007.

Despite these year-to-year shifts, as Figure 2-11 shows, outputs remain relatively flat over the six-year time period used for analysis.

	Average of 300 libraries included in trend analysis (2002-2007)	Average of 904 libraries included in PLDS 2007

Table 2-5: Difference between the Libraries Reporting Consistently between 2002 and 2007 and Those Libraries Reporting for PLDS 2007

	Average of 300 libraries included in trend analysis (2002-2007)	Average of 904 libraries included in PLDS 2007
Circulation	2,550,558	1,533,022
FTE Librarians	42	25
Population of legal service area	327,770 (167% of PLDS 2007 average)	196,111

Methodology

This study used data from Public Library Data Services (PLDS) surveys conducted between 2002 to 2007. The PLDS survey is an annual survey that has been conducted by the Library Research Center at the University of Illinois at Urbana-Champaign on behalf of the Public Library Association since 1988. More than 1,900 libraries in the U.S. and Canada are regularly invited and approximately 50%–70% of the invited libraries have participated in the survey annually.

In the profiles of public libraries section, aggregate characteristics of the 904 libraries that participated in the PLDS 2007 survey were described by descriptive statistics. For each of the continuous variables, the following statistics were obtained: number of reporting libraries, minimum, maximum, mean, and standard deviation. For each of the categorical variables, frequency and percentage of libraries were calculated.

In the subsequent sections, the variables of interest included financial and output per capita measures (circulation, holdings, library visits, program attendance, total income, total expenditure, reference transactions, in-library use of materials, and registrations) and three additional measures (percent registration of population, circulation per borrower, and collection turnover). Per capita measures were calculated by dividing the original measures by population that a public library serves. Circulation per borrower was calculated by dividing circulation by registrations. Collection turnover was calculated by dividing holdings by circulation.

The influence of population that a public library serves on financial and output measures was examined through the use of Multivariate Analysis of Variance (MANOVA). MANOVA is a statistical analytic method and is used to examine the effect of the population group on the multiple financial and output measures.

The output per expenditure measures were obtained by dividing the selected output measures by total operating expenditures. The output measures that were used included library visits, circulation, program attendance, reference transactions, in-library use of materials, and registrations.

Trend analysis was conducted for library visits per capita, circulation per capita, program attendance per capita, holdings per capita, income per capita, expenditures per capita, and collection turnover. Only the libraries that reported relevant statistics were included in the analysis. Yearly means are described.

Notes

1. Population estimates for the United States in July 1, 2006 in the U.S. Census used to calculate the percentage of patrons served in the U.S.: Annual Estimates of the Population (n.d.), Retrieved April 28, 2008, from www.census.gov/popest/states/NST-ann-est.html.
2. Population estimates for the United States in July 1, 2006 in the U.S. Census used to calculate the percentage of patrons served in the U.S.: Annual Estimates of the Population (n.d.), Retrieved April 28, 2008, from www.census.gov/popest/states/NST-ann-est.html.
3. Mustafoff, M. & Teffeau, L. (2007). Young adult services and technology in public libraries: An analysis of the 2007 Public Library Data Services. *Public Libraries*, 2008, 10–15.
4. For a more detailed examination of the technology questions for PLDS 2007, please refer to Mustafoff, M. & Teffeau, L. (2007). Young adult services and technology in public libraries: An analysis of the 2007 Public Library Data Services. *Public Libraries*, 2008, 10–15.
5. Mustafoff, M. & Teffeau, L. (2007). Young adult services and technology in public libraries: An analysis of the 2007 Public Library Data Services. *Public Libraries*, 2008, 10–15.
6. For a more detailed examination of the young adult library service questions for PLDS 2007, please refer to Mustafoff, M. & Teffeau, L. (2007). Young adult services and technology in public libraries: An analysis of the 2007 Public Library Data Services. *Public Libraries*, 2008, 10–15.
7. For a variety of annual figures and other statistics by population of legal service area, readers are referred to: Public Library Association (2007). *Public Library Data Services Statistical Reports 2007*. Chicago, IL: American Library Association.

About the Authors

Mijung Yoon has been a graduate research assistant for the Center for Informatics Research in Science and Scholarship (previously known as the Library Research Center) between 2005 and 2009, working on several research projects on Illinois and U.S. libraries and community surveys for public libraries. A native of South Korea who came to the United States for graduate study, she is currently working on her doctoral dissertation on evaluation practice at the University of Illinois at Urbana-Champaign.

Lauren Teffeau was a project coordinator for the Center for Informatics Research in Science and Scholarship (previously known as the Library Research Center) from October 2005 until February 2009. The center has administered the Public Library Data Service on behalf of the Public Library Association since 1988. Lauren has a master's degree in mass communication from the University of Georgia.

Chapter 3

No Easy Targets: Six Libraries in the Economy's Dark Days

Suzann Holland and Amanda VerPloeg

In the current economic climate, virtually no government agency is safe from financial hardships. Libraries all over the nation are feeling pain, often in the form of cuts to hours, programming, materials, or even staff. Now more than ever, people are turning to libraries for the services that they can no longer afford, such as media purchases and Internet access. The combination of library funding cuts and a growing library patron base has many libraries throughout the nation stretched thinner than ever before.

For this article, the authors talked to library administrators representing communities of varying sizes across the country about the difficulties they are facing and the ways that they are coping with their libraries' struggles. Most libraries are making difficult decisions about how to best prioritize the valuable and necessary services on which their patrons depend. Many library patrons are relying on services such as Internet access to apply for jobs, complete college applications, or work on homework—many things that they used to do from home.

According to a recent issue of *Time* magazine, 63 percent of the approximately one thousand people interviewed for the article have cut back on entertainment purchases due to the economy.[1] For better or worse, the perception of the public library is changing from that of an information source to an entertainment source, which can lead people to look at the library as an expendable resource. While many library patrons and staff know the important role libraries play in a community, many non-library users and municipality leaders may not see the value of the public library.

Despite the dark days many of America's libraries are facing, the directors of the profiled libraries consistently expressed hope for the future and optimism that things may be brighter than ever once the economy turns around.

The Libraries

Saxton B. Little Free Library

The Saxton B. Little Free Library (SBLFL) has been a presence in the small community of Columbia, Connecticut, since 1883. Staff members currently work to meet the needs of a population of just fewer than five thousand citizens. Though library funding has always been tight, recent years had seen small but steady gains in the budget. Director Su Epstein notes that in 2006, the library negotiated with the city for a substantial increase to take place over the course of several years. This additional funding was earmarked for much-needed salary adjustments for library staff. Once the economic crisis hit, the city reneged on this agreement, and made cuts to the library's budget.

In the fallout of the city's broken promises, Epstein and her staff had little choice but to reduce the level of service being provided to the citizens of Columbia. "While we have tried very hard to not cut, we have purchased less materials and reduced the number of programs offered," she said.[2] More service cuts may be coming.

Oskaloosa Public Library

The budget woes of the Oskaloosa (Iowa) Public Library (OPL) date back to 2004, when the state legislature made a $60 million cut to local governments. Like other cities and counties across the state, the city of Oskaloosa (population: 11,000) made across-the-board cuts that year. The city budget line item for library materials was slashed from $47,000 to $1,000. Left with few options, the library board and staff turned to "windfall money." These funds are primarily comprised of small special-purpose grants and memorial bequests.

OPL has tried to keep most of the cuts behind the scenes. The primary example of this came in February when the board voted to cease the library's RFID tagging program. The original equipment purchases were made with a large bequest, but the ongoing cost of supplies has been a financial burden.

The library's decision ushers in a new era with a new philosophy. No longer will ambitious new programs with substantial ongoing costs be initiated with windfall money. Generally, if the library's operating budget cannot support the fixed operating costs of a project, it's risky to commit the library to it.

Despite the change in philosophy, the point is almost moot, as available windfall money has been drained with little to replace it. OPL has to use the trickle of windfall money for materials, so it must find other areas in which to reduce operating expenses. Next on the horizon: a probable move from Sirsi-Dynix to a less expensive integrated library system.

Oak Lawn Public Library

Oak Lawn (Illinois) Public Library sits in the suburbs of Chicago with a population of just over 55,000. ALA Council member James B. Casey heads the library. Oak Lawn has not yet experienced the drastic budget slashes seen in other public libraries. Casey noted that the administrative team has been able to "hold the line in resisting budget cuts and has maintained a balanced budget through the current recession."[3] But this doesn't mean that the library isn't feeling the economic pinch.

The administrative team has been able to negotiate reductions in costs with vendors and service providers. However, the escalating cost of staff benefits has been difficult to absorb in a flat budget year. A partial freezing of salary increments accepted by staff has helped. Casey is noticeably proud of the library's employees for keeping staffing levels under control. "The increasing demand for service by the public has been met by astute management of existing staff by supervisors," he said.[4]

Washoe County Library System

Founded in 1904 as the Reno Free Public Library, the Washoe County (Nevada) Library System (WCLS) currently serves a population of 420,000 citizens and is led by Director Arnie Maurins. The situation in Washoe County is bleak. In the last two years, the system's budget has been reduced an astounding 40 percent, primarily because of the area's declining tax revenues. Maurins explained, "Sales taxes have been decreasing in Washoe County for over two years, and property taxes have been declining due to foreclosures and adjusted property values."[5]

Where are the cuts being made? Spending on materials and database subscriptions has been halved. A shared library with a middle school has been closed. Smaller branch locations, such as the one housed in Washoe County's Senior Center, have seen reductions in operating hours of up to 35 percent. The larger branches will likely see hours cut in the new fiscal year and more closures may be imminent. The coming year will also see mobile and outreach services significantly reduced.

Perhaps the hardest to swallow for Maurins and his staff is the closure of the partnership library with one of the area middle schools. He noted, "We had provided public library service in that facility for nearly thirteen years. Families in the immediate neighborhood now have to travel several miles to reach one of two alternative branches."[6] Staff layoffs may also be a difficult development on the horizon. "That would be an extremely painful decision, even if there are no other viable alternatives."[7]

Phoenix Public Library

The Phoenix Public Library (PPL) has been serving the public since 1898 and currently meets the needs of a population of 1.5 million. According to Director Toni Garvey, the facility has lost about 26 percent of its payroll budget in the last two years. Services have been hard hit. Much less adult programming takes place, although employment-related programming has been maintained, given the economic situation. Teen programming has been reduced from one per week to one per month. Gone are the school tours and the outreach program for the area's first graders, Grade One at the Library. The materials budget has been slashed by a million dollars. The hardest cut to make? Library hours, which have been decimated.

Before the cuts, every library in the system was open seventy-two hours per week, and each had the same hours, which included Sundays. Now Sunday hours only exist at half of the branches, and those libraries are open for four hours instead of the previous six. Each building operates one eight-hour shift per day, six days per week; bringing total open hours down to forty-eight per week. Garvey recalled, "For years we could say, 'we've got the best hours of service of any library in the country.'"[8] Bigger in geography than Los Angeles, Phoenix is served by a central library and only fifteen branches. "Accessibility was about the hours we were open, not a lot of buildings. We really redefined what access meant."[9]

Brooklyn Public Library

Brooklyn Public Library (BPL) Executive Director Dionne Mack-Harvin took the helm at a difficult time in the library's history. The institution has been open to the public since 1892, and currently serves a borough of 2.5 million citizens. Brooklynites are now watching helplessly as the library takes a city and state funding hit to the tune of $2.1 million. Early in the budget process, the library system is typically pegged for cutbacks, but funding has typically been restored during budget negotiations. Mack-Harvin noted, "This is the first time in several years that a proposed budget cut has gone through, and that is due to the state of the economy. Our operating budget, or spending ability, has also decreased—regardless of an actual budget cut—since funding has not increased along with inflation."[10]

All Sunday service throughout the system has been eliminated. Mack-Harvin said, "It's always a challenging decision to reduce hours of service, but in order to make the savings we need for the upcoming fiscal year, we closed six locations on Sundays at the beginning of this year. By eliminating Sunday hours, we've saved almost $1 million in operating expenses. A hiring freeze for nonessential positions is now in place, and the purchase of new materials has been severely curtailed."[11]

Increased Usage

While libraries all over the nation are feeling the effects of cuts to the budget line items for materials, programming, and staff, more and more people are flocking to libraries for entertainment and other needs.

Fall 2008 book sales were down about 7 percent compared to the fall of 2007.[12] With standard hardback books typically costing well more than $25, it is no surprise that people are cutting that expense out of their personal budgets and instead turning to their libraries. At the main library in Modesto, California, circulation of books, CDs, and DVDs is up about 15 percent.[13] The Boise Library saw a 61 percent increase in library card usage in 2008.[14]

These incredible increases in usage are great for libraries, in the sense that it seems like more and more people are realizing the value of the public library. Unfortunately, if the cuts get much worse, libraries may be forced to cut the very services that the patrons are using more than ever.

According to a January 2009 article in *The Boston Globe*, "at the Revere Public Library, circulation in fiscal 2008, which ended June 30, was up 20 percent over the previous year, according to library director Robert E. Rice Jr. He said usage has risen noticeably since then."[15]

In Seattle, the two primary library systems in the area—the King County Library System (KCLS) and the Seattle Public Library—loaned more than two million more items in 2008 than in the previous year.[16] KCLS is one of the busiest libraries in the nation, second only to the Queens (New York) Library.[17] KCLS saw an increase in circulation of about 6.5 percent in 2008.[18]

The American Library Association's (ALA) Public Information Office (PIO) reported that, as of September 2008, an estimated 68 percent of U.S. residents have a library card, up about 5 percent from 2006.[19] PIO also reported that 76 percent of U.S. residents visited their public library during the previous twelve months.[20] When compared to a study from 2006, this is a 10 percent increase in library visits.

In the same press release, PIO stated that in a recent poll of U.S. residents, 92 percent of the respondents felt that their library is a very important community resource.[21] Given these reported increases in visits and circulation, libraries are struggling to make sure that they can serve their communities in the best way possible.

Library materials related to the job search process have also seen spikes in circulation. At the Boulder (Colorado) Public Library, circulation of books related to job hunting has increased approximately 14 percent in the last year.[22] The Arlington Heights (Illinois) Memorial Library has seen an increase in homeless patrons appearing in business attire and spending long hours job hunting.[23] Despite the increases in the use of this category of materials, struggling libraries may have difficulty in updating their job seeking and résumé materials or replacing those materials when they become worn out from use.

More people are turning to their libraries as a substitute for entertainment purchases such as movie rentals and music. Cutting the entertainment budget may be easier for some families when they know that the library can provide them with the latest movies or most popular CDs. But with increased use comes increased replacement and mending costs. It may become more difficult for libraries to maintain an attractive collection of materials.

Of course, most library staff members love the increase of patrons and usage. After all, that is why the library is here, to be used! However, it must be acknowledged that the downturn of the economy, the stresses of layoffs, and the struggle to make ends meet is causing concern among library users and staff. More and more people that come into the library are already stressed to the breaking point. Little disappointments or unmet needs at the library can make their temperament or attitude take a downward turn.

Generally, crime rises when the economy sours. The increases in usage and stress have resulted in many libraries taking measures to make sure that their patrons and staff members are safe. At OPL, police officers have taken a proactive approach to safety—providing training to library staff and periodic walkthroughs of the library building by officers. They hope that showing that they are present and ready to respond to trouble will deter people from stealing or harassing staff and patrons. According to *The New York Times*, libraries all over the nation are facing increased security concerns and some may need to increase the measures they take to protect their employees and patrons, but they may not have the funds to do so.[24] The average cost of an unarmed security officer is about $26,000.[25] Many libraries do not have the money to pay for their current staff, let alone the additional expense of a guard.

Most libraries have seen or will see an increase in library use as long as the economic climate looks bleak. Hopefully, the vast majority of libraries will be able to maintain their collections, staff, and facilities until their funding increases. The interesting point will be seeing if the patrons that have discovered the value of their public libraries will continue to use library services after they are back on their feet.

Reduction Considerations

When there are no other choices other than to make cuts, how do we make these difficult decisions? Some rely heavily on statistics and make highly researched decisions; for others, the best choices are obvious.

With the vast majority of a library's budget going toward salaries and associated benefits, laying off staff might seem like the quickest fix. But few stones cause more ripples than staff reductions. Unless a library is overstaffed, which is unimaginable for most administrators, fewer employees means poorer service. Other devastating results can include shorter hours, fewer professional employees, longer waits for materials, and so forth.

Mack-Harvin noted that protecting staff positions was key for BPL. The system's administrative team recognizes that protecting staff positions and maintaining a high standard of customer service go hand in hand and are therefore top priorities for Brooklyn's library. "By cutting non-essential spending, not filling vacant positions and eliminating Sunday hours, we have been able to safeguard in fiscal year 2009 and preserve six-day service at our sixty libraries," she said.[26]

Staff of the PPL knew that hours must be reduced, and the administrative team worked to make the most informed decision possible. Formal usage studies were conducted to determine the foot traffic patterns for each branch location. The resulting data provided hour-by-hour, day-by-day information about the number of people entering the building and the circulation valleys and peaks. The ultimate goal was to reduce hours, yet still be available to patrons during the busiest times. Garvey learned that the hours from 11 a.m. to 7 p.m. are key, but steady morning traffic clearly indicated earlier hours were needed as well. Garvey said, "We're now open from 11 to 7 on Mondays, Wednesdays, and Fridays; 9 to 5 on Tuesdays, Thursdays, and Saturdays. Close to the same number of customers are now being served by 30 percent fewer staff." The system's visits-per-hour statistics show that the library is busier than before.

In light of the brutal cuts endured in Washoe County, Maurins considered a variety of factors. Primary on the list was the impact on the public. Geography was a strong consideration in closing a branch or reducing hours at others. The distance between branches and the open hours of each location was carefully studied. For staff reductions, the qualifications of employees were noted. Luckily, retirement incentives offered by the county reduced the number of layoffs. For other cuts, Maurins looked at the availability of outside funding to help with variable expenses. Funds from grants, donations, and support organizations are now part of the plan for supporting line items such as library materials.

For the smaller, single-location institutions of OPL and SBLFL, the decisions have been simpler. They have been made by a single person and have drawn heavily upon common sense and trusted instincts. The question has been, "How do we serve the most patrons with less money available?" At SBLFL, Epstein looked at "the amount and variety of patrons who utilize the material or service . . . It's common sense to eliminate something with little use but high in cost versus something highly used, but low in cost."[28]

Interestingly, none of the directors of the profiled libraries mentioned the dreaded three-letter word: fee. If pressure exists to take the "free" out of our libraries, administrators are not yet bowing to it. The idea of shutting our poorest patrons out of crucial services such as interlibrary loan with the institution of fees is reason enough. Logistics can also be a barrier. Charging a small fee to check out a feature film DVD could become a nightmare with self-check machines and more money to keep track of. Is the small amount worth the hassle? Do we want to start judging what materials or services are extraneous enough to warrant fees?

The Methodology of Service Prioritization

Unfortunately, the cuts that libraries have to make are not uniform across the nation. Libraries have to evaluate their communities' needs as well as their mission in serving the public. For example, in one community it may be obvious to cut the seldom-used job search classes, while in another community the job search classes are well attended and needed.

Many libraries have been forced to cut programming, which in turn may decrease the number of new patrons coming into the library. Libraries have to look at their own circulation records, library usage records, and successful elements in order to fully understand what cuts and sacrifices are needed.

At SBLFL they looked at what programs were most needed and used. They also tried to keep programs and services that cover the broadest of needs. By taking this approach SBLFL will, hopefully, be able to cut major costs without cutting vital services to its patrons.

OPL was able to use its remaining windfall money to cover the 2009–10 budget year. An operational efficiency committee was also created, consisting of a combination of board and staff members, to evaluate the everyday expenses of the library and make sure the library's money was being used in the best ways possible.

Maurins said Washoe County Public Library System did not use any special methods when making cuts, but rather followed a balanced scorecard strategic plan when deciding on a plan of action. The director also said that plan will likely be modified in the future to account for financial and human resources cuts.

PPL looked at its priorities and goals and decided that cuts that it would try to avoid would be preschool services and early literacy programs (preschool programs were eventually reduced in number). The library also had to adjust operating hours. In order to ensure that the new staff schedules would be manageable and effective, managers prepared sample schedules for various-sized branches to ensure that proposed staffing levels would be sufficient.

BPL's finance team created multiple budget models with possible cuts and some likely situations. After much evaluation the team decided that cutting Sunday hours would save the most money at the greatest rate.

Each of these libraries tried to look at all possible cuts and what sacrifices they were willing to make in order to make sure that they can still provide the best service to their communities without resorting to closing their doors. Ultimately, most libraries will, hopefully, look at all money saving avenues before being forced to cut staff.

According to an article in *The Tampa Tribune*, the Pasco County (Florida) Library System (PCLS) cut library hours across the county.[29] The cuts will result in the seven libraries being closed on Mondays and each library will be open for only forty hours per week. The county is likely to have a $30-million-dollar budget deficit next year. The libraries are also being asked to cut an additional 18 to 20 percent from next year's budget. The library has already had to cut seventeen employees, and it is looking like they will have to cut four more by September. PCLS's situation is a scary one that most library staff and patrons would hate to have their library face, but this story is not a lonely one. Libraries all across the country are being forced to make difficult and often unpleasant decisions.

While, hopefully, most people in any given community would hate to see their libraries close doors, there have been a small few who are calling for the removal of libraries all together. A notorious March 2008 editorial by George Elmore in *The Gainesville Sun* sent shockwaves through the library community.[30] Elmore claimed that libraries are basically useless and that if the library in his area were gone he would save roughly 5 percent on his property taxes. Elmore further asserted that the Internet and Google have replaced the library and that no real, or "serious research is carried on in the library stacks."[31] It would appear that Elmore is not a library user. If he were to visit his local library, I bet he would find a plethora of information, entertainment, and other services that he never knew were available to him. It also appears that Elmore has forgotten that many people, in the wake of lost jobs, rely on the free services of the library to find a job or develop new, helpful skills. Unfortunately, many of these free services that are so helpful to the residents of the community that cannot afford Internet access or other luxuries are being taken away and ultimately could mean removing many opportunities from the hands of our loyal patrons.

It truly is an ironic situation. While the need and demand for library services is on the rise, libraries are being forced to cut services, hours, staff, or even close the doors all together.

Utilizing Public Opinion

Only one of the libraries profiled in this article utilized direct public input in making services reduction decisions. Maurins described the efforts of the WCLS's administration to ensure the public had a voice. "For this most recent round of cuts, we are holding a series of town hall meetings at different branches, in order to solicit budget ideas, hear which services are most important to try to maintain, and also hear which days and hours our branches should be open to best serve the public," she said.[32] For those patrons unable to attend the town hall meetings, sharing their ideas and suggestions is still an option. The library system is providing special comment cards to gather patron input. Patrons are also encouraged to submit their comments through the library's Web site.

For PPL, the library's support groups are thought of as a focus group of sorts. Members are obviously very familiar with the library's wide array of services. During the recent round of cuts and reductions, their input was solicited. A secondary benefit of asking support groups for suggestions can also be realized—with the built-in advocate base that a library support organization provides, asking for assistance provides an excellent opportunity to educate the advocates.

Public input can also be quite casual and small in scale. SBLFL's strategy for selecting periodicals to discontinue demonstrates than an informal exchange of communication can yield highly relevant information. For those newspapers and magazines under consideration for elimination, staff members placed notes on the publications for the patrons reading them. Patrons were asked to let library staff know if they were reading a particular publication. This method also provides a little customized publicity about the library's financial plight and how it could directly affect the patron reading the note.

Garvey had other thoughts on patrons having a voice in PPL's reductions and cuts. The administrative team went back to the library's strategic plan for guidance in what services best met the library's mission and goals. "Though the input is indirect for reducing services, the patrons had quite a bit of input into our strategic plan," Garvey said.[33] Provided that a library has a current strategic plan partially or fully based on patron feedback, every time the resulting tool is used, patrons have a voice.

Turning to the frontline staff also sheds light on the pulse of a library's patron base. Frontline employees work with patrons every day. They hear the offhand remarks made by the public, understand which needs are being met, and those that still need to be addressed. The BPL administrative team utilized the direct input from frontline staff in making reduction decisions. Mack-Harvin said, "All changes to service were carefully discussed with our board of trustees and executive management, with input from library staff who serve the public directly."[34]

For the smaller communities of Oskaloosa and Columbia, the question of seeking out direct public input was academic. With a more limited array of services, fewer staff members, and less money to shift around, the service reduction choices were clear-cut. In libraries serving small communities, the administrative staff is likely to be comprised of just the library's director. Library directors in smaller communities more often have the opportunity to work directly with the public, thereby eliminating the middleman.

Sharing Difficult News

Early rumblings of service cuts usually spread quickly through the building. Keeping the library's staff well informed as events unfold is important for employee morale and will make things easier for patrons later in the process. Some administrators may feel that providing confirmation or denial for solutions under discussion is pointless. The "I'll let them know when we're sure" philosophy can lead to rumors that are far worse than reality. Meeting with a board committee to discuss reduction of service hours? A quick all-staff e-mail from the director announcing the meeting will help tremendously with information control. The hierarchy shouldn't matter. Every staff member, from maintenance to pages to catalogers, should receive the same information. Service or staff cuts impact everyone; take the time to get everyone on the same page.

Once the decisions are official, how do you tell the public the library is preparing to provide less service? In the current economic climate, the news is not surprising. Maurins said, "We have tried to maintain an objective tone, stating the dollar amounts of our cuts, the ideas we are considering, and the possible impacts to the public."[35] Epstein agreed: "I have been very straightforward. Our budget was reduced, our expenses have increased, we have had to make difficult decisions. We are trying to balance our cuts to minimize public impact."[36] With honesty, the script writes itself. Mack-Harvin noted, "We've been very straightforward that eliminating Sunday service, in which all staff were paid overtime, was the quickest way for us to make necessary savings to maintain six-day service across the borough."[37]

The local media outlets are an important tool in getting the word out. Notifying the public early and often will make upcoming changes unfold more smoothly and reduce the chances of anger and shock. Mack-Harvin had an enormous patron base to notify. "We are as disappointed as the public about having to cut our hours of service. With 2.5 million people living in Brooklyn, we decided a direct and far-reaching approach was the best way to disseminate the message. In December, we alerted media via press release that Sunday service would be eliminated within a few weeks," she said.[38] In addition to notifying customers through the press, staff posted signage in the system's buildings and a notice on the Web site.

Garvey has been careful to consider the needs of specific subgroups of people who might be impacted by the library's changes. Notification flyers were distributed to people entering the library so kids wouldn't be stranded unexpectedly. The police were notified. Local schools were alerted. Think not only of the patrons, but also of the organizations that may routinely refer the public to the library and its range of services.

Several libraries used special-purpose tools distributed within the library to communicate the message and reduce the amount of staff time spent answering the same questions repeatedly. At PPL on the day of the city council vote, a special communication plan was rolled out. It included an impressive variety of information-dissemination methods. Library staff members continue to distribute a printed "frequently asked questions" flyer within the building and an electronic version on the library system's Web site, detailing the budget cuts and the reasons behind them (see appendix at the end of this article).

BPL's administrative team uses the media not only to publicize cuts and reductions in library service, but also to help redefine the focus. Despite the lost hours, Mack-Harvin is quick to focus on what the library still has to offer, putting a positive spin on the situation. "Our customers can still conduct much of their library business on our Web site, such as place books on hold, renew library materials, get free homework help, and download e-books," he said.[39] Maurins said that while the library system's recent press releases convey unsettling news of massive cuts and reductions, the "primary message is that we will strive to provide the best service possible, whatever amount of resources we have."[40] Casey acknowledged the importance of "a strong and positive public relations effort providing local media and residents with announcements of new materials and program opportunities."[41]

Public Reaction

From all accounts, public reaction has been one of understanding. As our patrons suffer the consequences of the economy's downturn, they understand the prioritization that comes with making do with less. That is not to say they are accepting the changes with nonchalance. Garvey said that Phoenix patrons are enduring three and four-hour waits to use a computer. "They're understanding, not angry. But the frustration level is high."[42]

Are patrons too understanding? Maurins described a small minority in Washoe County who "shrug it off and think it's not a big deal or that libraries should be shut down completely."[43] Does public apathy make the problem worse?

Many of OPL's patrons have noticed a stark reduction in the purchase of materials. A handful of them have been vocal about the change. Most seem to shrug it off. Though circulation is very strong for a library serving a community of just more than ten thousand, very few seem willing to take steps to help the library or publicly support it to local officials. People express their frustration while they're in the library, but would never consider addressing a city council or county supervisors' meeting on its behalf.

Bright spots do exist. In some communities, patrons are working to improve the situation. Mack-Harvin tells of BPL's "Support Our Shelves" campaign. "We're asking the public to give what they can to help ensure our shelves are filled with books during these challenging economic times. In just the first thirty days of this three-month initiative, we've raised nearly $150,000 of our $300,000 goal, and received hundreds of postcards addressed to Brooklyn's elected officials pleading for library budgets to be restored," she said.[44]

Are Libraries Easy Targets?

Doesn't it often seem that when something must be cut, libraries come first? It's difficult to determine statistically if that's really the case. One interviewee cited the example of public schools. Many districts across the country have cut professional staff from their libraries or shuttered them entirely; despite all of the statistics that prove academic performance suffers in the absence of a library.

Are public libraries easy cuts for municipalities looking to reduce services? Maurins believes they are, clearly indicating who the favored children are:

> Unfortunately, I think that is true. In Washoe County, libraries were lumped together with parks and the law library in the lowest-priority tier of services, meaning that those departments are taking the biggest budget "hits" in terms of percentage reductions. Library service has always been rated very highly on the citizen surveys conducted by the County, and our library system has been able to get two ballot measures passed since 1994 that have provided revenue to expand from bonds and tax overrides. On the surveys, however, citizens' willingness to support libraries through the normal operating budget doesn't score as well compared to how other departments (such as the Sheriff) fare. Safety, security and health are at the top of most everyone's list of basic needs, so it makes sense politically to minimize funding cuts in areas such as public safety, health and social services, while allowing "non-mandated" services such as libraries to take a much larger share of the cuts. Until society as a whole values lifelong learning comparably to other needs such as survival and safety, it will be difficult to make the case that libraries and schools deserve as much (or more) funding as the agencies that are involved in law enforcement or public health.[45]

We know libraries are often undervalued and underfunded. But do those terms have much meaning when we can't think of a time when they weren't true?

A core group of vocal advocates can completely change the environment in which library cuts are made. Statistics and examples of the value of library service are proudly touted by library administration. Vitriolic support from those not in the employ of the library can carry even more weight and certainly garner more attention. Casey put things in perspective: "It helps to have respected and influential trustees representing the library's interests to their counterparts in the municipality, and for grass roots support to be represented by a vigorous and resourceful Friends of the Library."[46]

OPL and SBLFL face a problem common among public libraries in poorer communities—their primary users are not movers and shakers in the community, often not property owners, and often without a voice. Epstein contends that those who most need and use the public library are portions of the population that have little political power. "Although the public library is one of the few institutions that serves every member of the community, regardless of demographics, it is an institution that is often taken for granted," she said.[47] Many people seem to support the idea of a public library, but supporting it publicly is very low on the priority list.

In the absence of organized support, educating the patron base is key. The library can inform patrons without recruiting them. Both PPL and WCLS provided helpful, fact-based information to help patrons understand the budget issues and know who in government dissatisfied patrons could speak to about the library. Garvey noted that Sunday hours were originally eliminated during the council's budget slashes, but public comment during the budget hearings caused the council to rethink the decision. As a result, Sunday hours were partially restored at about half of the city's branches.

Casey and Garvey both understand that the burden of proving the value of libraries rests on the shoulders of the staff and patrons. Casey stated simply, "Our library has not allowed itself to be an 'easy target' for municipal funding cuts. The public appreciates the services provided by the library and voices that support in many ways during the course of the year."[48] Garvey added that any municipality department that cannot prove its worth is an easy target. "It is incumbent upon the both the library staff and the community to communicate the value of the library," she said.[49]

Speaking not only for BPL, but perhaps for libraries everywhere, Mack-Harvin said, "When you are an institution that solely exists to serve the public, there are no easy cost-cutting targets. Reducing costs hurts the entire public, whether it's decreasing the number of books we buy or deciding not to fill the vacancy of a staff member who helps children learn to read. Our customers are affected when our budgets are affected."[50]

Have the Roles of Public Libraries Changed?

Before the Internet boom of the 1990s and the instant access to seemingly endless amounts of information, the library was one of the primary public sources of information. Now, many public libraries fulfill less of an informational role and act as more of an entertainment hub. It has been said that librarians are the original Google—a statement with a strong basis in truth. Just fifteen years ago, the public's primary search portal for unknown information was the library.

This is probably where the idea of the library being a boring and dusty building was born. Libraries, however, are not immune to societal and cultural change, and to survive they have had to change their approach to public service. Casey believes that "the single most important factor assuring future development and public acceptance will be the library's willingness to invest the time, talent, and money needed to keep up with the technological innovations and trends that capture the public's interest."[51]

With all the recent cuts, many library administrators may be worried about whether or not they can afford to keep up with the ever-present changes in technology, or even maintain the equipment or resources that they have. The grants that some libraries receive through the Bill & Melinda Gates Foundation are certainly helpful, but may not cover all of the upgrades needed.

Regardless of what we believe is the primary role of a public library, we can't deny that things are changing. Ultimately, the directors of these profiled libraries see change, but believe the core roles remain the same. Epstein said, "I think the appearance has changed, the forms of media have certainly changed, but the function and role has not."[52]

OPL has also seen an increase in people, especially teenagers, coming in to use the library for the sole purpose of Internet access, primarily to use social networking sites.

Writing for *American Libraries*, Chrystie Hill noted, "more than 14 million people regularly use public library computers to access the Internet."[53] With this abundance of in-house Internet users, access to the Web as a resource is more important than ever. Libraries should not hesitate in adapting to the changes in technology. A library does not have to abandon its original mission to accommodate a growing desire and need for new forms of technology and media. In fact, it is core to a library's mission to meet the information and technological needs of the community.

Many libraries are even using social networking sites for free advertising. OPL, for example, has recently created profiles on social networking sites such as MySpace, Facebook, and Twitter. This demonstrates to the technologically savvy that the library is dedicated to remaining relevant. Some libraries, such as the Denver Public Library, have created MySpace pages dedicated to teens. They can post blog entries about upcoming events and other information that is pertinent to their teen users. The Birmingham (Alabama) Public Library also has a MySpace page where they post a calendar of events and videos. Michael Porter of Webjunction and David Lee King of the Topeka & Shawnee County (Kansas) Public Library offer the following list of possible uses for a Twitter account:

- connecting with patrons and colleagues;
- connecting with other organizations;
- advocacy;
- answering and asking questions;
- professional development;
- using it as a listening tool to "hear" what your community says about the library;
- broadcasting announcements;
- throwing ideas around;
- promoting services or events; and
- job postings.[54]

With many libraries making difficult cuts from their budgets, having resources such as MySpace, Facebook, and Twitter to use as free advertising can loosen up some of the money used for traditional advertising and maybe reach a much greater audience. Many of the sites let you search for users in your area, which allows you to reach out to the people of your community. BPL has found that Web 2.0 outlets create a dialogue between staff and customers that didn't exist before.

Internet access, while vital, is not the primary factor that has initiated the recent increase in public library use. Many people can no longer afford going to the movies, renting DVDs, buying CDs, or subscribing to cable television. The public library is, in a way, acting as a media outlet. This is a big change from even a few years ago when many libraries were only seen as an educational resource.

The changes in information delivery methods have led to changes in professional library staff. While some library staff members would rather refer to print resources than the Internet, the growing ease of services such as Google makes serving the patron much faster. With a younger generation of library staff members arriving on the scene, the methods are bound to change. A fresh-out-of-college library employee may be more comfortable using search engines, wikis, or online directories than using the traditional print resources that were the primary go-to of people only a generation or so older.

The public library has always been, and will continue to be, an organic entity. To best serve the public, library administrators must work to embrace evolving technology to find new and exciting ways to fulfill classic roles.

Hope for the Future

In the previously mentioned *Time* article, survey respondents were asked, "What is your best guess about how long it will take before the economy starts to recover?" Twelve percent said it would be six months, 26 percent said one year, 24 percent said two years, 9 percent said three years, 11 percent said more than three years, 14 percent see the current state of the economy as the start of a long-term decline, and a full 56 percent of respondents believe America's best days are ahead.[55]

Despite the bleak situation the libraries profiled here face in today's current economic climate, the common thread among their leaders is optimism about the coming years. "As public libraries are now playing a vital role in the recovery, they will secure an even greater place within the new prosperity," Casey said.[56]

When asked if she felt PPL would be able to return to its previous level of service, Garvey replied that it depends on how you define "level of service." Depending upon how long the library operates under the current circumstances, Garvey questions whether it's better to go back to the previous mode of operation or if perhaps it would better to "find another way to meet the community's needs."[57] Today's difficult situation offers her administrative team an opportunity to step back and take a fresh look at things.

Mack-Harvin is hopeful that library funding will be restored once the recession comes to an end so her team "can provide Brooklynites with the library service they deserve."[58] She acknowledges the broad spectrum of patrons who depend upon convenient library hours to meet their individual needs:

> Adding hours would mean that we can more effectively meet the needs of everyone in Brooklyn's communities, from the working adults who want to stop in before or after work to pick up a book they placed on hold to kids who come in after school for a safe place to hang out with friends and families who take advantage of our free cultural and recreational programs on the weekends.[59]

> Maurins is confident that WCPL will survive and thrive. An expansion fund passed by voters in 1994 will continue to produce a large stream of revenue until 2024. The administrative team hopes to utilize the resulting funds to build new libraries either as replacements or new branches in areas that currently do not have a library nearby. Maurins sees better times in the near future. "I believe we will surpass our previous service levels within five years, although our staffing patterns and delivery mechanisms may look significantly different than they do today," he said.[60]

Conclusions

We hope that we've seen the worst of the recession, as libraries across the nation are struggling. Librarians have always had a knack for stretching budgets and making do with less. The current economic crisis, while certainly difficult, is not the worst that libraries have endured. As in the past, we have stepped forward and made the difficult and often gut-wrenching decisions that must be made. When libraries suffer, communities suffer.

Although the focus of the interviews conducted for this article was on difficult economic circumstances and the resulting service reductions, each of the administrators of the profiled libraries spoke with hope. Rather than concentrating on what has been lost, they have chosen instead to focus on the many ways in which libraries can continue to meet as many of their patrons' needs as possible.

With diminishing funds, providing these services can be challenging, but rewarding. Libraries now, more than ever, are needed to help patrons with job searches, skill development, entertainment needs, or even just maintaining a sliver of normalcy in chaotic times.

The necessary cuts are often excruciating to make, but libraries all over the United States are using this opportunity to evaluate the needs of their communities and become more efficient than ever. Perhaps the silver linings are the valuable lessons learned. Our dedicated and loyal patrons want to see their libraries well supported and successful. Many are willing to head initiatives to raise money and awareness for their local institutions. In other communities, the support may not be as vocal, but the fierce loyalty that many people have for their libraries should be applauded. Without our patrons, no matter their demographics, libraries across the nation would cease to exist.

Libraries of all sizes from coast to coast are facing similar challenges. Through the combined efforts of dedicated staff and patrons, we will work to restore full service to our struggling institutions, making them more vibrant than ever before.

Notes

1. Nancy Gibbs, "Thrift Nation," *Time*, Apr. 27, 2009, 24.
2. Su Epstein, e-mail interview with the authors, Apr. 8, 2009.
3. James B. Casey, e-mail interview with the authors, Apr. 3, 2009.
4. Ibid.
5. Arnie Maurins, e-mail interview with the authors, Apr. 5, 2009.
6. Ibid.
7. Ibid.
8. Toni Garvey, phone interview with the authors, Apr. 10, 2009.
9. Ibid.
10. Dionne Mack-Harvin, e-mail interview with the authors, Apr. 8, 2009.
11. Ibid.
12. Motoko Rich, "Puttin' Off the Ritz: The New Austerity in Publishing," *The New York Times*, Jan. 5, 2009.
13. Derrick Z. Jackson, "The Library—A Recession Sanctuary," *The Boston Globe*, Jan. 3, 2009.
14. Freakonomics Blog, "The Public Library Renaissance," *The New York Times*, Jan. 7, 2009, http://freakonomics.blogs.nytimes.com/2009/01/07/the-public-library-renaissance/ (accessed June 16, 2009).
15. Jackson, "The Library—A Recession Sanctuary."
16. Mary Ann Gwinn, "Library Use Jumps in Seattle Area; Economy Likely Reason," *The Seattle Times*, Jan. 23, 2009.
17. Ibid.
18. Ibid.
19. American Library Association Public Information Office press release, "New National Poll Shows Library Card Registration Reaches Historic High," Sept. 23, 2008, www.ala.org/ala/newspresscenter/news/pressreleases2008/September2008/ORSharris.cfm (accessed May 26, 2009).
20. Ibid.
21. Ibid.
22. Jackson, "The Library—A Recession Sanctuary."
23. Ibid.
24. Freakonomics Blog, "The Public Library Renaissance," *The New York Times*, Jan. 7, 2009, http://freakonomics.blogs.nytimes.com/2009/01/07/the-public-library-renaissance (accessed May 26, 2009).
25. Payscale.com, "Salary Survey Report for Industry: Security Guard Services," www.payscale.com/research/US/Industry=Security_Guard_Services/Salary/by_Job renaissance (accessed May 26, 2009).
26. Mack-Harvin, Apr. 8, 2009.
27. Garvey, Apr. 10, 2009.
28. Epstein, Apr. 8, 2009.
29. Kevin Wiatrowski, "Pasco Cutting Library Services," *The Tampa Tribune*, Mar. 10, 2009.
30. George Elmore, "Pull the Plug on the Library," *The Gainesville Sun*, Mar. 3, 2008, www.gainesville.com/article/20080303/OPINION03/803030303 (accessed June 16, 2009).
31. Ibid.
32. Maurins, Apr. 5, 2009.
33. Garvey, Apr. 10, 2009.
34. Mack-Harvin, Apr. 8, 2009.

35. Maurins, Apr. 5, 2009.
36. Epstein, Apr. 8, 2009.
37. Mack-Harvin, Apr. 8, 2009.
38. Ibid.
39. Ibid.
40. Maurins, Apr. 5, 2009.
41. Casey, Apr. 3, 2009.
42. Garvey, Apr. 10, 2009.
43. Maurins, Apr. 5, 2009.
44. Mack-Harvin, Apr. 8, 2009.
45. Maurins, Apr. 5, 2009.
46. Casey, Apr. 3, 2009.
47. Epstein, Apr. 8, 2009.
48. Casey, Apr. 3, 2009.
49. Garvey, Apr. 10, 2009.
50. Mack-Harvin, Apr. 8, 2009.
51. Casey, Apr. 3, 2009.
52. Epstein, Apr. 8, 2009.
53. Chrystie Hill, "Inside, Outside, and Online," *American Libraries* 40, no. 3 (Mar. 2009): 39.
54. Michael Porter and David Lee King, "What Are You Doing Now? And Do Your Patrons Care? *Public Libraries* 48, no. 1 (Jan./Feb. 2009): 30.
55. Gibbs, "Thrift Nation."
56. Casey, Apr. 3, 2009.
57. Garvey, Apr. 10, 2009.
58. Mack-Harvin, Apr. 8, 2009.
59. Ibid.
60. Maurins, Apr. 5, 2009.

About the Authors

Suzann Holland is Director of the Oskaloosa (Iowa) Public Library.

Amanda P. VerPloeg is a Library Assistant at the Oskaloosa (Iowa) Public Library.

Appendix

Phoenix Public Library Budget Reductions—Frequently Asked Questions

Why has the library cut its hours?

By law, the city of Phoenix must maintain a balanced budget. Recent drops in tax revenues, resulting from the economic downturn, required the city to reduce its budget by more than $270 million. The majority of city departments (except public safety departments) were asked to reduce their budgets between 27 and 28 percent.

Did you cut other things before cutting hours?

Between 2002 and 2007, the city has reduced the library's budget by 16 percent. During this same time, library use has grown. Between fiscal years 2001–02 and 2006–07, the number of library visitors increased by nearly 13 percent while the circulation of library materials increased by almost 39 percent.

To increase efficiency, we have installed self-checkout machines at all locations, outsourced materials cataloging and processing and much of material selection, and reorganized library staffing. We have also deferred maintenance of facilities, delayed opening new branch libraries, and eliminated the library's print calendar of events. From 2006 to 2009, we reduced our materials budget a total of nearly $1 million annually.

How much has the library's budget been cut?

The library's budget will be reduced by nearly $10 million over a sixteen-month period, effective March 2, 2009.

Other than hours, what reductions will the library make?

The library has reduced its materials budget more than $500,000 annually. We have cut back on some programs (e.g., storytimes, computer classes, and GED/ESL classes) and eliminated other programs completely (e.g., Grade One at the Library).

How can the library build new facilities and renovate existing buildings while cutting hours, programs, and the materials budget?

Funding for operations (service hours, programs, and materials) comes from a different source than funding for construction and renovation. Most construction is funded through Citizen Bond Programs. Currently, the library is implementing projects approved by voters in the 2001 and 2006 Citizen Bonds. These funds cannot be used for operating expenses, such as salaries. Bond projects include the construction of Agave Library (2001 Citizen Bond), a community library in partnership with South Mountain Community College, and the improvement of the library's computer infrastructure, including additional public-access computers at many of our libraries. In addition, private funding is supporting the development of College Depot and additional renovations at Burton Barr Central Library.

If I have concerns about these cuts, to whom should I direct my inquiry?

You may submit comments/concerns to library management via Contact Us at phoenix-publiclibrary.org—see tab near top of page. If you would prefer to voice your concerns directly to city of Phoenix management, you may visit phoenix.gov and submit a comment through Contact Us—at the bottom of the page.

How can I help the library during these difficult economic times?

The library has several organizations that support its work. These include the Friends of the PPL and the Phoenix Public Library Foundation. The Friends and Foundation provide funding for library programs such as our summer and winter reading programs for children and GED/ESL classes for adults.

The library also welcomes volunteers. Please visit www.phoenixpubliclibrary.org for more information.

Excerpted from Phoenix Public Library Web site, www.phoenixpubliclibrary.org (accessed Apr. 15, 2009).

Chapter 4

Forming and Funding Public Library Foundations

Benjamin Goldberg

Foundation Basics

A foundation is a nongovernmental, nonprofit organization with funds and programs managed by its own trustees or directors and established to maintain or aid social, educational, charitable, religious, or other activities serving the common welfare, primarily through the making of grants.

Foundations in one form or another have been around at least since the ancient Egyptians and Greeks used charitable trusts to support religious and educational activities. The English legally defined them in their statutes in the 1600s. But it has been the Americans who have really developed the concept of the general-purpose foundation. Andrew Carnegie, a name familiar to all public librarians, established the Carnegie Corporation in 1911, and since then foundations with broad charitable purposes have flourished.

The word foundation is used quite loosely. An organization with the word in its name may not be a true foundation, while an organization that is a true foundation may not have used the word in its name. Most people think of a foundation as an organization funded by an endowment that gives grants, such as the Ford Foundation. However, when public libraries create foundations, the word has a different meaning. A foundation created by a library seeks funds and uses them to support that library. A library foundation will be identified by the Internal Revenue Service (IRS) as a separate 501 (c)(3) tax-exempt organization—this IRS tax status is critical to your library foundation.

Public and Private Foundations

Tax laws differentiate foundations into two main categories: public and private. As dangerous as it is to try to simplify tax law, there is a simple way to define the difference between the two. A foundation is public if it can meet at least one of the four tests outlined below; a foundation that meets none of these tests is private.

As defined in the IRS Publication 578, a public foundation must meet one of the following four tests:

- Is it a traditional organization, such as a church, school, hospital, or governmental unit? Most organizations formed to support one of these types of institutions are considered public. Usually library foundations fall into this category.
- Does it receive more than one third of its support from grants, contributions, gifts, and gross receipts, and less than one third from investment income? Here fall such groups as the local ballet or musical theatre company.
- Does it exist to support another public charity? An example might be if a wealthy individual leaves a million dollars to support the local library.
- Does it operate solely for public safety? This test does not pertain to library foundations.

For libraries, public foundations have many advantages over private ones. One of the major reasons for forming a public library foundation is to encourage donations that will help support the library. With a public foundation, a donor's gift is tax deductible to the extent provided by applicable law and regulations. An additional advantage is that public foundations are not subject to rules and penalty taxes, such as excise tax on investment income, that apply to private foundations. Also, because a public library foundation is a separate organization from the library, its assets are not subject to government scrutiny with regard to budgeting issues.

Private foundations tend to be company—or family—sponsored foundations that do not solicit publicly. By their very nature, private foundations are subject to a higher degree of regulation and reporting requirements than public foundations.

Benefits of a Library Foundation

To be sure, creating and maintaining a library foundation requires effort and thought, but there are definite benefits. Providing revenues to the library to enhance services is the most direct and observable activity of a library foundation, but a foundation has other advantages for your institution.

Budget Flexibility

A foundation can give the library alternatives it usually does not have in its budget structure. Public library directors and boards are well aware that the budgeting process takes place six to twelve months in advance. Sometimes during a tightly budgeted fiscal year an unplanned opportunity or necessary expense presents itself. A budget has little flexibility, but the foundation may have resources to meet the unforeseen need.

Accumulation of Funds

Many public libraries are limited in the amount of reserve or building funds they can accumulate. A foundation can be used for this purpose without interfering with annual budget proposals or negotiations. Foundation assets might be increased by gifts from Friends of the Library and the community, private grants, interest from foundation investments, and, where permitted, transfer of budget operating funds to the foundation when appropriate state and federal grants are received during the budget year.

Investment Opportunities

Some public libraries never have an option to invest their tax funds, and if they do they are restricted by laws as to location and safety of funds. Foundations may develop their own investment policies to maximize the benefit for the library, although a conservative investment policy is still recommended.

Community Support

Foundation boards include the best your community has to offer in the way of volunteer leadership. Through their involvement with the library foundation, board members will learn about the programs and resources provided by the library and serve as goodwill ambassadors throughout the community. This is a great advantage for library fundraising, bond issues, and the like.

Community Confidence

Another more subtle benefit is that people seem to have confidence in foundations. The word itself engenders feelings of safety and security, like the word "library." When the words come together in "library foundation," and respected citizens serve as board members managing the foundations, contributors feel comfortable in giving their support.

Grant Eligibility

Library foundations also have the advantage of being eligible for grants for which public libraries may be ineligible. Many major foundations and corporations have policies against giving money to tax-supported institutions, but will provide grants to public foundations with the 501 (c)(3) status.

Forming a Foundation

Before taking the legal steps to actually organize or establish a foundation for a public library, it is important to take time to do some planning, decision-making, and educating. The success of a foundation hinges on the reputation of the library in the community, the support of the staff and board of trustees for a foundation, and the composition of the foundation board.

Public libraries can approach this planning component in different ways. At the very least, staff meetings to educate library personnel on the idea should be held. Staff members are often the first people approached by the public for information. The library board must also be fully informed and enthusiastic. In addition to acceptance of the concept, the library should define its roles and develop a mission statement and strategic plan. A long-range plan can help identify library needs and provide a sense of purpose to the foundation.

Selecting the Board

Once the library staff and trustees "know their library,"they can begin to think about an initial organizational meeting and the appropriate choice of persons to approach as foundation board members. It is essential that foundation board members be influential and respected residents of the community. They will be able to personally provide financial and intellectual support as well as garner contributions from their individual and professional contacts. It is desirable that the foundation board has equal representation with respect to gender, include such professionals as an attorney or an accountant, and be representative of the community in such areas as age, race, and political affiliation. Members of civic groups with strong ties to the library should also be considered as prospective board members.

It is important for public libraries to communicate clearly to and maintain good relations with the appropriate governing body. Consider including an elected official, such as a city council member, or an appointed official, such as a finance director, on the foundation board. Such a board member will understand the inner workings of the library foundation and can dispel any impression that the library is hoarding dollars or withholding financial information. It can help at least one member of the governing body to have a more complete understanding of library needs at budget time.

Another group to consider for foundation board members is the local Friends of the Library. If an active group exists in the community, consider whether the foundation should be created by the Friends with strong Friends membership on the foundation board, thus combining the two organizations, or whether the foundation would function better as an independent association. At the very least, consider the appointment of a Friends board member to act as liaison between the Friends and the foundation. A Friends liaison board member can be an ex-officio member of the foundation board.

A decision will also have to be made as to how many, if any, library trustees will be on the foundation board. Some public libraries have only trustees on the foundation board, some have a mix of community people and trustees, some have no trustees. Each public library must look at its situation and service areas and decide what is best for itself, but it would be difficult to justify a foundation board with no community representation except for trustees. Again, at least one trustee to act as a liaison between boards is a good idea. The trustee can be an ex-officio member of the foundation board.

The size of the foundation board is optional. The more people involved with and aware of the library, the more potential support for the library. Too many people, however, may become unmanageable. Again, it is advantageous to have influential people involved in the library. Some boards are as small as seven, some as large as thirty-five. Consider your facility and community and decide on a reasonable number.

Organizational Meeting

Once the staff and library board of trustees have settled on a list of potential foundation board members, it is time to invite them to an organizational meeting.

This is a vital moment in the life and success of a foundation. Be clear and stimulating in your invitation—first impressions last. At this meeting the staff and trustees should present the roles, mission, and plan of the library. Outline the needs of the library as well as the role a foundation and its board can play in fulfilling those needs. Point out how valuable this coalition would be to the community. Be prepared. The people invited to serve are the best the area has to offer, and their questions will be intelligent ones. Finally, before adjournment gain a commitment from each individual candidate to serve on the foundation board. This is also a time to collect names of local attorneys so one can be recruited to serve as pro bono counsel for the foundation.

Articles of Incorporation

At this time the incorporation process can begin. To become a foundation, an organization must first incorporate as a nonprofit corporation with the state. A nonprofit corporation is a corporation that does not distribute any income or profit to its members, directors, or officers. In order to incorporate, articles of incorporation must be filed with the Secretary of State. To draft this document and others it is advisable to utilize the city attorney or a lawyer of your choice (hence the pro bono attorney mentioned before). An excellent source for model documents and advice of all kinds regarding the process of organizing a foundation is *Planning Tax Exempt Organizations* (Matthew Bender, 2002) by Robert Desiderio. There are also numerous examples available on the Internet; for example, the Foundation Center Web site (http://fdncenter.org) provides links to Web sites providing sample articles of incorporation.

Articles of incorporation should be brief and contain only the most essential facts about the organization. At minimum, these include the following:

- Name of the corporation. Usually it is the name of the library followed by the word foundation. However, it is not necessary to use foundation; some public libraries use "Friends of . . ."
- Duration of the corporation. In most cases the duration is perpetual.
- Purpose of the corporation. Here it is important to use the language needed later by the IRS: "The purpose of the corporation shall be to operate exclusively for charitable, scientific, and educational purposes as a nonprofit corporation."
- Address of corporation.
- Management of corporation. Include the number of board members and a statement to the effect that the affairs of the foundation will be controlled and determined by the bylaws.
- Name of registered agent. As this is a new organization, this is often the library director.
- Names and addresses of the initial board.
- Hold harmless clause. Protection for board members against legal claims.
- Provision of distribution of assets upon dissolution. Usually given to the library.

Each state's regulations may be slightly different, so each public library should check with its Secretary of State to determine exact requirements, filing procedures, and filing fee. Sometime after filing the library will receive a Certificate of Incorporation authorizing it to transact business as a nonprofit corporation. Articles of incorporation often cannot be amended without a resolution passed by the foundation board and forwarded to the Secretary of State along with the amendment.

The next step is to file a Form SS-4 with the IRS. This is an application for an employer identification number, which you will need for filing for tax-exempt status. The IRS will assign you a number and send you notification of the number. This identification will be used on all business accounts, tax returns, and related documents. The granting of the number does not mean you have gained tax-exempt status. You can download form SS-4 from the IRS Web site, www.irs.gov.

Bylaws

Bylaws flesh out provisions of the articles of incorporation and are therefore longer. They are the guidelines and procedures according to which the foundation will operate. They can be amended by the board without notifying the state. *The Nonprofit Board's Guide to Bylaws*, (BoardSource, 2003) by D. Benson Tesdahl offers a detailed discussion on creating bylaws for a nonprofit. At minimum, bylaws explain the following:

- Location of corporation.
- Members. A foundation may decide to have members in addition to the board of directors. If so, this clause should include qualifications for membership, rights of membership, terms, how members can resign or be terminated, and related matters.
- Board of directors. Describe its powers, number of members, tenure, and qualifications. If they must be residents of the library's service area, say so. Include such things as when they meet, attendance requirements, how vacancies are filled, and manner of acting.
- Officers. List officer's titles, methods of election, term of office, removal from office, vacancy filling, number of terms able to serve, and other relevant information.
- Committees. Most foundations have permanent committees, such as a development or fundraising committee, an investment committee, a nominating committee, or a marketing committee. Committee composition, duties, and responsibilities should be described here.
- Fiscal year.
- Dues. Use only if you have made the decision to have members other than a board of directors.
- Books and records. Describe what books and records, such as minutes, will be kept and where they will be kept.
- Contracts, loans, checks, and deposits. Include such items as authorization for entering into contracts, restricting loans to certain situations, and establishing who can pay bills or make deposits.

- Dissolution. Explain what happens if the foundation disbands.
- Amendments. Establish provisions for changing the bylaws.
- Rules of order. Consider adoptions of guidelines, such as Robert's Rules of Order, for governing meetings.
- Waiver of notice. It is prudent to include a provision for an alternative to issuing notices required elsewhere in the bylaws.
- Indemnification. This clause states that directors will be held harmless or protected from legal responsibility for the actions of the organization.

As with the articles of incorporation, this document should be written in consultation with an attorney. The Foundation Center (http://fdncenter.org) offers online samples of bylaws. Also, many local organizations have bylaws that can be used as models. The bylaws must be prepared in time for discussion and adoption at the first meeting of the foundation following the organizational meeting. At this first meeting, the foundation board also should consider adopting its own mission statement.

Applying for Tax-exempt Status

Once the organization has incorporated with the state, received an employer identification number, and adopted bylaws, it is ready to file for recognition of exemption from federal income tax. The magic number at this stop is 501 (c)(3). This is the pertinent section of the IRS code that will give the library foundation all the advantages outlined earlier, including tax deductibility for its donors. To apply, fill out IRS Form 1023. You can download Form 1023 from the IRS Web site, www.irs.gov. Applying for tax-exempt status can be done while waiting for certification from the state and should be completed or reviewed by an attorney. The form asks the following:

- Signature of an authorized person.
- Employer identification number.
- Previous tax returns (only if the organization has been in operation for a while).
- Balance sheet of receipts and expenditures for current and preceding three years or a proposed two-year budget.
- Description of anticipated activities.
- Bylaws.

This form is filed with the district IRS office. Even if the application is thoroughly completed, it is not unusual for the IRS to ask for additional information. Supply what is requested and wait for their reply. Expect to wait five to six months for the IRS to respond with a Letter of Determination. This is not a problem because the tax-exempt status is retroactive. It is also common, especially for new foundations, to receive a temporary determination, or, as the IRS terms it, an "advance ruling period." After this period, perhaps eighteen months, a determination is made as to whether the requirements have been met in actual performance. In any event, the public library foundation can expect a declaration of tax exemption six to twenty-four months after organizing. The IRS offers several resources online (www.irs.gov) to help with the process, including the Tax-Exempt Organizations Tax Kit and Tax Information for Charitable Organizations.

About the Author

Benjamin Goldberg is the Library Development Officer at the Williamsburg Regional Library in Virginia. He holds degrees from Bard College and the College of William and Mary.

Part II

An Advocacy Mini-Toolkit

You've probably been hearing a lot about library advocacy lately. In these turbulent economic times, libraries are under more pressure than ever to prove their value and relevancy. The selections that follow will not only help you become an effective advocate for your library, but also will provide ideas for building and sustaining partnerships and more.

In "Advocacy Basics" from the PLA publication *Libraries Prosper with Passion, Purpose, and Persuasion!* you'll get an excellent overview of advocacy basics and tips for getting your own advocacy efforts started. In "Advocate for More: Focus on Legislative Funding," Stephanie Gerding describes how to use community members to advocate for the library. In "A+ Partners in Education: Linking Libraries to Education for a Flourishing Future," Valerie Gross details how her library was positioned as a full partner in the education of the county's youth, heightening the library's visibility and building the next generation of library supporters.

These brief but information-packed excerpts and articles will give you and your library advocates ideas for refining or developing an advocacy plan or partnership to demonstrate the value of your library.

Chapter 5

Advocacy Basics

Metropolitan Group with PLA @ Your Library Taskforce

Communications is a core need for libraries of all sizes in all locations. Good communication is two-way, which means listening to community needs and developing library programs and services that respond to what you have heard from the community. Communication practices we commonly use in libraries include marketing, public relations and advocacy.

Marketing, public relations, and advocacy are all approaches to telling the story of the library in your community on an ongoing basis and increasing perceived value among library constituencies for the library and the valuable resources, programs, and services it delivers every day. PLA's Smartest Card project is an example of these types of approaches.

This toolkit focuses on advocacy, but it's helpful to understand how advocacy is different from other efforts and what types of challenges are best addressed by each practice. When combined, the approaches below are the foundation of a successful, ongoing communication program that ensures your library is top of mind in your community.

Marketing: Focused on creating a transaction between a customer and the provider of a service, program, or product. Marketing is best used by libraries to do some of the following things:

- Increase program participation
- Increase the number of card holders
- Reach special populations
- Engage specific audiences to use key services

Public Relations: Focused on creating mutually beneficial relationships between an organization and the audiences that are the keys to its success. Public relations is best used by libraries to create and sustain long-term relationships with stakeholders, friends, funders, voters, community leaders, potential partners and others whose influence and contributions are necessary. It supports marketing and advocacy efforts because it is focused on the long-term impact.

Advocacy: Webster simplifies it this way: to support or urge by argument, especially publicly. Advocacy is creating an argument in support of a specific proposal and getting your audience to say "yes." Advocacy is best used by libraries to advance specific proposals such as your budget and is best for addressing challenges such as funding or policy questions and advancing issues (e.g., literacy, freedom of speech/press information, privacy rights, etc.).

Why Do You Need to Be a Library Advocate?

You need to be a library advocate because if those closest to the library aren't championing the library's role in the community, why should anyone else?

You need to be advocates because you and those who work in your library are the first line of defense against claims of irrelevance, displacement by technology, demotion on the list of community priorities, declining literacy, and ultimately, erosion of the memory of our collective communities.

Who Can Be an Advocate?

The more passionate voices you have to tell your library story the better. As an advocacy champion, your job is to encourage staff, Trustees, Friends, stakeholders, community partners and leaders to join you in becoming the voice of the library within your community. Remember, others can say things you can't and can be more direct than you in advocating for your library. As you work your way through this toolkit, you will learn how to do just that. Some examples of people you can help enlist as library advocates include:

- You
- Staff (professional staff, pages, etc.)
- Customers
- Community partners
- Teachers and other education professionals
- Friends of the Library
- Board members/Trustees
- Foundation board members
- Volunteers
- Community and business leaders
- Political leaders
- Health care professionals
- Realtors and developers
- Community development staff in your city or county

About the Authors

Metropolitan Group with PLA @ Your Library Taskforce. The Public Library Association (PLA), a division of the American Library Association (ALA), worked with the Metropolitan Group (MG) to develop the publication,

Libraries Prosper with Passion, Purpose, and Persuasion! A PLA Toolkit for Success. The Metropolitan Group is a strategic communications and resource development firm with offices in Portland, Oregon; Chicago, Illinois; and Washington, DC.

Chapter 6

Advocate for More:
Focus on Legislative Funding

Stephanie Gerding

The normal focus of the "Bringing in the Money" column is alternative funding sources, such as grants, library cafes, and book sales, but these strategies should never be employed without ensuring that more traditional revenue streams are safeguarded. One way to do this is to enlist the support and assistance of library advocates to speak on behalf of your library. We may think of going to our local city council for funding support, but we should also not forget the large amount of state and federal dollars that are allocated for libraries each year; for example, consider the $262,240,000 that was the IMLS 2007 budget appropriation for library programs.[1] According to ALA's handbook for advocacy, "Keeping legislators informed about library concerns, trends, and successes is the best way to turn them into supporters and even library champions."[2] Reinforcing the value of our libraries to our elected officials and community leaders can help support local, state, and federal library revenue.

Finding the Right Advocates

First, you should determine who should represent the library. If the thought of meeting with elected officials or other funders sends you in a panic, remember that a library advocate can be the perfect person for this task. If you think of the true meaning of an advocate, it is someone who speaks on behalf of another, for example, a child advocate or an attorney that represents the interests of someone else. We can advocate for ourselves, for our libraries, but it is not nearly as effective as when someone else does.

The claim is sometimes made that the person delivering the message can be more important than the message itself. If you think about how likely you are to listen to a political telemarketer regarding an issue versus a family member, friend, or coworker, you can see the importance of having the right people delivering the library's messages.

"Bringing in the Money," a regular column in *Public Libraries*, presents fund-raising strategies for public libraries. Many librarians are turning to alternative funding sources to supplement shrinking budgets. Fund-raising efforts not only boost finances, but also leverage community support and build collaborative strategies.

In Arizona we've seen the power of library advocates. The Arizona State Library initiated a statewide program for strategic planning using PLA's *The New Planning for Results*.[3] In 2002, Sandra Nelson, the book's author, trained twenty librarians who were then charged with taking another library through the strategic planning process. Each library formed a community committee. This committee was made up of stakeholders, representatives of all major segments of the local populace. The committee was involved in the initial steps of the process, a needs assessment of the community that focused not on the library but on the local situation and the true issues the community was facing. These leaders became engaged in the work and the purpose of the library; many are now true library advocates. The success stories of the strategic planning process have been compiled, and a recurring theme has been an increase in budgets and funding to the libraries. Often requests from library directors that previously were not funded were realized when the appeal was made by a community member instead of a library employee.

The right person to be your advocate will vary according to what the message is. A library advocate communicates the value of the library to their audience. And that value will depend on what is important to the individuals present. A mother who brings her child to storytime every week values the library for different reasons (her sanity?) than someone who is beginning a home business and is using the library's computers for research and to write a business plan. Decide what audience you want to target first and then find advocates from their peer groups. For example, some libraries are finding great success in using teen advocates to speak in their classes and to other groups about the resources a library can offer rather than having a librarian who may have less influence. While you probably don't want to appeal to teens for funding, they can be great advocates to take with you on library legislative day to tell their stories of why the library is valuable.

We know what amazing outcomes public libraries produce every day, but many community leaders don't. Most of them will share with you their happy memories of going to the library as a child. But they also think that by working in a library, you spend most of your day reading books, right? Many adults who don't use the library have no idea what the library is doing today besides providing books. They aren't aware that libraries are in need of funds and support.

As GladysAnn Wells, Arizona state librarian, has said, "Build connections before you need them. Think of your contacts as a savings account. Determine well in advance of your need: who might be willing to help you, who can stop you, and what each of them might want that you could supply."

The American Library Association has an online advocacy resource center (www.ala.org/ala/issues/issuesadvocacy.htm) with a lot of helpful information, including the *Library Advocate's Handbook* (www.ala.org/ala/advocacy-bucket/libraryadvocateshandbook.pdf).

Mobilizing for Legislative Action

The most influential role of an advocate can be to mobilize people to a course of action. An important action is, of course, to direct finances to support and maintain libraries. By educating and organizing advocates, libraries can influence legislative actions. And advocating for a particular cause is a huge component in the democratic process.

When thinking of whom you should invite to meet with a legislator or accompany you as a delegate, think of whom those elected officials consider the most important people. Of course, it is the voter who is the most important. Other VIPs include campaign supporters and donors, local leaders, newspaper editors or other media executives, and personal friends or acquaintances. Think of who you know that can champion your library's causes.

Some libraries even advertise online for library advocates. Providing a few tip sheets and having some structured meetings, which can even be run by your Friends group or a board member, can be a simple way to increase community support.

Meeting with Elected Officials

There are many ways library advocates can help you increase funding for your library. Let's examine just one of these—contacting elected officials.

There are many ways to contact your elected officials. These tips describe effective methods for making an impact. Attorney Roberta Voss, past lobbyist for the Arizona Library Association and a former three-term legislator, provided them. Use one of several modes of communications to get your message across. Remember to focus on the people in your community and their needs.

In-person Meetings with Elected Officials

Prepare for the Meeting
- Arrange for a small group of people who share your concerns to participate; this can include members of your community.
- Decide what the group will say and who will speak on each issue.
- Limit your visit to one or two topics.
- Determine what you hope to get out of the meeting—an agreement to sponsor a bill, for example.
- Find out if there are any personal, professional, or political connections to the elected official among your advocates.

During the Meeting

- Be prompt and patient; schedules often change.
- Present your case. Explain what you want your legislator to do and why. Keep it short and focused; you may have only ten minutes.
- Give personal and local examples of the impact the proposed legislation will have on your home state or district.
- If you don't know the answer to a question, offer to find out and send the information back to the office later.
- Keep control of the visit. Don't be put off by long-winded answers or avoidance. Your appointment time is limited.
- Find out if your legislator has heard opposing views. If so, find out what the arguments are and what groups are involved.
- Do not confront, threaten, pressure, or beg.
- Leave a brief position paper or fact sheet when you leave.

Follow-up

- Send a thank-you note that reiterates the important points of your issue.
- You can always invite your elected officials to participate in your library's activities. You might ask them to address a group, present them with an award, or have them tour a facility. These events leave a lasting impression about the library and build a relationship with the legislator that can be useful.

Telephone Calls

A phone call is a good way to let your legislator know how you or your organization feels about a particular issue. Elected officials pay close attention to these calls as a measure of voter sentiment. An outpouring of calls can sometimes change the vote of a legislator; even a small number of calls can make a difference.

When you call, ask if your senator or representative could send you a written response. This will help ensure that your call gets counted. You can also ask if the office has received other calls from constituents on the same issue, and if so, what position most of the callers took on the issue.

Letters

Letters can also make a difference. Legislators rely on letters to find out what the people in their districts are thinking. Letter-writing can be the first step in building an ongoing relationship with your legislators. Here are some guidelines to follow when writing:

- Spell the legislator's name correctly.
- Write legibly or type your letter.
- Address your legislators properly; for senators or representatives, use "The Honorable [insert name]"
- For a salutation, use "Dear Representative [last name]." If you know your legislators at all, use their first names; your letter will receive more attention.

- Use your own words. Personal letters are far more effective than preprinted postcards or petitions.
- Clearly state the topic you are writing about and your position on it in the opening sentences. For example, "I'm writing to oppose steep cuts in education and libraries."
- Refer to bills by name and number if possible.
- Stay on one topic. If you want to write about other issues, send another letter at a later date.
- Give reasons for your position. As appropriate, use personal experience or a concrete example to make your case.
- Raise questions. A well-formulated question can get a personal response.
- Keep it short. One page is best. Use two pages if necessary and for completeness.
- Be polite, positive, and constructive. Don't plead, and never threaten.
- Be timely. Write before decisions are made and action is taken, but do not write too long before the vote or it may be forgotten.
- Use your name and address on both the letter and the envelope. This helps the legislator in replying and identifies you as a constituent.
- Write to thank your legislators when they take actions with which you agree. It's surprising how few letters of appreciation are received at capitols. If staff members are particularly helpful, thank them by mentioning your gratitude in the letter to your legislator.

E-mail
You can e-mail your legislators to save time and stamps. Keep e-mails short, and make sure you let them know if you are a constituent.

Editorials
Writing editorials can be an effective way to develop community support and drum up editor interest in your position. Comments are more likely to be published if concisely and thoughtfully written.

Finding Your Elected Officials
ALA provides a **database of elected officials and media outlets** (www.capwiz.com/ala/dbq/officials) that includes background information and contact details that you can search by state or zip code. If you wish to call a Washington, D.C. office, you can reach your senator or representative through the Capitol Switchboard. Simply dial (202) 224-3121 and ask for your member of Congress.

Many state library associations help coordinate a library legislative day. This can be a great time to meet with your governmental representatives. Usually there will be a meeting for librarians that will summarize the legislative agenda and give tips on advocating for library issues and legislation of importance to the library community.

ALA coordinates the National Library Legislative Day, a spring event in which people who support libraries go to Washington, D.C. and participate in advocacy and issue training sessions, interact with Capitol Hill insiders, and visit congressional offices to ask Congress to pass legislation that supports libraries.

Notes

1. IMLS budget, www.imls.gov/about.shtm (accessed June 15, 2009).
2. ALA, The Library Advocate's Handbook, www.ala.org/ala/aboutala/offices/ola/libraryadvocateshandbook.pdf (accessed June 15, 2009).
3. Arizona State Library, Archives and Public Records, "Arizona Public Libraries Planning for Results," www.lib.az.us/extension/planningForResults.cfm (accessed June 15, 2009).

About the Author

Stephanie Gerding is a librarian, author, and trainer. She presents workshops around the country and online on grants, leadership, and technology topics. She is coauthor of *Grants for Libraries: A How-To-Do-It Manual* (Neal-Schuman) and the library grants blog (librarygrants.blogspot.com).

Chapter 7

A+ Partners in Education: Linking Libraries to Education for a Flourishing Future

Valerie J. Gross

In September 2002, Howard County Library and the Howard County Public School System in Columbia, Maryland, announced the formation of A+ Partners in Education, a formalized partnership designed to position the public library as a full partner in the education of the county's 48,000 public school students. The partnership promotes scholarship, assists with eliminating student achievement gaps, and expands the academic opportunities for each student. The partnership also heightens the visibility and importance of the library and school media centers, shapes the role of librarians as educators, links libraries to a commonly understood definition of education, and builds the next generation of library customers and supporters, ensuring the future of the library.

A few years back, a young journalist called me, eager to ask questions for a feature article. As the director of the Howard County Library (HCL), I was happy to oblige, and spoke with her for more than an hour about A+ Partners in Education, a newly implemented initiative between HCL and Howard County Public School System (HCPSS).[1] Nearly three years later, I can still hear her concluding comments: "Wow! I grew up in Howard County. I wish all of this had been in place to help *me* when *I* was in school!"

In fact, much of it had been available—she simply had not realized it. And it is likely that her teachers and parents had not viewed the library as playing a major role in education either. Yet we, and most public libraries, have provided academic assistance that supports school curricula for years. Indeed, all library services and programs fall under the umbrella of lifelong education.

A+ Partners in Education capitalizes on the value the community places in education and serves as a catalyst to change public perceptions of the library. We repackaged traditional services for students and enhanced our overall program with innovative ideas and cutting-edge components. A comprehensive network of communication serves to connect the library with the entire school system. If our young journalist were starting school today, I am confident she would view HCL as an integral aspect of her twelve years of required education.

Now in its third year, the partnership has resulted in extraordinary gains for both the schools and the library. The schools benefit from students' improved academic performance. For the library, the partnership augments visibility and links libraries to a commonly understood definition of education and its indispensability, which we can then expand to our services for all ages. At the same time, the partnership is leveraging public funding, making school media center and public library jobs more rewarding, and developing new generations of library customers who will value and support the library.

The Essence of the Partnership

The overall essence of the partnership can be summarized with the example of a student, "Sara," who is just entering kindergarten. When Sara's parents register her for school in March, they will be asked to complete a HCL card application along with school forms. Sara will receive her new library card in the mail, along with an incentive to register for the Summer Reading Program and an invitation to "Kindergarten Here We Come!" at her liaison library. Sara and her parents will hear library staff speak at Sara's Back to School night. In October, Sara's class will take a field trip to the library as part of the full-day kindergarten curriculum. Throughout the year, Sara will experience library staff presentations in her classroom, and she will return to the library for additional curriculum-related field trips arranged by her teacher. Sara, her parents, and her siblings will have an opportunity to attend family night at the library hosted by her school's Parent-Teacher Association (PTA). Through the schools, Sara will learn about extracurricular library services and children's programs; for example, children's books in Chinese or author programs featuring popular writers such as Linda Sue Park, Lemony Snicket, and Jack Gantos.

As years progress and homework mounts, Sara will learn that in addition to guidance from her school's media specialist, she can receive assistance from professionals at the public library, who will be able to plan ahead for Sara's projects thanks to Assignment Alerts her teachers forward to HCL. Sara will learn that her library card provides her access to full-text databases available from school, home, or the library. To help her with specific homework questions, Sara will learn that she has access to a personal online tutor—for free— from 2 p.m. to midnight, seven days a week, in the core subjects of math, science, social studies, and English. If Sara does not have Internet access at home, she will be able to use any of the library's 325 public-access computers during prime homework time (after school, evenings, and weekends) and that word-processing programs are also available at each branch for projects that must be typed.

The Partnership in the Making

Before the A+ Partnership, HCL had worked with twelve of the county's sixty-nine schools at varying levels. Activities included setting up library tables at back-to-school nights, periodic library card drives, and taking library programs into the schools. Some schools also brought students into the library. Nevertheless, relations were less than ideal with many schools, where it was our perception that there was little interest in working together. In addition, any communication, brochure, or flyer we sent to the schools for dissemination required individual approval, delaying the process and chilling outreach efforts.

We began imagining a countywide partnership where working relations and communication with media specialists, principals, faculty, and staff would be ideal, where students would receive library cards through the schools, and where library staff would be viewed by the schools as adjunct faculty. We pictured a world where students, faculty, and the community would view the library as critical to education.

After securing the support of the superintendent of schools, library staff, media specialists, and key school administrators met with us to begin plans. We set out to convince the schools (especially media specialists) that this program would supplement and enhance existing school and media center programs, and that we could implement the partnership with our existing staffs and budgets. A handful of ideas blossomed, and over the course of one year, we shaped the partnership's vision, mission, and objectives.

Each of the county's schools was assigned a liaison public library, along with a staff member responsible for regular communication.

After the signing of an official agreement, public library staff met individually with principals, assistant principals, media specialists, and reading specialists at all sixty-nine schools to explain how the collaboration would enhance student achievement. Each meeting generated more enthusiasm. One hurried principal, who said she only had thirty minutes for the meeting, was still envisioning ideas two hours later. Another principal, who initially did not want to meet, requested one thousand library card applications for her school. She also said she would require students to use the library for certain assignments. The designated library's branch manager and partnership liaison (a children's or teen specialist) represented HCL at each of these meetings.

A+ Vision

The A+ Partners in Education vision promotes scholarship and expands the educational opportunities for Howard County's public school students, providing each student the best possible chance of overall academic success.

The mission includes ensuring that every student has and uses an HCL card and developing programs that encourage reading and assist with the completion of school assignments. The initiative applies a comprehensive approach to working with the schools, providing for a solid, unified, county-wide program.

In short, we are taking the public library into *all* schools, and we are bringing the schools—students and faculty—into the public library to assist with eliminating achievement gaps and improving grades. Working from school, at the library or from home, all students have the same access to databases, online tutoring, and professional assistance with projects and assignments. With the passage of the No Child Left Behind Act of 2001 and the revised SAT test that includes an essay component, this initiative is especially important, as schools are focusing on improving student test scores, especially in reading and writing.

Key Components
The following components of the partnership play a major role in its success.

Library Cards
Students receive library cards through school registration. School personnel place public library card applications in kindergarten and new student registration packets, then collect and send the completed forms to the library. Library staff mail the cards to the students' homes. We have processed more than 14,000 library cards through the partnership, as well as 800 A+ Teacher cards, a special program for teachers that we instituted. While this systematic approach will eventually end the need for library card drives, until such time, the schools are coordinating drives, with many principals aiming for 100 percent participation.

Sometimes we get additional help. The grandfather of a third grader reported that a librarian had visited his grandson's class, asking how many of the children had a library card. All students, except his grandson, raised their hands. Hearing that his grandson was the only one who did not have a library card, the grandfather gave all of his grandchildren library cards as gifts. When asked how old his grandchildren were, he replied, "Five weeks to eleven years old. I guess I should start the little one now—I don't want her not to have something that all children have."

Commitment from Both Organizations
Commitment from both organizations contributes to the success of the partnership. One of the strongest indications of the commitment and value the schools place in the partnership occurred this past year. The school system decided to add an annual field trip to the library to its kindergarten curriculum. In support of this decision, HCPSS superintendent Sydney L. Cousin said, "Establishing this academic connection with the library at the beginning of each child's twelve years of education can only further one of our major goals: bridging achievement gaps among students."[2]

Assignment Alerts
Teachers communicate with media specialists and library staff about upcoming assignments through online Assignment Alerts. One alert informed staff that 117 fourth graders would be assigned a Native American folktale to read. Advance notice allowed staff to bolster the branch's collection with copies from

other branches. One hundred books were checked out to the students. Another alert allowed preparation time to assist seventh graders with a history project. A student wrote, "Thank you for helping me receive an 'A' on my Cleisthenes project. Without your assistance, I would have spent twice the time getting half the work done."

Online Tutors

Through the library's Web site, students have access to online tutors—for free—from 2 p.m. to midnight, seven days a week. Tutors—who are graduate students, retired teachers, or teachers desiring supplemental income—assist with homework questions in math, science, English, and social studies. Students also may request homework help en Español. Students key their school, grade, and library card number into a computer, which launches a virtual classroom. Although students log on for tutoring in all available subjects, most log on for assistance in algebra, geometry, calculus, trigonometry, and chemistry. Feedback has been overwhelmingly positive from the nearly 20,000 sessions recorded since September 2002, as evidenced by the following sampling of comments:

- "Excellent tutor; great service. I'm glad my library is offering it!"
- "This was very helpful in the proofreading of my essay."
- "A great resource when you're stuck on something."
- "[My online tutor was the] best math teacher I ever had."
- "Never, ever, stop this. My mom does not remember algebra and I would be lost without this."

In true partnership spirit, the schools share in the expense of providing this service. Assistant superintendent of curriculum and instruction Robert O. Glascock stated, "I truly believe that the more we can engage kids around libraries, the stronger their overall education will be. Online homework assistance through the library plays an important part in accelerating student success as we work toward the goal of eliminating achievement gaps among student groups."[3]

Full-text Databases

Online tutoring complements two other remote-access services available through the library's Web site. Available 24/7, students search full-text databases for their research needs (for example, *Encyclopedia Americana, Groves Dictionary of Art, Biography Resource Center, Access Science,* 125,000 full-text poems, and thousands of newspapers and magazines), and use AskUsNow!, Maryland's statewide virtual reference service.

Two-way Communication

Library liaisons place high priority on maintaining ongoing communication with their counterpart school liaisons. School liaisons disseminate partnership information to the school's faculty and administration, who, in turn, communicate the information to students and parents through school newsletters,

Web sites, meetings, and classroom announcements. Numerous principals send e-mail to their entire faculty, emphasizing the importance of students capitalizing on the partnership, especially library databases and online tutoring assistance. Principals ask teachers to give extra credit to students who use library resources and encourage them to forward assignment alert forms to the library. In addition, the A+ Advisory Committee, comprised of school and library staff, meets monthly to continue cultivating close working relations, review progress, and discuss new ideas. We also keep board members at both the library and the schools informed through regular updates, and library staff serve on the school system's district planning team, media advisory committee, and technology advisory committee, which keeps the partnership visible among key school administrators.

Publicity
Publicity continues to build momentum. We promote the partnership through public speaking, television segments, newspaper articles, library publications, school newsletters, and conference presentations. (At a PTA council meeting last year, the audience of PTA presidents and school representatives seized every last packet of materials I had brought along the instant I finished speaking.)

At the conclusion of the first and second years of the partnership, we hosted celebrations that were attended by elected officials at federal, state, and local levels; library and school board members; community dignitaries; and leaders and representatives from the Maryland Department of Education and the American Library Association. The events featured presentations from school media specialists and library staff who shared stories illustrating the benefits of the partnership. At this year's celebration, Nancy Grasmick, Maryland state superintendent of schools, described the partnership as "enhancing educational excellence." Irene Padilla, Maryland superintendent for libraries, announced a $25,000 continuation grant in addition to the initial $52,000 grant for the development of the partnership during its second year, emphasizing the importance of producing an A+ Tool Kit for the benefit of other public libraries wishing to replicate the program.

Connecting with Students, Faculty, and Parents
By bringing the library into the schools and vice versa, we have connected with more than 150,000 students, faculty, and parents since the partnership's inception. The first year of the partnership, we said "yes" to nearly every program idea that teachers and media specialists brought to the table. The second year, we developed a catalog of programs that outlined available library staff presentations from which teachers could choose to supplement their courses, all of which correlated to elementary, middle, and high school curricula. Programs, which we present either at the schools or in the library, include Computer Resources, Geography to Go, Spirit of America, Middle East Cultural Enrichment, and Law Day Mock Trials. In addition, we offer book talks and

story times (such as Multicultural Medley and Dr. Seuss on the Loose) relating to ongoing themes during the school year. Responses from media specialists and teachers to these programs have been overwhelmingly positive. The schools value the lineup of choices, and library staff appreciate that the catalog provides variety within parameters to facilitate consistent quality and adequate preparation time.

Library staff are frequently invited to present customized partnership programs for teachers. For instance, when speaking to English instructional leaders, we focused on assistance available to students working on research papers at both the media centers and at the public library; they were so impressed that we have been invited back to present the same program for *all* high school English teachers at their in-service day!

We aim to be responsive to teachers' needs. When teachers at an elementary school reported they were having difficulty motivating third-grade students to complete their curriculum's twenty-five-book reading requirement, we developed a reading game as an incentive. The game featured the school's mascot walking through the woods, encountering books along a path. As they read, students received prizes. Library staff visited the class, booktalking and bringing books the students could borrow. The school also brought the class to the library. As a result, all students are now on target for their mandated reading requirement. This program will be made available to all elementary schools in the county. The game board can be modified to feature the school's mascot, and the liaison branch library can provide ongoing assistance through booktalks and visits.

Also in response to teacher requests, we initiated an A+ Teacher Library Card. The card gives teachers who are employed in Howard County schools special borrowing privileges for materials used in preparing lessons or assisting students with assignments. Teachers may borrow materials for six weeks and renew materials once; they are given a ten-day grace period for fines. The cards were an immediate success. In the past eight months, we issued eight hundred A+ Teacher cards—including two hundred the first day of teacher orientation!

We are especially pleased about the increased opportunities we have to connect with parents. We now are invited to speak to parents about the partnership as part of the program agenda at First Day of School and Back-to-School Night meetings. In addition, family nights at the library sponsored by the schools' PTAs provide opportunities to inform parents of the academic support the library provides for their students. While classroom presentations and PTA events grant us opportunities to connect with students and parents, we have also implemented the following programs.

Dogs Educating and Assisting Readers

In partnership with Fidos for Freedom, the schools, and the Friends of HCL, the library offers Dogs Educating and Assisting Readers (DEAR). Third graders visit the library on Saturday mornings to read to a loving, nonjudgmental audience: therapy dogs. One parent wrote, "My daughter was a shy reader who blossomed into a confident one. She fell in love with 'her' dog and believed that the dogs needed to be read to as much as she needed to read." Students begin the program reading two to five levels below their target level and usually read at or above grade level upon completion. Fidos for Freedom won Howard County's Community Organization of the Year award for this joint program with the library.

Book Club for Boys
We initiated a successful program for middle-school boys, Book Club for Boys. With statistics showing that boys score lower on standardized reading and writing tests than girls, it is especially important to facilitate programs intended to get boys excited about reading. The boys meet weekly after school. Mystery books are the most popular.

A+ Summer Reading Program Promotional Video
Our jointly produced A+ summer reading program promotional videos now bolster the in-person summer reading marketing we do each year in May. Library staff, school faculty, and students (who receive class credits for the projects) write and produce three videos—one each for elementary, middle, and high school students. The Maryland State Department of Education's Division of Library Development and Services funded this year's videos and distributed them to library systems throughout the state.

Spelling Bee
The new HCL Spelling Bee is inspiring students to improve their spelling, increase their vocabularies, learn word etymology, and develop correct English usage. Winners from the forty bees held in fall 2004 at public schools, private schools, and home school associations participated in HCL's Spelling Bee on March 18 before an audience of 800 people. The overall champion represented Harford County at the National Spelling Bee in Washington, D.C., all expenses paid. Sponsored by *The Baltimore Sun,* the HCL Spelling Bee is organized as a regional bee under the rules of the Scripps-Howard National Spelling Bee.

English for Speakers of Other Languages
To assist with bridging achievement gaps among English for Speakers of Other Languages (ESOL) students, we expanded our outreach to the ESOL community, coordinating numerous tours and introducing library resources and programs to these students and their parents. The schools' ESOL office translates library card applications, brochures, and other library publications into the top four languages spoken in the county: Spanish, Chinese, Korean, and Urdu. This past year, the summer reading program game board was translated into three languages. We also are targeting schools with high ESOL populations for on-site summer reading program registration. Additionally, we visit Newcomers classes (high school courses for first-generation immigrants) every two

weeks, bringing books at appropriate reading levels on topics suggested by the teacher. The classes also visit the library, and interested students participate in an evening program at the library with their parents. Teachers say the increased contact with the library has resulted in these students reading more and achieving better English skills.

Measurable Outcomes

While principals, teachers, and students have credited the partnership with contributing to improved grades, higher test scores, and increased reading levels, it is important to produce measurable outcomes that support these assertions. To this end, four schools have agreed to serve as models for purposes of evaluation. Serving as a model school involves a greater commitment on the part of the schools' principals and media specialists to work closely with the library. Teachers submit assignment alerts allowing the library to measure the benefits of having staff prepared to assist with specific projects. Library staff is conducting pre- and post- surveys of students and faculty to find out how library use has changed since beginning the partnership. Measurable outcomes will support the assertion that the partnership helps bridge achievement gaps, increase reading, and assist in improving grades and test scores. The Institute of Museum and Library Services (IMLS) funded the outcome-based evaluations we are using.

A+ On the Rise

As the partnership progressed, library staff offered a number of presentations to the library community. We talked about the partnership's successes at the 2004 PLA conference, at a 2003 meeting of the YALSA executive board, and at numerous Maryland events, which led to inquiries from libraries across the state and across the country.

At PLA's conference, HCL led a session called "Changing Perceptions: Public Libraries As Partners in Education." One of the attendees wrote, "I think the time spent at your program was worth the price of admission to PLA all by itself."

The Wadsworth (Ohio) Public Library has launched its own A+ initiative. Director C. Allen Nichols confirms the remarkable benefits of the program, noting, "We will not likely discover a partnership that provides more benefits for our efforts than A+ Partners in Education."[4] Commenting on changed perceptions, he added:

> Now that Wadsworth Public Library is connected with education in this visible way, we are seeing far more students and parents using library resources. Just as important, the general public is beginning to view library staff as educators and is placing a higher value in the library and its contributions to quality of life in the community.[5]

Charles County (MD) Public Library director Emily Ferren, who is in the process of implementing a comprehensive partnership with the schools, observed:

Teachers, students and parents appreciate the variety of library programs that also reinforce the school curriculum. Even though our partnership is still in its infancy, we are already reaping the benefits of strengthened relations with the schools and with the Charles County community including private schools and those home schooled.[6]

Extraordinary Gains

Howard County has seen extraordinary gains for both the schools and the library. The schools have acquired access to research materials, databases, online tutors, and an additional band of adjunct faculty (library staff) who provide homework assistance to students. Schools also benefit from the training and programs library staff provide for teachers and students. The partnership expands the resources available to media specialists, who now view the library as an extension of their services. Branch library hours extend student research and homework assistance time into evenings, weekends, and school vacations.

Although library professionals also care about more complete homework, better projects, improved test scores, and increased reading, there are other significant gains for school media centers and public libraries—and for the library profession in general. School media centers and media specialists have been recognized time and again since the launch of the partnership as an essential component of students' overall education. Carol Fritts, coordinator of media and educational technology for HCPSS, recommends the partnership to schools. "All schools should take advantage of the opportunities offered by the A+ Partnership because it greatly increases the resources available to students and teachers in our schools," she said.[7]

From HCL's standpoint, a library system that serves a county of 270,000 people, the gains beyond contributions to student academic achievement have been astonishing. Over the past three years:

- visits to the library more than doubled—from 1 million to 2.1 million;
- borrowing soared from 3 million titles to 5 million;
- program attendance climbed nearly 200 percent, from 60,000 to 177,000 participants;
- reference questions increased 41 percent, from 760,000 to 1,072,000;
- electronic visits nearly tripled—from 5 million to 12 million; and
- summer reading program participation rose by 50 percent.

In addition, 95 percent of Howard County residents now hold library cards—more than 10,000 cards have been issued through the partnership.

While many library systems across the country experienced budget cuts in 2004, Howard County government raised taxes to support education, the definition of which included libraries. The tax increase funded three additional full-time positions at HCL and an 8 percent salary increase for library staff. County executive James N. Robey justified the tax increase by focusing on the need to fund the county's school and library systems. He stated, "the tax increase is vital to keep Howard County's schools and libraries top-notch."[8]

Since the launching of the A+ Partnership, HCL has won the Howard County Chamber of Commerce's Non-Profit Business of the Year Award and the school system selected the library for its Accelerating Academic Achievement (Triple A) Partnership award. Additionally, one of the strongest and most visible statements of the impact the partnership has had in linking the library with education came when Hope Chase, HCL's head of youth services, was chosen as Educator of the Year by the Howard County Chamber of Commerce. For the first time ever, the Chamber of Commerce allowed public library educators to be nominated for this prestigious award, along with educators from public schools and the community college.

The most remarkable benefit the partnership brings to libraries is the highly visible link to education, shaping an overall image that libraries are an integral part of the education process. This is important because people understand and value education—even people who have never set foot in a library. Being linked with education can only further elevate our profession. Our jobs are more satisfying because more people understand what we do, and we gain more recognition for what we have been contributing all along. When linked with education as most people define it, libraries and librarians become more valued in the eyes of the community, assisting us as we advocate for increased funding.

A much longer-term benefit is the way the partnership is building a solid base of customers. If students, as part of their education, use and value the library, we will be constantly building the next generation of library customers and supporters, who will link all that we do to an expanded definition of education, assuring libraries an important role in the future.

Notes

1. For further details regarding how the partnership began, the planning process, and struggles along the way, see also "A+ Partners in Education: Positioning Libraries As a Cornerstone in the Education Process," *Children and Libraries* 1, no. 2 (Summer/Fall 2003): 27–31.
2. Sydney Cousin, opening remarks, A+ Partners in Education Celebration, Oct. 7, 2004.
3. Robert O. Glascock, kindergarten curriculum staff meeting, Sept. 1, 2004.
4. C. Allen Nichols, personal correspondence with author, Apr. 12, 2004.
5. Ibid.
6. Emily Ferren, personal correspondence with author, Nov. 30, 2004.
7. Presentation at Statewide Invitational Leadership Conference, sponsored by the Council of Educational, Administrative, and Supervisory Organizations of Maryland and by the Maryland Department of Education, Nov. 5, 2004.
8. "Tax Referendum Petitions Submitted," *Baltimore Sun,* July 23, 2003.

About the Author

Valerie J. Gross is Director of the Howard County Library in Columbia, Maryland.

A+ Partners in Education: Addendum, May 19, 2009

This fall will mark the beginning of the eighth year of A+ Partners in Education, the comprehensive partnership between Howard County (MD) Library and the county's schools. The partnership, as well as Howard County Library's overall alignment with education, have since expanded significantly and continue to thrive.

What's new with A+? The partnership now officially includes Howard Community College (HCC) in addition to Howard County Public School System (HCPSS). As with HCPSS, HCC students receive Howard County Library (HCL) cards through the school's registration process. While HCL Children's and Teen Information Specialists and Instructors serve as A+ liaisons for each elementary, middle, and high school, HCL's Adult Instructors connect with HCC liaisons in each of its academic divisions (e.g., Mathematics, Science and Technology, Arts and Humanities, English and World Languages, and Business and Computer Systems). Since the partnership's inception in 2002, interactions between library staff members and HCPSS and HCC students, parents, and faculty total 422,000. To date, 34,000 A+ library cards have been processed, of which 2,800 are educator cards.

Also notable, HCPSS has added links to the A+ Assignment Alert Forms on its Web site for teachers, and A+ *Curriculum Enhancement Guides* describing available A+ classes taught by HCL instructors (either in the school classroom or at HCL) are now compiled for elementary, middle, and high school faculty.

To ease the transition from pre-K to Kindergarten, HCL began offering Kindergarten, Here We Come! A+ classes. Held in August, students listen to stories about Kindergarten, participate in activities, and practice boarding a real school bus courtesy of HCPSS and the Friends of HCL. Moving Up to Middle School was also added to the line-up of A+ classes for students entering sixth grade. Students meet at HCL to hear study tips, learn about their specific school, and meet other students attending their new school.

Perhaps the most impressive addition to A+ since 2005, Battle of the Books is a glorified reading exam sponsored by the Friends of HCL and the Rotary Club of Columbia. The academic competition attracts audiences exceeding 1,000, who flock to the event to watch some 60 teams of five fifth grade students compete for the gold medal. Guided by a coach, each group prepares for months, reading and studying 16 assigned books that cover a range of interests, including adventure, folk tale, memoir, poetry, biography, science, and civics. The "Battle" comprises 50 questions for which students are given 30 seconds to answer. Runners in each aisle collect the answer sheets and judges tally the scores. Elected officials clamor to be the judges who bestow "Best Costume," "Best Team Name," "Best Team Spirit," and "Best Civility" awards.

Launched in 2007, Choose Civility continues to gain momentum, receiving major press coverage locally, nationally, and even internationally—as far away as *The Times of India*. The initiative includes nearly 100 partners and supporters representing a cross-section of the community. HCPSS and HCC have been major partners in this initiative, sponsoring poster contests, developing anti-bullying policies, hosting civility-related workshops and seminars, and cosponsoring major events. Representatives from both institutions serve on the Choose Civility Board of Advisors.

What else is envisioned for A+? As part of our new Miller Branch & Historical Center, currently in the final phases of design, we are planning to bring history to life in an unprecedented fashion, which includes students and their local history curriculum. The new branch will also be an ideal place to focus on students' environmental education. In addition to the building's LEED Silver Certification and outdoor classroom space, discussions are underway for an organic garden that would involve the area's PTAs and students, as organic food is a growing passion in the area.

Plans are also under way to strengthen and augment A+ Partners in Education by establishing formal partnerships with all Howard County schools—including the Chinese and Korean schools—and postsecondary institutions.

Lastly, while A+ Partners in Education was the first step in HCL's positioning as a major component of Howard County's strong educational system, HCL has aligned its *entire program* under education—because education is, without fail, the highest priority of any elected official's budget.

Through consistent advocacy, HCL has been moved to the Education Section of Howard County's Operating and Capital Budgets (previously under Community Services). While symbolic, the move to the Education category has served as yet another avenue to elevate HCL's perceived value, and to connect public libraries with education, which drives economic advancement and quality of life.

Part III

Ideas and Tips for Better Directorship

As a busy public library director, you are used to juggling many responsibilities at once and likely have limited time for professional reading. In this section, you'll find a few fairly brief but info-packed articles from *Public Libraries* as well as some excerpts from PLA publications. These articles were chosen by public librarians with directors in mind, and each addresses some aspects of the director's job.

In "Staffing Public Libraries: Are There Models or Best Practices?" Jeanne Goodrich summarizes the results of a staffing survey and also sheds more light on public library standards. "Leadership and Generosity" by PLA Past-President Daniel L. Walters is a short, thought-provoking essay on the importance of mentoring your staff. "Retaining and Motivating High-Performing Employees," will show you how important it is to build a library culture and work environment that leads to employee commitment, loyalty, and retention. "High-Impact Retention," from *Human Resources for Results*, by Jeanne Goodrich and Paula M. Singer, reveals how to create and sustain a culture of positive employee relations. In "Great Expectations: An Interview with Jim Collins" you'll hear how to take your library from good to great. "Branch Management" by Chad Lubbers takes a detailed look at the roles and competencies of branch managers. "Getting Your Money's Worth: How to Hire the Right Consultants" by Paula M.

Singer and Sandra Nelson is a straightforward look at hiring consultants, and, finally, "The Library Balanced Scorecard" by Joe Matthews explains the "Balanced Scorecard" concept and shows how it may be used to identify the most important performance measures for library management.

Chapter 8

Staffing Public Libraries: Are There Models or Best Practices?

Jeanne Goodrich

How do public libraries make staffing allocation decisions? Are there models or best practices that could be adopted to help the libraries make these critical decisions? This article summarizes the findings of a recent staffing survey conducted by the Public Library Association (PLA) Workload Measures and Staffing Patterns Committee and provides insight into why standards are not practicable despite some PLA members' desire for them.

Staff costs—salaries, wages, benefits—account for the lion's share of most public library budgets. At 50 to 80 percent of an operating budget, the amount spent on staff far exceeds what is made available for library materials, facilities, technology, and all the other resources necessary to provide services to the communities being served. Library managers want to be sure that they are spending this money wisely and fairly. But what does that mean? Is it possible to know for sure how best to allocate staff resources? Are there standards or models or best practices that can be located and adopted to assure local library managers and the decision-makers to whom they report that they are using the best approach?

These questions came to a head in PLA's Strategic Plan, approved by the PLA Board of Directors at the 2002 ALA Annual Conference. One of the strategies under the Staffing and Recruitment goal is to "Create an open dialogue forum for the purpose of collecting best practices and raising questions on staffing issues."

The Workload Measures and Staffing Patterns Committee quickly took on this assignment and commissioned a professionally designed Web-based survey (funded by PLA) to ascertain staffing practices in public libraries. Committee members also asked the co-authors of *Staffing for Results* (Diane Mayo and Jeanne Goodrich) to assist them in developing questions and analyzing the results of the survey.

The Survey and Findings

The survey was made available on the PLA Web site during the latter part of 2003, and libraries were invited to respond to it. Since it was not administered to a randomly selected number of public libraries, the findings are not scientifically valid. The committee intended the survey to be a beginning point in gathering information about how libraries make staffing decisions and a first step in finding out what models or techniques libraries might be employing to make these decisions.

Respondents were asked fifteen questions about how they made various staffing decisions and five identifying questions, designed to ascertain the size of the library (in terms of population served, number of facilities, and number of full-time equivalent [FTE] staff members), the configuration (whether the library had a central library and branches), the size of annual circulation, and the size of operating budget.

Eight hundred seventy-eight usable responses were received. Of these respondents, about 60 percent were from libraries with one to five branches, employing fewer than fifty FTEs. At the other end of the spectrum, 13 percent of the respondents have forty-one or more branches and 9 percent employed more than 300 FTEs (see Figure 8-1).

The composition of those libraries that returned surveys differs significantly from the makeup of public libraries in the United States.[1] Whereas 80 percent of the libraries in this country serve fewer than 25,000 people, only 46 percent of

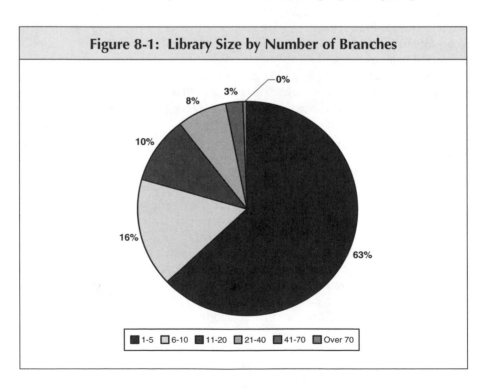

Figure 8-1: Library Size by Number of Branches

0%
3%
8%
10%
16%
63%

■ 1-5 □ 6-10 ■ 11-20 ▨ 21-40 ■ 41-70 ▨ Over 70

the respondents were from libraries serving this size population. Looking at a wide middle swath of libraries serving 25,000 to 250,000 people, 42 percent of survey respondents came from libraries of this size compared to there being only 19 percent of libraries of this size in the country. And, at the top end, 12 percent of the respondents serve 250,000 to a million or more people, whereas only 2 percent of the libraries in the country serve a population that large (see Table 8-1).

The analysis of the survey responses focused on several key factors to determine whether variations in size or configuration made a significant difference in the staffing decisions made by the reporting libraries.

A number of questions were asked to find out how public libraries determine the number of hours they need to staff branch and central library facilities. Staff groupings were broken down into clerks, shelvers and pages, and librarians. Across all sizes of libraries, hours of operation was the number one factor used to determine the number of public service (librarians and library paraprofessionals), clerical, and shelver and page hours needed to operate both branch and central libraries.

The second factor most often cited, again by all sizes of libraries, was patron traffic expected. The committee and consultant assumed that this was interpreted by responding libraries to mean their best judgment of what usage would be like by time of day, day of week, and so on.

Actual usage factors, such as the number of circulation transactions, reference transactions, or the number of checkouts usually came in third, with

Table 8-1: Service Populations of Survey Respondents versus Public Libraries in the U.S.		
Population Group	**% of Workload Survey Responses**	**% of U. S. Public Libraries**
1,000,000 and over	2.67	0.26
500,000 to 999,999	4.53	0.57
250,000 to 499,999	4.53	0.99
100,000 to 249,999	11.16	3.56
50,000 to 99,999	12.09	5.75
25,000 to 49,999	19.07	9.66
10,000 to 24,999	22.60	19.19
5,000 to 9,999	11.28	16.15
Less than 5,000	12.09	43.86

physical factors such as the building lay-out (number of floors, meeting rooms, and so on) and the number of service points (reference and other public service desks, check out stations) being the final top deciding factors. None of this seems particularly surprising, except that the impact of changes often cited as a result of increased use of technology in libraries are not yet seen as major determinants of staffing requirements. For example, despite the large increase in public access PCs in libraries, this had little influence on staffing decisions. Respondents rarely mentioned the number of holds and reserves processed, despite the very large increases in workload that the advent of patron-placed holds has meant to libraries that offer this service. It may be that this service is still relatively new or underutilized by library users in many of the libraries that offer it. When asked what data sources were used to determine staffing levels needed, respondents indicated that automated reports, experience, estimates based on observations or sampling, and supervisor requests were all quite important. However, as libraries increased in size and complexity, automated reports and experience outweighed supervisor requests noticeably. It may be that staffing allocations are managed so closely through the budget process that supervisor requests are not utilized (or even allowed as an option) in these larger systems.

The role and influence of unions often comes up when discussing staffing, workload measurement, and other topics related to work management and employee utilization. Seventy-three percent of respondents indicated that they were not unionized. On the other hand, all of the large libraries (those with more than 750 employees) that responded are unionized (see Table 8-2).

Where there are unions, influence is mixed. Some contracts require a prescribed number of consecutive days off in a designated work period. A few contracts (14 percent among the larger libraries) specify a certain staff mix and level by rank or status (a librarian must always be present for a facility to be open, for example). The percentage of respondents indicating that management and the union make staffing level decisions collaboratively ranged from 5 percent at the smallest libraries to nearly 30 percent at the largest.

Since the presence of unions is often cited by managers as an impediment to their reviewing work assignments and processes, it is interesting to note that 43 percent of the respondents from very large libraries indicated that the union had little or no influence in staffing decisions. Only 12 percent of the respondents from libraries employing fifty or fewer FTEs made this response, however. This large difference may be reflective of the comparatively closer working relationship and easier and more perceptible communication that can take place among a smaller work force. It may also stem from a more formalized sense of the term "influence" in the larger library settings.

Library managers, employees, and human resources specialists often ask if there are standards for the number of hours employees work on the public service desks. The survey asked whether the library defined a minimum or maximum number of hours that employees were to work on circulation or

Table 8-2: Bargaining Units Contracts' Influence on Staffing Decisions

	All (%)	<50 FTEs (%)	50-99 FTEs (%)	100-199 FTEs (%)	200-299 FTEs (%)	400-499 FTEs (%)	500-749 FTEs (%)
Not unionized	73.0	81.0	57.0	54.0	33.0	46.0	14.0
Contract language requires x number of consecutive days off	5.0	3.0	10.0	10.0	21.0	23.0	29.0
Contract language indicates a certain staff mix and level by rank or status	1.0	0.5	2.0	3.0	*	*	14.0
Library Management works with union to make staffing level decisions	6.0	5.0	6.0	3.0	17.0	15.0	29.0
Union has little or no influence in staffing decisions	18.0	12.0	38.0	33.0	46.0	23.0	43.0
Other	4.0	2.5.0	3.0	10.0	4.0	15.0	14.0

"Other" included contract specifies hours of work, procedural requirements like posting schedules, contract specifies number of people who must be in a build ng, only custodians a e in the union, only the library director is in the union (in two cases).
* No response on survey.

Table 8-3: Staffing Standards

	All		<50			50-99			100-199			200-299			400-499			500-749		
			FTEs			TEs			FTEs			TEs			FTEs			TEs		
	Yes (%)	No (%)		Yes (%)	No (%)		Yes (%)	No (%)		Yes (%)	No (%)		Yes (%)	No (%)		Yes (%)	No (%)		Yes (%)	No (%)
Minimum/maximum number of hours on circulation desk?	17	83		16	84		26	74		19	81		24	76		31	69		33	67
Minimum/maximum number of hours on reference desk?	16	84		13	87		31	69		26	74		24	76		33	67		17	83
Minimum/maximum number of hours on combined circulation/ reference desk?	7	93		7	93		6	94		10	90		12	88		8	92		29	71

reference desks. The vast majority (83 percent overall) said no (see Table 8-3). The answer shifted, however, as the size of the library grew. By the time the size reached more than 500 FTEs, about one-third of the respondents indicated there were standards for circulation or combined circulation/reference desks, and 17 percent indicated there were standards for the reference desk.

Respondents were asked to explain their answers to the questions about minimum and maximum staffing standards. The responses were voluminous. For example, there were forty-seven pages of text for libraries with one to five branches and fifty-one pages for libraries employing fewer than fifty employees, the largest groupings.

Reviewing these explanations shows that there is absolutely no pattern in the public libraries of the United States. In many smaller libraries, everyone is "on deck" all hours the library is open: staffing public service desks, working the floor, and doing whatever is required of them. In some libraries, staff work an hour on and an hour off the desk throughout the day. In others, two-, three-, or four-hour shifts are the norm, while some staff work on a public desk eight hours a day (see Table 8-3).

In some systems, branch managers are given discretion to make up desk schedules as they deem appropriate to meet local needs. In other systems there are norms as to the number of hours a day or week that staff members work on public desks. These norms may or may not be reinforced by bargaining unit contracts (see Table 8-2). Sometimes shift length and percentage of time on the desk is determined by employment status, with part-time staff members usually working longer shifts or a larger percentage of the time.

Whatever norms exist are typically built on past practice and can vary within a multi-facility system and even floor to floor or work unit to work unit within large central library buildings.

Standards History

It's been nearly forty years since prescriptive library standards were promulgated on the national level. *Minimum Standards for Public Library Systems, 1966*, published by the American Library Association in 1967, marked the last attempt to quantify the ingredients for at least minimum quality public library service. In almost cookbook fashion, the book itemized for practitioners, board members, and governing officials what it took to have an adequate library—two to four books per capita, one MLS-degreed librarian per x thousand population served, buildings of so many square feet per capita served, and so on.[2]

Over the decades this approach was used, problems emerged. No one was really sure what a "standard" was. Most viewed them as statements of a level of effort to be achieved, but for some libraries the minimum level floor became a ceiling beyond which they could not move. These standards focused largely on inputs, such as the number of books, staff hours, square feet, with scant reference to the realities and needs of local communities. Public librarians knew how such a quantitative approach had failed school libraries, often filled with the required number of books without regard to the timeliness or relevance of the titles in the collection. They didn't want to find themselves in the same situation. Ultimately the profession concluded that this approach had to be abandoned.

> Future standards for public libraries must flow from the needs of the institution. This means that goals and specific quantifiable, measurable objectives must be determined by each public library and system in terms of local community concerns and needs. . . . Library performance must be measured by its outputs or services rendered, rather than by its inputs (budgets, materials added, personnel positions, buildings). In measuring performance, continuous effort must be made to clarify relationships between output and input.[3]

Out of this realization came a series of planning approaches and models that focused on learning about local community composition and needs, identifying service priorities to address these needs, and then intentionally marshaling resources to fulfill local goals developed to meet these needs. The latest incarnation of this approach to planning and delivering responsive local public library services is embodied in *The New Planning for Results: A Streamlined Approach.*[4]

As this local, community-needs-based concept has evolved, PLA has published what has come to be a highly regarded series of planning management books, the Results series: *Managing for Results: Effective Resource Allocation for Public Libraries, Technology for Results: Developing Service-Based Plans, Staffing for Results: A Guide to Working Smarter*, and *Creating Policies for Results: From Chaos to Clarity.*

All titles in the *Results* series reinforce these important messages:

1. Excellence is defined locally.
2. Effective library planning involves community leaders, staff members, and board members.
3. Library plans should identify public service priorities.
4. Library managers and boards must identify measures that show progress toward meeting the library's service priorities and that are meaningful to local leaders.
5. Effective resource allocation occurs when resources are deployed to accomplish the library's service priorities.

A logical but not often comprehended extension of this set of principles is that if excellence is defined by meeting locally identified and defined needs, then there can be no "one size fits all" answers or externally defined standards. Even "best practices" have to be used gingerly, identified and applied based on a clear understanding and appreciation for the local situation and the locally selected service priorities. Questions of effectiveness (are we doing the right things?) and efficiency (are we doing things right?) can only be answered by examining whether the library is carrying out activities and utilizing resources in a manner that is consistent with its service priorities.

Notes from the Field

Several libraries provided the committee with detailed information about their staffing: spreadsheets indicating staff and their duties, pages from personnel manuals stipulating staffing levels by size of branch (determined usually by hours open each week), and, in a few cases, detailed staffing formulas with accompanying spreadsheets.

Most of the libraries in the United States are small and operate out of small buildings. As mentioned earlier, 80 percent of the public libraries in this country serve fewer than 25,000 people. Forty-six percent of the survey respondents were from these libraries. They responded because they are desperate for guidelines and standards, but acknowledge the realities under which they operate. "Staffing is based more upon staff safety than patron needs at peak periods," wrote one director of a small library. "Thus, how staff time is allocated has nothing at all to do with the workload documentation you were seeking and everything to do with the hours of operation. Period."

This view was borne out by libraries of all sizes and compositions selecting "Hours of operation" as the number one factor used to determine staffing needs. For small libraries, "floor" or "threshold" levels of staffing are basically the norm.

A few large, multibranch systems have developed staffing allocation formulas to assist them in determining the number of staff hours needed and to help provide "balance" or "equity" (always a slippery concept). These formula-driven allocation systems typically define workload factors (such as circulation or door count) and occasionally environmental factors (building layout or size, special needs of target customer groups). Sometimes these factors are weighted. Usually a concept of "floor" or "threshold" staffing to meet practical (coverage for breaks and meals) and safety considerations is included. In one case, benchmark productivity is identified for facilities of various sizes within the system, and comparisons are then made to this benchmark. In another case, a benchmark was derived from looking at statistics of similar libraries outside the system. All of the formulas involve a number of calculations and comparisons that ultimately result in a "gap analysis," which shows facilities with more staff than the factors would require or fewer than appear to be required. Rebalancing (through reassigning staff or hours) is then implemented. Some libraries perform this analysis and rebalancing on a regular basis; others have done it once and have no set plans for reanalyzing staffing.

Conclusion

There is clearly no one approach or standard that will work for all libraries. There are simply too many variables. Even libraries that have borrowed an approach from another library make significant adjustments to the factors and weights in the formulas they develop. As library systems undergo building projects and adopt new technologies they find that they must make additional adjustments to their statistics, factors, and weights.

It is worth noting that the factors and data sources (for example, hours of operation, expected traffic, and experience) employed to make staffing level decisions are traditional and intuitive, rather than based on hard data. Even with the huge impacts that technology (whether from user-generated holds or public PCs) have made, few libraries cited these factors as among the top ones that influence their staffing decisions. In other words, one library thinks x clerk hours are needed for each hour open and another library believes that y hours are needed. They just "know" that they need this level of staffing.

Some libraries are heavily influenced by another factor not identified in the survey or mentioned by respondents: local politics. This issue came up when the survey results were reviewed and discussed by committee members and is borne out by evidence encountered in the field. For some libraries, hours of operation and even staffing levels and makeup are mandated by local politicians who desire to see resources equally allocated. This can mean that all branches must be open the same number of hours a week, despite differences in usage patterns and neighborhood populations (such as the number of people actually living in the service area, the number of school age children in the service area, and so on). Or it can mean that every branch must have a full-time children's librarian, regardless, again, of the number of children actually living in the branch service area or the number of schools to be served, among other factors.

Such requirements typically result in the squandering of resources rather than truly supporting the concept of equitableness. Libraries finding themselves having to deal with such political pressures on staffing will have to work hard to develop strong, data-driven arguments around expanding the concepts of what is fair and what constitutes good library service for an entire jurisdiction as well as for a particular council member's constituents.

What has the community told the library they need?

Analyzing the real content of work and then determining what job classification is required to do it can benefit libraries of all sizes. One responding library system, for example, reported that it had conducted a reference study and found that 80 percent of the time the professional librarians and paraprofessionals spent on the reference desks was to explain technology, instruct in Internet and database usage, and manage the public computers. Coupling this knowledge with how the telephone and Web-based reference services are used will help this library make appropriate staffing decisions. For the very small (or one-person) library, analyzing what work is done and how long it takes is an exercise akin to time-management analysis. It can be illuminating and definitely is needed for the librarian who is trying—or has—to do everything.

While it may be a dream of some library managers that PLA provide guidance on how many circulation and reference staff members they need if they serve a community of 25,000 people, there are simply too many local variables to make such a pronouncement prudent, or even truly helpful. Who are the people in the community? A community of upper-income retired professional people is very different from a community of mostly non-English-speaking, lower-income workers with young families. What has the community told the library they need? One group may want access to a wireless network, investment and travel planning materials, and multiple copies of popular titles. Another may place a high value on having homework help services for their children, family literacy activities, and materials in both English and the language they speak at home. Another variable will be local capacity. What can be done with a support level of $58 per capita is very different from what can be done with a support level of $25 per capita.

Looking for ideas and best practices (so long as you know how you have defined the best performers and know that their best practices will undoubtedly have to be modified for your own setting) outside your own library are critical performance improvement concepts. Learning how others have struggled to make staffing allocation decisions and finding ways to incorporate workload and performance measures into your own decision-making process will certainly help you work more efficiently to provide services you know are most important to your community. The Workload Measures and Staffing Patterns Committee will continue to gather information and provide conference programming on this topic. But defined standards or recommended models with the PLA stamp of endorsement? No. This would be a step back of nearly forty years in planning theory and practice. The thrust will continue to be to find tools, techniques, and methodologies that will help each local library determine its own best model or standard, based on *its own* unique needs and resources.

Notes

1. Library size data as reported by Patricia Elaine Kroe, *Public-Use Data File: Public Libraries Survey, Fiscal Year 2000* (NCES 2002-341) (Washington, D.C.: U.S. Department of Education, National Center for Education Statistics, 2002).
2. Public Library Association, *Minimum Standards for Public Library Systems, 1966* (Chicago: ALA, 1967).
3. Public Library Association, *Goals, Guidelines and the Public Library Mission Statement and Its Imperatives for Service* (Chicago: ALA, 1979), 10.
4. Sandra Nelson, *The New Planning for Results: A Streamlined Approach* (Chicago: ALA, 2001).

About the Author

Jeanne Goodrich is an independent consultant based in Portland, Oregon.

Chapter 9

Leadership and Generosity

Daniel L. Walters

My first job as a librarian was in rural Washington State at the North Central Regional Library District. North Central has twenty-eight branches that serve a vast, five-county area bordered on the west by the Cascade mountain range and stretches from the center of the state north to the Canadian border. Its service area extends east and south across portions of the great basalt Columbia Plateau, an area marked by orchards and fertile farmland made possible by water from Columbia Reclamation Project reservoirs. The striking southeast quadrant's arresting desert topography is riddled with coulees formed by the age-old torrential floodwaters that swept across the plateau from Glacial Lake Missoula. Rural public libraries can be found in towns and hamlets throughout this expansive area. Just the place for a wide-eyed librarian fresh from library school.

I started out at the headquarters branch in Wenatchee, and during the course of the five years I spent at the district, I had the good fortune to try my hand at a variety of tasks in reference, adult services, and management of the branches. Microfiche catalogs were a new technology in those days, and the district was one of the first rural libraries to convert its catalog so that all branches could have access to district resources. There were only five ALA-accredited librarians, including the director at the time, and it turned out that the only limits to gaining professional experience were those that were self-imposed. I was the beneficiary of a generous and tolerant boss in now-retired director Mike Lynch, who was open to letting this young librarian have enough room to experiment, while tempering that freedom with a quick yank of the rope when necessary. And it was necessary, from time to time.

When I took the job out of library school, some of my colleagues were skeptical about starting a career in a cash-strapped rural system that was isolated from an urban center without ready access to the university and contact with other state-of-the-art urban libraries. Those urban and suburban systems generally had larger budgets, were implementing new technologies, and were viewed as "more sophisticated." But those systems usually had slots in larger departments for their new recruits. It turned out that instead of starting in a large system with caste-like departmental assignments in reference or adult services where advancement opportunities often hinged on seniority, I was not as affected by internal organizational constraints at North Central. Although we had a smaller budget, I learned many things at the district, and many from wise staff who were not ALA matriculates. Mike was quick to teach that the term "nonprofessional" had no place in the lexicon of a public library staff where the MLS was by no means the sole benchmark for dedication to public library service.

I met up with Mike last summer when vacationing in Washington State, and a lingering discussion over dinner has contributed to my thoughts that leadership characterized by generosity is essential to assure the growth and development of future leaders. Mike's tutelage during those years at North Central (and my continued access to exceptional public library leadership during the following years under the guidance of now-retired King County Library System director Herb Mutschler and now-retired deputy director Enid Griswold in Issequah, Washington) provided experiences that set high standards for trust and responsibility. I have come to realize that Mike, Herb, and Enid were not really looking the other way when I was trying something, and I hope others coming through the ranks have the good fortune to experience such generosity of leadership in their careers. I didn't know it then, but I was being "mentored," although it was a much less formal and less intentional activity than we currently seek to provide as a critical component in leadership development within our institutions and professional associations.

While I did not come of age in the horse-and-buggy stage of the profession, there are a number of changes that have altered the context in which library administrations can provide substantive opportunities for staff development. Larger institutions often have less flexibility than smaller organizations to provide options outside of "normal" assignments for individual staff development. Bargaining unit rules may also limit staff members with less seniority from participating in development activities. Opportunities for existing staff to pursue formal education such as a master's in public administration or other degrees require a significant investment from the individual staff member and flexibility from the employer to adjust work schedules when necessary. Institutional travel and continuing education budgets are often inadequate for staff to participate at national ALA and PLA conferences, or even state meetings in many cases. The looming Baby Boomer retirements point to future open positions throughout the profession and across the country at a time when salaries and the cost of moving may inhibit librarians from relocating as their predecessors have done in the past. In addition to these hurdles, increasing diversity within our communities requires an institutional commitment to extend leadership opportunities to diverse staffs if our institutions are to be viewed as both relevant and open to the communities we serve.

Despite these difficulties, public libraries must create and invest in systems that provide opportunities for staff development. If funding is very tight locally, there are often scholarships available at the state and national level for participation at national conferences, including opportunities available through ALA and PLA. New extension MLS degree programs are now available to those who do not live near an accredited university, and some programs do not require time on campus from students who do not live nearby. The Laura Bush 21st Century Librarian initiative has already assisted with funding that has added new ALA-accredited librarians to the workforce across the country, including employee graduates who have been willing to obtain the degree in order to advance within their libraries and the profession. Library leaders should be aware of these opportunities so they can assist staff and others in their communities who may be interested. We must convince our governing authorities that investments in staff development are critical components of our annual budgets in order for our libraries to be able to serve our communities in the years to come.

There are also strategies that don't require funding, but they do require a similar attitude of generosity and support that was provided to me and to many of my peers by our mentors and leaders. Mentoring systems can be established and maintained within our libraries at little expense other than dedicating the time and commitment that in turn expresses value in our employees. Seasoned librarians can be teamed with staff members who are considering obtaining the MLS or currently enrolled in a degree program. Every new initiative undertaken by the library administration can also be a vehicle for mixing newer staff with seasoned veterans on planning and implementation committees.

Perhaps the greatest benefit that library leaders can extend to their staffs is simply the good will, tolerance, and patience that should be an abiding characteristic of leadership. After all, most of us in leadership positions have advanced through the generosity of others, even if we may have chafed under the yoke from time to time.

About the Author

Daniel L. Walters is Executive Director of the Las Vegas–Clark County Library District in Las Vegas, Nevada.

Chapter 10

Retaining and Motivating High-Performing Employees

Paula M. Singer and Jeanne Goodrich

Retaining talented employees is becoming increasingly difficult. As information technology (IT) has become indispensable to the functioning of libraries, human capital requirements for effective librarians have shifted. Libraries are now forced to compete in a broader arena than ever before for talented, IT-savvy, and interpersonally skilled library workers. In addition, libraries face a decreasing pool of leadership, owing to the relatively older workforce. Today, 57 percent or more of librarians are at least forty-five-years old (if not older).[1] The American Library Association (ALA) estimates that only 7 percent of librarians are currently ages twenty to twenty-nine.[2] ALA projects that nearly 60 percent of current librarians will reach retirement age by 2025.[3] In the midst of these talent-siphoning factors, salaries in the public sector are low and library degree-program graduation and job-growth rates are flat and are projected to remain so.[4] In this article we address some ways to motivate and retain high-performing employees.

For the reasons mentioned previously, retention is becoming an acute issue for libraries. An effective retention strategy is an investment that pays for itself in almost any organization. Turnover of trained staff is expensive and creates additional costs and extra work. Let's look at these costs. They are higher than you may think, and they include:

- the cost to hire (advertising, time spent screening resumes, interviewing candidates);
- costs due to lost productivity;
- training costs—yes, it is expensive to get a new employee up to speed. Even the most experienced new hire will have a learning curve; and
- the costs from colleagues spending their time orienting their newest team member.

If your library is required by union or civil service rules to pay "acting pay" to a staff person who assumes the tasks of the departing employee, that will add to costs as well. Human resources experts estimate that the cost of filling a vacancy is one-and-a-half to two times the salary and benefits of the person who leaves. In addition, there are less tangible costs of turnover. The library system loses the knowledge and institutional history the departing employee takes with him or her. Projects might not be completed on time, priorities not met, and colleagues might feel the burden of additional work piled on top of their already overscheduled workday.

As you can see, it is truly advantageous to build a culture and work environment that leads to employee commitment, loyalty, and retention. How, then, can a library generate and maintain commitment among its employees? We pose this question in the context of current employer and employee expectations, listed in Figure 10-1. These expectations reflect today's employment reality and are quite different from the expectations that many staff with fifteen or twenty years' tenure brought to their jobs.

We approach building and maintaining employee commitment as a process, one that begins before recruitment and ends after retirement. We do not assume that library workers stay in one position for the duration of their careers—the opposite is more often the case—but this approach allows us to capture the full spectrum of employee experiences as they relate to employee commitment.

Figure 10-1: Expectations Imposed by Today's Labor Market	
Employer	**Employee**
Your education alone does not qualify you for this job	I know my job stability will be based upon my reputation for performance
We are not offering a job for life, and we don't expect you to spend your lifetime here	I will be responsible for managing my own benefits
Your workmates may change during your employment here	I will continue to hone my skills and grow professionally
You will be part of many self-managed teams, each responsible for a range of tasks	I will embrace *intrapreneurship*
Your assignments will provide learning experiences that will enhance your employability	I will always be open to new jobs and opportunities inside the library and elsewhere
We expect you to support our vision and values passionately while employed here	

Building Commitment

Employees report that they stay with an employer for the following reasons:

- They feel valued: their concerns, ideas, and suggestions are genuinely sought and listened to.
- They enjoy a feeling of connection and that they make a difference: they know how the work they do helps the library accomplish its mission.
- They have opportunities for personal and professional growth: formal education, workshops, on-the-job training, new assignments, job rotation, attendance at conferences.
- The work environment promotes continuous learning: growth opportunities, jobs that are designed to be interesting and stimulating, and the opportunity to participate on committees and task forces.
- Good management: a bad supervisor is often cited as the reason employees leave an employer.
- Fair pay and benefits: even though many work in libraries because they love libraries and support the mission, most employees have to receive pay and benefits that allow them to live a reasonably comfortable life.

With employee loyalty and job security lower than ever, building commitment means responding to workforce needs and expectations. Fair compensation and benefits, career development, involvement in decision-making, and recognition are all areas of the work experience that play a role in whether an employee leaves or stays.

Retention can be improved by considering employee preferences and capabilities. Managers can build employee commitment, and with it retention, through responsiveness in each of the following areas.

Compensation

Some of the most obvious elements of employee retention are also the most important. Compensation and benefits must be addressed as key issues enhancing initial recruitment and continued retention. Base pay is the foundation for total compensation because it establishes the standard of living. Employees with good IT and interpersonal skills demand a competitive salary. Libraries' capacity to offset this demand with benefits unique to their government affiliations is generally difficult. The ALA established the Better Salaries and Pay Equity Task Force to address library workers' comparably lower average level of compensation. ALA's "Advocating for Better Salaries and Pay Equity Toolkit," published in 2003, can be helpful in this arena, but does not provide short-term relief for libraries facing recruitment and retention problems.[5]

What, then, can libraries do? Libraries must enlarge as much as possible the quality of the work experience and work environment. This begins with recruitment and carries through the orientation period and beyond.

Recruitment and Orientation

An employee's experience of a place starts with recruitment—that is, *before* he or she is actually hired. Recruitment, orientation, and assimilation processes provide chances to emphasize the personal elements of a prospective employee's connection to the organization. For instance, by dispensing with paperwork and procedural tasks in advance of the actual orientation, helping with relocation, inviting new hires to introduce their partners or families to the library and vice-versa, and matching them with such local services as babysitters, an orientation process fosters the sort of personal connections that most employees value.

Orientation should include such basic elements as introducing the new employee to fellow workers, having the workspace ready, providing instruction on the use of office equipment and basic information about where to put coats, lunches, and so on. It should also cover the employee's specific job and give him or her a more general introduction to the library as a whole. A checklist of points to cover can be helpful to a harried manager so the most mundane and the most critical points can be remembered. Adding a few extra touches (balloons at the desk, a mug with the library's logo, the director stopping by to introduce him or herself) can make the new employee feel even more welcome and valued.

A library can improve its induction process by surveying reactions to orientation at 30, 60, and 120 days and sharing the feedback with library leadership and then making changes. This process also communicates to new hires that the library values their input. First impressions are extremely important, and taking the time to find out if the library is making a positive and productive first impression will pay off in increased feelings of inclusion and loyalty.

A new employee's assimilation into the library workplace can be enhanced through developing standards and practices that support the process. Managers need to know that they are expected to assist new employees throughout their first few months of employment by purposefully creating ways for them to become engaged members of their work unit. Publicizing and recognizing creative ways of doing this can inspire other supervisors and managers and will create an environment that is seen to value the thoughtful induction of new employees.

Structuring Benefits and Work Environment

Elements of the orientation process dovetail with retention strategies. A buddy or mentoring system does not lose its value just because someone has passed his or her probationary period. A mentor can provide career guidance, constructive criticism, and act as a sounding board for employee frustrations or ideas with regard to how the library functions and organizational politics.

Like mentoring, employee rotations through different functions, branches, programs, or departments need not end with the official end of orientation. Exposing employees to different aspects of the library's work and giving them an opportunity to acquire skills, knowledge, and experience in a variety of areas can hold their interest, make them more effective team members, and make them better candidates for greater responsibilities or promotion.

Treating rotations as a chance for skill-acquisition and recruiting from within enables employers to link skills, expectations, and rewards.

Different employees value different aspects of their compensation and benefits and certainly respond differently to opportunities, expectations, and rewards. Career development, health benefits, and the work-life balance are areas to which keen attention should be paid. Younger employees may be more interested in career development than, say, health screening or retirement plans, and may benefit more from mentoring than more mature or experienced personnel. In addition, career development generally means different things to newer, and often younger, employees interested in skill acquisition than it does to employees seeking management experience or pursuing an advanced degree. For employees nearing retirement, mentoring or teaching opportunities may be the preferred form of career development. Supporting career development not only gives a library a means of aligning its goals with that of its workers, it also offers challenges to employees—a proven factor in building loyalty and retention.

Health benefits also mean different things to different employees. For some, access to a fitness center is an important health benefit. For others, subsidized health screening or family insurance coverage is prized. To a still greater degree, helping employees to strike a balance between work and home life means tailoring paid time off and benefits to their preferences, capabilities, and level of responsibility both at home and in the library.

A responsive work environment is another crucial source of employee commitment and thus retention. The keywords here are *communication, accountability*, and *recognition*. Creating and maintaining effective forums for employee input can connect leaders to staff at all levels. Employee involvement in making decisions—made possible by open but structured communication—invests everyone in positive *and* negative outcomes, such that all are accountable to all. Finally, accountability is indivisible from recognition for contributions and achievements. Whether in the form of a small bonus or thanks and applause at a staff meeting, the universality of forms of recognition in public and private sector organizations is a testament to recognition's importance for cementing employee commitment.

It is critical to train managers and supervisors in the value of a work environment that appreciates and fosters employee participation, involvement in decision-making, initiative, and creativity. A manager or supervisor who is familiar and comfortable with the old "command and control" environment will not necessarily embrace this new approach nor know how to make it work effectively. The work environment and employee culture desired by library leadership will not exist if those in middle management and supervisory positions are not supportive of it.[6]

Work-Life Balance

Helping employees balance work with life is critical in the twenty-first century. The expectation of a balanced life is a given among many of our younger colleagues. It is not, as frequently mentioned by Baby Boomers, that younger employees do not have the same work ethic their older colleagues do; they just define it differently. The work gets done: just not necessarily in the same way, in the same style, with the same tools, or even in the same place.

What are some ways to create an environment that tries to balance both work and life? There are some ways to demonstrate and acknowledge the differences in employees. They include:

1. Define the work in terms of what is to be accomplished. Do not just say "our working hours are from 8 a.m. to 5 p.m. Be there" (except for when an employee needs to cover a desk or attend meetings). Focus on the project or the program. Ask "what needs to be done," and "what is the work?" Think about whether it really needs to be completed only onsite during regular business hours.
2. Provide flexible work schedules, allow for job sharing and out-of-the box ways of meeting customer, employee, and library needs.
3. Provide flexible benefits and cafeteria plans. To the extent you can, align what employees want with what they get.
4. Evaluate alternative work places and telecommuting as options.
5. Appreciate dilemma of child care, elder care, and multiple individual roles.
6. Allow voluntary demotions. Of course your library allows voluntary demotions, but what we are saying is that it is important to create a culture where a demotion—or a change of direction—is safe and acceptable. A culture where an employee can take a risk, and change his or her mind.
7. Appreciate diversity of personal values and priorities . . . and demonstrate that acceptance.

Surveying Employees

Employees leave for other—possibly higher-level or more lucrative—library jobs, for jobs in other sectors, and to retire. Managers should learn from each scenario.

Exit interviews can provide an invaluable source of information, especially if an employee leaves for another library system. There is less at risk for exiting employees, allowing them to be honest and open in their criticisms and suggestions. Whether exit interviews yield specific or general comments, managers would do well to learn more about what prompted a resignation— what pull another job had and possibly what pushed the employee to leave his or her current job. If you are having trouble retaining key staff, carefully and systematically explore the causes. Losing staff is a symptom. Doing something about it demands an understanding about the true causes. Not waiting until employees leave to get their opinions about life and work at the library is an even more proactive way to understand the wants and needs of the workforce.

Many organizations (and a few public libraries) conduct confidential employee climate or opinion surveys—and make changes based upon what they discover.

Retaining Talent As They Age

Phased retirement is an important way to mitigate the impact of an employee exit on a given organization. By making schedules and tasks more flexible for those considering retirement, managers can retain a talented pool of mentors without taking on new compensation costs and without overburdening full-time employees. As retirees, former full-time employees can provide a reliable, flexible, knowledgeable, and affordable addition to the library's workforce.

Inducements for phased retirement could include flexible hours or assignments so retirees can travel or pursue other personal interests but still be available during parts of the year or week, or for projects of several months' duration. Some library employers are finding ways to capture and celebrate the many years of experience and the deep knowledge base their most senior employees possess. Others are developing ways for senior staff and managers to take larger periods of time off while still retaining their employment status or to phase out by working part-time or on temporary assignments before they ultimately retire completely. This latter option is most attractive when future retirement benefits are not adversely impacted by preretirement reductions in hours.

The Commitment Keys

These strategies are all about building commitment to the job and the employer, since productivity and retention are greatly increased when employees are committed. This is especially important today since job security and loyalty to the library—to any employer—are much lower than ever before. Retention strategies must be *intentionally designed* so employees know what they need to do and what is expected of them; so they are involved in decisions that affect the work they do and the services they provide to library users; so they have opportunities to learn and grow; so they earn recognition for good performance; and so they know that they are responsible for their performance and will be held accountable if performance is lacking. Strategies developed with these factors in mind will result in the best and brightest employees choosing to stay with the library in capacities that allow them to contribute, learn, and grow.

In sum, productivity and employee retention are greatly increased when employees are committed. To enhance retention, remember these five keys:

Focus: employees know what they need to do and what is expected of them;
Involvement: people support most what they help to create;
Development: opportunities for learning and growth are encouraged;
Gratitude: recognition for good performance (formal or informal); and
Accountability: employees are responsible for their performance and lack thereof.

Notes

1. Arlene Dorm, "Gauging the Labor Force Effects of Retiring Baby Boomers," *Monthly Labor Review* 123, no. 7 (July 2000): 19.
2. Mary Jo Lynch, "Age of Librarians," 1999, www.ala.org/ala/aboutala/offices/ors/reports/ageoflibrarians.com (accessed June 15, 2009).
3. Mary Jo Lynch, "Reaching 65: A Lot of LibrariansWill Be There Soon," *American Libraries* 33, no. 3 (Mar. 2002): 55–56.
4. Olivia Crosby, "Librarians: Information Experts in the Information Age," *Occupational Outlook Quarterly* 44, no. 4 (Winter 2000/2001): 1–15.
5. ALA, "Advocating for Better Salaries and Pay Equity Toolkit," www.ala-apa.org/toolkit.pdf (accessed June 15, 2009).
6. Christi Olson and Paula Singer, *Winning with Library Leadership: Enhancing Services through Connection, Contribution, and Collaboration* (Chicago: ALA, 2004).

About the Authors

Paula M. Singer is President and Principal Consultant of The Singer Group, Inc., a management consulting firm she founded in 1983. She provides strategic planning and alignment, organization design and development, performance management, leadership development, compensation, coaching, and other services to clients in the public, private, and nonprofit sectors. She is coauthor of *Winning with Library Leadership: Enhancing Services Through Connection, Contribution and Collaboration* (with Christi Olson), *Human Resources for Results* (with Jeanne Goodrich), and *Designing a Compensation Plan for Your Library* (with Laura Francisco). Paula is a frequent speaker at ALA, PLA, and state library association conferences and has written a number of articles for library and other publications.

Jeanne Goodrich is an independent consultant based in Portland, Oregon.

Chapter 11

High-Impact Retention: Retaining the Best and the Brightest

Jeanne Goodrich and Paula M. Singer

Milestones

By the time you finish this chapter you will be able to

- understand why employees want to stay employed in a library
- create and sustain a culture of positive employee relations
- accommodate generational differences when designing retention and development programs
- develop employees through formal and informal means
- build and maintain effective feedback and recognition systems
- confidentially solicit employees' opinions about their job satisfaction, needs, and wants

How can a library generate and maintain commitment among its employees? This has always been a challenging process and is becoming more difficult every year. Many of the people currently working in libraries have been employed by the same library for 5, 10, 15, or even 20 years. It is not uncommon to find that over 50 percent of the employees in a library have never worked elsewhere. However, the realities of library employment are changing rapidly, and these fresh challenges are quite different.

In this new world a person's education alone does not qualify her for a job. Instead, library managers are writing job descriptions that focus on a prospective employee's knowledge, skills, and abilities, and they may also define her needed competencies.

Library jobs are no longer immutable. The work is continually evolving and the way the work is managed is also changing. The old bureaucratic and hierarchical structure is being modified and replaced with one that is flat, networked, and nimble. More libraries are moving toward cross-functional and self-managed teams, with each team responsible for a range of tasks. Employees expect to be included in discussions about the library's future and want to have a voice in making important decisions.

Library staff are expected to continue to develop their KSAs while on the job and should be given opportunities to do so. In turn, their job tenure depends on their ability to perform. This continual growth and development makes the employee more valuable in her current and any future position in the library. Employees are expected to actively support the library's vision and values. When they can no longer do that, they are expected to look for new opportunities in other libraries, or other organizations.

These expectations reflect today's employment reality and may be very different from the expectations that staff brought to their jobs twenty or even five years ago. The psychological contract of a "job for life" has been broken. Public libraries twenty years from now will not be employing the person they hired last year or will hire next year. That person is likely to have had seven jobs by then—in three different careers! We are increasingly seeing an exchange of lifelong employment for "mutuality of purpose," where an employee can be expected to do a great job for an employer as long as she is provided with challenges, opportunities, and work/life balance.

Building and maintaining employee commitment is a process, one that begins during recruitment and ends after retirement. The key question, then, is how to go about this process of retaining the best and the brightest. The easiest place to start is with yourself. Think about your needs and wants. Ask yourself this question: What keeps me at my library? Think also about why your employees accept a job with your library and why they remain once they are hired.

There has been considerable research on this topic. Employees report that they stay with an employer for these reasons:

They have a feeling of connection and know that they make a difference; they know how they and the work they do fits in and how they help the library accomplish its mission.

They feel valued; their concerns, ideas, and suggestions are genuinely sought and listened to.

They are respected and recognized for the work they do. There is a feeling of safety in the work environment.

They have opportunities for personal and professional growth : formal education, workshops, on-the-job training, new assignments, job rotation, and attendance at conferences.

The work environment promotes continuous learning: jobs that are designed to be interesting and stimulating, and the opportunity to participate on committees and task forces to create and implement improvements.

There is good management as well as good communication with senior management. A bad supervisor is most often cited as the reason why employees leave an employer.

There are fair pay and benefits. Even though many work in libraries because they love libraries and support their mission, employees have to receive pay and benefits that allow them to live a comfortable life. While pay does not motivate an employee to stay, pay that is not fair, especially in relation to peers, is a demotivator.

Today's reality is that the library cannot afford a culture of entitlement, nor can it afford to lose employees who add value. The truth is that today your employees have choices as to where they work; they are not limited to the library in the community in which they live. It is incumbent on library leadership to create a culture that supports the retention of the right employees. Management training is key, as is knowing and responding to what employees want.

Task 5: Develop and Implement a Retention Plan

Task 1: Assess Required Staff Resources
Task 2: Describe the Job
Task 3: Identify the Right Person for the Right Job
Task 4: Develop and Implement a Performance Management System
Task 5: Develop and Implement a Retention Plan
   Step 5.1: Plan the project
   Step 5.2: Understand workforce needs and expectations
   Step 5.3: Create the culture
   Step 5.4: Define expectations
   Step 5.5: Provide training
   Step 5.6: Build commitment

Using your own experiences as well as research, you can begin to develop and implement a retention plan that fits your library, its culture, and its employees. The plan starts with knowing the members of your library's workforce and engaging them to high performance and commitment.[1] It is also important to be cognizant of the political environment in which you work, as well as any civil service rules and union contracts that may affect the library's ability to "create the culture." Talk to your union representatives as well as local government HR staff. Get them on board with helping you make changes to your library's culture to the extent possible.

Step 5.1: Plan the Project
This information will help you plan the project, determine whether you need a committee, and if so, select committee members, create a charge, and formulate a communications plan.

Step 5.2: Understand Workforce Needs and Expectations
Earlier in this chapter, there was a discussion of how the expectations of employees and supervisors have changed. One of the key changes is the demise of the hierarchical "command and control" organizational structure in many libraries.[2] It is critical to train managers and supervisors to support a work environment that fosters employee participation, encourages involvement in

decision-making, and cultivates initiative and creativity. Even with training and development, a manager or supervisor who is familiar and comfortable with the more traditional bureaucratic management structure will not necessarily embrace this new approach or know how to make it work effectively. The work environment and employee culture desired by library leadership will not exist if those in middle management and supervisory positions are not also supportive of them.[3]

For this to happen, supervisors should be able to answer "yes" to each of these statements with regard to every person on their team:

1. I inquire about how to make work more satisfying for my employees.
2. I realize that I am mainly responsible for retaining the talent on my team.
3. I know my employees' career ambitions.
4. I take steps to ensure that my employees are continually challenged by their work.
5. I respect the work/life balance issues that my employees face.

Getting to know something about each person who works with you shows respect and concern and is highly correlated to retention. Employees want to know that you know who they are, that you've considered their needs as you make decisions, and that they have been heard.

Generational Diversity

There has been a lot of discussion about the differences between the various generations that work in libraries (or anywhere else) today. What follows is not meant to stereotype these generations, but rather to acknowledge some broad generalizations about their experience, behavior, expectations, and worldview. While each employee must be understood as an individual, understanding the four generational groupings—Traditionalists, Baby Boomers, Generation Xers (GenXers), and Millennials—can provide insight into factors that influence their approach to work and to the ability to manage and retain these employees in your library.[4]

Two approaches to understanding generational differences are relevant here. The first focuses on the events shaping the lives of each generational cohort, and thus shaping the culture, expectations, and worldview of its members. This is referred to as the Event Theory of Generations. The second approach is the Career Stage Theory, which states that the differences we perceive in the actions and behavior of the generations are attributed to their career stage, rather than to life events. Both viewpoints have implications for human resource management, policies, and practices. Both offer insights into the retention of employees at every age and career stage.

The Four Generations and Events Shaping Their Lives. The four generations in the workplace today can be briefly characterized as follows.

Traditionalists. These employees were born before 1946. Traditionalists value hard work, dedication, and sacrifice. They respect rules and authority and they believe in duty before pleasure, self-sacrifice, and pulling oneself up by one's bootstraps. Loyalty to their employer, hard work, and honor are very important. The Great Depression, the New Deal, and World War II were the events that shaped the worldview of this generation.

Baby Boomers. Born between 1946 and 1964, many of these employees have come to librarianship as a second career. They tend to be more concerned with clarity of organizational structure, opportunities for growth and challenge, and rewards than Traditionalists, GenXers, or Millennials. Boomers seek stability, wear their values on their sleeves, possess a driven work ethic, value relationships, and often have a love/hate relationship with authority. They want to be involved, are competitive yet have a team orientation, and seek personal gratification and personal growth. They are optimistic and success oriented. The worldview of the Boomers was shaped by the cold war, the civil rights movement, the Vietnam War and the antiwar movement, and the sexual revolution.

GenXers. Born between 1965 and 1981, these employees are results-oriented, value a work/life balance, are relatively unimpressed with authority, technologically literate, loyal to managers who treat them well, resourceful, self-reliant, pragmatic, independent, and are more mobile than stable in their job history. The members of this generation grew up in a time of reduced economic growth, and many of them were latchkey kids. Their worldview was influenced by Watergate, the women's liberation movement, the end of the cold war, and the first Gulf War. Some are described as "slackers" who do not live up to their potential, some as young people who work hard and play hard. Members of this generation have been characterized more by concern for individual growth and less with loyalty to their employer.

Millennials. Born between 1982 and 2000, these employees are collaborative, openminded, achievement-oriented, confident, optimistic, inclusive, and technically savvy. They respect diversity, have high expectations, value public service, and are seen as more positive and more realistic than the GenXers.[5] Key events shaping their worldview were the rise of high technology and the Internet, growing up in a child-focused world, the terrorist attacks of September 11, 2001, and the second Gulf War. Many grew up in structured settings and value family and multiculturalism. This generation has also been referred to as GenY, the thumbers, the MySpace generation, and the 9/11s. Figure 11-1 provides additional insight into the differences among these groups.

Challenges among the four generations arise at the library because of each generation's differing attitude about work, the meaning of work, and the perceived value of the job being performed. There are seven areas of potential conflict: respect for authority, time on the job, advancement, recruiting and retention, skill building, work/life balance, and recognition.[6] While it is beyond the scope of this book to examine each in detail, a few potential conflict situations and tips on managing members of the four generations in the library follow.

Figure 11-1: Generational Differences				
	Traditionalist Before 1946	**Baby Boomer 1946-1964**	**GenXer 1965-1981**	**Millennial 1982-2000**
Outlook	Practical	Optimistic	Skeptical	Hopeful
Work Ethic	Dedicated	Driven Balanced	Ambitious	
View of Authority	Respectful	Love/hate	Unimpressed	Relaxed, polite
Leadership by	Hierarchy	Consensus	Competence	Achievers
Relationships	Personal sacrifice	Personal gratification	Reluctant to commit	Loyal
Perspective	Civic	Team	Self	Civic

The most significant differences exist between GenXers and members of the Baby Boom generation, first because the preponderance of most libraries' employees fall into one of these two groupings, and second, because the disparity between each group's life events and experiences is wide, thus creating the largest level of misunderstandings and tension.

Feedback is a major area of work/life clashes. We know of the importance of feedback in the performance management process, yet there are major differences between the generations in the content and style of feedback sought and given. Traditionalists tend to believe that "no news is good news" and are surprised, and sometimes bewildered, when their younger managers comment on their work. This is true of Boomers as well, who are accustomed to once-a-year feedback supported by lots of paperwork. In contrast, GenXers, and to a greater extent Millennials, expect feedback on a frequent basis. They also give immediate and honest feedback, which can be seen as pushy, arrogant, and inappropriate by others. GenXers need positive feedback and coaching to know they are on the right track. They will ask for it, and will sometimes interrupt to check for it. Millennials will ask as well. Many seek constant feedback, and in real time. They often interpret silence as their having done something wrong or as disapproval. They need to know how they are doing, right and wrong. Boomers often give but rarely receive feedback, and Traditionalists do not seek lavish praise, but they do appreciate acknowledgment of their efforts and accomplishments.

Authority is another area where differences in behavior are observed. Many Traditionalists and Boomers do not question the status quo or authority. This can cause confusion and resentment among GenXers and Millennials, who have been encouraged to challenge authority and make their voices heard. Boomer and Traditionalist managers too often view this challenge as a personal threat to them and their authority. These managers believe that they earned the right to make decisions and that their seniority and roles deserve respect. GenXers believe respect should be earned. Many Boomers managing GenXers feel challenged by this. At the same time, because their styles are different, too often GenXers and Millennials fail to listen actively to Boomers and Traditionalists, consequently losing the opportunity for gathering important information, perspective, mentoring, and guidance.

What can you do? If you are a Boomer or Traditionalist manager, go out of your way to engage, encourage, and capitalize on the KSAs, perspectives, and talents of the newer, younger members of your library. You will gain credibility and trust by developing and mentoring them. GenXers and Millennials need to acknowledge and respect Boomers' experience and abilities. GenXer staff should pursue learning opportunities and make managers aware of their willingness to take on new areas of responsibility, when ready. Millennials should seek mentors or coaches throughout the library, learn how to ask good questions, and listen patiently.[7]

Tips for Managing Members of Each Generation. Traditionalists are at or near retirement age, but for a variety of reasons they may choose to continue working. They may be looking for a position that allows them to take advantage of the skills and networks they've developed over their working life, but with a schedule that gives them freedom to enjoy the activities they anticipate pursuing in retirement. If you are managing Traditionalist employees, be open to part-time employment and flexible working hours. Capitalize on their talents and institutional knowledge and provide them with the opportunity to coach and develop new talent. This is also critical for succession planning and to ensure a smooth transition of knowledge to the leaders of the future.

Some tips for managing a Boomer are to give her public recognition, provide her with opportunities to prove herself, show appreciation, let her know she has special contributions to make to the library, provide perks, acknowledge and reward her work ethic, explain the benefits of changes, and show respect for her experience and knowledge. Saying "I need you to do this for me" goes a long way to motivate a Boomer.

GenXers like challenges, new learning opportunities, specific feedback, flexible work options, and strong working relationships. GenXers like to do things their way; it's best to set the parameters of a project or activity and let them do the job their way. Don't micromanage, just coach and monitor progress. The work will be done. Include the members of this generation in decisions that are made and let them offer their ideas and opinions. GenXers want a mentor relationship with their boss, so finding the time for regular coaching and feedback is critical. To promote retention, remember that GenXers value a fun and informal work environment.

The members of the Millennial generation, the newest and fewest members of the library's workforce, are often compared to the Baby Boomers, who share a partiality for public service and volunteer activities. Many persons in this generational group thrive on learning opportunities and constant challenges. They want meaning in their job and often choose to work for organizations whose mission they value and for leaders who are honest and have integrity. You can best manage them with very regular feedback, flexible working options and schedules, and by acknowledging their ideas. Invite them to serve on committees and reinforce how the library, and their job, contribute to the community. Emphasize the meaningfulness of their role for the public and the services they provide to many people.

What else can you do? Think about the differences we've discussed as you consider the generations of employees working in the library. Talk about them with others. Ask yourself and others the following questions:

1. What were some defining historical events for each generation?
2. What was "cool" for each generation (movies, TV programs, music, toys, clothes, etc.)?
3. What are the core values of each generation?
4. Which generation predominates in the library?
5. What are the differences between members of the different generations who work at the library?
6. What is the best way to bring the generations together at work?
7. What advantages are there to having multiple generations working at the library?
8. Which generation do you admire the most at work and why?
9. What can each generation teach others?
10. What can each generation learn from others?

The Career Stage Theory. An alternative approach is to analyze generational differences based on where each employee is in his or her career. From this perspective, one would expect 60-year-olds to be more interested in retirement policies and 20-year-olds to focus on vacation policies, regardless of the historical events and challenges faced by their generational cohort.

Career development generally means different things to newer, and often younger, employees interested in skill acquisition than it does to employees seeking management experience or pursuing an advanced degree. And for employees nearing retirement, mentoring or teaching opportunities may be the preferred form of career development. Supporting career development not only gives a library a means of aligning its goals with those of its workers, it also offers challenges to employees, which is a proven factor in building loyalty and retention.

Do not make assumptions about what employees at any point in their life cycle or career really want or need. To find out, be direct and ask them. Talk to employees frequently about their learning goals, their desire for personal and professional development, and their career at the library. This information should be captured in the employee's self-evaluation and discussed during the performance review meeting.

Career development is not a one-time process; it must be ongoing. It's about continuous learning and development and should not be viewed in the context of promotion alone. Especially in today's flatter organizational structures, there are fewer promotional opportunities, but many lateral opportunities offering challenges or new experiences. Most important, career development should be about both the individuals' needs and the library's needs. It's about linking and matching employee skills with the library's strategic priorities.

Step 5.3: Create the Culture

Why create, or change, a library's culture? The most important reason is to ensure that the library is able to attract and retain a committed workforce that is engaged and therefore gets the required work done in an effective and efficient way.

To ensure a committed workforce, the library needs to create the right intangibles—the culture—that not only attracts but also retains a talented workforce. It's not as hard as you think, but it is more time-consuming than you'd hoped! You start by understanding the workforce's needs and expectations. Then you work to align how you treat employees, to the fullest extent you can, with their needs (not yours, theirs) and your mission.

The term workforce refers to each and every one of your employees, from the young high school graduate in his first job to the veteran librarian with her thirty-year pin with the tiny emerald stone. Knowing what each employee wants and needs doesn't mean that you can give everyone what they want and need. It's about paying attention to each, "hearing" them, and doing what you can to support their needs, goals, and aspirations, all within a largely inflexible (public sector) framework. The challenge is to figure out ways to be more flexible.

Some of the ways to respond require little more than listening, hearing, and being creative. For example, it is important to keep in mind that different people define success differently. While one of your newest library school graduates might aspire to be the library director in a few short years, the other one who just joined your staff is defining her success in terms of work/life balance. She wants a traditional family. She exercises at the gym three mornings a week, does a lot of volunteer work during the week and on weekends (at the soup kitchen on Wednesday, and building a house with Habitat for Humanity on weekends), and plays soccer or volleyball at 5:30 p.m. twice a week.

And yet both of these Generation X librarians want to be continually learning and challenged. Both want to know the latest technology and trends. Both expect to be in on all decisions affecting their work and are committed to working in an organization that has meaning. It is important to create a culture that emphasizes

- participation
- shared decision-making
- sense of purpose and value
- initiative
- feedback

- creativity
- social aspects of the workplace
- balance

You also need to acknowledge that this environment is intended to support the library's goals and objectives, which always come first. Work, after all, is called work for a reason. The items in the preceding list are good things to have if they do not adversely affect the delivery of services.

You might ask, "How do we do this?" The first step is to train supervisors, train supervisors, and train supervisors! While many supervisors are very effective and well trained, others are not. Those supervisors are not malicious or evil; they just do not know how to create the culture described. They haven't been trained and they often have bad habits: habits learned from their own supervisors in their first job after graduating from library school. In many cases our profession has taken its best librarians and made them poor branch and department managers. Developing well-trained supervisors and managers is clearly the bedrock of creating a culture that supports retention. Developing a well-designed supervisory and management training program is essential, a strategy that must be adopted to ensure that the right employees are doing the right work in support of the library's goals and objectives.

Creating a Culture That Values Work/Life Balance

There are many ways to create an environment that tries to balance work with life, including the following ones. As you consider these, be mindful of what is written in your union contracts, civil service rules, and city or county policies. Not all of these strategies are possible in every library.

Define the work in terms of what is to be accomplished. Don't just say, "Our working hours are from 8 a.m. to 5 p.m. . . . be there." Unless an employee needs to cover a desk or attend meetings, focus on the project or the program. Ask: "What needs to be done?" or "What is the work?" Think about whether the work really needs to be completed on-site and only during regular business hours.

Provide flexible work schedules. Allow for job sharing and out-of-the box ways of meeting customer, employee, and library needs. Many public libraries have developed a part-time workforce to cover evening and weekend shifts. It may be that other forms of flexibility can also be accommodated. A study conducted by Catalyst showed that two-thirds—67 percent—of Generation X employees would like to work a compressed workweek, though only 6 percent actually did, and 36 percent would like to work part-time, while only 4 percent did.[8]

Provide flexible benefits plans. If possible, align what employees want with what they get. If your library controls the health benefits you offer employees, consider alternatives. Health benefits mean different things to different employees. For some, access to a fitness center is an important health benefit. For others, subsidized health screening or family insurance coverage is prized. To a still greater degree, helping employees to strike a work/life balance means tailoring paid time off and benefits to their preferences, capabilities, and level of responsibility both at home and in the library. Consider creating a cafeteria benefits plan. Look into the new consumer-driven health plans, which give employees a fixed dollar amount and make them responsible for managing their health care. While new, these plans are starting to gain acceptance.

Are your employees permitted to use sick leave to care for a sick child or parent? It's better for everyone involved if a sick leave policy recognizes this eventuality and allows employees to care for family members rather than lie about how they are using their sick leave. Have you thought of a paid time-off plan, where all time off except holiday leave is combined and employees spend it as appropriate for their needs and lifestyle? It's likely that the newer members of your workforce don't have enough vacation time, and those with many years of service can't find the time to take the time off that they earn! Paid time off can be a way to balance this equation. Figure 11-2 provides an illustration of one model for providing paid time off.

Evaluate alternative workplaces and telecommuting as options. Most library service takes place in the library building, but there's a strong tradition of taking services outside the building as well. Think beyond bookmobiles and traditional forms of outreach services and ask yourself if all the work of the library needs to be accomplished at the library. Could telephone reference

Figure 11-2: Paid Time Off	
Paid time off (PTO) provides staff members with paid time away from work that can be used for vacation, personal time, personal illness, or time off to care for dependents. PTO takes the place of sick time, personal time, and vacation. The benefit of PTO is that it promotes a flexible approach to time off. Staff members are accountable and responsible for managing their own PTO hours to allow for adequate reserves if there is a need to cover vacation, illness or disability, appointments, emergencies, or other needs that require time off from work. PTO must be scheduled in advance and have supervisory approval, except in the case of illness or emergency. All time away from work should be deducted from the staff member's PTO bank in hourly increments (some exceptions for exempt staff) with the exception of fixed holidays and time off in accordance with the library's policy for jury duty, military duty, or bereavement.	Accrual Example: **Years of Service PTO Accrual** 0-6 years 23 days/year or 15.33hours/month 7 years + 28 days/year or 18.66 hours/ month The amount of accrual can be increased for senior-level positions. A specified amount of accrued hours can be carried forward at the end of the year (example: 40 hours maximum may be carried forward). When a staff member resigns, the accrued PTO can be paid to the employee. Part-time staff members will have pro-rated PTO. For example: If a staff member works 20 hours per week, she will earn 50 percent of the above accruals.

questions be answered at a more convenient location? Where do Web projects need to be developed? Could question-answering and research be conducted from an employee's home? Could committee work be done by telephone or videoconference? Could e-mail and intranets be used effectively to avoid having to call a meeting at all? New technology and new definitions of acceptable work locations and activities have broadened the possibilities for answering these questions for libraries of all sizes and means.

Appreciate the dilemmas of child care, elder care, and employees playing multiple roles. The reality is that you and your employees often have family obligations. There will always be sick children, pregnancy leave, and aging and ailing parents. Accept it and to the fullest extent you can, plan for it. Recruit, train, and work to retain a qualified substitute pool (perhaps retired librarians or library school students) and treat them like valued members of your staff. Create internships or work-study programs with your local college. Create two "staff pools" of librarian and circulation staff in each region of your service area. Let employees float between branches to fill in when the need arises. Do the same for departments in your central library. Create policies and practices that anticipate and support these life-cycle events. Employees will appreciate not having to feel guilty when they must take time off to care for a child or parent.

"Allow" voluntary demotions. Your library may "allow" voluntary demotions, but it is important to create a culture where a demotion or a change of direction is safe and acceptable. What you want is a culture where an employee can take a risk and change her mind without penalty or humiliation. When Mary Sue realizes that she really doesn't like supervising employees or all the paperwork associated with an administrative position, make it easy for her to return to a job where she was competent and celebrate the fact that she tried and learned. If her former job has been filled maybe she can't return to it, but perhaps there is another vacancy that fits her and the library's needs better. She may realize that she isn't ready for a supervisory position but would like to try again in the future, or she may realize that supervision really isn't for her. Whatever she learns, it should be accepted and appreciated for what it is without a negative value being attached to it.

Appreciate the diversity of personal values and priorities. Demonstrating an acceptance of personal diversity can take a variety of forms. Accepting and supporting family obligations are one form, but there are others. Increasingly, HR specialists are writing about the employees without family responsibilities who want time to do what interests them. Their interests might range from taking windsurfing lessons to traveling, performing a community service, or taking a class. Could this time be built into the employee's and library's schedule? If not, why not? Paid time off and personal leave options might encourage both the recruitment and retention of the high-performers who want a position that allows them to pursue personal interests.

Wonderful ideas, you say. But how can I implement them in my library? My library operates under the mandates of our local jurisdiction. "No creativity allowed here!" is the refrain heard in between the lines when we suggest a new program. Don't despair. There are ways to have your voice heard, but it will take some time and work. Here are some tips.

1. Get involved. If your local jurisdiction is creating a bargaining team, studying benefits, or assessing the workforce or the climate of employees, volunteer to serve on the committee. You will learn what is happening and a great deal more; you will be the "go to" person for issues pertaining to the library's workforce; and most important, you will gain their respect, so that they will listen to your suggestions when you want to try something new.
2. Take the long view. Most local jurisdictions are bureaucratic, and changing the course, even allowing for some flexibility, can take a considerable amount of time.
3. In the meantime, keep reinforcing your credibility and stay in dialogue. Be a team player and don't bad-mouth the process or the bureaucracy. Remember, when you are ready, you want them to accept your ideas at least provisionally, if not enthusiastically.
4. When you see the time is right, meet with the HR director of your local jurisdiction. Turn her into an ally. Be prepared. Share the information you learned from this book, other resources, and conferences. Anticipate resistance. Have answers to the questions she will ask that pertain to best practices for recruitment and retention as well as to how your plan for workforce flexibility fits in to the library and its workforce. Offer to sponsor it as a pilot, so the local jurisdiction doesn't have to make a complete policy change. Tell the HR director that you will share the library's learning and even help make a case to the county executive, civil service commission, union, staff association, or other group.

Being part of the team and understanding your local jurisdiction's needs and resources will make you a valuable member of that team. You will learn and understand its needs as well. You will then be able to clearly articulate your case in a way that would make it difficult for anyone to turn you down!

Step 5.4: Define Expectations

It seems obvious, but performance problems are frequently the result of the work not being clearly defined. It is very critical for the employee to have clear answers to the following questions:

What is my job?
What must I accomplish?
To what level of quality/quantity/time frame? How will I know I've been successful?
What resources are available to help me (including the supervisor, the library's intranet, city/county/library resources online, a mentor, the HR department, training materials, peers, etc.)?

Most employees just want to be told "the bookends," that is, the scope of the work. What needs to be done? What are the expected results or outcomes? Tell them, and then let them put their own imprint on "how" the work gets done.

Many supervisors have a hard time letting go of the "how" to do the job. These supervisors have done the job for a long time and just "know" the best way. While it may be the best way for the supervisor, the new employee might have a better way, or at least a way that works really well for her . . . and fulfills her individual performance plan. An individual performance plan lists the activities each employee will engage in over the course of the year in order to fulfill assigned goals linking to the library's service priorities. It lists the time frame for accomplishing each activity, the measures of success for it, and any resources that will be needed.

Rewards and Incentives

Motivated workers make the difference between failure and success, turnover and loyalty. What employees want most is interesting work and appreciation for their efforts. Lack of recognition or appreciation is one of the top reasons why high-performing employees leave their jobs. Yet many employers neglect to use this simple management tool.

Some libraries create written, formal recognition programs. For the most part, simplicity reigns. A library leader saying a sincere, personal "Thank you!" to the employee is great, especially if done on the spot or at the time of the accomplishment. Referencing a specific accomplishment adds value. Sending a handwritten thank-you note to an employee is silver medal territory, and offering a specific "Thank you" in front of other employees is gold. Celebrate a library accomplishment as a group and you've hit platinum.

Over the years, recognition programs have changed. Until recently they were formal, centrally (HR) run, infrequent, based in cultures of entitlement, and selectively used for the few very top performers. The norm now is multiple recognition programs and activities that are leader-oriented, informal, frequent, and flexible. They are shaped by cultures of performance and are available to reward everyone.

If your library does not have a recognition program, you'll be amazed to see how productivity and morale increase by implementing even the simplest one. A few guidelines for starting a program are:

Make the program meaningful; the things that are recognized should be worthwhile and not trivial.

Focus on the areas that have the most impact. Involve employees.

Develop clear, objective criteria and recognize all who hit them. Develop the logistics (i.e., schedules, time frames of events). Announce the program with fanfare.

Publicly track progress; "if you don't measure it, you can't manage it!" Have lots of winners.

Allow flexibility of rewards.

Renew the program as needed; build on successes and learn from mistakes. Link informal and formal rewards.

The program can be low-cost and still yield high-impact results. A medium-sized public library offers "Everyone Counts" spot awards which can be used for video coupons, branch sale items (such as tote bags), store gift cards, book sale items, summer reading T-shirts, or books sold at the circulation desk. The vouchers are valued at $1.50 each and can be accumulated for a larger item. A supervisor or coworker can hand one to any employee on the spot. Ten-dollar vouchers for a gift basket, breakfast, or gift card are also presented on the spot to employees who handle an emergency or a difficult librarian-in-charge situation, fill in on another job, complete a special task, or consistently present a positive attitude that inspires or gives time and assistance to an area or staff person outside the assigned department or area of responsibility. This library system also provides more formal incentives and recognition with its Customer Service Spirit and Service awards twice a year. The awards are $200, and two each are presented at Staff Day each year.

In addition to providing formal awards, a large public library offers "Applause" awards that are spontaneous and can be given at any time by any employee to any other employee. They are awarded as a way to say "Thank you!" for going beyond expectations and doing a great job. These are used to say, "I know the terrific job you did/are doing and I appreciate your efforts." These spot awards consist of a certificate and a $5 gift or premium. This system also offers two large incentive awards ($500) for employees who demonstrate an ongoing commitment to quality customer service, create a major project, practice innovative thinking resulting in a significant improvement in library operations or customer services, are willing to undertake new responsibilities or to participate in activities not usually included in the job description, or produce an extremely high volume of quality work output over an extended period of time.

Other libraries provide suggestion programs with cost savings shared by the employee and library. You can also have celebratory bragging sessions where employees share their progress with library leadership; start staff meetings with good news and praise for employees who deserve it; read thank-you letters from customers; schedule self-recognition or recognition days; or send a card on an employee's anniversary date noting her accomplishments for the year and how important the person is to the department. You are limited only by your creativity. If you need a boost, read *1001 Ways to Reward Employees*.[9] It will help spur your creativity. Recognition programs are a very low-cost way to show employees respect and appreciation. They focus on performance, help make work fun, and lead to retention of top talent.

Step 5.5: Provide Training
When you hear the words staff development you probably think of formal training programs, and these are certainly an important component of staff

development. However, they are not the only component. Developing your employees starts with orientation and doesn't end until retirement. It includes both formal and informal learning opportunities and it focuses on the needs of individual employees.

An employee's experience and impression of a place start with recruitment; that is, before he or she is actually hired. Recruitment, orientation, and assimilation processes provide chances to emphasize the personal elements of a prospective employee's connection to the organization.

Employee Orientation
Orienting new employees to the library and their job continues to be one of the most ignored functions in libraries. Too often it is not conducted at all, and when it is, it is often done poorly: paperwork overload, boring lectures, and overwhelming amounts of information. Too often the new employee is left to sink or swim. New employee orientation should be conducted within the first thirty days of employment.

Why Conduct An Orientation Program? Orientation is not just a "nice to have" function. Since new employees make their decision to stay or leave the library within their first ninety days, it is an important component of the recruitment and retention effort and serves several key purposes:

1. To make the employee feel welcome and help her get up to speed on the job quickly
2. To reduce the employee's anxiety about the new job and eliminate the stress of guessing how she should respond to easy-to-answer questions
3. To reduce turnover by showing that the library values the employee and provides the tools for success
4. To save the time of managers and peers by providing consistent information that all employees need
5. To develop realistic job expectations, convey an understanding of the library's values and goals, and help the employee see where she fits into this picture

There are two types of orientations, and both should be provided: an overview of the library and an overview of the job.[10] The first provides the basic information a new employee needs to get started and includes detail on the library and its context in local government, the employee's department or branch, important policies, information about compensation and benefits, safety issues, employee and union issues, and physical facilities. This type of orientation can be conducted by the human resources department or by a skilled librarian or other staff person, since it is generic information that is not related to any one job.

The second type of orientation must be handled by the supervisor or manager. It pertains to the library's goals and how the employee and her job fits in: her job responsibilities, performance expectations, and duties; policies and procedures; how the supervisor likes to work with and communicate with employees; and an introduction to coworkers and others.

You should consider completing paperwork and procedural tasks before the new employee orientation. That allows the employee to actually think about what she is experiencing during the orientation rather than worrying about all of the paperwork details that accompany a new job. If the employee is moving to your area, helping with relocation, inviting the new hire to introduce her family to the library and vice versa, and matching her with local services (e.g., babysitters) foster the sort of personal connections that most employees value.

The orientation should include basic elements (introducing the new employee to coworkers, having the work space ready, providing instruction on the use of office equipment and basic information about where to put coats, lunches, etc.) as well as the employee's specific job and a more general orientation to the library as a whole. Creating a checklist of points to cover can be helpful to the harried manager, so that both the most mundane and the most critical points can be remembered. Adding a few extra touches (balloons at the desk, a mug with the library's logo, the director stopping by to introduce herself) can make the new employee feel even more welcome and valued. One director sends a "welcome card" to new employees. She writes in it: "At the end of some days you'll feel elated; after some you'll feel completely drained; but may you always leave the library knowing you contributed to our organization!"

It can be helpful to survey new employees to get their reactions to the orientation after they have been on the job for 30, 60, or 120 days. Share the feedback with library leadership and then make adjustments to the orientation process as needed. That way you can improve your library's induction process while also communicating to new hires that their input is valued. First impressions are extremely important, and taking the time to find out if the library is making a positive and productive first impression will pay off in increased feelings of inclusion and loyalty.

Going beyond surveying reactions to orientation is an important next step. Talk to employees about what they are doing and about their thoughts and feelings toward the library and their job. Managers and peers could also provide important information about what is going well and what is not. Rather than leaving it to chance, assign a staff member to this function. Taking the time to interact in a genuine way with new employees is vital. Research shows that most new employees decide within their first ninety days if they will remain on the job.

A new employee's assimilation into the library workplace can be enhanced through consciously acknowledging this process and developing standards and practices that support it. Managers need to know that they are expected to assist new employees throughout their first few months of employment by purposefully creating ways for them to become engaged members of their branch or work unit. Publicizing and recognizing creative ways of doing this can inspire other supervisors and managers and create an environment that is seen to value the thoughtful induction of new employees.

Tips for Designing An Orientation Program. Plan an orientation program that develops loyalty, enhances morale, and supports retention. This reinforces the fact that you must consciously plan a new employee's introduction to your library and make sure that someone is assigned to each piece of the orientation process. This plan should be reviewed and updated regularly in order to ensure its continued accuracy and relevance.

However, before redesigning or creating an orientation program, gather input from employees (both long-term and those recently hired), managers, and others and ask the following questions:

> What does the new employee need to know about this library and its work environment to make her feel more comfortable?
>
> What impression do we want to make on the employee's first day? What key policies and procedures must the employee be aware of to avoid mistakes in her first weeks and months of hire? Focus on key issues. What special things (desk, work area, equipment, special instructions) should be provided to make the new employee feel comfortable, welcome, and secure? What specific things can supervisors and managers do so the employee begins to know her coworkers?
>
> What positive experience can I provide for new employees that they could discuss with their families? The experience should be something to make the new employee feel valued by the library.[11]
>
> What can we do to make sure this process is fun and welcoming?

Strategies for Developing Staff

Whether your library is large or small, there are a number of things you might consider to help your staff grow and develop. Keep in mind any programs provided by your jurisdiction, as well as requirements in your civil service rules or union contract. These programs include the following.

Grow your own workforce. Provide support for employees seeking a bachelor's degree or an MLS. Give tuition assistance to employees who are working full-time while attending college or library school (any little bit helps), as well as some time off to study every week. Just an hour or two makes a huge difference to a working student.

Promote MLS students to an interim job-grade level. After the student has successfully completed half of her degree program, reclassify her job from library associate to librarian trainee or another title. Award a grade increase, as well as a salary increase. The employee will value your appreciation and show it in her work, as well as in her loyalty and her decision to remain in the library after graduation.

Develop a program of job rotation and cross-training. Have staff swap jobs for three to six months. All will return with increased job knowledge, vitality, perspective, and appreciation of the library, its work, and workforce.

Do it as part of a structured program where the staff keep a journal or record questions they encounter and discuss the key things they have learned with their peers or a coach.

Job rotation does not have to be this extensive. Alternatively, you can rotate library associates assigned to the central library into a branch for a week or rotate employees among branches, if you have more than one building. Cross-train public service, technical services, and business office employees. Not only will these assignments develop the individuals involved, but cross-training provides the library with a more flexible and capable workforce, eliminating work stoppages or backlogs when a vacation is taken or someone is out on extended sick leave.

Develop employees by asking them to serve on task forces or in interim job assignments. Do not repeatedly ask the same people to serve on task forces or committees. For each new task force or job assignment, seek out a promising person who hasn't been given an opportunity to participate. Ask her to serve. If she agrees, provide support and watch her blossom.

Implement a 360-degree feedback program. In a 360-degree feedback program, performance data is obtained from peers, subordinates, and the supervisor in order to provide an assessment of an employee's performance up, down, and sideways in the organization. It provides full circle, or 360-degree, feedback. This type of evaluation process offers employees a learning tool and feedback mechanism to promote employee growth and development. There are a variety of ways to conduct a 360-degree feedback program. As with other approaches to employee performance evaluation, it is essential that everyone involved understand the purposes of the evaluation and receive thorough training in applying the process.

Create a dual career-ladder system for librarians. Career ladders allow employees to focus on their expertise as an individual contributor (e.g., a children's librarian) without having to take on a management role to earn more money. In this scenario, an employee might advance from Librarian I to II by taking on more responsibility in collection development, conducting research, or designing new programs in early childhood learning. Other options might include the Librarian I moving up by becoming a specialist in literacy readers' advisory, information technology, or training. There are many ways to acknowledge and reward your staff for increasing their responsibility and value to the library outside of advancement to a management position.

While the library might ultimately place the employee in a higher grade level and pay her a higher salary, that amount will be far less than the cost of replacing her if she goes elsewhere, or the cost of low morale and mistakes if she takes a management job she doesn't really desire just to earn more money.

Assign mentors to both new and longer-term employees. This is especially important when an employee is promoted or assumes a new role. Mentoring can be a powerful tool in employee development. An effective mentoring process takes some thought and preplanning. It is important to match the mentor and the mentee carefully. Their personal styles and interests should be compatible. Allow a trial period for the relationship to settle in, and if there are problems, make needed adjustments.

You will want to identify clear expectations for the mentoring relationship. Define the results you expect and discuss responsibilities, roles, and expectations with both the mentor and mentee. Provide training for mentors. Monitor and evaluate progress and reset expectations as the relationship grows and changes. The formal mentor/mentee relationship is not intended to be permanent. The last phase of the formal relationship should be to encourage independence at the appropriate time. Lois Zachary's *The Mentor's Guide: Facilitating Effective Learning Relationships* is a wonderful resource for developing a mentoring program or relationship.[12]

Step 5.6: Build Commitment
The suggestions in Step 5.5 will help you build a workforce of competent and effective staff members. Every organization wants to retain the best and brightest members of its staff, but that is becoming increasingly difficult. Today's employees are more mobile than ever before. The typical employee starting in the workforce now will have seven or more jobs in her lifetime and in several different careers. Library managers need to think about ways to build commitment in their employees.

Exit Interviews
Employees may leave for other, possibly higher-level or more lucrative library jobs, for jobs in other sectors, or for retirement or personal reasons. Managers should learn from each situation. Exit interviews can provide an invaluable source of information, especially when an employee is leaving for a job in another library system. Managers need to learn more about what prompted a resignation. What pull did another job have, or what pushed the employee to leave her current job? If you are having trouble retaining key staff, carefully and systematically explore the causes. Losing staff is a symptom. Doing something about it demands an understanding of the true causes.

The exit interview should be performed by human resources staff, an ombudsperson, or a neutral person. The employee should be assured that the information she shares will be confidential and used only as summary feedback to help improve retention at the library. The exit interview should not be conducted by the employee's supervisor or anyone in her chain of command, in case supervision or leadership is the reason the person is leaving the library's employment. Even in large libraries, to the extent possible, you should conduct exit interviews of employees at all levels, including pages and clerks. All those separating from the library at their choice can be an important source of information about library and management practices, as well as compensation, benefits, and the work environment. While face-to-face interviews may elicit more information, they are more time-consuming and harder to schedule. An online survey, hosted on the library's intranet or by SurveyMonkey.com or some other source, is a realistic alternative and may even provide more candid information.

Employee Climate Surveys
Not waiting until employees leave to solicit their opinions about life and work at the library is a proactive way to understand the wants and needs of your workforce. Many organizations (and a few public libraries) conduct confidential employee climate or opinion surveys and make changes based upon what they discover. You can study a variety of issues, depending on the conditions in your library. The typical topics involved in how employees think and feel about their workplace include

- job satisfaction
- leadership
- training
- compensation and benefits
- technology and tools
- customer services
- communications and information received
- supervision
- understanding the library's vision and service priorities
- job expectations

Conducting a climate study is not as daunting as you might think. Start by creating and chartering a "climate study" committee. Include a cross-section of employees and managers on the committee. Invite representatives from branches, the central library, technical services, business services, and the union or staff association, as well as newer employees, long-term employees, women, men, people of color, and so on. Strive for diversity on this committee. Clarify if it is an advisory or a steering committee in terms of the types of decisions the group will be authorized to make.

Decide what topics you wish to study and how you plan to collect the data. Will some members of the committee conduct interviews or focus groups? Will you use a consultant or local faculty member to help? What about collecting quantitative data via a Web-based survey? You could easily pick a handful of topics and ask 10 to 20 questions on your intranet. If confidentiality is a concern, go to SurveyMonkey.com. For a very low fee, you can purchase one or two months of this resource. SurveyMonkey, Zoomerang, and other Web-based survey companies will walk you through the design of the survey and will also tabulate the data.

Write the questions to include in your survey. Think carefully about what you want to know. It is easy to tabulate and analyze data from multiple-choice questions, but it is much more challenging to code, tabulate, and analyze data from open-ended questions. Now is the time to decide how you want to understand the survey responses when it comes time to analyze the data. Do you want to be able to look at answers by department, branch, or unit, by gender, race, tenure, age? If so, you have to ask the respondents to identify themselves by those categories when they are taking the survey.

Always test the questions in your survey with a small group of the people who will be taking the survey before you distribute the survey to the entire staff. You may be surprised by how differently respondents interpret questions that you thought were perfectly clear. After the pilot test, review the surveys and talk to the people who were your testers. Ask them if they understood the survey instructions and if the questions were clear. You might also ask if the testers want to tell you about something that was not included in the survey. Revise the survey and ask the testers to review the revised questions to make sure they reflect the needed changes.

When the survey instrument is finalized, you are ready to publicize and conduct the survey. Communication should be sent from the library director letting employees know who the members of the committee are, the purpose of the survey, and what will be done with the data. Confidentiality should be stressed, as should the commitment by the director to review and implement findings as feasible. Implementation issues and approaches will depend on the purpose of the survey.

After the closing date for returns, you are ready to analyze the data and act on what you learn. Always report the survey results to employees, even if the results are not positive. If you don't report the results of a survey, you can be sure that the grapevine will assume the worst and employees will resent your starting a project without bringing it to closure. Use simple bar graphs and pie charts to show the data to employees. Start by asking them if there are any surprises or anything missing in the results. Get employees involved in making changes suggested by the survey data.

The director should also provide one-to-one feedback on departmental findings to each department head. Based upon their feedback, the committee and director should plan and prioritize next steps and develop an action plan. Keep the committee active as action is taken and changes are made, or if appropriate, appoint new committees to manage projects that result from the survey. Review lessons learned at every stage; celebrate, monitor, evaluate, and survey employees again. Making changes based on what you learn from the survey can be a powerful force for showing employees that you value what they say. As a result, it creates a culture that is conducive to retention. Whenever possible, it is often best to hire outside consultants to do these kinds of surveys. The outsiders have more credibility and the staff is often more comfortable about confidentiality issues.

There are four tool kits in *Demonstrating Results: Using Outcome Measurement in Your Library* that will also be helpful as you develop, tabulate, and analyze your surveys: Tool Kit C, Sample Confidentiality Forms; Tool Kit D, Tips on Developing Questionnaires; Tool Kit E, Data Preparation, Coding, and Processing; and Tool Kit F, Sampling.[13]

Retaining Talent As They Age

Phased retirement is an important way to mitigate the impact of employee exit on the library. By making schedules and tasks more flexible for those considering retirement, managers can retain a talented pool of mentors. In a phased-in retirement or as retirees, former full-time employees can provide a reliable, flexible, knowledgeable, and affordable addition to the library's workforce.

Inducements could include flexible hours or assignments so that retirees can travel or pursue other personal interests but still be available during parts of the year, parts of the week, or for projects of several months' duration. Some library employers are finding ways to capture and celebrate the many years of experience and the deep knowledge base their most senior employees possess. Others are developing ways for senior staff and managers to take longer periods of time off while still retaining their employment status, or to phase out by working part-time or on temporary assignments before they ultimately retire completely. This latter option is most attractive when future retirement benefits are not adversely impacted by such preretirement reductions in hours.

Retirees can be a great source of desk coverage or coaching. Keep them informed and connected. Have them work in an on-call arrangement. Give them a cell phone, a computer, and a coaching assignment!

You should review your local government's civil service rules and personnel policies to ensure that retirees can continue to work. Retirement rules vary by state and local jurisdiction. In some locales, retirees cannot continue to work at all in the organization from which they retired. It is considered to be "double dipping" from the local government. In other jurisdictions it is acceptable, and in other instances where full-time work is not permitted, hourly or consulting work is allowed, so check the details, as well as the regulations pertaining to benefits, pensions, maximum salary permissible, and so on. Provide assistance to these employees through local financial planners or retirement counselors to ensure that they are comfortable with the arrangements, particularly if they are able to collect Social Security.

The Keys to Commitment

A responsive work environment is a crucial source of employee commitment and thus retention. The keywords here are

- communication
- accountability
- recognition

Creating and maintaining effective forums for employee input can connect leaders to staff at all levels. Employee involvement in decision-making, made possible by open but structured communication, invests everyone in positive and negative outcomes, such that all are accountable to all. Finally, accountability is inseparable from recognition for contributions and achievements. Whether it is just a "Thank you" and applause at a staff meeting or a promotion or some other substantial acknowledgment, the universality of forms of recognition in public- and private-sector organizations is a testament to recognition's importance for cementing employee commitment.

These strategies are all about building commitment to the job and the employer, since productivity and retention are greatly increased when employees are committed. Retention strategies must be intentionally designed so that employees know what they need to do and what is expected of them; are involved in decisions that impact the work they do and the services they provide; have opportunities to learn and grow; receive recognition for good performance; and know they are responsible for their performance and are held accountable if performance is lacking. Strategies developed with these factors in mind will result in the best and brightest employees choosing to stay with the library that allows them to contribute, learn, and grow.

In sum, productivity and employee retention are greatly increased when employees are committed. This is especially important today, since job security and loyalty to an employer are lower than ever. To enhance retention, remember these five keys:

1. Focus. Employees know what they need to do and what is expected of them.
2. Involvement. People support most what they help to create.
3. Development. Opportunities for learning and growth are encouraged.
4. Gratitude. Recognition (formal or informal) is given for good performance.
5. Accountability. Employees are responsible for their performance.

Notes

1. Marcus Cunningham and Curt Coffman, *First Break All the Rules: What the World's Greatest Managers Do Differently* (New York: Simon and Schuster, 1999).
2. Christi Olson and Paula Singer, *Winning with Library Leadership: Enhancing Services through Connection, Contribution, and Collaboration* (Chicago: American Library Association, 2004).
3. Ibid.
4. Lynne C. Lancaster and David Stillman, *When Generations Collide: Who They Are, Why They Clash, How to Solve the Generational Puzzle at Work* (New York: HarperCollins, 2002).
5. D. Doverspike and A. O'Malley, "When Generations Collide: Part 1," *International Public Management Association for Human Resources newsletter*, February 2006. www.ipma-hr.org.
6. Doug Brown, "Understanding Four Generations in the Workplace," *Fort Worth Business Press*, June 27, 2003, 11.
7. Carolyn A. Martin, "Bridging the Generation Gap(s)," *Nursing* 34, no. 12 (December 2004): 62–63.
8. Catalyst, Inc., "Workplace Flexibility Isn't Just a Women's Issue," Viewpoints, August 2003. www.catalyst.org/files/view/Workplace%20Flexibility%20Isn%27t%20Just%20a%20Women%27s%20Issue.pdf.
9. Bob Nelson, *1001 Ways to Reward Employees*, 2nd ed. (New York: Workman, 2005).
10. Bacal and Associates, "A Quick Guide to Employee Orientation—Help for Managers and HR," www.work911.com/articles/orient.htm.
11. Judith Brown "Employee Orientation: Keeping New Employees on Board," http://humanresources.about.com/od/retention/a/keepnewemployee.htm.

12. Lois Zachary, *The Mentor's Guide: Facilitating Effective Learning Relationships* (San Francisco: Jossey-Bass, 2000).
13. Rhea Joyce Rubin, *Demonstrating Results: Using Outcome Measurement in Your Library* (Chicago: American Library Association, 2006), 104–12.

About the Authors

Jeanne Goodrich is an independent consultant based in Portland, Oregon.

Paula M. Singer is President and Principal Consultant of The Singer Group, Inc., a management consulting firm she founded in 1983. She provides strategic planning and alignment, organization design and development, performance management, leadership development, compensation, coaching, and other services to clients in the public, private, and nonprofit sectors. She is coauthor of *Winning with Library Leadership: Enhancing Services Through Connection, Contribution and Collaboration* (with Christi Olson), *Human Resources for Results* (with Jeanne Goodrich), and *Designing a Compensation Plan for Your Library* (with Laura Francisco). Paula is a frequent speaker at ALA, PLA, and state library association conferences and has written a number of articles for library and other publications.

Chapter 12

Great Expectations: An Interview with Jim Collins

Lisa Richter

Jim Collins has authored or coauthored four books, including 1994's *Built to Last: Successful Habits of Visionary Companies* and 2001's *Good to Great: Why Some Companies Make the Leap . . . and Others Don't.*

Both are bestsellers that explore the characteristics of success based on extensive research of the business sector. Recently, he released *Good to Great and the Social Sectors: A Monograph to Accompany Good to Great*, which explores the *Good to Great* principles as they apply to the social sector, and, by extension, building a meaningful life. The ideas in this companion piece, which states upfront that business thinking is not the answer, just might surprise you.

Public Libraries: One of the hallmarks of your work is the thoroughness of your research and a commitment to evidenced-based ideas, even when they are contrary to accepted beliefs. Yet you've published this monograph on the social sector without the usual obsessive research into this specific subset. Why?

Jim Collins: I was getting inundated with readers from the social sectors asking a series of questions about the application of *Good to Great* ideas to their world. They had already established for themselves that the ideas applied. This interest came as a delightful surprise—how quickly and extensively *Good to Great* reached into the social sectors. I had hoped that would happen, but I did not expect that it would happen to the extent that it did. In fact, I thought it would take hold less in the social sectors than *Built to Last*, because *Built to Last* is inherently about mission-driven, vision-driven organizations, which I thought clearly would appeal to social sector enterprises. As I kept getting more calls, cards, e-mail, questions, and invitations, I felt that I really owed our readers an attempt to try to answer their most frequently asked questions. So that's where the whole thing really began. That and a passion that I have for social sector questions; I never thought of myself as a business writer. I just happened to use business as my starting point.

The second answer is that I stuck very close to the *Good to Great* ideas, and I did that because they are research-driven ideas. It's a treatise on the *Good to Great* concepts in the context of the social sectors. It is entirely possible that, if you did a massive research project, you would find some additional insight and maybe even key concepts that you don't find from the *Good to Great* research. In fact, I would suspect that you might. I don't think they would subvert what we found, but I think you would find some additional things.

In fact, I've been very excited to see that people in the social sectors are taking our research method and applying it into their particular arenas. Any given study is going to take years. There's only so many silver bullets that I have in my life, but I can serve as a bit of a thesis adviser. So, perhaps the biggest contribution that we might be able to make is to give people the method and say, "You know, you can do this in medical centers, libraries, police departments, or in communities." Because, someday I'm not going to be here, and I would love the method to be left behind as something that people can use in their own world.

PL: Some of the concepts in *Good to Great and the Social Sectors* seem almost counterintuitive. For instance, the front cover states "Why Business Thinking Is Not the Answer." Why isn't it?

JC: Sometimes well-intentioned businesspeople join boards or serve as advisers to social sector enterprises, and, in an attempt to be helpful, bring with them a sense of what I would call business parochialism: "Let us businesspeople show you how to do it because we know how to deliver results and you need to be more like a business." But from what I've seen, that actually is a counterproductive approach because social sector leaders might be put off by that attitude. Thus, my first objective was to speak to businesspeople and give them a bridge to say, this isn't about imposing business on the social sectors, this is about creating a shared language around the principles of what separates great from good. Then a social sector leader and a business leader can both agree that what they are trying to do is create great outcomes and whether those are great sports outcomes, crime reduction outcomes, chronic homelessness reduction outcomes, orchestra outcomes, educational outcomes, or whatever, we all agree that what we want to do is embrace the principles of greatness as distinct from feeling like it's an imposition of business on social sectors.

The second is this: It's just tautologically true that most businesses are average. I mean just by definition. So to say that we're going to export the average practices of businesses into the social sector is to say that we are exporting averageness. Why do we want to do that? As it says in the monograph, the critical question is not the difference between business and social, but between great and good.

PL: Another idea that seems illogical is that, to achieve greatness, an organization must first find the right people and put them in the appropriate place before it decides where it is going. Why is that?

JC: I came in with an expectation that what we would find is that to take a company from good to great you would have somebody who would set a vision or a direction and would really galvanize people to go there. And, that's just what comparison companies did. Our comparison companies tended to have people who first set the direction and then tried to get people to go there. But the empirical observations found that *Good to Great* companies did not do that. They said, "First, we made sure we had the right people, and then we figured out where we were going to go." So it isn't so much a point of view as it was an empirical finding of the difference between the two sets of companies. That said, you have to stand back and puzzle. Well, why would that be?

Number one, in an uncertain world, and that is the world that we live in, your ultimate hedge against uncertainty is not your plans but your people. To use an analogy from climbing, my good friend, Jim Logan, did a climb called the Emperor Face on Mount Robson (Canadian Rockies) in the 1970s. It's been almost thirty years since that climb was done, and, since then, it has never been repeated. I asked Jim, "Why were you able to get up this thing?" He said: "Because I knew that above a certain point on the climb, where no one had ever been, it was entirely uncertain what the mountain would throw at us. We didn't know how big the cracks would be, we didn't know what the ice would be, whether we could be hit by a storm. There were so many variables that we couldn't possibly plan for because we didn't know what the mountain would give us. So the most important decision I made was picking my partner. I picked Mugs Stump. I went up there with a great confidence that, if I couldn't do a certain pitch, Mugs could. And Mugs had confidence that, if he couldn't do a certain pitch, I could. The ultimate plan for the route was who I climbed with."

Secondly, what really separates a great organization from a good one is the discipline of being able to not only see clearly what needs to be done but to actually execute and execute well. Therefore, even if you did have the right decision about which direction to take things, it's not going to make any difference if you haven't populated the bus with the right people in the first place; they will not be able to climb the pitches.

PL: How do you know if you've got the right people and how do you find them?

JC: How do you find them? I'll come to that question second. That's a harder question actually. In terms of what makes for the right people, obviously, of course, it varies from type of industry or type of situation. If you were to have a great surgical operation, for example, your people better know something about surgery. But, what are some of the generic things? Number one, they have to be someone who fits your core values. Not that they've learned your core values intellectually, but rather they have in their DNA a fit with the core values. People often ask me, "How do you get people to share your core values?" The answer is, you don't. You find people who already have a disposition to sharing your values, and you create a culture that is so tight around those values that those who don't share them find themselves very uncomfortable and generally self-eject like a virus. Number two is the right people understand that they don't have a job; they have responsibilities. Now in the social sectors this is even more important because a lot of people who work in social sector enterprises by definition don't have a job, they're volunteers. But even in a for-profit situation, the same idea applies. You need people who think in terms of what is my responsibility as distinct from what are my tasks. Let me underscore, by the way, that I'm talking about key seats. Obviously, you can't necessarily get a perfect hit rate on all of these criteria for every seat on your bus. You have to do it for the seats that really matter. Third is that the right people don't really need to be tightly managed. The moment you feel the need to tightly manage someone, you might have made a mistake. They need to, of course, be guided and taught and led and all of those things, but tightly managed? Probably not.

Collins' Concepts

Throughout *Good to Great*, Collins coins terms for its main concepts. Here are some highlights.

Level 5 Leadership: Level 5 leaders are ambitious for the cause—not themselves—and they have the fierce resolve to do whatever it takes to make good on that ambition. A Level 5 leader displays a paradoxical blend of personal humility and professional will.
First Who . . . Then What: Those who build great organizations make sure they have the right people on the bus, the wrong people off the bus, and the right people in the key seats *before* they figure out where to drive the bus.
The Stockdale Paradox: Retain unwavering faith that you can and will prevail in the end, regardless of the difficulties, and, at the same time, have the discipline to confront the most brutal facts of your current reality.
The Hedgehog Concept: An operating model that reflects understanding of three intersecting circles: what you can be the best in the world at, what you are deeply passionate about, and what best drives your economic or resource engine.
The Flywheel: In building greatness, there is no single defining action, no one killer innovation, no solitary lucky break. Rather, the process resembles relentlessly pushing a giant, heavy flywheel in one direction, turn upon turn, building momentum until a point of breakthrough and beyond.

Excerpted from *Good to Great and the Social Sectors: A Monograph to Accompany Good to Great*, by Jim Collins, reprinted here with permission from Jim Collins.

Fourth, the right people deliver on their commitments; they do what they say, which means two things. They are very careful with what they say, and they don't fail to deliver on what they say they're going to deliver. There is just simply no room in key seats in a great organization for people who fail to deliver on their commitments, just no room.

And then the last thing I would point to is an emerging ability to have window and mirror maturity. In the Level 5 chapter in *Good to Great*, we write about the window and the mirror. The essence of it is this: If you are mature with the window and the mirror, you point out the window to apportion the credit to forces, factors, and people outside of yourself. But when things go badly, and this is where the maturity really comes in, you don't point fingers at factors outside of yourself. You stand in front of the mirror and say, "Yeah, I'm responsible. It wasn't circumstance, it wasn't this, or that, I'm responsible." Now, how do you find those sorts of people? The best place to look for people for key seats is in your own organization. You may have somebody who has been working in a much smaller seat for a while, but you look at them and you say, yeah they have the core values, they don't need to be tightly managed, they seem to understand the notion of responsibility, they've fulfilled their commitments, and you know they really seem to have a sense of that window-mirror maturity. Maybe there is somebody who you can grow into that bigger responsibility. That's a much lower risk game because they're a tested quantity; they may not yet have the skills, but they've demonstrated some of the character you're looking for.

How then do you find people for seats, small seats, big seats, volunteer, or nonvolunteer, whatever? This may sound completely trivial, but it's not. How is your daily calendar organized? If you are responsible for this bus, are you spending your best hours obsessing on the question of finding and getting and hanging onto and developing the right people for your key seats? If you're not spending more than one-third of your time and somewhere around two-thirds of your best hours on that question, you're not going to succeed at it.

PL: Given the constraints of an organization such as a public library—limited financial resources, diffuse power structure and, often, little to no control over who "stays on the bus"—how can anything like greatness be achieved?

JC: Let me give you an example. You want to talk about an environment full of constraints? Let's talk about underfunded schools with poor kids. You don't have the money you'd like to have. You don't have the class size you'd like to have. You don't have the parental involvement you'd like to have. You don't have the ability to change the bus because of the teachers union. I mean there are all these reasons why you couldn't deliver outstanding results. And yet Juli Peach, the principal of Alice Byrneis standing up and saying, "There are all kinds of reasons why we can't succeed, but we refuse to capitulate, and we're not going to capitulate." She refuses to capitulate on the fundamental goal, which is one thing: 100 percent of the kids are going to read by the end of grade 3. She's a total hedgehog: Kids are going to read. So then she and her teachers make obsessive use of data to track each kid, week by week, month by month. She got all of her teachers involved with the data. She couldn't change the people, but she could change the conversation around actual results. Then, of course, a big chunk of this is the hedgehog focus on one thing: The kids are going to read, all of them. If Juli Peach, standing on the island of her little school in Yuma, Arizona, can basically refuse to capitulate to mediocrity on the variables that matter, then it should give all of us hope that we are not imprisoned by our circumstances. I just get so inspired by what she does. That to me is, in the end, what our work is all about, showing that Juli Peach is possible.

PL: How can any of these concepts apply to my everyday life when I'm not in charge of any big organization, I have little power?
JC: The incredible beauty of the story we were just talking about is that, sure, you may have even less to work with than a small elementary school in Yuma, Arizona, but even that's a pretty contained circumstance. I always like to say to people, look, you have a minibus. It may only be a four-seat minibus, but the principles of deciding what the standards are that you are not going to capitulate on and then the discipline to try to either change those seats or, if you can't change the seats, to use the brutal facts (Stockdale Paradox) to begin to engage people in the conversation of how do we do a better job of achieving those standards. Those are things that can apply. Really they can apply down to a seat of one. You might be the whole bus yourself as an individual, although most people have at least a small group.

A good example from my own life is when my wife was ill (she's healthy now). Prior to *Good to Great*, I would have focused much more on what we should do. But since this happened after *Good to Great*, I found I focused more on who should be the doctors. It sounds like something very simple, but it's huge when the Stockdale Paradox is an approach to life. I mean, life throws curve balls. Life can really be a pretty awful experience sometimes for any number of reasons, and the Stockdale Paradox can really make a difference. I had a woman come up to me yesterday at a gathering and asked me to pass along a thank-you to the Stockdale family because the Stockdale Paradox really helped her get through her son's illness. She said, "We had to have faith that we could get through it and prevail, but we had to confront the brutal facts and not think we were going to be 'out by Christmas.'" (James Stockdale maintained that it was those people who believed they would be out of the prisoner of war camp by Christmas—the optimists—who were the ones who "died of a broken heart.")

It is also helpful in life to think about the Hedgehog Concept. What are you passionate about? What are you genetically encoded for? What can you contribute that is of economic value? How can you put those three things together so that you have an economic engine for yourself, you're building off of your genetic encoding, and you're doing something you're really passionate about?

Also relevant is the notion of a Flywheel—that life is about a consistent building of momentum as opposed to looking for the single big strike, which is so very American, but it's not generally how great things happen.

These things come back in a lot of different guises so I encourage people to think broadly about the idea because we discovered them by studying the difference between big corporations in contrast to average corporations, of course, but that doesn't change the fact that we were comparing great to good and that can be scaled up as well as down.

About the Author

Lisa Richter is a freelance writer based in Evanston, Illinois.

Chapter 13

Branch Management: An Analysis of Minneapolis–St. Paul Area Public Libraries

Chad Lubbers

With a librarian shortage forecast for the immediate future, the role of the public library branch manager will become increasingly important to the successful administration of public library systems. The Metropolitan Library Service Agency conducted a survey in August–October 2003 to create a profile of current branch managers in the Minneapolis–St. Paul metropolitan area, with the intent of addressing some of the management staffing issues that will affect public libraries in the years ahead.

Most public librarians are familiar with the popular McDonald's statistic, which states that there are more public libraries in the United States than McDonald's restaurants.[1] Of the more than sixteen thousand public libraries, approximately nine thousand are members of a multibranch library system.[2] In these nine thousand libraries, there is typically a single library manager who exercises a degree of supervisory authority over the staff, collection, and daily operations of that library facility. In this study, that person is identified as a public library branch manager.

The catalyst for the initiation of this project was Ken Haycock's insightful presentation, "Exemplary Public Library Branch Managers: Their Characteristics and Effectiveness," at the 2002 PLA conference in Phoenix. Haycock's study confirmed the importance of this area of study while also demonstrating—by attracting a standing-room-only audience—that there is significant interest about the competencies and roles of public library branch managers.

Methods

In August 2003, two surveys were distributed to library employees of nine Minneapolis–St. Paul area (Twin Cities) public library systems. All nine library systems are members of the Metropolitan Library Service Agency (MELSA). These nine library systems included a total of one hundred individual libraries at the time the surveys were distributed.

The first survey group comprised ninety-two branch managers. For the purpose of this study, the term "branch manager" was used to describe the individual who had supervisory authority over the collection, staff, and daily operations of a single library facility, including central libraries, which may be perceived as the largest branch of a given library system.

Within this branch manager survey pool, several managers were identified who supervised more than one library. These managers were surveyed only once. There were also two branch management vacancies in MELSA libraries at the time of survey distribution.

The branch manager survey consisted of sixty-three questions on a variety of topics, including education, previous work experience, current responsibilities, professional activity, and career development.

The second survey group consisted of the sixteen administrators of the nine MELSA library systems. For this study, the term "administrator" was defined as the individual who functions as the director or assistant director of a multibranch library system. Two of the nine MELSA library systems do not employ staff in an assistant director capacity. The administrator survey contained twenty-six questions based on the same general categories listed above in the branch manager survey.

Results

The survey return rate was 83 percent (seventy-six out of ninety-two) for the branch management survey and 88 percent (fourteen out of sixteen) for the administrator survey. Data were recorded in a Microsoft Access database to allow for analysis and data mining within the collected results.

Education

There was a wide range of educational backgrounds represented by the MELSA branch managers. The seventy-six survey respondents reported ninety-seven undergraduate degrees from twenty-seven discrete majors. However, 58 percent of the total undergraduate degrees came from just four disciplines: English (literature), history, library science, and education.

Administrators' undergraduate education patterns were largely consistent with those of library managers. The most numerous undergraduate degrees among administrators were also English, education, history, and library science degrees (see Figure 13-1).

Sixty-three of the seventy-six branch managers (83 percent) reported having a master's degree in library and information science (MLIS). Library administrators in the Twin Cities were slightly less likely to have an MLIS than the branch managers who work for them. But administrators were more likely to have postgraduate degrees in fields outside of library and information science (see Figure 13-2).

When managers were asked "When did you receive your MLIS?" the average response was 1982. Slightly more than half of the branch managers'

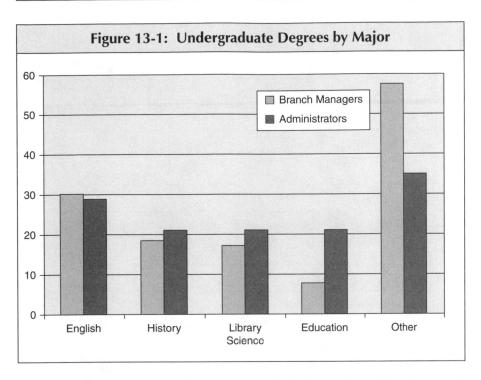

Figure 13-1: Undergraduate Degrees by Major

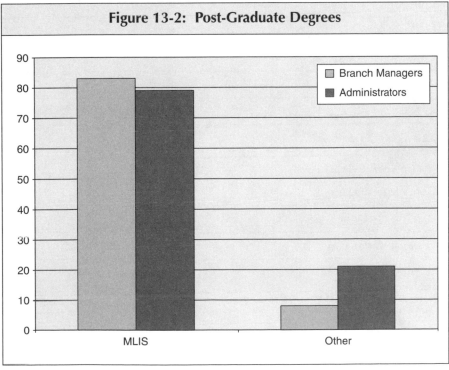

Figure 13-2: Post-Graduate Degrees

Figure 13-3: Branch Manager MLIS Degrees by State

MLIS Program	State	Graduates
Univ. of Denver	CO	2
Catholic Univ.	DC	1
Univ. of South Florida	FL	1
University of Iowa	IA	4
Dominican Univ.	IL	2
Rosary College	IL	2
Univ. of Illinois	IL	1
Indiana Univ.	IN	3
Simmons College	MA	1
Univ. of Michigan	MI	1
Univ. of Minnesota*	MN	22
College of St. Catherine	MN	3
St. Cloud State	MN	2
Univ. of North Carolina	NC	1
Rutgers	NJ	1
SUNY	NY	1
Case Western Reserve	OH	1
Univ. of North Texas	TX	1
Univ. of Washington	WA	1
Univ. of Wisconsin	WI	9
Unspecified Program		3
TOTAL		63

*The University of Minnesota eliminated its MLIS program in 1985

MLIS degrees were received from library and information science programs outside of Minnesota (see Figure 13-3).

Previous Work Experience

Managers reported having been librarians for an average of twenty-one years. Twenty of the seventy-six respondents had been librarians for more than thirty years. Approximately one-third of the managers reported working full-time in a profession other than librarianship for more than a year, and 55 percent worked in libraries that were not public libraries.

Managers and administrators were asked which departments they had worked in prior to becoming branch managers. The overwhelming majority— 72 percent of branch managers and 78 percent of administrators—reported previous work in reference or information departments. Fifty-one percent of the managers and 11 percent of administrators reported full-time posts in children's services. Twenty-two percent of library administrators worked as catalogers, compared to just 7 percent of branch managers who reported former posts in cataloging (see Figure 13-4).

Nine of the fourteen administrators were branch managers earlier in their careers. Administrators who had been branch managers supervised a combined total of thirty libraries while working as branch managers. Each of these nine administrators with previous branch management experience supervised an average of 3.3 branches before entering posts in administration.

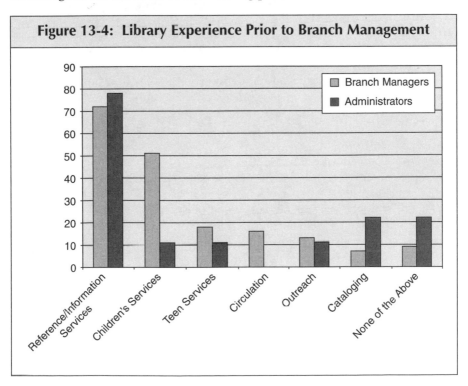

Figure 13-4: Library Experience Prior to Branch Management

Current Work Responsibilities

The majority of the questions in the branch management survey fell into this category and were not duplicated in the administrator survey. Managers were questioned about staffing, library facilities, supervision and management roles, outreach activities, work schedules, and personal workloads. Eighty-two percent of managers reported working with unionized staff, while only 29 percent of the managers were themselves unionized. Sixty-four percent were managers of a building that had undergone renovation, and 51 percent reported that the current building they supervised was also the first building they had supervised.

When asked about personal work schedules, 75 percent indicated that they were contracted to work a forty-hour week. Sixty percent of those with forty hour contracts work more than forty hours a week on a regular basis. More than 80 percent of the branch managers surveyed regularly work weekend and evening shifts. More than 60 percent of managers indicated that they left the library they supervised on a weekly basis for training, committee work, meetings, or outreach activities.

Managers were also questioned about a variety of tasks pertaining to library work, including both professional and paraprofessional duties. Specifically, managers were asked to identify the frequency with which they performed these tasks. Of the duties listed, those performed most frequently (on a daily basis) included reference work, reader's advisory, troubleshooting computers, bibliographic instruction, and circulation.

Again, referring to the above figure, managers were asked which of the above tasks occupy the majority of their time. The most time-consuming tasks included staff scheduling, community relations, and collection weeding.

When asked which of the above tasks they enjoyed the most, managers identified reference work, reader's advisory, and collection building as their favorite activities. Activities enjoyed least were complaint resolution, troubleshooting computers, and performance reviews.

Career Development

Seventy-one percent of the surveyed managers reported that librarianship was their first career choice. When given a list of possible reasons for entering the ranks of branch library management (see Figure 13-5), almost half identified "diversity of duties" as the chief attraction of the branch manager position.

For 53 percent of the managers in this survey, branch management was the first management experience of their careers. Six of the nine administrators (67 percent) who reported being branch managers earlier in their careers indicated that branch management was also their first supervisory experience in public libraries.

Branch managers and administrators ranked six criteria they considered to be the most important measures of effective public library branch management (see Figure 13-6). The top two responses for both groups were "user satisfaction" and "employee satisfaction," respectively. Both groups ranked "adherence to policy" near the bottom of the list.

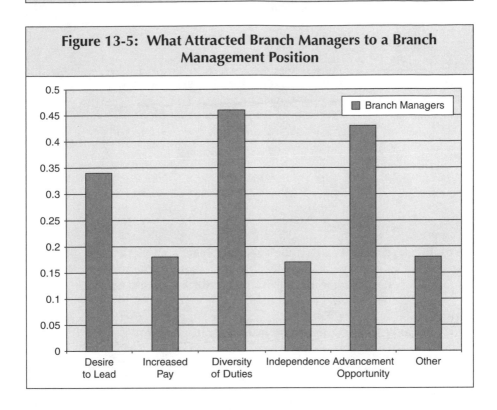

Figure 13-5: What Attracted Branch Managers to a Branch Management Position

Figure 13-6: Most Important Measures of Successful Branch Management

Administrator's Rank	Measures	Branch Managers
1st	User Satisfaction	1st
2nd	Employee Satisfaction	2nd
3rd	Circulation Statistics	4th
4th	Reference Statistics	5th
5th	Adherence to Policy	6th
6th	Problem free branch operation	3rd

Managers and administrators were also asked which of sixteen supervisory or management skills were the most important professional qualities of public library branch managers (see Figure 13-7). The top four responses of the branch managers were, in order: interpersonal communication skills;

Figure 13-7: Most Important Professional Qualities of Branch Managers

Flexibility	Innovation	Interpersonal
Assertiveness	Team-building skills	communication skills
Leadership ability	Poise under pressure	Problem-solving ability
Analytical skills	Organizational skills	Professionalism
Accessibility	Decisiveness	Initiative
Resiliency		Knowledge of
		the community

flexibility; leadership ability; and problem-solving ability. The administrators' top four responses were, in order: interpersonal communication skills; problem-solving ability; leadership ability; and team-building skills.

Eighteen percent of branch managers in Twin Cities libraries intend to retire within five years. Forty-three percent plan to retire within the next ten years. Exactly half of the library administrators surveyed intend to retire within five years. Eighty-six percent plan to retire within the next ten years.

Trends

Several trends emerged during the analysis of the two surveys. Just more than half of the branch managers who reported holding MLIS degrees obtained their graduate educations in a state outside of Minnesota. (The University of Minnesota eliminated its MLIS program in 1985.) Thirty-eight percent of these managers reported working in libraries outside of Minnesota at some time in their professional careers. These figures suggest a fair amount of geographic mobility within the ranks of public library branch managers.

While it is common to find nationwide job postings for library administrators, it is less common to see national advertisements for branch management positions. The mobility demonstrated by this group of branch managers suggests that nationwide recruiting may be a viable alternative to local recruiting efforts for vacant branch management positions. Hiring committees concerned about a stagnant pool of applicants for management positions may find success with nationwide job postings.

Newly hired, first-time branch managers in the Twin Cities have one significant distinction from their predecessors who supervised public library branches: they are significantly less experienced as librarians than their predecessors were when they became branch managers.

Librarians in the Twin Cities who received MLIS degrees in the 1960s worked as librarians for an average of seven years before becoming a branch manager for the first time. Librarians who received their MLIS degrees in the

1970s were librarians for an average of fifteen years before becoming managers, and librarians who received degrees in the 1980s spent eleven years in the profession before becoming managers. Librarians who earned degrees in the 1990s, however, were librarians for an average of just three years before entering the ranks of branch management (see Figure 13-8).

These new managers do not have as many years in the trenches as their branch manager predecessors did. And although no questions pertaining to age were included in this survey, it may be reasonably assumed, given the above data, that the average age of current public library branch managers is also decreasing from what it was in the 1970s and 1980s.

In his 2002 PLA conference presentation, Ken Haycock referred to a management bottleneck, which built up in the profession throughout the 1960s and '70s, delaying advancement for many librarians. This bottleneck, Haycock claims, was created by the massive influx of baby boomer librarians who entered the profession during those two decades.

One result of this bottleneck was that librarians who first became managers in the 1970s and 1980s were significantly more experienced librarians, having worked in the profession for more than a decade, on average, before becoming branch managers. But because these librarians were forced to wait so long for advancement opportunities to become available, they were generally older and had fewer years ahead of them in the profession when they finally did become branch managers.

With the onset of retirement, this boomer bottleneck in library management is now loosening—with positive and negative results. On the positive side, new librarians will face more advancement opportunities at an earlier stage in their careers than did many of their immediate predecessors. Employers hiring these less-experienced managers may find themselves supervising managers

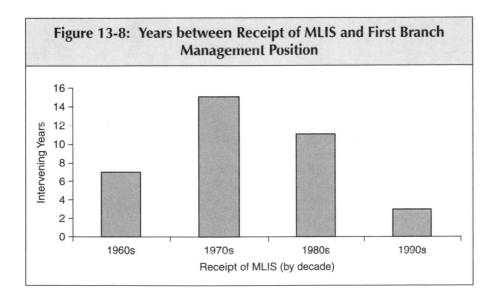

Figure 13-8: Years between Receipt of MLIS and First Branch Management Position

who lack the biases and entrenched thinking that occasionally results from long-term employment in a single library or department.

However, for these same employers, it may now be unreasonable to expect five to ten years of librarianship experience in applicants for branch management positions. And it may be necessary to provide more training and continuing education opportunities for these new managers, who simply have not logged the same number of professional hours as their predecessors did in the 1970s and 1980s.

Because so many of these baby boomers will retire in the near future, there will be fewer and fewer senior managers for those newer branch managers to consult for advice and input on the job.

Current branch managers in this study also followed an interesting pattern in regard to children's services. Just over half (58 percent) reported previous employment in children's departments before becoming branch managers. Yet 72 percent of the current managers indicated that, at some point as a branch manager, they were responsible for presenting a storytime program to children. These statistics further affirm the need for training in children's services—and not just for youth services librarians.

In 1998, Somerville suggested that youth services coursework be mandatory in graduate programs with public librarianship tracks.[3] Given the number of branch managers who have performed storytime programs for children regardless of education or training in children's services, this idea continues to have real merit.

Those future librarians who are currently in or seeking enrollment in an MLIS program should be aware that experience in children's services will be an asset for those who are considering advancement within the profession. Even if experience in children's services is not a specific requirement for advancement, it remains a skill set they are statistically likely to use should they become a branch manager.

Continuing education patterns, whether they are in children's services or otherwise, were also a significant component of this study. Managers were asked where they sought information for continued professional development once they became branch managers. Ninety-one percent indicated that professional workshops provided the most information. Seventy-eight percent indicated that other branch and department managers were good sources for information, and 61 percent claimed that trial and error was an important method of on-the-job learning.

When asked which specific skills these managers would like to develop through continuing education, the top response was conflict resolution skills. This response correlates readily to the 70 percent of library branch managers who find themselves in complaint-resolution situations on a daily or weekly basis. Mentors were also identified as another information resource for continuing education and professional development. One-fourth of the managers identified their mentor(s) as a continuing education resource, and one-fourth of the branch manager respondents indicated they would like to further develop their own mentoring skills.

While this may not seem like a very high rate of interest, consider that 57 percent of library administrators indicated the presence of a mentor earlier in their careers. This contrasts with just 30 percent of branch managers reporting the presence of a mentor earlier in their careers. These numbers suggest that mentoring does indeed play a role in leadership development. Statistically, librarians with mentors are more likely to advance into the highest ranks of library administration than those librarians without mentors.

Yet the presence of a mentor was not the only critical distinction between administrators and branch managers. Administrators and managers varied widely in their professional memberships and activities. Library directors and assistant directors were almost twice as likely to belong to national library organizations, such as the American Library Association and the Public Library Association, than were library managers (see Figure 13-9). Administrators were also more than twice as likely (57 percent versus 21 percent) to have published in professional journals, magazines, and newsletters.

This trend suggests that librarians who are active and contributing members of professional library organizations are more likely to advance into posts in library administration than those who are not.

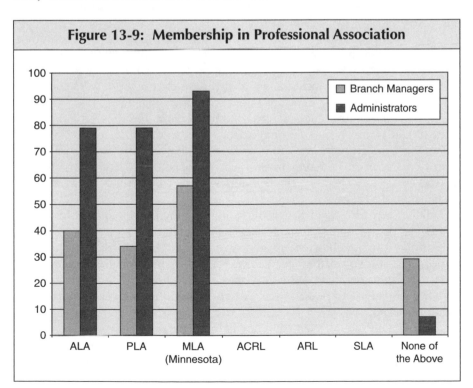

Figure 13-9: Membership in Professional Association

Conclusion

The 2000 U.S. Census reports that more than 25 percent of librarians in the United States will reach retirement age by 2009.[4] This survey suggests higher retirement rates for branch managers and administrators. While a flagging economy may postpone retirement decisions for some, this postponement is, at best, a temporary delay.

Two other issues further complicate these alarming retirement statistics. The first is that the forecasted number of retirements will exceed the number of new librarians produced by graduate programs in the near future. Secondly, fewer of these new librarians are electing to enter public library career paths as private industry draws increasingly from the pool of MLIS graduates.

This shrinking pool of entry-level librarians, coupled with the high rates of retirement suggested by this study, will create a high number of advancement opportunities within the profession.

Will the shrinking pool of librarians entering public library careers be prepared for the management roles that they may soon find themselves in? The survey results provided earlier in this article identify many of the skills and work responsibilities current branch managers consider most important in their current positions. This information may be of use to new librarians who wish to identify the skills and abilities that they should most actively develop to prepare themselves for the leadership roles they will need to fill in the immediate future.

Yet it is not just newer librarians who will face an increase in the number of advancement opportunities available to them. As administrators retire, current branch managers will also have the opportunity for advancement.

The majority of branch managers in this study, however, were content to continue in their current capacity as branch library managers. Just 18 percent indicated a desire to become a library administrator, and 7 percent claim that they would transfer out of management or leave the profession completely, given the opportunity. For those professionals who intend to continue as branch managers for the remainder of their professional careers, this study attempts to identify a variety of work duties, skills, and activities that can serve as benchmarks to measure themselves against.

This study also identified professional characteristics shared by branch managers and by library administrators as a means of encouraging managers to consider the possibility of advancement. Nine of the fourteen administrators in this study were branch managers prior to becoming library administrators. Eight of these nine indicated that their branch management experiences helped prepare them for the work they currently perform as administrators.

Given a choice of seven roles normally associated with management, administrators and branch managers both identified most strongly with "problem solver," "planner," and "decision maker" roles. Similarly, given a choice of seven supervisory roles "administrators and managers both identified themselves most strongly with "motivator," "project leader," and "coach" roles.

This mutual identification with the same management and supervisory roles indicates a degree of overlap between the management and supervisory skills requisite for both branch management positions and posts in library administration.

With this in mind, hiring committees faced with the difficult task of replacing administrators may need to look no further than the ranks of branch managers to identify potential candidates with the core aptitudes necessary for successful library administration. Nor should branch managers shy away from considering this seemingly large advancement step. As this study indicates, the majority of directors and assistant directors surveyed in this study were, at one time, branch managers themselves.

The high retirement rates forecasted in our profession for the years ahead will create numerous opportunities for professional development and advancement at all levels within the profession. The MELSA Branch Management Study is an attempt to analyze one important position that will be impacted by the shift in workplace demographics in the near future.

While numerous publications address the skill sets and aptitudes of library administrators, describe the qualities of effective reference librarians, and offer career development for children's librarians and catalogers, public library branch managers have often been neglected.

This study, in addition to quantifying many of the duties and responsibilities of branch managers in the Twin Cities, is an attempt to formally recognize the complex, important work performed daily by the thousands of public library branch managers around the country.

Notes

1. American Library Association, "Quotable Facts: America's Libraries,"@ your library®: The Campaign for America's Libraries, 2004. Accessed Feb. 20, 2004, www.ala.org/ala/aboutala/offices/ola/quotablefacts.cfm.
2. United States, National Center for Education Statistics, *Public Libraries in the United States: Fiscal Year 2001* (Washington, D.C.: U.S. Department of Education, 2001), iii, 94–105. This report identified 16,421 stationary library outlets in the United States. Of these, 7,353 were identified as single- (or zero-) outlet libraries. The difference between these two figures (9,068) represents the number of libraries that are part of a multiple-outlet (multibranch) library system.
3. Mary Somerville, "Facing the Shortage of Children's Librarians: Updating the Challenge," *American Libraries* (Oct. 1998): 50.
4. John Berry, "Addressing the Diversity and Recruitment Crisis," *American Libraries* (Feb. 2002): 7.

About the Author

Chad Lubbers is Branch Manager of the Carver County Chanhassen (MN) Library; clubbers@carverlib.org. For further information about this study, please refer to the Executive Report of the MELSA Branch Management Study, available for download at www.melsa.org/media/MELSABranchStudy.pdf.

Chapter 14

Getting Your Money's Worth:
How to Hire the Right Consultants

Paula M. Singer and Sandra Nelson

The process of selecting a consultant can be challenging even for experienced library managers. This article provides guidelines for writing effective Requests for Proposals (RFPs), distributing those RFPs to the appropriate consultants, evaluating the proposals that are received, and working with the consultants who are selected.

The environment in which library managers operate is becoming more complex every day. As a result, more managers from libraries of all sizes are making use of outside consultants to help with strategic planning, automation projects, Internet and Web applications, program and service development, and productivity assessments, to name a few. Ten years ago there were relatively few library consultants. Today there are dozens of individuals and firms providing a wide variety of consultant services for public libraries.

The process of hiring a consultant can be challenging, even for managers who have hired consultants in the past. Many libraries are required to go through a formal RFP process to solicit proposals from consultants for every project, or for projects that will cost more than a specified amount of money. Other libraries can develop their own methods for selecting a consultant. The basic steps for either process are the same. The primary difference is that the RFP process normally requires staff to use a predetermined outline and to request specific information from the consultant. This article uses the term RFP as a general term referring to all processes used to solicit proposals or bids from consultants.

The key to writing an effective RFP is to start by defining "effective." Too often an RFP is considered effective if it contains all the elements required to be approved by the library's governing authority—and in some libraries that can be a significant achievement. However, that is not the way to measure the effectiveness of an RFP. You are issuing an RFP to find the most qualified consultant for your project. The way to measure the effectiveness of your RFP is to see if it contains the information needed to encourage qualified consultants to respond.

It can be helpful to think of your RFP as a combination of job posting and advertisement for your library. You are posting a position for a consultant and you want to get proposals from the most qualified applicants. Well-written RFPs attract qualified and experienced consultants. Poorly written RFPs are often ignored by those consultants. The RFP process has three steps: write the RFP, distribute the RFP, and evaluate the proposals you receive.

Write the RFP

Four key elements need to be included in an effective RFP: project description and scope, consultant roles and job description, project timeline, and project budget.

Project Description and Scope

The RFP should contain a clear description of the project, including the scope of work, the deliverables (what you expect the consultant to produce), and the major milestones. Having a clear scope of work that is understood by the library staff and the consultant is critical. Projects and relationships have been known to crumble when "scope creep" occurs (by either the consultant or client), especially if neither funds nor time have been allocated for additional tasks. Reporting relationships need to be defined, and everyone needs to agree on who the client is. The client may or may not be the individual to whom the consultant reports. The line of authority and reporting relationships need to be clear and understood by everyone involved in the project.

It is a good idea to include library decision makers and representatives from key constituencies in the process of developing the project description and scope. This helps to ensure that there is general consensus about the expected outcomes, processes, and responsibilities. This is the time to think not only about the what, but the how and who of the project as well. How should the project be conducted? Who should be involved: the board, the staff, the community? Do you want to create an internal review or steering committee? Who are the final decision makers? These decisions are critical to the success of your project and should be included in the RFP. The more information potential consultants have about your project, the more likely they are to develop a proposal that will meet your unique needs.

It is often helpful to include a brief description of the library as a part of the project description. In the best of all possible worlds there would be no surprises for the consultant or client during a project. This being the real world, we all know that there are always some changes and some surprises. These can be minimized if the RFP includes a description of the library and potential project constraints, such as limited budget, short turnaround time, civil service issues or union restrictions, political environment, or internal issues (major facility renovation, union campaign, installation of new technology, layoffs, new leadership, etc.).

Consultant Roles and Job Description

Consultants can play many different roles, depending on the scope of project and the needs of the hiring library. You will have to identify the primary role or roles you expect the consultant to play before you develop a consultant job description and write the RFP. Common consultant roles include:

- Facilitator: Objective-neutral to manage meetings, offer input, resolve a grievance, or help settle conflicts.
- Researcher: Information gatherer when there is no internal expertise or if a project is too time-consuming.
- Extra pair of hands: Help when you are short-staffed.
- Expert: Specialist to provide information and expertise.
- Political cover: Outsider to deliver politically sensitive information or recommendations.
- Coach: Teacher who provides one-to-one guidance and support for one or more managers.
- Trainer: Teacher who helps groups of staff develop skills or change behaviors.
- Evaluator: Assessor to provide feedback and recommendations to library managers about a program or service.

While the consultant can take on many roles, the consultant is not the manager—that is the job of the client. The consulting relationship is that of a partnership. The consultant can provide coaching, walk the client through options, envision and practice alternative scenarios, role play, and help the client sort through values and options, but in the end the client remains the manager. The manager is the person who makes personnel and value-based decisions, implements recommendations, and deals with the consequences of actions.

When you have identified the role or roles the consultant will play in your project, you are ready to decide what skills you want the consultant to have. Be realistic; no consultant will be able to be or do everything, although most have a number of skills and areas of expertise. The skills you seek in a consultant should be a function of the scope of the project and actions that are required to successfully complete the project. It is probable that you will require the consultant to have more than one major skill. For example, you may want a consultant with subject matter expertise, the ability to assess needs, and the ability to analyze data. You should expect the consultant, regardless of the project, to possess skills in three areas: the subject matter that is the focus of the project (e.g., strategic planning, performance management, library technology, etc.); interpersonal skills; and consulting skills (contracting, feedback, etc.).

After you have determined the consultant's roles in your project and identified the skills the consultant will need, you are ready to develop a consultant job description. The job description, much like the job description of any employee, should include the following:

- project summary
- roles of the consultant
- responsibilities of the consultant
- required knowledge, skills, experiences, and competencies to complete the project.

This job description should be included in your RFP and serve as the basis for evaluating the proposals you receive.

Time Line
The third key element in an effective RFP is the time line. When you define the time line for the project, make sure you allow enough time for consultants to respond. Good consultants are busy people working with multiple clients and multiple deadlines. It is unreasonable to expect them to drop everything to prepare a proposal immediately upon receipt of an RFP. When setting the deadline for receipt of proposals remember that it can take up to two weeks for an RFP to reach a consultant after you issue it. Therefore, the minimum turnaround time for proposals should be one month, and six weeks is preferable.

The consultants are not the only people operating under time constraints. Library staff are also fully occupied. It is important to leave sufficient time to evaluate the responses to your RFP before the project start date and to build enough into the project timeline to complete all project activities. If a project has budget implications and needs to be finalized by April and you think it will take about six months to complete the project activities, then estimate a nine month project (it almost always takes longer than you think) and make sure that you will be able to award the project by August of the prior year. Generally, that implies issuing the RFP in May, requesting responses thirty to forty-five days later and issuing an award or notice to proceed to the consultant selected in July. If your board does not meet in July, you would need to change these dates to accommodate the board schedule.

Budget
The fourth key element in your proposal is the budget for the project. It is important to let potential consultants know how much money you have available for your project. If you cannot include specific dollar amounts because of restrictions by the library's governing authority, at least provide consultants with some sense of the scope of your budget parameters. You might include a range of dollars available or a "not to exceed" amount. If the consultants understand your financial restrictions, they can develop and design a methodology that fits within your budget and meets your needs. If your budget is lower than might be expected, the consultant might suggest tasks that could be eliminated, performed by qualified members of the library, delayed, or even moved to the following budget year. If your RFP includes no budget parameters, you are going to find it difficult to evaluate the proposals you receive, because each consultant will develop a methodology based on his or her best guess of your resources.

Another budget issue to consider when developing your RFP is how you want to pay the consultant. Do you want the consultant to propose a fixed fee for the project, or do you want an hourly or daily fee? Do you expect the consultant to charge travel and expenses separately and, if so, what kinds of receipts do you need? Do you want the consultant to present a single budget for the entire project, or would you prefer that each section of the project be priced separately? As noted above, if you want to be able to evaluate comparable products from the consultants who develop proposals, you will have to provide the consultants with enough information to allow them to start from the same place.

Distribute the RFP

Once you have completed your RFP, you will need to find consultants to send it to. There are a number of ways to identify potential consultants for your project. Call your State Library Agency to see if it has a list of consultants who have done work in your state. Ask your colleagues for recommendations. Post a request for recommendations on state or national library discussion lists. Ask consultants you know from other projects for recommendations. Announce the availability of your RFP in ads in *Library Journal*, *Library Hotline*, *American Libraries*, and *Public Libraries*, and ask that interested consultants get in touch with you to request a copy of the RFP.

There are also two online lists of consultants that you should check. The first is a general list of library consultants that can be searched by name, geographic area, and specialty: **Library Consultants Online** is available at www.libraryconsultants.org. The second is a **list of library building consultants** maintained by LAMA which can be searched for a small fee and is available at https://cs.ala.org/lbcl/search/.

You can use these online sources to develop a targeted list of consultants to receive your RFP.

Evaluate the Proposals

Finally, you have to decide how you will evaluate the proposals you receive and what criteria you will use as the basis for your evaluation. Many libraries use a committee to evaluate proposals to bring different points of view and different areas of expertise to the evaluation process. The committee normally reviews all of the proposals, selects the top two or three proposals, checks references, and then conducts interviews in person or by telephone before making a final selection.

The committee will probably use a variety of criteria to evaluate the proposals. The first and most important criterion should be whether or not the consultant meets the requirements of the job description included in the RFP. Next the committee members will want to look for a consultant or firm whose proposal demonstrates an understanding of your needs as described in the RFP and presents an approach to the work that seems logical and appropriate. They will want to avoid consultants or firms who provide general work plans that could apply to any library. Remember the old saying "if all you have is a hammer, then every problem is a nail." Give preference to consultants or firms who use a broad range of "tools" and will select the ones best for your issue, situation, problem, and culture.

The committee will also want to consider whether the person or firm will be able to convey credibility to staff, senior management, and the board. The consultant or firm must be available to complete the work during your time frame and must suggest realistic fees that match your budget and needs.

Finally, it should go without saying that the consultant or firm that is selected should have great references—and that references will be checked.

Planning Is the Key to a Successful Project

As you can see, careful planning is the key to selecting and using a consultant. The planning starts by working with representatives from all stakeholders to write a clear and complete RFP. It continues when you identify qualified consultants and send them the RFP. Your planning is completed when you establish a process to evaluate the proposals that you receive and determine which consultant will best meet the unique needs of your library. By following these simple steps you will create a framework that will guarantee that you will indeed *get your money's worth* from the consultant you select.

General Guidelines for Using Consultants

- Remember *you* are the client.
- Define the consultant/client relationship.
- Make sure that responsibilities and timelines are clearly defined.
- Identify the client liaison and the lines of authority.
- Assign staff to work with the consultant to learn new skills.
- Make sure the consultant has all of the relevant information. Remember, no surprises!
- Give the consultant feedback about his/her performance throughout the project.
- Hire consultants you can trust—and then trust them!

About the Authors

Paula M. Singer is President and Principal Consultant of The Singer Group, Inc., a management consulting firm she founded in 1983. She provides strategic planning and alignment, organization design and development, performance management, leadership development, compensation, coaching, and other services to clients in the public, private, and nonprofit sectors. She is coauthor of *Winning with Library Leadership: Enhancing Services Through Connection, Contribution and Collaboration* (with Christi Olson), *Human Resources for Results* (with Jeanne Goodrich), and *Designing a Compensation Plan for Your Library* (with Laura Francisco). Paula is a frequent speaker at ALA, PLA, and state library association conferences and has written a number of articles for library and other publications.

Sandra Nelson is a consultant, speaker, trainer, and writer specializing in public library planning and management issues. During her career, Nelson has worked in both large and small public libraries and in state library agencies. She is the author of *The New Planning for Results* (ALA, 2001) and is co-author of *Creating Policies for Results: From Chaos to Clarity* (ALA, 2003).

Chapter 15

The Library Balanced Scorecard

Joe Matthews

Author's note: The Institute of Museum and Library Services (IMLS) awarded funds for a Library Balanced Scorecard Project to the Carlsbad (Calif.) City Library. Any views, findings, conclusions, or recommendations expressed in this article do not necessarily represent those of IMLS.

Primarily for historical reasons, the vast majority of public libraries collect a plethora of performance measures and statistical information. Some of these measures are reported to the library's stakeholders, some are used to complete ad hoc surveys or annual surveys required by the state library, and sadly, many are gathered but then ignored.

The goal of the Library Balanced Scorecard (LBS) is to assist the public library in determining what performance measures and metrics are important within a broader context of strategic planning and management. These important measures should focus on what defines the success of your library and show the difference it makes in your customers' lives. LBS provides a framework for assessing the library's performance and communicating the value of the public library to its community of stakeholders.

The scorecard approach is well suited to complement the planning process detailed in *Planning for Results*.[1] However, it is not a requirement that a library complete the processes outlined in *Planning for Results* prior to developing its own scorecard.

Origins of the Balanced Scorecard

Robert Kaplan, a Harvard accounting professor, and David Norton, a consultant, collaborated on a project to develop a set of performance measures that would complement the heavily weighted financial measures found in almost all company annual reports.[2] Financial measures by their very nature are backward-looking or lagging measures and reflect results of the prior month, previous quarter, or past year. The result of this project was development of the balanced scorecard.

The performance measures selected for the balanced scorecard should reflect the vision and strategies of the organization and include four perspectives: financial, customer, internal business processes, and innovation and learning (sometimes called organizational readiness, learning, and growth or potentials). Within each perspective, three to five measures are chosen to reflect the strategic goals and vision of the organization. The balanced scorecard is shown in graphic form in Figure 15-1.[3] Originally developed to fit the needs of for-profit companies, the balanced scorecard has been successfully adapted by many government and nonprofit organizations.

As shown in Figure 15-2, the balanced scorecard is read from the bottom to the top. In effect, the scorecard requires the organization to create a cause-and-effect relationship between the perspectives. For example, if a company invests in additional training for its staff and provides the necessary information technology (IT) infrastructure (the organizational readiness perspective), then the staff members will be better able to develop improvements in procedures and processes (the internal processes perspective) and thus work more productively. The staff will also be better able to respond to customer needs and requests that will lead to more satisfied customers (the customer perspective), which in turn will lead to higher revenues and better profits (the financial perspective).

The four perspectives are designed to balance:

- the financial and non-financial;
- the internal and external; and
- current performance with the future.

Once an organization can clearly articulate its strategy, it should create a strategy map, a graphic method for showing how its strategy is reflected in each

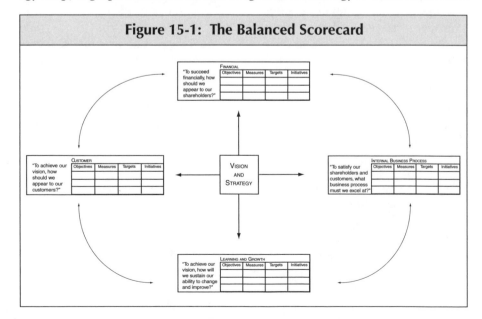

Figure 15-1: The Balanced Scorecard

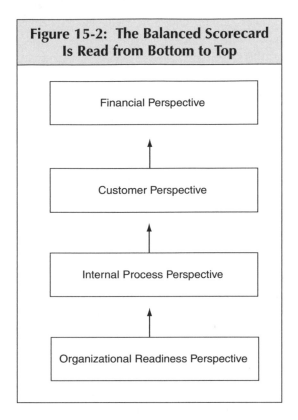

Figure 15-2: The Balanced Scorecard Is Read from Bottom to Top

perspective. The organization then selects performance measures to reflect the chosen strategies; it should also identify both short- and long-term targets for each measure. The balanced scorecard requires collection of data for each measure (data may be collected by an automated system as the result of each transaction, or sampled periodically), and the scorecard typically should be updated on a quarterly basis.

The Organizational Readiness Perspective

This perspective, sometimes called learning and growth, innovation and learning, or potentials, is designed to assess the organization's ability to compete in the future. The organization may assess the skills of its employees to determine if the right mix and depth of skills are present to meet the changing competitive environment. IT readiness assessment is designed to ensure the IT network and software applications meet the needs of the organization today and into the future. The organization may also wish to determine whether its organizational culture will support change and action as reflected in such measures as employee morale and staff turnover rate. This perspective attempts to answer the following type of questions:

- Are staff members equipped with the right skills to deliver quality services?
- Are new technologies being tracked so that skills likely needed in the future are being identified?
- Do staff members possess the proper tools and training to perform their jobs in an excellent manner?
- Is the organization's IT infrastructure (local-area network, link to the Internet, and application software) adequate to meet the needs of the library today and into the near-term future?
- Are the morale and motivation of library staff members high?
- Does the organization have a culture that is willing to carefully and systematically assess the quality of services currently being delivered?

The Internal Process Perspective

The goal of the internal process perspective is to understand the processes and activities critical to enabling the library to satisfy the needs of its customers and add value in their eyes. In developing its balanced scorecard, the library should be identifying and implementing strategies that allow it to offer distinctive and sustainable competitive advantages.

Costs, quality, throughput, productivity, and time measures are usually included in this perspective (Figure 15-3). Quality-improvement initiatives attempt to monitor and improve existing library practices and processes by streamlining workflows and eliminating nonvalue-added work. Nonvalue-added work is tasks that may be done for some time but do little to improve access to the collection, such as catalogers penciling in the first three characters of the author's name for the fiction call number. In developing its own scorecard, the library may identify new services and processes at which it must excel in order to meet customer expectations and changing conditions of the marketplace.

While the library may focus on the continuous improvement of existing internal processes and procedures, it may decide that it needs a radical process reengineering such as advocated by Michael Hammer and James Champy.[4] The focal point of process reengineering is not efficiency (although efficiency will most likely be improved), but rather effectiveness: discovering what will add value for the customer. In a majority of process reengineering projects, tools such as activity modeling, data modeling, statistical quality-control techniques, activity based costing, and cost-benefit analysis can be used to help achieve breakthrough results.

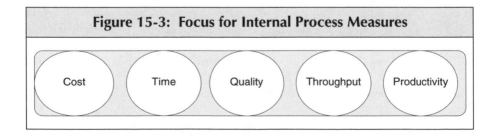

Figure 15-3: Focus for Internal Process Measures

Cost — Time — Quality — Throughput — Productivity

The Customer Perspective

For any organization, the heart of its business strategy is the customer-value proposition that allows the organization to differentiate itself from competitors. The performance measures or indicators chosen for this perspective show the extent to which the company is serving its potential market (market share) and how well the customers' needs are met by the product or service being delivered (customer-satisfaction measures).

Customers generally evaluate a product or service by considering three discrete categories of benefits: product or service attributes, a relationship, or its own image.

Possible product or service attributes of interest to a customer are:

- **Availability.** Does the organization have the product or service when requested by the customer? For a library, this translates into determining whether the desired item is on the shelf or if the service can be delivered. For a library, an availability study or fill-rate survey is generally used to determine how often the library is able to provide the desired item.
- **Selection.** Some companies compete by providing a wide variety of product or service choices (for example, Nordstrom in the retail sector) while others offer fewer choices and compete using other service attributes.
- **Quality.** Some companies compete in the marketplace on the basis of high quality (for example, Mercedes or Lexus in the automobile sector). It is important to note, however, that a great many organizations have been spending considerable time and energy in quality improvement projects so that high quality is now often an assumption made by customers.
- **Functionality.** Some companies find that providing a greater amount of product functionality—for example, a software application—will differentiate them from their competitors. The challenge for those that wish to compete by using functionality is that the bar is constantly being raised, and what is currently superior functionality becomes the minimum standard in a year or two.
- **Time.** Assuming the customer decides to physically visit the library, the time and energy required to retrieve the desired material or receive the desired service may be considerable. The customer may also need to wait in a line for assistance or to receive services. Ultimately, the customer determines whether the effort involved exceeds the likely value of the information or materials being sought. The determination of customer value versus effort in a library setting has been formalized as Mooers' Law, which states: "An information retrieval system will tend not to be used whenever it is more painful and troublesome for a customer to have information than for him not to have it."[5]
- **Price.** The customer incurs a cost to fulfill an information need, even if the materials or information service is free, as in a public library. Given the low price of using the tax-supported public library, an important question to consider is why more citizens are not using the library. While it is obvious that the answer involves a number of factors, competition is clearly one of the more important concerns.

The relationship that exists between the customer and an organization can be manifested in one of two ways:

- **Service.** The service provided by an organization to its customers may be one of the most important differentiating factors in the customer-value proposition. For example, some of the higher-priced four- and five-star hotels maintain an extensive customer profile so that customer preferences are anticipated and provided without any action on the part of the guest. The goal is to develop a level of customer intimacy such that the customer would never consider staying at a different hotel. The customers are willing to share more and more information about themselves with the hotel because their stay will be more relaxing and refreshing. Some people in marketing circles call this willingness of customers to divulge increasing amounts of personal information an opt-in personalization service.

- **Partnerships.** An organization may develop a vital and important relationship with one or more of its customers. This relationship is sometimes taken beyond the normal supplier relationship when both the organization and customers can foresee developing a win-win relationship. And finally, an organization can define its customer-value proposition using its image or brand name. Some brand names have a lot of value and are quite old (consider Coca-Cola or Pepsi), while other valuable brands have relatively recent origins (for example, Google or Amazon.com). Rethinking and modernizing branding can be useful for an organization as well. For example, the library district in London's East End decided to close seven traditional branch public libraries and replace them with seven radically new "Idea Stores." The library district saw the transition as an attempt to change the general perception of the library as a quaint, outdated, and obsolete institution to one that is vibrant, relevant, and hip.[6]

The Financial Perspective

The bottom line for any for-profit company is to choose a set of strategies that deliver long-term shareholder value by increasing the growth of revenues (and profits) as well as increasing its overall productivity—that is, improving its asset utilization. Thus, in a company's annual report you will see the presentation of information about market share, revenue growth, profitability, and so forth. A public library can use the financial perspective to assess the amount of local support for the library using a variety of measures such as budget per capita, growth in budget compared to inflation, a share-of-the-pie measure, and so forth.

Integrating the Perspectives

The power of the balanced scorecard is that it allows the organization to focus on identifying the impact of its strategies using each of the perspectives. That is, using a logic model, the company is able to formulate a cause-and-effect relationship between the perspectives. For example, consider the normal balanced scorecard, as shown in Figure 15-4. Four broad assumptions about the interrelationships are hypothesized in a general cause-and-effect scorecard.

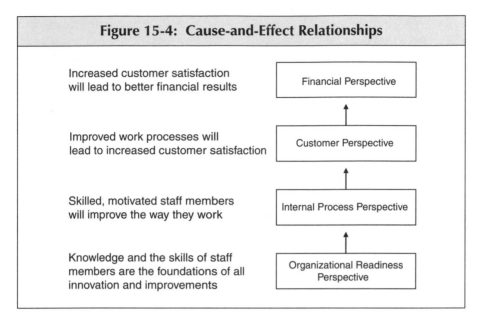

Figure 15-4: Cause-and-Effect Relationships

Increased customer satisfaction will lead to better financial results → Financial Perspective

Improved work processes will lead to increased customer satisfaction → Customer Perspective

Skilled, motivated staff members will improve the way they work → Internal Process Perspective

Knowledge and the skills of staff members are the foundations of all innovation and improvements → Organizational Readiness Perspective

The strength of the scorecard is demonstrated by its balance—showing how well you have been doing (lagging indicators), how well you are doing (current indicators), and can expect to do in the future (leading indicators). Using a balanced scorecard will assist an organization in focusing on the factors that create long-term value for its customers. Research has validated the underlying structure of the scorecard. For example:

- increased employee satisfaction leads to higher performance;
- service quality is correlated significantly with customer satisfaction; and
- rework and waste significantly affect performance.[7]

Experiences in Using the Balanced Scorecard

Due to its flexibility, many companies, whether small or large and in almost every sector of the economy, have used the balanced scorecard quite successfully. The scorecard's framework provides the necessary structure, but the detail can be tailored to fit the needs of any organization. The results of introducing and using the balanced scorecard can often be quite dramatic and generate very positive results.

The use of a scorecard is not a one-time event but rather must be integrated into the fabric of the organization so that it influences how people perform their jobs on a daily basis. The scorecard's popularity is attested to, in part, by the fact that the Balanced Scorecard Technology Council has more than ten thousand members.[8]

Organizations are using the scorecard to:

- clarify, update, and communicate strategy;
- link strategic objectives to performance measures with associated long-term targets;

- broaden management's focus on issues that affect sustainable long-term performance;
- provide a focus for continuous process improvement efforts and quality-enhancement initiatives;
- identify and align strategic initiatives;
- identify critical employee competencies;
- learn about those capabilities critical to realizing strategic intent; and
- demonstrate accountability.

One of the primary reasons for the balanced scorecard's success is that it assists an organization in translating its vision and strategies into concrete actions by its staff. In short, selecting the correct performance measures will show how well the organization is doing in terms of implementing its strategy. When used in this way, the scorecard becomes a strategic management tool rather than simply a new format for monitoring performance. Strategic management is a system's approach to identifying and making necessary changes and measuring the organization's performance as it moves toward its vision. Rather than merely a collection of performance measures or a wish list for continuous improvement, the scorecard prescribes a plan for strategic execution.

The balanced scorecard assists the organization in answering two very fundamental questions:

- What do we want to achieve and what must we do to achieve it?
- Are we doing what we set out to do?

Organizations that have successfully adopted the scorecard concept have found that:

- It is important to recognize that developing and implementing a scorecard is an ongoing and iterative process and not a one-shot project.
- The scorecard becomes the central focus for management meetings, and the perspectives are often used as a means of focusing the agenda of meetings.

The use of multidimensional perspectives found in the balanced scorecard will change the focus of the library's performance—*away* from past performance and *toward* what the library seeks to become.

The Library Balanced Scorecard

Nonprofit and government organizations have adjusted the sequence of the perspectives and added one or more perspectives. A general purpose Library Balanced Scorecard (LBS) is shown in Figure 15-5. A new perspective called information resources is included, because the library's physical collection and provision of access to electronic resources are the raison d'être of the public library.

After selecting three to four performance measures for each perspective, the library then selects improvement targets for each measure. In some cases,

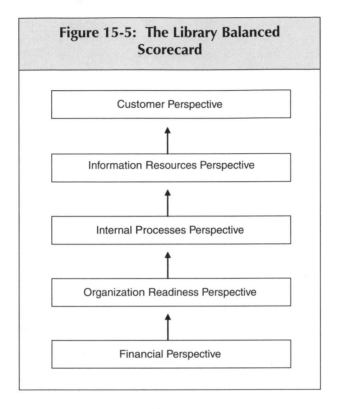

Figure 15-5: The Library Balanced Scorecard

Customer Perspective

↑

Information Resources Perspective

↑

Internal Processes Perspective

↑

Organization Readiness Perspective

↑

Financial Perspective

the library may decide that staff members need to participate in improvement projects or initiatives to achieve the desired targets.

Other scorecard models have been suggested, but none of these approaches have achieved anywhere near the popularity of the balanced scorecard.[9]

The LBS Project

The other participating project libraries, all located in California, are Cerritos Public Library, Chula Vista Public Library, and Newport Beach Public Library. The LBS Project has two phases. Phase One activities involve working with the four project libraries to develop their own LBS. In addition, a workbook detailing the process that any public library may follow to develop its own scorecard has been prepared and can be downloaded from the project's Web site, www.ci.carlsbad.ca.us/imls.

Phase Two involves a number of large and small public libraries from across the United States testing the workbook by developing their own LBS. This phase began in September 2005, and each participating library developed and updated their scorecards. In summer 2006, a survey was distributed to the stakeholders of these libraries to determine their assessment of the value and utility of LBS. Libraries interested in participating in or learning more about LBS are encouraged to visit the project Web site or send an e-mail to the project consultant, Joe Matthews (joe@joematthews.org).

Notes

1. Ethel Himmel and William James Wilson, *Planning for Results: A Public Library Transformation Process* (Chicago: ALA, 1998). See also Sandra Nelson, *The New Planning for Results: A Streamlined Process* (Chicago: ALA, 2001).
2. The Balanced Scorecard was first introduced in a January 1992 *Harvard Business Review* article. A whole series of articles by Kaplan and Norton followed over the succeeding years further expanding and explaining the scorecard concepts.
3. Robert S. Kaplan and David P. Norton, "Using the Balanced Scorecard As a Strategic Management System," *Harvard Business Review* 74 (Jan./Feb.1996): 76.
4. Michael Hammer and James Champy, *Reengineering the Corporation: A Manifesto for Business Revolution* (New York: HarperBusiness, 1993). See also David Osborne and Ted Gaebler, *Reinventing Government: How the Entrepreneurial Spirit Is Transforming the Public Sector* (New York: Addison-Wesley, 1992).
5. Calvin N. Mooers, "Mooers' Law or, Why Some Retrieval Systems Are Used and Others Are Not," *American Documentation* 11, no. 3 (1960): 204.
6. Thomas Patterson, "Idea Stores: London's New Libraries," *Library Journal* 126, no. 8 (May 1, 2001): 48–49.
7. James R. Evans and Eric P. Jack, "Validating Key Results Linkages in the Baldridge Performance Excellence Model," *Quality Management Journal* 10, no. 2 (Apr. 2003): 7–26.
8. Visit the Balanced Scorecard Technology Council Web site at www.balancedscorecard.com (accessed Sept. 28, 2006).
9. See, for example, Steve Montague, *The Three R's of Performance: Core Concepts for Planning, Measurement, and Management* (Ottawa, Canada: Performance Management Network, 1997); Andy Neely, Chris Adams, and Mike Kennerley, *The Performance Prism: The Scorecard for Measuring and Managing Business Success* (London: Prentice Hall, 2002); Andy Neely and Chris Adams, "The Performance Prism Perspective," *Journal of Cost Management* 15, no. 1 (Jan./Feb. 2001): 7–15; Andy Neely, Chris Adams, and Paul Crowe, "The Performance Prism in Practice," *Measuring Business Excellence* 5, no. 2 (2001): 6–12. Information about The Big Picture Framework is available at www.thebigpic.org.uk (accessed Sept. 28, 2006).

About the Author

Joe Matthews is a consultant who lives in Carlsbad, California.

Part IV

A Communications Primer for Public Library Directors

Communications skills are essential to your success as a public library director and can also increase the effectiveness of your library. Regardless of the size of the library you are managing, you will need to confidently relay your message to both individuals and groups. This section of the *PLA Reader* will help you to understand how to communicate your message in the best possible way.

"Library Communication," "Identifying Options for Groups," "Reaching Agreement with Groups," and "Presenting Data" are all excerpted from *The New Planning for Results: A Streamlined Approach* by Sandra Nelson and will provide a thorough, concise look at achieving not only effective library communication, but also more effective output from groups. "Assessing Your Library's Physical Message," an excerpt from *Managing Facilities for Results* by Cheryl Bryan, will help you look at your facility with fresh eyes and understand how the way your library looks communicates a message to your community.

Chapter 16

Library Communication

Sandra Nelson

Issues

If practice really did make things perfect, we would all be master communicators. We certainly spend a large part of everyday communicating, both as senders and receivers: we chat, write, advise, and phone; we leave and receive voice mail, and send and receive e-mail; we remind, read, page, meet, listen, lecture—and on and on. In spite of all this communication, many people still feel uninformed, out of the loop, and misunderstood, particularly in their work environments. There are many reasons for this apparent dichotomy.

Some of the reasons are quite basic. Many people don't fully understand the communication process itself. They are also unclear about the differences between personal and organizational communication and about the functions of communication in a work environment. Even people who are familiar with communication theory can have problems putting it into practice. Most people deal with dozens or hundreds of messages every day and find it increasingly difficult to process all of the information they receive. Furthermore, there are more ways than ever to transmit information, and people don't always choose the best medium for the messages they are sending. The medium is not the only thing that can get in the way of successful communication. The message itself can be distorted by either the sender or the receiver—or by both. Sometimes the problem is not communication but the lack of communication, or having the wrong people involved in the communication loop. These issues are discussed in more detail in the sections that follow.

Defining Communication

Many people think of communication as sending a message. In fact, that is only the first part of the communication process, and even that is not as simple as it might appear on the surface. As shown in Figure 16-1, before a person can send an effective message, he or she has to understand the message. That should go without saying, but unfortunately it does not. Think about the number of times you have listened to a speaker who seemed to be confused or

163

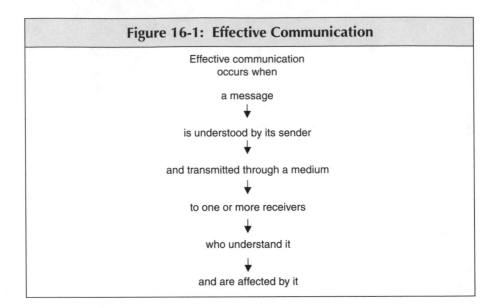

Figure 16-1: Effective Communication

Effective communication
occurs when

a message
↓
is understood by its sender
↓
and transmitted through a medium
↓
to one or more receivers
↓
who understand it
↓
and are affected by it

unsure of his or her message. If the sender doesn't understand the message, it is virtually impossible for the receiver to understand and act on it.

Once the sender understands the message, he or she has to transmit it through some medium. People can't read our minds (and it is just as well they can't), so we have to tell them what we are thinking. The medium we choose to transmit our message will affect how the message is received. (There is more information on matching the medium and the message later in this tool kit.) The communication process does not end when a message is sent. For effective communication to occur, there must be one or more receivers who understand the message and are affected by it. Philosophers have long debated the question, "If a tree falls in a forest and no one hears it, does it make a sound?" There is no such debate about communication. If you send a message and no one receives and understands it, you have not communicated.

People sending messages tend to blame the receivers when a message isn't understood or acted upon. However, that's not entirely fair. The responsibility for ensuring that the communication is completed rests with the sender. The person who initiates the communication has a reason for the communication and expects something to occur as a result of the communication. The receiver, who did not initiate the communication, must understand and accept the message in order to provide the expected response. While this is true in both formal and informal communications, it is more often a problem in the formal communication environment. Informal communications usually occur between two people or in small groups where it is easier to provide feedback and evaluate whether the message has been received. Formal communications, on the other hand, are often third-party communications that go through several layers of the organization. Therefore, there is less opportunity for feedback, and it may take longer to see if the message has been received, understood, and acted upon.

There are two main types of formal communication used in public libraries. One type includes all of the communications the library has with the public. The second type includes all internal communications among library staff members. It is this second type of formal communication that is the focus of this chapter.

Internal communications in public libraries have five main functions. They are used to

> obtain information to make decisions
> clarify job duties and provide feedback to staff
> evaluate services and programs
> maintain control (both formal and informal) by defining values and sharing the expected norms
> meet the social and emotional needs of the staff

When any of these functions are not addressed adequately, library managers and staff find it difficult to provide quality library services.

Managers can do several things to help staff understand the importance of communication within the library. The most obvious is to provide training at all levels. Most staff have attended one or more programs on customer service, and as a part of that training they have received some basic information about communicating, particularly with difficult library users. However, it is also very helpful for all staff to attend at least one training program that focuses on the specific elements of effective communication. A program like this can provide tools to help staff develop messages that are clear and appropriate to the intended receiver, select the best medium for the message, and identify ways to get feedback to ensure that the message was received and understood.

All library managers and supervisors should also receive training in the functions of formal communication, including discussions of how well each function is being addressed in the library. Follow up this training with meetings among managers to identify ways to improve formal communication in the library. Finally, the library director should include an ongoing review of the status of formal communication in the library as a part of regularly scheduled management meetings. This will help to identify problems early and to resolve them before there are serious consequences.

Sorting through the Cacophony

One of the biggest problems that we all have in receiving, understanding, and acting on incoming communications is that we receive so *many* messages. The sheer volume of information makes it difficult to sort out the messages that are important or urgent from those that are trivial or irrelevant. As already noted, it is up to the sender to help the receiver make these distinctions. The sender can do several things to help the receiver. By far the most important is to select the right medium for the message.

The Message and the Medium

Today there are more ways than ever before to "reach out and touch someone," and most of us haven't given a lot of thought to which way is the most effective in a given circumstance. Consider several things as you match the message and medium:

Does the intended receiver have easy access to the medium being considered? Is the message complex, or is it fairly straightforward?

Is the message important, or is it routine?

Is the content ephemeral, or does it need to be maintained as a permanent record for documentation purposes?

Is the message confidential?

How soon does the message need to be received?

Think about these issues in relation to e-mail communications. Many library managers use e-mail as their prime method of communicating with library staff members—regardless of the message. There are several problems with this, not the least of which is that only in rare libraries do all staff members have personal e-mail accounts. Staff do not think of messages sent to a generic agency or unit e-mail address as personal messages. E-mail is also not a good medium to send long messages. As one staff member said, "I hit page down, page down, delete no matter how long the message is. I am not going to read a ten-page memo one screen at a time." E-mail is an ephemeral medium. Most people don't print out e-mail messages, and they don't file them electronically either. Therefore, it is difficult to refer back to an e-mail message if questions arise later. Finally, e-mail isn't a good medium to use for private or confidential messages. It is far too easy to hit the wrong button and send the message to a group instead of a single person, or for one person to forward the message to another with a single keystroke.

Figure 16-2 lists ten common media used to transmit messages in public libraries in the left column and six criteria to consider when matching the message and the medium across the top of the table. Some of the decisions about matching the medium to the message are based on local conditions or the message itself, and they are labeled with a question mark. For instance, someone wanting to deliver a message to a library director and using a phone as the medium has every reason to assume that the director has easy access to a private phone. However, there is no reason to assume that a page or a part-time circulation attendant has that same easy access. As another example, a complex message could be delivered effectively to a small meeting of people who are directly affected by the message, particularly if the meeting is long enough to allow for thorough discussion. The same complex message could not be delivered as effectively to a large group of people consisting of some who are affected by it and others who are not.

It can be helpful for library managers to develop general guidelines concerning the media to be used to transmit certain types of messages. For instance, managers might decide that all messages dealing with human resource issues should be transmitted in written form, either through personal or group memoranda. Sometimes the guidelines will be more general. The managers in

Medium	Access	Message					
	Receiver has easy access	Message is complex	Message is important	Permanent record is required	Message is confidential	Message is urgent
Face-to-face conversation	✓	✓	✓		✓	✓
Telephone conversation	?		✓		✓	✓
Meeting	?	?	✓	?		?
E-mail	?	?		?		✓
Individual letter or memo	✓	✓	✓	✓	✓	✓
Videotape or audiotape	?	?	?	✓		?
Group letter or memo	?	?	?	✓		
Policy and procedure manual	?	✓	✓	✓		
Web page	?			?		
Notice on a staff bulletin board	✓					

Figure 16-2: Match the Message and the Medium

one library developed the following preliminary guidelines for the types of messages that should be sent using e-mail:

- general information that can be sent quickly and easily
- nonconfidential messages
- short and concise messages (simple, ephemeral)
- messages that serve as means to send attachments
- scheduling for collaborative projects or meetings
- messages that don't require immediate feedback
- follow-ups to other communications
- reminders

These might not be the guidelines that you would develop in your library, but they can provide a starting place for discussion. The point is that library managers and staff should talk about how communication works in your library environment and what would make it more effective.

Repetition Works

Most experienced public speakers follow this traditional rule: tell the audience what you are going to say, say it, and then tell the audience what you said. Many speakers also provide the content of their presentation in multiple formats, using both verbal messages (the presentation) and written messages (handouts, overheads, or PowerPoint presentations). These speakers have learned that people need to hear and see information several times before they can fully understand or accept it. This is particularly true if the message contains information that is completely new to the receivers or if the message contains information that the receivers aren't particularly pleased to hear.

It will be worth your time and energy to follow the example set by these speakers. Send important messages several times using several different media. No matter what media you use, remember to rephrase the key points several times and summarize the message in the final paragraph. This improves the odds that the receiver will not only get the message but will understand it and be affected by it. It also provides an opportunity for receivers to verify the information being transmitted. They can check the different versions of the messages they receive to be sure they understand what is being said. One caveat: don't rephrase so much that receivers look for differences, thinking they're getting a new message.

Dealing with Distortion

A message can be distorted by the sender or by the receiver or by both. The sender can distort a message by deliberately filtering the content. For example, a staff member who is unhappy about a new policy might send her supervisor a memorandum describing in detail the complaints she received from two library users about the policy but not mentioning the positive comments she received from ten other users. The sender can also accidentally distort the message in a number of ways. The sender might assume incorrectly that the receiver has certain background information and thus not provide needed data, or the sender might not understand the content clearly and therefore highlight the wrong data. Finally, there is the message's language itself. Because most words have several meanings, some people will interpret a message one way and some another. The easiest way to avoid misinterpretation is to keep professional messages clear, complete, and concise. Use short words and short sentences. Ask several people to review important messages before they are transmitted to the receivers to be sure that the main points are unambiguous.

Receivers can also distort messages. Everyone perceives things a little differently based on their own experiences, needs, and interests. Emotional reactions may be the most common reason that messages are distorted by receivers. When people are involved in personal crises, they are less likely to pay attention to messages that don't deal directly with the crisis at hand. When people are angry or frustrated, they are often not responsive to messages from the people or groups that they blame for their anger or frustration. What this means, among other things, is that messages that are likely to evoke strong emotions—especially messages that deal with significant change—have to be even more carefully written and broadly disseminated than other messages.

Lack of Communication

Not all communication problems deal with how a message is framed and delivered. Many staff members say that the biggest problem with communication in their libraries is too little communication. Perhaps the most common reason for lack of communication is simple oversight. We are all busy, and most of us feel overwhelmed on occasion. It takes time to communicate, and time is one of our most precious commodities. We also have a tendency to think, "If I know it, everyone must know it." The corollary to that is, "I don't know it, but everyone else must know it because no one else is asking." These two assumptions keep us from transmitting important information to others and from asking for the information that we need to do our jobs.

Sent but Not Received

Sometimes "lack of communication" doesn't mean the message wasn't sent; it may mean that an important message was sent once through a single medium. The sender may feel that the message has been delivered, but, as noted previously, the intended receivers may not have actually received the message. Perhaps the message was sent to branch or department managers who were instructed to pass the message on to their subordinates. If there is no requirement for feedback built into the process, there is no way for the original sender to know if all of the managers in the middle transmitted the message as instructed. It is not uncommon for a branch manager to return to the branch from a meeting with information that is to be passed on to all employees. Too often this is what happens:

The manager sees employee 1 and gives her the complete message. The manager sees employee 2 ten or fifteen minutes later and gives him most of the message. Employees 3 and 4 run into the manager in the break room and get an abbreviated version of the message. Employee 5 doesn't see the manager at all that day and is given a very brief summary the next morning. Employee 6, who is out sick all week, never gets the message.

It is clear that employee 6 has been completely cut out of the communication loop, but even employee 1, who received the whole message, has no way of validating what she was told. Everyone but employees 3 and 4 was told something slightly different.

Sent Too Late
Sometimes information is disseminated too late to be useful to a specific audience. Consider this scenario:

January 15	The administrative team considers a policy change and an individual, committee, or task force is asked to develop a draft of the new policy.
March 1	The draft policy is reviewed by the administrative team.
March 15	The draft policy is sent to senior managers for review and comment.
April 15	The administrative team discusses reactions from the senior managers and makes changes in the draft as needed.
May 15	The draft of the policy is sent to branch/department managers for review and comment without explicit instructions that they should share the draft with staff. Consequently some managers share it, and some don't.
July 1	The administrative team discusses reactions from branch/department managers and makes changes as needed.
August 1	The policy is officially approved by the chief administrator and sent to all units.
August 15	The policy is officially scheduled to be implemented.
August 16	Frontline staff, who actually have to implement policy, complain that they were not informed. Managers can't understand what staff are talking about. After all, the new policy has been under discussion for more than nine months.

Variations on this scenario are played out in libraries across the country over and over again. It is critical to involve the staff who will be affected by a new policy in discussions about that policy early in the planning stages and to be sure that the staff who have to implement policies and procedures are fully trained before the implementation process begins.

Library Intranets
Some library managers are using the library's intranet to provide staff with the information they need to do their jobs more effectively. The intranet can be used to provide access to a broad array of information, including policies and procedures, committee or task force information (membership, agendas, minutes, reports), staff directories, training schedules, job postings, public relations announcements, and so on. The most important benefit to providing information through the intranet is that all staff have access to it, and they can access it whenever it is convenient. The second benefit is that information can be loaded on the intranet fairly easily and can be updated without a lot of trouble. This is particularly important for library policies and procedures, which are very difficult to keep current at the unit level in paper formats. A third benefit is that,

with proper design, most information on the intranet can be searched by keyword. This makes finding and using the information much easier.

Evaluating Communication Processes

Four general models that describe the way information is transmitted in libraries are downward communication, downward-and-upward communication, horizontal communication, and diagonal communication. None of these models is intrinsically superior to the others. At times each is appropriate to use. The important thing to remember is that in libraries with effective communication, all four of these models are used regularly. Four measures can be used to help you decide which model will be most effective for a given situation: distribution of information, ability to verify information, need for acceptance from the receiver, and time required for the transmission.

Distribution of Information

The first measure to use when deciding which model is appropriate is how widely the information needs to be distributed. Does everyone in the organization need to know? Do you need to have some verification that the message has been received? Remember, the more ways you send a message, the more likely it is that the people you are targeting will actually receive, understand, and be affected by the information in the message.

The Ability to Validate Information

The second measure to use when deciding which model is appropriate is the need for the receiver to validate the information being received. Most people have no desire to validate simple messages or messages of little importance. However, people often need to be able to corroborate messages that are complex or messages that contain information they are unfamiliar with or unhappy about.

Need for Acceptance from the Receiver

The third thing to consider when selecting a communication model is the degree to which it is important that the receiver accept the information in the message. Some messages are purely informational, and it doesn't matter a lot to the sender if the receivers accept or reject the information. The announcement that the library board will be holding its regularly scheduled meeting on July 21 is an example of such a message. However, in some instances it is critical to the sender that the receivers not only understand the message but that they accept the information in the message as accurate and valid and act upon the information in a specific way. Suppose a message is disseminated announcing a new policy and procedures for managing patron reserve requests. Staff who receive the message must not only understand the new policy and procedures, they must also put them into practice on a specified date. This is far more likely to occur if staff are familiar with the changes, understand why the changes are being made, and agree that the changes are reasonable and necessary. In general, the more involvement the staff have in the decision-making process, the more accepting they are of the final decision. Therefore, communication models that allow for discussion and interaction are the most effective ways to deal with issues that require staff acceptance.

Time Required

The fourth thing to consider when selecting a communication model is time. If there is only one way to do something or if a decision has already been made, then it makes sense to transmit the message in the fastest way possible. Communication processes that allow for staff feedback and staff involvement in decision making are time-intensive. The more participation you allow, the more time-intensive the process becomes. If the issue under consideration is important and staff involvement is critical, then invest the time needed to resolve it effectively. You will probably find that the initial investment in time pays off in significant time savings during the implementation phase.

Methods for Communicating in Your Library

Downward Communication

Downward communication is also known as "bureaucratic" communication. Messages are sent down the chain of command throughout the library. In many libraries, this is the most frequently used communication model. Downward communication often reflects a centralized managerial style in which decisions are made by senior managers; middle managers and staff are expected to implement those decisions with little or no input. It is rare for centralized decisions that were communicated downward to have a high level of staff acceptance.

> Distribution of information:
> Moderate
> Ability to verify information:
> Low
> Acceptance of receiver:
> Low
> Time required:
> Low

The most significant benefit of downward communication is efficiency. It is by far the fastest and easiest of the four communication models. However, this efficiency has a price. There is no way for the sender to be sure that the message was distributed throughout the library, nor is there a way for the intended receiver to know that he or she didn't receive the message. This is important because there are often breaks in the bureaucratic delivery chain. Some of these breaks are accidental—a manager might be out sick for several days and unable to send the message—but others are deliberate—a manager might disagree with the information in the message and not pass it on. Part-time workers are often unintentionally excluded from the downward communication chain because they aren't at work when messages are being delivered to the rest of the staff. Even messages that are delivered to all intended recipients may be garbled as they move from one level in the organization to the next. Remember the game of "Telephone" in which a message that is passed through a chain of ten people is changed completely by the end of the chain?

When to Use

Downward communication can be used effectively to send simple messages that are intended to distribute general information that requires little or no action on the part of the receiver.

What to Do

1. Make it explicitly clear to managers that they are responsible for ensuring that all downward communications reach all employees.
2. Put all messages to be sent throughout the library in writing.
3. Number each message consecutively, and keep a copy for reference.
4. Clearly label all messages sent downward through the library as "For Your Information."
5. Check periodically to see if messages are being transmitted throughout the library by asking a sampling of people at all levels if they received a given message.
6. Keep each message brief.
7. Start the message with the most important information and then provide supporting data, if needed.
8. Focus on a single topic in each message. If you have several different kinds of information to share, send several separate messages.
9. Post copies of all messages sent downward through the library on the library's intranet so that employees can refer to them easily.

Downward-and-Upward Communication

Downward-and-upward communication is also known as "two-way" communication. It follows the chain of command in the library but includes formal processes for ensuring that information flows in both directions. General staff meetings in which downward communications are presented and discussed are one common example of two-way communication.

> Distribution of information:
> Moderate to high
> Ability to verify information:
> Moderate
> Acceptance of receiver:
> Moderate
> Time required:
> Low to moderate

The most important benefit of two-way communication is that it gives the receivers a chance to verify the data in the message to be sure that they understand it. Downward-and-upward communication provides a mechanism for receivers to formally express their opinions about the information in a message to the people who sent the original message. If the receivers believe that their opinions are taken seriously, they are more likely to accept the content of the message.

There are, however, a number of drawbacks to downward-and-upward communications. Because the process usually follows the structure of the library bureaucracy, the successful transmission of the communication in both directions is dependent on individual managers to provide a conduit for two-way information. Unfortunately, most libraries have at least one manager who blocks the flow of information rather than facilitating it. Even managers who make a good-faith effort to promote two-way communication have differing communication skills and attitudes. As a result, the staff in each unit of the library probably get slightly different messages. This model provides no way for staff to validate information among units.

When to Use

Three main categories of messages can be effectively disseminated using two-way communication processes. First, all formal employee-supervisor communications should be both downward and upward. One example is the performance appraisal process, in which employees and their supervisors discuss goals and objectives at the beginning of the year and then evaluate progress at the end of the year. Another example is the formal grievance process.

The second category includes all messages that transmit decisions that will affect staff duties and responsibilities. Some of these decisions, such as city or county policies or information about the library budget, will have been made without significant staff input. Other decisions will have been made after extensive discussion using horizontal and diagonal communication processes. Sometimes the participants in committee and task force meetings forget that not everyone has been as involved in the decision-making process as they have. As a result, decisions are made but not formally shared with the entire staff. It is appropriate to share these final decisions using a downward-and-upward communication process. Be sure to include a brief description of the participative process used to reach the decisions in your message.

The final category of messages that can be delivered using downward-and-upward communication are messages containing suggestions from staff and the public for improving services or changing policies. These are messages that originate with staff and are passed up through the chain of command for action. When the recommendations have been acted upon, messages are sent back to the originating staff to inform them of the action taken.

What to Do

1. Personnel communications
   a. Review your performance appraisal process to be sure that it provides a mechanism for two-way communication.
   b. Require supervisors to communicate with employees about their performance regularly throughout the year.
   c. Ensure that all staff are aware of the grievance process.
2. Disseminating decisions
   a. Make it explicitly clear to managers that they are expected to serve as conduits for information—both downward and upward.
   b. Provide training to help managers improve their communication skills and learn to facilitate group discussions.
   c. Clearly label messages that are intended to be discussed by managers and staff as "For Discussion."
   d. Include a date by which feedback and questions about the information in the message are due to be submitted to a single person.
   e. Develop a specific format for managers to use to submit feedback, and use it consistently. For example:

Issue discussed
Date discussed
With whom
General reaction
Questions
Suggestions

   f. Prepare and distribute a final message that summarizes the feedback and describes what actions, if any, have been taken to respond to the feedback.

   g. Monitor the feedback that is received over a period of time. If you notice that some managers rarely provide feedback, speak to them to determine why.

3. Suggestions from the staff and the public

   a. Develop specific forms for staff and for public suggestions and make the suggestion forms readily available.

   b. Provide a link on the library Web site to a public suggestion form and make sure someone is assigned to retrieve and process the suggestions.

   c. Provide an electronic version of the staff suggestion form on the library intranet.

   d. Consider posting selected staff and public suggestions on the intranet for staff to review. Include some indication of the disposition of the suggestion.

   e. Make sure that staff and the public know when actions are taken as a result of a suggestion.

Horizontal Communication

Horizontal communications in libraries normally take place in regularly scheduled meetings of people with similar positions who work in different units of the library. Common examples include children's librarian meetings, circulation attendant meetings, branch manager meetings, and main library unit manager meetings.

> Distribution of information:
> Low to moderate
> Ability to verify information:
> High
> Acceptance of receiver:
> High
> Time required:
> Moderate to high

Horizontal groups provide peer support for their members and can significantly improve staff morale. They are the ideal forum for developing new and innovative services or programs and for solving problems in specialty areas that affect more than one library unit. Horizontal groups also provide a mechanism for staff in various library units to verify all kinds of messages that have been distributed downward through the organization.

However, horizontal groups are not always the best way to disseminate information to other staff members in the library. Often the members of the group place far more value on communicating with each other than on communicating with non-group members. This can cause real problems for library managers who expect horizontal group members to share information with other staff in their units. If a library manager announces a change in circulation policy to the members of the circulation attendant group and asks them to pass the word, that manager cannot assume that everyone who needs to know about the change will be informed. In fact, it is highly probable that some group members will not pass on the message and that some unit managers will be irritated (to say the least) that they were not informed directly.

The primary drawback with horizontal groups is the time they take staff from other activities. Horizontal meetings usually occur monthly. Someone has to plan the meeting, and participants have to travel to a single location for their meeting and then spend one to three hours in the meeting before traveling back to their library units. Next, someone has to write the minutes from the meeting and pass on any recommendations from the group to the managers who can act on the recommendations. Many library managers resent the scheduling problems that result from staff participation in horizontal meetings.

When to Use
Most participants of horizontal groups benefit from their participation in those groups and use their meetings to discuss ways to improve the services they offer. However, many libraries offer the opportunity to participate in a horizontal group only to selected staff members, generally children's staff and unit managers. Library managers should discuss the benefits that would result from encouraging members of other horizontal groups to meet regularly. Some possibilities to consider are reference staff, staff who serve people with special needs, technical support staff (formal or informal) in each unit, paraprofessional staff, and staff with materials selection responsibilities.

What to Do
1. Provide an opportunity for members of any horizontal group in the library to meet if they wish to and if they can explain the benefits that will result from their meetings.
2. Make sure that all members of a horizontal group are given equal opportunity to meet with the group.
3. Establish a regular schedule for each group to meet.
4. Identify a group leader. This can be an appointed or elected position and can remain the same year after year or change annually.
5. Develop a standard format for horizontal group agendas and minutes, and expect all groups to use it.
6. Ask each group to prepare an agenda (using the standard format) for each meeting and distribute it to all participants and all managers at least one week before the meeting. If you have a library intranet, post all agendas there.

7. Ask each group to have someone responsible for preparing minutes from each meeting (using the standard format) and distributing them to all participants and all managers within one week of the meeting. If you have a library intranet, post all minutes there.
8. Establish a formal process for reviewing the recommendations received from horizontal groups and for acting on those recommendations.
9. Disseminate the final actions taken on recommendations from horizontal groups to all staff members using the downward-and-upward communication model. If for some reason a decision is made not to implement one or more of the recommendations, be sure to explain why.

Diagonal Communication

The most common diagonal communication models in libraries are cross-functional work groups that include people with different job classifications who work in different units of the library. The two types of cross-functional groups are task forces and teams. Cross-functional task forces are normally convened for a specific purpose; when the task is completed, the task force is disbanded. Cross-functional teams, on the other hand, generally have continuing responsibilities. For example, a task force might be appointed to coordinate the selection of a new automation system for the library. When the system has been selected, the task force will have completed its work. On the other hand, a cross-functional team might be appointed to monitor library safety issues. The members of the team might change, but the team itself would be ongoing.

Distribution of information: Moderate to high
Ability to verify information: High
Acceptance of receiver: High
Time required: High

Cross-functional teams and task forces are the most open of the communication models. They encourage communication among all staff at all levels. This in turn allows staff to verify messages received through any of the other models. Cross-functional teams and task forces also give staff members a very real voice in the decision-making process, which significantly increases staff acceptance of the final decisions.

While cross-functional groups have strengths, they also have some drawbacks. The most obvious drawback is the time it takes to bring disparate people from all over the library system together to discuss a problem and identify possible solutions. In addition, some members of these groups might find it difficult to remember they were appointed to represent a specific constituency and instead promote their personal views. The reverse can be true as well. Sometimes the members of a constituent group don't trust the person selected to represent them. Furthermore, some task forces do not include people with the skills and knowledge required to accomplish the task. Others include people with diametrically opposed positions who refuse to consider compromise. Teams and task forces function most effectively if they are led by an experienced facilitator who has credibility with the members of the team and other stakeholders.

When to Use

Most libraries use cross-functional teams and task forces differently. Cross-functional teams are appointed to discuss ongoing issues that affect all staff and to make recommendations when appropriate. Different libraries will have different teams, depending on local conditions. Examples of teams include the safety team mentioned previously and staff development teams. Generally the membership of a team changes each year, but the team charge remains the same. Teams give staff members a forum to discuss issues of ongoing interest or concern and provide managers with recommendations for action and with feedback about staff attitudes.

Almost all task forces address some aspect of decision making. Some task forces provide the information needed to reach a decision. Other task forces are responsible for determining how to implement a decision that has been made. Still other task forces are responsible for actually implementing a decision. The members of each task force must understand both their responsibility and their authority clearly.

Task forces should be used when the decision under consideration or being implemented will have a significant effect on the way most or all staff members do their jobs. Never appoint a task force to consider an issue that you, as a manager, know how you want to handle. More than one library manager has appointed a task force firmly believing the task force would recommend a specific action. When the task force made a different recommendation (and they almost always do), the manager had a serious problem: He could either adopt the task force recommendation even though it was not at all the way he wanted to solve the problem, or he could do what he intended to do all along and alienate the members of the task force and the rest of the staff. Neither option is attractive.

What to Do

1. Identify a clear charge for each task force or team that is appointed.
2. Determine which library constituencies should be represented on the task force or team. Make it clear to everyone that the people asked to be members of the task force or team are expected to represent their specific constituencies and not their own personal points of view.
3. Require task force and team members to report regularly to the constituent groups they represent.
4. Establish a time line for each task force that includes a deadline for the receipt of recommendations and a deadline for taking action on those recommendations.

5. Disseminate the charge and membership of every team and task force to all staff. Include information on the time lines for all task forces. If any of this information changes, notify all staff that the changes have occurred. If you have a library intranet, this information can be posted there.

6. Develop a standard format for task force and team agendas and minutes, and expect all groups to use it. Consider using the same form used for horizontal groups.

7. Ask each task force and team to prepare an agenda (using the standard format) for each meeting and distribute it to all participants and all managers in the library at least one week before the meeting. If you have a library intranet, post all agendas there.

8. Ask each task force and team to have someone responsible for preparing minutes from each meeting (using the standard format) and distributing them to all participants and all managers within one week of the meeting. If you have a library intranet, post all minutes there.

9. Establish a formal process for reviewing the recommendations received from task forces and teams and for acting on those recommendations.

10. Disseminate the final actions taken on task force and team recommendations to all staff members using the downward-and-upward communication model. If for some reason a decision is made not to implement one or more of the recommendations, be sure to explain why.

About the Author

Sandra Nelson is a consultant, speaker, trainer, and writer specializing in public library planning and management issues. She has presented hundreds of training programs in forty-eight states during the past three decades. During her career, Nelson has worked in both large and small public libraries and in state library agencies. She is the author of *Implementing for Results* (2009), *Strategic Planning for Results* (2008), and *The New Planning for Results: A Streamlined Approach* (2001). She has co-authored a number of other publications and serves as Senior Editor for the PLA *Results* series.

Chapter 17

Identifying Options for Groups

Sandra Nelson

Issues

Library managers must make decisions every day. Sometimes they make those decisions alone; sometimes they give the responsibility for making a decision to a committee or task force. In either case, the first step in any decision-making process is to identify the options to be considered. Regardless of whether the ultimate decision will be made by a single person or a group, it is usually more effective to involve a number of people in the process of identifying options. The greater the number of viable options that decision makers have to consider, the more likely they are to make effective decisions.

At first glance, it would seem that identifying options would be fairly easy. After all, almost everyone seems to have opinions about almost everything. In reality, when you begin to work with groups to help them identify options, you discover that people's preconceived ideas make it more difficult, not easier, to identify a range of options. Other problems include the tendency to think there is only one right answer to every question, the difficulty in identifying new options for old problems, the dominance of the group by one or more members, and the effect of peer pressure on group activities that results in a tendency among group members to minimize the appearance of conflict. Finally, it is important to remember the old computer acronym GIGO (garbage in-garbage out). It applies here, too. You need to have the right people involved in the process to identify effective options. The right people, in this instance, include people with some understanding of the problem and some experience or knowledge that provides them with a basis for suggesting solutions. Each of these issues is discussed in greater detail in the following sections.

Searching for the One Right Answer

It is important for the group leader to lay the groundwork carefully for the process to be used to identify options, stressing the need to look at a variety of points of view. Many people are uncomfortable with ambiguity and find the concept of multiple, valid options difficult to understand. Instead they search for the absolute answer to any question. They are inclined to make premature

181

decisions to avoid having to deal with uncomfortable choices. Most groups need periodic reminders that the purpose of this part of the decision-making process is to identify as many options as possible, and that even ideas that seem wildly unrealistic at first glance may lead to new insights or choices.

Thinking "Inside the Box"

In general, the more familiar people are with a situation, the more difficult they find it to consider the situation objectively or creatively. This can be a particular problem in libraries because so many staff members have worked in the same system for decades. The group leader will want to encourage people to look with new eyes at the issues under consideration. This might be done in at least three ways.

Move from the specific to the general. Encourage group members to broaden their frames of reference. For instance, instead of thinking about the public library as an institution, broaden the definition to include all libraries, and then broaden it again to include all information providers. Remind the participants of the story of the railroad company executives who defined their business as "railroading." Not much later the competition from trucking and airfreight had pushed them close to bankruptcy. If the executives had understood that they were in the transportation business and not just the railroad business, they might well have been able to identify alternative options.

Look at what is happening beyond our own field. We can learn a lot from other organizations, both profit and nonprofit ones. For instance, many library managers have benefited from management books written by such authors as Stephen Covey and Peter Drucker, even though their books were intended primarily for businesspeople. The United Way has been very involved in helping nonprofit organizations define the results of the services they provide, and the United Way manual *Measuring Program Outcomes: A Practical Approach* would be a valuable tool for any library manager.[1]

Question everything. James Thurber once said, "It is better to ask some of the questions than to know all of the answers." When someone says, "We've always done it this way," ask "Why?" When someone says, "We can't do that" ask "Why not?" Why can't we provide off-site access to information? Why can't we let users access their e-mail accounts on library equipment? Why can't we use e-book technology to deliver current materials more quickly and cost-effectively? Why can't we use wireless technology? Why can't we collaborate with another organization to provide a service?

Dealing with Dominant Behaviors

Every group has one or more dominant members. The source of their dominance varies: some people control a group by sheer force of personality. Others are dominant because of their positions. Yet others use their expertise (real or perceived) to control a group. Finally, some people dominate groups because they are bullies and attack anyone who disagrees with them or tries to express an alternative point of view.

It is critical for the group leader to make it clear to all group members that each person's opinion is important. This message may have to be repeated several times during the process. Then the group leader must control the behavior of the dominant members in the group. This can be done by waiting until others have spoken before asking the dominant members for their opinions. Another possibility is to divide the group into smaller subgroups, which has the effect of minimizing the impact of the dominant members. These techniques will work in many situations but may not be effective with bullies. It is possible that the group leader will have to talk to the bully privately during a break or after the meeting to ask him or her to respect the opinions of the others in the group. If this direct intervention doesn't work, the leader should consider asking the person who made the appointments to the committee to talk to the bully about his or her disruptive behavior.

Dealing with Peer Pressure

Most people are more comfortable if they feel they are part of a group and not an outsider. Therefore, people have a tendency to go along with what they think the group believes or values, even if they don't necessarily agree. This can lead to "groupthink," in which the members place a higher value on agreement than on identifying multiple options. This problem is easiest to deal with at the very beginning of the process by making it clear that the group's task is to identify multiple options. The leader should assure the group that the purpose is not to make the final decision, and that success will be defined by the number and creativity of the options identified. This in turn creates a group norm that supports and encourages diverse points of view.

Involving the Right People

Several things should be considered when determining whom to involve in the identification of options. First, of course, you want to include people who have something to contribute to the discussion. Their contributions may be based on specialized skills or expertise, on background or experience, or on position or authority. Second, you want to include people who care about the issue being considered. Third, you want to include people who will be affected by whatever option is ultimately selected. Finally, you want people who are reasonably open to change and willing to consider a variety of points of view. If you are careful in your selections (and lucky), most of the participants in whatever process you use to identify options could be included in at least three of these four categories.

Evaluating Methods of Identifying Options

Four methods you might use to help a group identify options are general group discussion, brainstorming, Nominal Group Technique, and the Delphi Method. Each of these methods can be used effectively in certain situations. The important thing is to match the method and the situation. Four measures that can be used to help you decide which method will be most effective for a given situation include the desired:

- level of participation from the group,
- range of the options identified,
- skill required of the facilitator/leader, and
- time it takes to make the decision.

Level of Participation

The first measure to use when deciding which method to use for identifying options is how much participation you need to identify the options for a specific decision. If the options you are to consider relate to a significant change in policy, you will probably want to use a process that encourages the maximum level of participation. On the other hand, if you are developing options for dealing with a situation in a single unit or dealing with a relatively minor change, you may not want or need extensive participation.

Range of Options Identified

The second measure is the range and creativity of the options that are identified. Some problems are intrinsically more difficult to address than others. Consider two committees: one responsible for identifying options for ways to integrate a new technology into the ongoing operations of the library, and the second responsible for options for improving the activities in the annual staff-day training event. Both are important, but the first will require considerably more flexibility and creativity than the second.

Leadership Skill Required

The third measure is the skill required to develop and lead the process to be used to identify the options. Some of the methods described in this chapter are relatively easy to manage; others require more specialized skills or knowledge.

Time Required

The final measure is the length of time it will take to identify options. The identification of options is just the first step in the decision-making process. There is not much point in expending so much effort on this part of the process that there is no time left to reach agreement on the most effective option to select before the deadline for implementation. Furthermore, some decisions are fairly simple or can only be addressed in a limited number of ways. As a general rule, select the easiest and quickest process that will produce the level of participation and range of options you need.

Methods for Identifying Options

General Group Discussion

General group discussion is probably the most common method used for identifying options in libraries. Group discussions often occur during meetings that have multiple agenda items. Someone will raise an issue, someone else will suggest a solution, there may or may not be a little discussion, and the suggestion is adopted. The other common setting for group discussion is a special committee meeting called to review a problem and to identify possible solutions.

General group discussions present a number of problems when used as the means to identify options. Because general group discussions often occur extemporaneously, people don't have time to think about the problem and bring suggestions to the meeting. Instead, they are expected to think of options very quickly. The negative effects of peer pressure and the dominance of one or more members of the group are most likely to occur in this situation. Furthermore, the process of identifying options tends to end the first time someone suggests a solution that sounds reasonable to the other members of the group. There is no reward for prolonging the identification process, and there is often considerable pressure to move on to the next item on the agenda.

> Level of participation:
> Varies, often low
> Range of options identified:
> Low to moderate
> Leadership skill required:
> Low
> Time required:
> Low

When to Use

Generally, library managers overuse group discussion. However, group discussion can be an effective way to identify options in several circumstances. The first is when the decision to be made is confidential and the number of people involved in the process of identifying options is small. Two or three people would probably find it difficult and obtrusive to use any of the other methods to identify options. It is also appropriate to use general group discussions to identify options when the group is one that meets regularly and has a shared knowledge base. Branch managers, for instance, often identify options for addressing common problems during their monthly meetings. However, in both instances, the people responsible for leading the process need to be very aware of the problems presented in the preceding paragraph and work with the members of the group to avoid them.

What to Do

1. Identify the issue or question to be addressed.
2. Select the group to address the question. It may be an existing group or committee, or it may be a group convened specifically for this process.
3. Prepare a brief (one-page) description of the issue to be addressed and send it to the members of the group at least one week prior to the meeting at which it will be discussed. Ask the participants to come to the meeting ready to suggest ways to address the issue.
4. At the meeting, briefly review the issue and ask the members to suggest options. Write the options on flip-chart paper as they are presented. Encourage the group to provide as many suggestions as possible. Ask participants to clarify any options that seem ambiguous. Encourage people to combine options that are similar. Do not evaluate the suggestions as they are proposed.

5. When it becomes clear that everyone is finished presenting options, review the list and ask if there are questions or additions. Make needed changes and develop a final list of options.
6. Use the options as the starting point for making a decision about the issue under review.

Brainstorming

Brainstorming is a method used to identify multiple options by generating a large number of ideas through interaction among team members. The intent is to break free of preconceived ideas by exploring as many alternatives as possible and building on each other's ideas.

Level of participation:
Moderate to high
Range of options identified:
Moderate
Leadership skill required:
Moderate
Time required:
Low to moderate

As shown in Figure 17-1, in this process a group of people creates a list of ideas by having each member make a suggestion in turn, and the suggestions are recorded with no comment or discussion. Members are encouraged to build on each other's ideas. The actual brainstorming is best done in groups with six to eight members, but large groups can be divided into smaller groups for the initial brainstorming activity, and then the suggestions from all of the small groups can be combined.

This is a relatively easy process to manage and, by its very nature, makes it difficult for a few people to dominate the discussion. It is a process that many people enjoy; participants often find the fast-paced generation of ideas by a variety of people stimulating. However, the fast pace of the process can be a problem too. Brainstorming doesn't provide much opportunity for reflection. Participants are encouraged to think of options very quickly, which may mean that more complex or unusual options are never identified. Participants may also hesitate to make an unusual or creative suggestion for fear that others will laugh at them or think they are strange. There may be a tendency to follow the lead of the first two or three people who offer options rather

Figure 17-1: Rules for Brainstorming

1. Be creative; push the limits.
2. Never criticize anyone's ideas. There are no right answers or wrong answers.
3. The more ideas you contribute the better. Quantity is more important than quality.
4. Free-associate ideas; build on the ideas of others.
5. Don't discuss ideas or stop for explanations.
6. Record all ideas exactly as they are stated.
7. Take turns making suggestions. Contribute one idea each time it is your turn.
8. Pass your turn if you have no further suggestions.

than suggesting alternate ones that may be perceived as being in conflict with earlier recommendations.

When to Use
Brainstorming is a good method to use to generate a lot of ideas from a group in a fairly short period of time. It works best when it is used to consider a single, focused topic. For example, brainstorming can be an excellent way to identify a list of possible activities to achieve a predetermined goal and objective. However it is probably not the best way to identify the options for addressing the myriad of issues surrounding access to pornographic sites on the Internet. In the first case, the staff of the library probably have all the information they need to make suggestions, and any grouping of several dozen possible activities could be used to accomplish the goal and objective. In the second case, there aren't dozens of good answers. In fact, there aren't any answers that satisfy everyone involved. Having people with little knowledge of the legal issues or the political environment make suggestions is probably not going to be useful.

What to Do
1. Identify the issue or question to be addressed.
2. Decide whom to include in the process. This may be an existing group or committee or it may be a group convened specifically for this process.
3. Decide if you want to have official recorders for each group or if you want to ask the participants to share the responsibility for recording.
4. Write a short issue or problem statement. This should be specific enough to help participants focus on the issue but open-ended enough to encourage creativity. The statement could include a list of questions that would encourage exploration of the topic.
5. At the beginning of the brainstorming session, review the problem statement with the participants.
6. Prepare a handout with the rules for brainstorming (see Figure 17-1), and distribute it to all the participants.
7. If the group has more than eight people, divide it into smaller groups.
8. Establish a specific period of time for the initial brainstorming activity, usually around twenty minutes.
9. If there is more than one group working on the problem, combine their suggestions into a master list on a flip-chart.
10. Review and discuss the items on the master list, clarifying when necessary and combining when possible.
11. Use the options on the master list as the starting point for making a decision about the issue under review.

Nominal Group Technique
The Nominal Group Technique is used to generate a large number of ideas through the contributions of members working individually. Research suggests that more ideas are generated by individuals working alone but in a group

environment than by individuals engaged in group discussions.[2] In this process, group members start by writing down their ideas on note cards and posting them for others to read. Members get an opportunity to ask questions to clarify other members' ideas, and then they participate in group discussions about all of the ideas presented. Finally, each group member reassesses the ideas presented and selects those that seem most effective. These conclusions are then posted for a final discussion.

Level of participation:
Moderate to high
Range of options identified:
Moderate to high
Leadership skill required:
Moderate
Time required:
Moderate

The Nominal Group Technique is both more time-consuming and more structured than brainstorming. The investment in time is often repaid because this process generally produces a greater number of more developed and creative ideas than are produced in a group discussion or brainstorming process. However, people generally feel more comfortable with the fast-paced and open brainstorming process than with the Nominal Group Technique, at least partly because people are more familiar with brainstorming. The Nominal Group Technique structure can be perceived by group members as artificial and restrictive. Participants may feel that the process drives the content, rather than the other way around, and as a result, they may question the validity of the final list of options.

When to Use

The Nominal Group Technique is a good method to use with a group that has some very strong or opinionated members. Because each participant writes down his or her ideas privately before any discussion begins, the responses are less likely to be driven by the dominant members of the group. Because the facilitator reads the suggestions aloud, the process allows suggestions to be evaluated on their own merits rather than being prejudged based on who made them. The Nominal Group Technique also can be used effectively to identify options for addressing issues that are potentially controversial. For instance, you may be considering how to revise your circulation policies so they support the goal of meeting the public's demand for materials on current topics and titles. This opens up some interesting possibilities, including extending your loan period, allowing patron reserves, and so on. Each of these possibilities has proponents and opponents. Using this process, you can develop a comprehensive list of options without a lot of arguments. You can also get a sense of which options are perceived as having the potential to be the most effective ones.

What to Do

1. Identify the issue or question to be addressed.
2. Decide whom to include in the process. This may be an existing group or committee or it may be a group convened specifically for this process.

3. Write a short problem statement. This should be specific enough to help participants focus on the issue but open-ended enough to encourage creativity. The statement could include a list of questions that would encourage exploration of the topic.

4. At the beginning of the session, describe the process to be used and review the problem statement with the participants.

5. Give the participants five to ten minutes to write down their ideas on note cards without any discussion with others. Ask participants to use a new card for each idea.

6. Collect the cards and read the ideas, one at a time. Write the ideas on flip-chart paper as they are read, so that everyone can see them. There is no discussion during this part of the process.

7. After all of the ideas have been recorded, encourage participants to discuss them. Participants may be asked to clarify their suggestions. They can express agreement or disagreement with any suggestion.

8. Give participants several minutes to select the five options they think are the most effective.

9. Tabulate the choices and indicate which options received the most votes. One quick way to tabulate the choices is to use the dot exercise, described in the Groups: Reaching Agreement tool kit.

10. Discuss the final list of options.

11. Use the options as the starting point for making a decision about the issue under review.

Delphi Method

The Delphi Method was developed by the RAND Corporation as a way of eliminating the problems of generating ideas in groups: dominant behaviors, peer pressure, and so on. In this process the participants never meet face-to-face, and they normally don't even know who the other members of the group are. The participants are presented with a list of general questions about a specific topic and asked to prepare a written response. The responses are sent to a coordinator who edits and summarizes them into a single report. This report is returned to the participants with a second list of questions intended to clarify differences, and participants are again asked to respond. The responses from the second round are edited and summarized and sent to the participants one final time. In this third round, participants are provided with statistical feedback about how the group responded to particular questions, as well as a summary of the group's comments. This makes the participants aware of the range of opinions and the reasons for those opinions. The group is then asked to rank the responses one final time. A final report is developed and sent to all participants.

Level of participation:
High
Range of options identified:
Moderate to high
Leadership skill required:
High
Time required:
High

This is by far the most complex of the methods for identifying options, and most library staff members have never participated in a process that used the Delphi Method. The drawbacks are obvious. The method is quite time-consuming for the participants and extremely time-consuming for the coordinator. Furthermore, this method, more than any of the others, can be seriously compromised if the wrong people are included as participants because their involvement is so much more intensive. However, real benefits can be gained from using the Delphi Method as well. It can be used to gather options from people with significant subject expertise regardless of where they live. It can also be used to facilitate communication among individuals who disagree strongly about the issue being discussed.

When to Use

The Delphi Method is a process that library managers should use sparingly. It is simply too complex and too expensive to be used as a regular tool. However, in some circumstances the effort might well be worth the time and energy invested. For instance, let's say you are the director of a library in a community with a growing Hispanic population. You want to provide services for this new population group, but you don't know where to start. Some board and staff members feel that you don't have the resources to provide quality services to your "regular" client groups already, and it would be foolish to reach out to new groups. In this instance, using the Delphi Method to generate options from board members, staff members, members of the Hispanic community, and librarians in other communities with established service programs for Hispanics might be quite effective. It would minimize the potential for open conflict and maximize the number of options that could be considered. All points of view would be presented, and everyone involved would have a chance to respond. Because the responses are anonymous, participants might be more responsive to other points of view and more open to revising their initial suggestions.

What to Do

1. Identify the issue or question to be addressed.
2. Select a coordinator to manage the Delphi Method, preferably one who has coordinated a similar process before or at least participated in such a process.
3. Select the people to be involved in the process. The majority of Delphi studies have used between fifteen and twenty respondents.[3]
4. Send the participants a description of the process, and include the time frame. Participants have to agree to respond to three sets of questions.
5. Prepare a brief description of the issue or problem to be addressed and develop a short list of questions to be answered. Send both to each of the members. The initial questions will probably be general and open-ended.
6. Edit the responses and develop a set of follow-up questions based on the answers to the first questions. These follow-up questions will be

more specific than the first open-ended questions. Send the edited responses and the second questions to the participants.

7. Tabulate the responses to each question, edit the comments, and prepare a third report. Send this to the participants for review, and ask them to answer the questions one final time.

8. Tabulate the responses into a final report. Send copies to all participants. Use the information in the report as the starting point for making a decision about the issue under review.

Notes

1. United Way, *Measuring Program Outcomes* (Alexandria, VA: United Way of America, 1996).
2. Center for Rural Studies, "Guidelines for Using the Nominal Group Technique," http://crs.uvm.edu/gopher/nerl/group/a/meet/Exercise7/b.html.
3. Barbara Ludwig, "Predicting the Future: Have You Considered Using the Delphi Methodology?" *Journal of Extension* (October 1997), available at www.joe.org/joe/1997october/tt2.html.

About the Author

Sandra Nelson is a consultant, speaker, trainer, and writer specializing in public library planning and management issues. She has presented hundreds of training programs in forty-eight states during the past three decades. During her career, Nelson has worked in both large and small public libraries and in state library agencies. She is the author of *Implementing for Results* (2009), *Strategic Planning for Results* (2008), and *The New Planning for Results: A Streamlined Approach* (2001). She has co-authored a number of other publications and serves as Senior Editor for the PLA *Results* series.

Chapter 18

Reaching Agreement with Groups

Sandra Nelson

Issues

Most public libraries make extensive use of committees and teams to explore options, make recommendations about future services, and review and evaluate existing programs. No matter what their purpose, all committees and teams have one thing in common: to be successful, their members must be able to reach agreement on the issues under consideration. As anyone who has ever served on a committee knows, this isn't easy. Problems include lack of a clear committee or team charge, groups that are too large or too small, group leaders with poor facilitation skills, group members with competing agendas, lack of accountability, and the absence of official action on committee recommendations. These issues are discussed in more detail in the following sections.

The Charge

Every committee or team should have a clearly stated charge, and every member of the committee should understand that charge. The charge should include:

- an explicit description of what the committee is expected to accomplish the time frame for the committee's deliberations
- the person or group that will receive the committee's report
- the process that will be used to review and act upon the committee's work the time frame for that review and action

Group Size

Committees and teams can range in size from two or three people to as many as twenty or thirty people. The decision concerning the size of the group is a trade-off. Smaller committees are usually easier to work with because fewer people are involved. Communication is quicker, orientation takes less time, discussion and consensus may move more quickly, and smaller committees are less expensive to support. However, smaller groups may be open to potential criticism of narrow thinking or elitism. If the workload you envision for committee members is heavy, a small group may be overwhelmed and burn out before the committee completes its work.

Larger committees usually reflect a wider range of interests and can include people with a variety of expertise. Because the interests of the members may be more diverse, a wider scope of issues might be addressed. On the other hand, meetings will require more time for discussion and reaching consensus. Some committee members may feel lost in the crowd and lose enthusiasm. Large groups are also more difficult to lead. If the group will have more than twelve members, it is advisable to make arrangements for a trained facilitator to be the leader.

Leadership

Committees and teams are most effective when they are led by people who understand how groups work and have strong facilitation skills. Most library committees and teams are responsible for problem solving or information gathering. In these types of group activities, leaders are responsible for involving all members of the group in the work and ensuring that everyone has a say in the group's decisions. Generally, group members participate more and take a greater level of responsibility for the group's decisions if the leader focuses his or her energies on facilitating participation rather than on providing answers. See Figure 18-1 for more information on group leaders' roles.

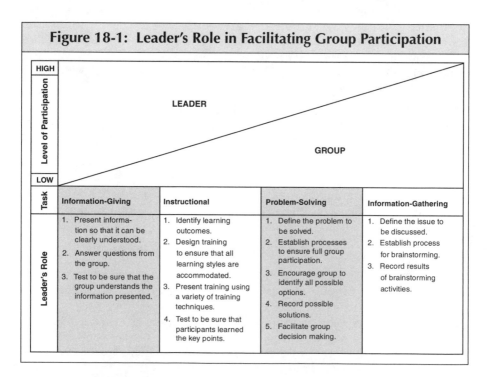

Figure 18-1: Leader's Role in Facilitating Group Participation

	Information-Giving	Instructional	Problem-Solving	Information-Gathering
Leader's Role	1. Present information so that it can be clearly understood. 2. Answer questions from the group. 3. Test to be sure that the group understands the information presented.	1. Identify learning outcomes. 2. Design training to ensure that all learning styles are accommodated. 3. Present training using a variety of training techniques. 4. Test to be sure that participants learned the key points.	1. Define the problem to be solved. 2. Establish processes to ensure full group participation. 3. Encourage group to identify all possible options. 4. Record possible solutions. 5. Facilitate group decision making.	1. Define the issue to be discussed. 2. Establish process for brainstorming. 3. Record results of brainstorming activities.

Membership

A committee or team is only as strong as its members. Group members normally play one of three roles:

Builders. These people are interested in the work of the committee and focus their energies on the successful completion of the group's charge.

Blockers. These people get in the way of the work of the committee by behaving in ways that block progress. There are dozens of behaviors that can derail an effective meeting. See Figure 18-2 for more information on blockers.

Maintainers. These people are more interested in maintaining relationships than in the work of the committee. They are the bridge between the builders and blockers.

Every committee needs builders and maintainers, and unfortunately almost all committees have at least one blocker. It is the leader's responsibility to see to it that the members of the group, no matter what their primary motivation, work together effectively.

Accountability

Committees and teams should be held accountable for their actions, just as individuals are. All too often the old saying, "When everyone is responsible, no one is responsible" comes into play with committees. It is not only possible but desirable to make it clear to a group that they are collectively responsible for specific results.

Action on Recommendations

If you ask any committee or group member what was the most frustrating thing about the group experience, far too many of them will say that they never saw any results from all of their work. Submitting a group report is often likened to Henry Wadsworth Longfellow's words: "I shot an arrow into the air, it fell to earth, I know not where." Library managers who appoint committees or teams to make recommendations have to establish processes for reviewing and acting on those recommendations. All group members should be aware of the review process and be kept informed of the status of the review from the beginning to the point at which a final decision has been made.

Evaluating Methods of Reaching Decisions

Three general approaches to reaching agreement in groups are consensus building, voting, and the forced-choice process. Each of these decision-making approaches can be used effectively to lead the group to a decision. The important thing is to match the approach to the situation. Four measures can be used to help you decide which approach will be most effective for the situation: the importance of the quality of the decision made; the time it takes to make the decision; the level of support the members of the group have for the decision; and the learning that takes place while the members make the decision.

Figure 18-2: Problem Behaviors in Meetings

Problem	Behavior	Suggested Solution
Latecomer	Always late	Start meetings on time—don't wait for stragglers. Do not recap meeting when Latecomer arrives, but offer to provide a recap during the first break.
Early Leaver	Never stays until meeting is adjourned	Set a time for adjournment and get a commitment from all members at the beginning of the meeting to stay until that time.
Clown	Always telling jokes; deflects group from task at hand	Laugh at the joke and then ask the Clown to comment on the topic under discussion. If the Clown responds with another joke, again ask for a comment on the topic.
Broken Record	Brings up same point over and over again	Write the Broken Record's concern on a flip-chart sheet and post it to provide assurance that the concern has been heard.
Doubting Thomas	Reacts negatively to most ideas	Encourage all group members to wait to make decisions until all points of view have been heard. Let Doubting Thomas express his concerns, but do not let him argue with others who do not share his negativity.
Dropout	Nonparticipant	Try asking Dropout's opinion during meeting or at break. Break group into groups of two or three to encourage everyone to participate.
Whisperer	Members having private conversations	Make eye contact with Whisperers. Pause briefly until you have their attention and then begin to speak again.
Loudmouth	Must be center of attention; talks constantly	Acknowledge the Loudmouth when he begins to talk and let him have his say. Then, if Loudmouth interrupts others, remind him that he has had his say.

(Cont'd.)

Figure 18-2: Problem Behaviors in Meetings (Continued)

Problem	Behavior	Suggested Solution
Attacker	Makes very critical comments, often directed at leader	Thank the Attacker for his/her observation, and then ask other group members what they think. If attacks are directed at another group member, the leader has a responsibility to intervene. It is best to resolve these conflicts privately and not in front of the whole group.
Interpreter	Often says "In other words" or "What she really means	Check this in public with the original speaker.
Know-It-All	Always has the answer	Remind the group that all members have expertise; that's the reason for meeting. Ask others to respond to Know-It-All's comments.
Teacher's Pet	Tries to monopolize the leader's attention	Be encouraging, but break eye contact. Get group members to talk to one another. Lessen your omnipotence by reflecting "What do you think?" back to the Teacher's Pet.

Quality of the Decision

The first measure is the importance of the quality of the decision that is produced. For example, a group that decides very quickly to vote to select priorities may not make as informed a decision as a group that spends the time needed to explore all of the options in detail before making a decision. On the other hand, not all situations are equally critical. Decisions such as where the group will eat lunch or when the next meeting will be held don't require extensive discussion.

Time Required

The second measure is the time it takes to reach the decision. To continue with the preceding example, the group that voted quickly obviously made a decision in less time than the group that explored options more fully. There is often a trade-off between the length of time a group spends on a decision and the quality of the final decision. However, that is not always true: at times groups get stuck in a seemingly endless process of data collection and discussion and never make any decision—good or bad.

Level of Support

The third measure is the desired level of support the group will have for the decision that has been made. Consensus building, by its very nature, creates the highest level of group support for the decisions being made because everyone has to agree with the decisions before they become final. On the other hand, the forced-choice process, which averages the choices made by group members in order to determine priorities, has the potential to result in decisions that none of the group supports wholeheartedly.

Development of Expertise

In some cases, it is important that the group members be given an opportunity to develop expertise in the area under consideration. For instance, if a team is going to be involved in making decisions about technology issues for the library for the next year, it is clearly important that the members of the team become knowledgeable about technology options and stay aware of changes in the field. In other cases, there is no need to support the development of such expertise. A committee of children's librarians who are responsible for developing and presenting a puppet show to publicize the summer reading program will probably have the expertise they need to accomplish their charge.

Methods for Reaching Agreement

Consensus Building

Consensus building is a process by which group members seek a mutually acceptable resolution to the issue under discussion. Note that consensus does not mean that everyone agrees that the solution is the best of all possible answers. A group has reached consensus when everyone can and will support the decision.

Quality of decision:
Normally very good
Time required:
Time-intensive
Group support for decision:
High
Development of expertise:
High

When to Use

This approach is best suited for making important decisions. Consensus promotes hard thinking that really gets at the issues. It can be slow, and it is occasionally painful; however, when a group finally reaches consensus, it has developed a solution that will have the support needed for implementation. Since consensus requires so much energy, the group should agree that the outcome of the decision is worth the effort. Such outcomes might include long-range planning, the development of a new program or service, or the revision of the library's job descriptions. In each of these situations, people probably care deeply about the outcome, and their support will be required to successfully implement the decision.

What to Do

People reach consensus by talking about issues in a fair and open environment. This means that the group leader will have to ensure that each member of the group has an opportunity to be heard, that no idea is discarded without a thorough review and discussion, and that all members of the group take responsibility for finding a mutually agreeable decision.

The national best seller *Getting to Yes: Negotiating Agreement without Giving In* identifies four steps to reaching consensus.[1]

Separate people from the problem. People often feel strongly about issues under discussion, and discussions can shift quickly from issues to personalities. It is important to keep the discussion firmly focused on the problem under review.

Focus on interests, not positions. Positions are the opinions that each group member brings to the discussion before the discussion begins. These positions get in the way of reaching consensus because they tend to be "all or nothing." To reach consensus, group members will have to focus on the problem and their mutual interest in resolving it, and not on their preconceived positions.

Generate a variety of options before deciding what to do. There is no one right way to do anything. Consensus building involves identifying and discussing all of the ways the problem might be resolved. This is surprisingly difficult. Most people see problem solving as narrowing the options, not expanding them.

Base decisions on objective criteria. This is a critical step in the consensus-building process. The group members must be able to define the criteria they will use to evaluate the options they have identified. If they can't agree on criteria, the group members are likely to revert to their positions when reviewing the options.

Voting

When people think about group decision-making processes, the first process that comes to mind is voting. Our whole society is based on the premise that the majority rules. We have all been voting on things since we were children. Voting is democratic, it's generally fair, and it's always quick and easy. However, there are some potential problems with voting. It can short-circuit consideration of all of the options, and if the issue is particularly contentious, it can split the group into winners and losers.

When to Use

If the decision under discussion is not critical and not worth a lot of discussion, it may be easiest to vote with a simple hand count. It is perfectly acceptable to take a hand count to decide where the group will have lunch. Hand counts can be used to make procedural decisions (how long the meetings will last, when the next meeting will be held, etc.).

Quality of decision:
Varies
Time required:
Low to moderate
Group support for decision:
Moderate
Development of expertise:
Low to moderate

If the decision is important, the dot-exercise voting process is more flexible and allows group members to express their opinions in more detail. It also provides a visual summary of the group members' preferred choices. The dot exercise might be used to identify activities that would help the library achieve the goals and objectives in the long-range plan, or to identify the topics for a staff-day program.

What to Do: Dot Exercise

The basic dot exercise process is quite straightforward. The process allows a large number of people to vote on a variety of options in a short period of time.

1. The leader first lists all of the options on flip-chart paper with enough space next to or between the items to allow committee members to place adhesive dots.
2. Each participant is given five self-adhesive colored dots.
3. The group members vote by putting dots on the flip-chart sheets next to their choices. Members may vote for five separate items, or they may load their vote, or "bullet vote," by giving an item more than one dot.
4. Count the votes by totaling the number of dots by each item.
5. Share and discuss the outcome of the voting exercise. Does the outcome seem to reflect the earlier discussion? Are clear priorities and a consensus emerging? Ask those who voted for items under discussion that received few votes to talk about their reasons for selecting those items.

A variation on the basic dot exercise helps to balance the effect of "bullet voting," which occurs when members place more than one of their dots by a single option. If the group is large, the bullet votes of one or two people will not have much impact, but if the group is small, those one or two people can essentially set priorities for the entire committee. With a small group, you might consider avoiding the impact of bullet voting by asking that committee members use a star to indicate their top priority. Then count votes by totaling the number of dots by each item and the number of stars by each item. Next, they share and discuss the outcome of the voting exercise. What is the difference, if any, between the priorities reflected by the dots and the stars? Does the outcome seem to reflect the earlier discussions? Are clear priorities and a consensus emerging?

Forced Choice

Most people find it virtually impossible to compare the relative merits of more than three or four items. The forced-choice process allows people to compare any number of items, each against the other, to determine which are the most important.

> Quality of decision:
> Varies
> Time required:
> Low
> Group support for decision:
> Low to moderate
> Development of expertise:
> Low

When to Use

The forced-choice process is an effective way of helping groups that have become mired in discussion to look at the options under review in a different way. The process does just what its name says: it forces people to make decisions from among a number of competing possibilities. The process also provides the information needed to place the options in priority order, based on the average ranking by each group member. That, however, is also the main weakness in the process. Because the priority of the options is determined by averaging, it is quite possible that the final list will not reflect the opinions of any single individual in the group. However, the process does identify items with little support. These can be excluded from the discussion, and one of the other processes discussed in this chapter can be used to allow the group to move forward to reach final agreement on the remaining options.

What to Do

1. List the options under review and number each. It is easier for the group members to vote if each of them has a copy of the options.
2. Prepare a forced-choice workform (see Figure 18-3) and make a copy for each group member.
3. Each of the group members will complete the forced-choice process. (See Workform N, Forced-Choice Process, for directions.)
4. After each group member totals the number of times each option was circled, the option with the highest total is the one with the highest priority for that person.
5. The leader will help the group to see how the group members' selections compare with one another. This may be done in one of two ways:

   • Total the points for each choice from all of the group members. The choice with the highest total score is the most important; the next is the second most important, and so on.
   • Determine where each of the group members ranked each option by asking how many ranked a given option as the highest priority,

Figure 18-3: Workform N: Forced-Choice Process—Example

Instructions

Assign a number to each of the items you are prioritizing. This worksheet will help you evaluate up to 15 items against every other item on the list, each time determining which of your choices is the more important. Begin in Column A below. Compare the first and second items and circle the number of the one you think is more important (1 or 2). Continuing in Column A, compare the first item and the third item, again circling the service response you think is more important (1 or 3). Continue through all of the columns.

A

   B

1 2   C

1 3   2 3   D

1 4   2 4   3 4   E

1 5   2 5   3 5   4 5   F

1 6   2 6   3 6   4 6   5 6   G

1 7   2 7   3 7   4 7   5 7   6 7   H

1 8   2 8   3 8   4 8   5 8   6 8   7 8   I

1 9   2 9   3 9   4 9   5 9   6 9   7 9   8 9   J

1 10 2 10 3 10 4 10 5 10 6 10 7 10 8 10 9 10   K

1 11 2 11 3 11 4 11 5 11 6 11 7 11 8 11 9 11 10 11   L

1 12 2 12 3 12 4 12 5 12 6 12 7 12 8 12 9 12 10 12 11 12   M

1 13 2 13 3 13 4 13 5 13 6 13 7 13 8 13 9 13 10 13 11 13 12 13   N

1 14 2 14 3 14 4 14 5 14 6 14 7 14 8 14 9 14 10 14 11 14 12 14 13 14

1 15 2 15 3 15 4 15 5 15 6 15 7 15 8 15 9 15 10 15 11 15 12 15 13 15 14 15

To score your ratings, add the number of times you circled each number and place the total by the appropriate line below. Note that you must add vertically and horizontally to be sure that you include all circled choices. The service response with the highest number is the one you think is most important.

1. _____   4. _____   7. _____   10. _____   13. _____

2. _____   5. _____   8. _____   11. _____   14. _____

3. _____   6. _____   9. _____   12. _____   15. _____

how many ranked it as the second-highest priority, and so on. In this case, the option with the highest average ranking becomes the highest priority.

Note

1. Roger Fisher, William Ury, and Bruce Patton, *Getting to Yes: Negotiating Agreement without Giving In*, 2nd ed. (New York: Penguin Books, 1991), 10–11.

About the Author

Sandra Nelson is a consultant, speaker, trainer, and writer specializing in public library planning and management issues. She has presented hundreds of training programs in forty-eight states during the past three decades. During her career, Nelson has worked in both large and small public libraries and in state library agencies. She is the author of *Implementing for Results* (2009), *Strategic Planning for Results* (2008), and *The New Planning for Results: A Streamlined Approach* (2001). She has co-authored a number of other publications and serves as Senior Editor for the PLA *Results* series.

Chapter 19

Presenting Data

Sandra Nelson

Issues

Public library staff and managers collect a wide variety of information about library services and programs. In theory, five main reasons for collecting all of this data are to

- measure progress toward accomplishing the goals and objectives in the library's strategic plan
- document the value of library services
- make resource allocation decisions
- meet the requirements of a grant project
- meet state library data-collection requirements

In practice, much of the information that is collected in libraries is never used at all, and when managers attempt to use the information they collected, they often have problems presenting the information effectively.

The first and most basic problem with presenting data concerns the selection of which data elements to use to support the intended outcomes. This is trickier than it appears. Too little data is unhelpful; too much data is overwhelming; and the wrong data is misleading. The second problem is the difficulty some people have in organizing data. This was a more serious problem when we had to use adding machines and ledgers to analyze data; today we have a variety of computer software programs that help to manipulate and organize data. However, we still have to have a coherent reason for the organizational decisions that we make; otherwise, the data won't make sense. The third problem has to do with the layout and design of the data. It doesn't do any good to select the right data elements and organize the data elements in a logical pattern if you don't present them in a clear and attractive manner. These issues will be discussed in more detail in the following sections.

Selecting the Right Data

Before you can begin to select data for any purpose, you have to know who your audience is and what that audience needs to see in order to make a decision or reach a conclusion. If you are making a presentation intended to encourage seventh-grade students to use the library, there isn't much point in telling them about the increase in the number of senior citizens who use the library for personal development and ongoing learning. If you are making a presentation to senior citizens about the opportunities for lifelong learning at the library, they probably won't be interested in the number of hits on your homework help Web page or the rapidly increasing circulation of game cartridges.

Knowing your audience goes beyond understanding their interests. You also have to have some idea of what they already know and what they don't know. If you present information on document delivery to library managers, you can reasonably assume they will know you are talking about interlibrary loan, reserves, and the delivery of requested items among the various units in the library. If you present information on document delivery to the members of the city council, they may well assume you are talking about services to the homebound.

There are two kinds of data: quantitative and qualitative. Quantitative data is numeric and measures how much of something there is or how often something happens. Most library data is quantitative (circulation figures, number of reference questions, number of users who log on to the Internet, number of online searches, etc.). Qualitative data comes from observations or interviews and results in patterns or generalizations about why something occurs. The information obtained from a series of focus groups on business services is qualitative data. Both types of data can be effective. Figure 19-1 lists nine common purposes for collecting data and suggests which type of data would be most effective in each case.

No matter which types of data you decide best meet your needs, be selective about the specific data elements to include. Too much data is worse than too little. However, once you select the data elements you want to use, be sure to include the entire data set for each element. Let's say you want to explain to the members of the library board the relation between increased use of electronic resources and decreased print and media circulation. After reviewing all of the possible data elements, you might select circulation figures and number of electronic searches as the two data elements that would best illustrate what is happening. The data set for circulation includes all of the different categories of circulation you count. You may not want the board to focus on the increase in the circulation of media items, but once you decide to use circulation figures you have to include them all. In the same way, to present an accurate picture of the number of electronic searches, you will have to include all electronic searches that take place using library equipment, both on- and off-site, and both CD-ROM and Internet. It is equally important to include the full set of data elements when you use qualitative data. If you

Figure 19-1: Quantitative and Qualitative Data		
Reason	**Quantitative Data**	**Qualitative Data**
Measure number of people who use a service or program	✓	
Show reasons for current use		✓
Show trends in the numbers of people who use a service or program	✓	
Show relations between trends in current use	✓	
Show reasons for trends in current use		✓
Measure user satisfaction		✓
Measure units of library service delivered	✓	
Show trends in units of library service delivered	✓	
Measure cost per unit of service delivered	✓	

decide to report on public reaction to a new service, you have to report all of the reactions, not just the positive ones.

The key to all this is to be as honest as you can with the statistics you select and present. You will want to be able to explain why you chose the data elements you are using and the source of each. It is also important that you check and double-check your numbers. If one number is inaccurate, it doesn't matter how carefully you selected the data elements you included or how accurate the rest of the numbers are: the single inaccurate number will taint the entire report.

Organizing the Data

Once you have selected the data elements to use, you have to decide how to organize the information so that it is clear and easily understood. Three basic organizational models that you might want to consider are historical order, priority order, and narrative logic. Your choice from among these three options depends on what you are trying to accomplish, what data elements are available, and which of the three options seems most logical to you.

What you want to avoid is the fourth option—no particular order. This is just what it sounds like—data elements are arranged without pattern and in no conscious order. This makes it difficult for the person using the data to deliver a coherent presentation and makes it even harder for the audience to understand what is being presented. Think about how hard it would be to follow a presentation about library services that started with juvenile circulation figures, moved to general budget numbers, took a side trip to present data about attendance at the summer reading program, then talked about adult circulation, and finally ended with information about the cost of new electronic resources.

Historical Order

When you use the historical order organizational model, you present information about trends in the areas being considered. These trends provide a context in which to consider data about current services or programs. This is a particularly useful model when you are presenting information about programs or services that are experiencing significant changes. If adult nonfiction circulation has dropped 20 percent in the past five years, that is important information to have when you are considering your materials budget. If media circulation has increased by 15 percent during the same period, that is also important to know. Of course, you can't use historical order if you don't have historical data, which is often the case when you are presenting data about new services or programs.

Priority Order

When you use priority order as the organizational model, you present the most important data first and then provide less important supporting data. It is a useful model if you are presenting a number of different data elements to support a specific proposal. Let's say you are reporting on the use of the library's electronic resources during the eighteen months since you began to allow users to dial in from off-site to use the library's databases and connect to the Internet. The most important data element would be the number of log-ons from off-site, and you would start your report with that. You might then choose to include data on the number of searches and the number of items retrieved to give the audience an idea of how the off-site access is actually being used.

Narrative Logic

When you use narrative logic as the organizational model, you arrange the data to tell a story. This model can be very effective when trying to sell a new idea or program. It allows you to create a script that moves the audience from one step to the next until they finally reach the conclusion you want them to reach. Often the story starts with information that the audience already knows (once upon a time . . .). Confirming prior knowledge builds credibility into the sales process. Then you select and present the data that best supports each of the key points in your story.

Designing the Document

The final thing to consider when presenting data is the layout and design of the data. In some ways, this is the most important part of the process. After all, if no one looks at the data you have selected and organized, all of your efforts will have been wasted. The first step in the design process is to create a document that is attractive and visually appealing. The document will have to look inviting enough to encourage busy people to take time to pick it up and start reading it. Next you want to be sure that the information in the document is clear and easy to read. Most of the people in your audience are too busy to spend a lot of time trying to decipher a jumble of confusing words and charts.

Graphic design is managing visual information through layout, typography, and illustration to lead the reader's eye through the page. The layout of the document is the first thing readers will see. They will observe the balance of white space and text and the proportion of text and graphics. A page that has little or no white space is not user-friendly; neither is a page filled with a jumble of graphics. You are looking for a balance between text and graphics surrounded by enough white space to provide an effective frame.

Create a basic layout and style sheet and use it consistently throughout the document. Select a single, readable font to use for text and graphics. Match your text and your graphics and try to keep the size of the visuals proportionate. A number of excellent books on graphic design are available that will provide additional suggestions and illustrations to help you create an effective document. Remember, in graphic design, as in so much else, simple is always better. You want the audience to focus on the content, not on the graphics.

Evaluating Methods of Presenting Data

Most library managers present data in three main ways: narrative descriptions, tables, and graphs and charts. Each can be used effectively in certain circumstances. You can also use two or all three of the methods together to improve the chances that your audience will receive and understand the information you are presenting. To help you select the best method or combination of methods for your purpose, think about the following:

> How long will it take to develop the presentation, and what level of skill will be required?
>
> How important is it that the information be presented in a visually attractive and interesting way?
>
> How easy will it be to read and understand the final product?
>
> Will the audience be expected to understand the relationships among various data elements?

These questions are addressed in more detail in the following sections.

Time and Skill

The first issue to consider when selecting a method of presentation is the time and skill required to develop the presentation. It can take considerable time and technical skill to create high-quality charts and graphs. Narrative descriptions and tables are normally much easier and quicker to develop. Consider the following questions when deciding how much time and energy to invest in developing a presentation:

Is the target audience internal or external? Normally, library managers are willing to invest more time in presentations for external audiences.

Is the data being presented for informational purposes, or do you want it to result in a decision? It makes sense to spend more time on presentations that are intended to help people reach a decision.

How frequently will the final product be used? Some presentations will be used a number of times, while others will be used just once. It is worth investing the time and energy needed to ensure that the template for your monthly report to the city manager is a high-quality product because you will be using it repeatedly.

What is the easiest and simplest method that can be used to achieve what needs to be accomplished?

Visual Appeal

The second issue to consider when selecting a method of presentation is the need to present the information in a visually attractive manner. It is always important that information be readable, but if you are presenting information to staff, you may be less concerned about making it attractive and interesting than you would be if you were presenting the same information to the members of the chamber of commerce. Most library managers routinely "clean things up" for external use. Visual presentations tend to be more appealing and interesting than text presentations. They also usually take considerably longer to develop.

Simplicity and Clarity

The third issue to consider when selecting a method of presentation is the ease with which the data can be read and understood. Some kinds of data are easier to understand than others. A single data point can be presented very nicely using a narrative description. On the other hand, as you will see in Figure 19-2, it is difficult to use narrative description to present complex historical data about several different categories of information.

Depiction of Relationships

The last question to consider when selecting a method of presentation is whether there are relationships among the data elements that you want to highlight. Most people find it easier to see such relationships when they are presented in graphs and charts rather than in narrative form. The old saying "A picture is worth a thousand words" is as true about data as it is about describing a sunset.

Figure 19-2: Narrative Description

Circulation by Type of Material

The circulation patterns in the library have changed over the past five years. The most significant change has been in the circulation of nonfiction materials. In 2004, 28 percent of the total circulation in the library came from adult nonfiction items and approximately 12 percent came from children's nonfiction; the combined circulation of children's and adult nonfiction items represented almost 40 percent of the total circulation. In 2008, the circulation of adult nonfiction materials was 19 percent of the total circulation and an additional 9 percent came from children's nonfiction. The combined circulation of children's and adult nonfiction materials was only 28 percent of the total circulation. That represents a 12 percent decrease over a five-year period.

On the other hand, the circulation of nonprint materials increased from 13 percent to almost 20 percent of total circulation between 2004 and 2008. The change in the percentage circulation of fiction materials has been more moderate. In 2004, 25 percent of the total circulation came from adult fiction materials and 22 percent of circulation came from children's fiction; total fiction circulation was 47 percent of the overall circulation. In 2008, 27 percent of the circulation came from adult fiction materials and 25 percent came from children's fiction; total fiction circulation was 52 percent, a 5 percent increase.

Methods for Presenting Data

Narrative Descriptions

Narrative descriptions use text to present quantitative and qualitative data and to describe the relationships, if any, among data elements. Before library managers had easy access to personal computers and spreadsheet programs, they presented a great deal of library information using narrative descriptions. Even now, some managers rely heavily on narrative descriptions because they are quick and easy to prepare and do not require any special computer skills.

Time and skills:
Low
Visual appeal:
Low
Simplicity and clarity:
Low to moderate
Depiction of relationships:
Moderate

At times narrative descriptions can be effective (especially for qualitative data that is itself narrative in form), but they have some serious drawbacks when used as your primary presentation method. The most obvious problem is that blocks of text aren't very attractive or interesting. It can also be confusing to read about a variety of data elements with no easy way to keep track of them. Although you can use narrative descriptions to describe the relationship among several data elements, the relationship would probably be clearer if you included a table or graph.

Figures 19-3 through 19-6 present the same data in a variety of ways. Read the description in Figure 19-2, and then look at the table in Figure 19-3 and the graphs and charts in Figures 19-4 through 19-6. Which of the options do you think presents the information most effectively? Why?

When to Use

Narrative description can be an effective way to present information gathered through focus groups or other qualitative data-collection processes because qualitative data is often narrative rather than numeric. Narrative descriptions can also be used effectively to present a few simple statistics and to discuss the relationships among them. You might also find narrative descriptions helpful when you are presenting information that is new or unfamiliar to your audience. The narrative process makes it easy to include background and introductory information.

Whenever you use narrative description to present data, read the final product carefully to see if your points would be clearer if you included one or

Figure 19-3: Sample Table

Circulation by Type of Materials					
	2004	**2005**	**2006**	**2007**	**2008**
Media (DVDs, CDs, etc.)	38,900	46,650	60,877	63,450	65,980
Adult fiction	78,090	79,950	82,074	85,375	87,430
Adult nonfiction	88,098	84,650	76,220	70,580	63,250
Children's fiction	67,991	71,600	76,909	81,649	83,230
Children's nonfiction	36,500	36,480	34,815	32,112	30,980
Total	**309,579**	**319,330**	**330,895**	**333,166**	**330,870**

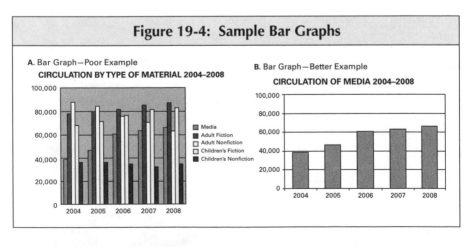

Figure 19-4: Sample Bar Graphs

A. Bar Graph—Poor Example
CIRCULATION BY TYPE OF MATERIAL 2004–2008

B. Bar Graph—Better Example
CIRCULATION OF MEDIA 2004–2008

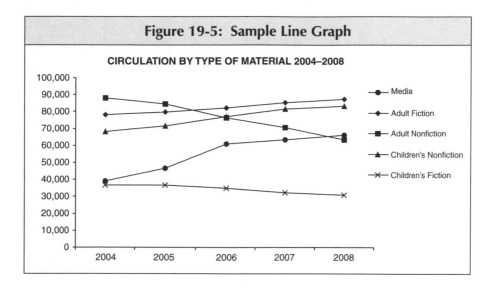

Figure 19-5: Sample Line Graph

CIRCULATION BY TYPE OF MATERIAL 2004–2008

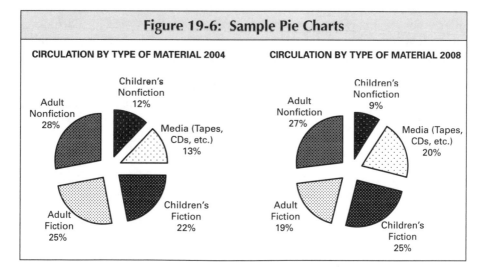

Figure 19-6: Sample Pie Charts

more tables or charts. In general, narrative descriptions work best when used in conjunction with one of the other methods of presenting data.

What to Do

1. Treat the narrative description as you would any other written presentation. Include an introduction, a body, and a conclusion. If the description is longer than a page, consider using heads and subheads to break up the text.

2. If it takes more than one short paragraph to describe the actual data, consider including a table or graph.
3. Keep it simple. Use short words and sentences.
4. Be very aware of layout and page design. Large blocks of text are boring and can be intimidating.
5. Include the date when the narrative description was written.

Tables

Tables present information in a grid format (see Figure 19-3) and provide a relatively easy way to display a considerable amount of information. Library managers often use tables to present data because tables don't require sophisticated computer skills to prepare and can be put together fairly quickly.

> Time and skill:
> Low
> Visual appeal:
> Moderate
> Simplicity and clarity:
> Moderate
> Depiction of relationships:
> Low

Tables are more visually interesting than text, but they can be harder to read and understand than charts or graphs. It is often difficult to identify trends and relationships among the data presented in a table, particularly if the table includes a lot of data. State libraries publish public library statistical reports annually. These reports present data about public library services and resources in tabular form. The tables typically have five or more columns, and they can have hundreds of rows—one for each public library in the state. These endless rows of numbers are very difficult to read, and it is virtually impossible to use them to identify trends or relationships. Most state libraries are now making this statistical data available electronically, which allows the user to manipulate the data to create more focused tables and to develop charts that illustrate trends or relationships.

When to Use

You can use tables to present a variety of information, both numeric and textual. Tables work best when you are dealing with a limited number of data elements and a small set of data. The table in Figure 19-1 is effective because it presents relatively simple data in an easily read and understood format. If the same information were presented in a narrative description, it would have taken more space and been more difficult to understand. Figure 19-1 also provides a visual break in a full page of text.

What to Do

1. Select a brief title that clearly identifies the focus of the table.
2. Put borders around tables to make them easier to see and read.
3. Number tables if you are using more than one.
4. Label each row and column clearly using simple words or short phrases.

5. Use different kinds of lines to separate labels from data when possible.
6. Identify the source of data for each table.
7. Round off numbers to the nearest whole number.
8. Use bold or italic type to indicate totals and subtotals.
9. Include the date when the table was prepared.

Graphs and Charts

Graphs and charts are visual depictions of numeric data. If you can't count it, you can't graph or chart it. Every graphic item in a chart represents two pieces of information:

1. The name of a measurable item (called a category), which is identified on the chart by a label
2. The quantity associated with the item (called a data point), which is plotted on the chart as a value[1]

Today, almost all charts and graphs are created using computer software programs, which provide templates for dozens of different types of charts and graphs. Microsoft Word includes fourteen standard chart styles and an additional twenty custom chart styles. Specialized chart and graph software packages provide even more options. Because all of these software programs take time to learn and use, graphs and charts are the most labor- and skill-intensive of the three presentation methods. However, if the message is important and the data is complex, the investment in time required to create graphs and charts is worthwhile.

The three main types of charts and graphs that most libraries use are bar graphs, line graphs, and pie charts. These three styles are illustrated in Figures 19-4–6. In general, bar graphs are used to rank the relative size or importance of something over a period of time. Line graphs illustrate trends in several data elements over a period of time. Pie charts show the relationships of parts to the whole; pie charts always present 100 percent of a single category of data.

When to Use

Use graphs and charts when it is important that the audience understand the relationships among various types of information. The most effective graphs and charts focus on a single theme or message and contain only the data needed to deliver the message. Be sure to select the right type of graph or chart to present your data. Use graphs to show the relationship between two or more variables. Charts are used to represent data with a single variable.

Bar graphs work best when you want to present data about two variables, normally the changes in a single data element over a period of time. Look at the two graphs in Figure 19-4. Bar graph A is difficult to read and confusing because it tries to present data about multiple data elements over a five-year period. Bar graph B, which presents data on one data element over the same five-year period, is much clearer and easier to understand.

Line graphs work well to illustrate the trends in multiple data elements over a period of time. Figure 19-5 presents exactly the same data as Figure 19-4A.

However, most people would agree that Figure 19-5 is easier to read and understand than Figure 19-4A. The horizontal lines make it easy to follow the trend in each category of circulation during the five-year period under consideration.

Pie charts are used to present data with a single variable. As noted previously, all pie charts reflect 100 percent of the data in the variable under consideration. Figures 19-6A and 19-6B illustrate the circulation of materials (the variable) in 2004 and again in 2008. To present the circulation data for 2005, 2006, and 2007, you would need to create three more pie charts. Pie charts are not normally the best format to present multiyear data. However, they are an effective way to illustrate the proportions of the pieces of any given data element.

What to Do
1. Select the right type of graph or chart for the data you are presenting.
2. Keep each graph or chart focused on a single message or theme.
3. Select a brief title that clearly identifies the focus of the graph or chart.
4. Put borders around graphs or charts to make them easier to see and read.
5. Number graphs or charts if you are using more than one.
6. Identify the source of data for each graph or chart.
7. Keep the background clear, and select simple contrasting patterns to fill bars or slices of a pie chart.
8. Round off numbers to the nearest whole number.
9. The x axis (bottom) and y axis (left) should meet at 0 for bar and line graphs.
10. Include the date when the graph or chart was prepared.

Note
1. Michael Talman, "Charts and Graphs: Visualizing Data," chap. 10 in *Understanding Presentation Graphics* (San Francisco: Sybex, 1992), www.talmanassociates. com/upg/ch10/ch10.html.

About the Author

Sandra Nelson is a consultant, speaker, trainer, and writer specializing in public library planning and management issues. She has presented hundreds of training programs in forty-eight states during the past three decades. During her career, Nelson has worked in both large and small public libraries and in state library agencies. She is the author of *Implementing for Results* (2009), *Strategic Planning for Results* (2008), and *The New Planning for Results: A Streamlined Approach* (2001). She has co-authored a number of other publications and serves as Senior Editor for the PLA *Results* series.

Chapter 20

Assessing Your Library's Physical Message

Cheryl Bryan

Issues

Routine assessments of the condition of your building and the message your building projects to users are part of facilities management. The vision and the mission and the image the library staff has of itself are demonstrated in the routine care for the library facility. The public library's image is part of the community's image. The physical message of your library is as important as the programs and services provided. The way your library looks, feels, and smells affects people who come to the library even before they begin to access the resources you provide for them. If the message of your building is one of neglect, a stale appearance, and a lack of attention to cleanliness, users may turn away long before you can show them the services you would like to provide.

Looking at the facility with fresh or "new eyes" from time to time is important. If you have unsuccessfully struggled with a problem like cracked foundations, or peeling paint that must be refinished every four years, you may find yourself overlooking those problems that are apparent to someone entering the library for the first time who only sees the unattractive feature but doesn't understand why it exists. For this reason it is well worth the time invested to ask someone not connected with your library's organization to conduct a walk-about assessment. The lists below can help someone conduct an impartial assessment of your building.

Assessing the Exterior

Before users can enter a library, they must find out where it is and when it is open. How easily can new users determine where your building and main entrance are located? Congratulations if your library has attained the users' ideal of 24/7 service hours; but if it is only open during designated hours, how easily can a user determine whether your building is open for business and when it will be open? Can they conveniently get this information from their car? Other questions to ask when reviewing the building's exterior are the following.

Signage
- Is there a sign for the library clearly visible from the street?
- Is the sign in good repair?
- Can the hours be read from the street?

Landscaping
- Is the exterior of the library attractive and inviting?
- Do the lawns need mowing?
- Is the landscaping trimmed back away from the road and walkways to enable good sight lines around the building, and does the landscaping contribute to a welcoming appearance of the library?
- Do the library grounds and building exterior meet or exceed community standards?

Parking
- Are driveways and parking areas well lit, and are walkways to entrances safely out of the flow of traffic around the library?
- Are there a sufficient number of parking spaces for the users of your library to have easy access, and are they well marked?
- Is the pavement cracked or broken?

Building Exterior
- Does the foundation have any visible cracks or water seepage?
- Are the doorways clearly marked, in good working order, and unobstructed by signs, book returns, and landscaping?
- Are all entrances to the library ADA–compliant, with appropriately pitched ramps and appropriate hardware on all doors so they can be opened from a wheelchair with a minimum amount of resistance? (For further information, visit www.access-board.gov/ada-aba/.)

Assessing the Interior
Visitors to your library will be most successful in using its resources if they can easily find their way through the building. Good design involves an orientation point within ten to twenty feet of the entrance where a first-time user can figure out the basic layout of services. More than signage, people depend on visual cues to direct them through the building. Has anyone on your staff ever complained that no one reads your signs? That is most people's first response. Visual cues are actually more significant than signage in directing people through a new or unfamiliar space. These cues include path carpeting, walls painted in unique colors for the various departments and services in the library, placement of shelving and furnishings,

and different lighting or styles of furnishings; these can all send a message to users about the purpose of an area of the library before they locate and interpret the signage. This is not to imply that you should not also make every effort to provide clear directional signage throughout the building.

Lighting can affect the feel of the library, and many contend that lighting also affects the mood and health of those who spend long hours there. Many libraries in areas of the country where winter means short, dark days for many months of the year invest in full-spectrum lighting for high-intensity-use areas like information services and circulation/user services.

Some questions to ask when reviewing your library's interior are the following.

Directionals
- Is the entryway clean, well lit, and inviting?
- When new users enter the building, can they easily find their way to an information or public assistance desk?
- Do visual cues lead users through the building so they can find the services sought (i.e., path carpeting, walls painted in unique colors for the various departments and services, placement of shelving and furnishings, and different lighting or different styles of furnishings)?
- Is there adequate and consistent signage guiding users to services?

Lighting
- Does your library make the best use it can of natural light?
- Are your window treatments clean, in working order, and consistent throughout the individual areas of the library?
- Are there adequate light levels, so index labels on books on the bottom rows of shelving can be easily read and identified?

Walls
- Is sound controlled in high-use areas (such as the children's programming area), and have measures like extra carpeting, fabric wall panels, or acoustical tiles been installed to prevent noise from bouncing around on the hard surfaces of the library?
- Are the walls in good repair and clean?
- Are windows or glass partitions clean and in good repair?
- Are decorations like wall hangings, plants, or local art cleaned regularly and well kept?

Ceilings
- Are the ceilings in good repair?
- Are ceilings painted light colors and well lit to reflect back the most light possible?
- Is there dirt around the air flow vents?

Floors
  • Do the library's floors feel solid?
  • Do the floor treatments contribute to the appearance of a well-maintained building?
  • Are rugs securely fastened down?

Facilities Policy and Maintenance Plan

Policy

Libraries should have and keep current a policy about building maintenance. A list of questions that must be addressed in developing this policy is provided in Appendix A of *Creating Policies for Results*, a companion volume in the *Planning for Results* series.[1] Preventive maintenance can prevent costly and inconvenient facility breakdowns. This is accomplished by scheduled inspections conducted at regular intervals and by the systematic scheduling of cleaning, lubrication, repair, and replacement of parts of building systems. Cost-effectiveness is the justification for maintaining a preventive maintenance schedule. The maintenance staff or someone in library administration will want to keep accurate records of maintenance tasks so the schedule reflects realistic needs for the systems in your building. It is also helpful to keep an up-to-date list of those who regularly service the systems in your library like the plumber, electrician, those who maintain the HVAC, elevators, and snow removal (depending on where you are in the country). A single list of names, numbers, and last maintenance task and date will serve the facilities coordinator well as a handy reference.

Maintenance Plan

A maintenance plan should describe the maintenance duties of staff on all levels and will contain general guidelines or standards. The purpose of the maintenance plan is to clearly lay out what is expected, how frequently, and by whom. Staff members responsible for programming may not be expected to vacuum their rooms after use, but if food or glue land on the carpet they may be expected to clean it up as soon as possible. This role clarification can increase the life of the carpet by preventing food or debris from being ground in and becoming more difficult to clean.

Most libraries don't have an abundance of maintenance time available to them, so it is wise to establish a list of prioritized maintenance tasks to assist the maintenance crew in setting priorities and moving through these weekly, monthly, and annual inspections. The following table is an example of a sample preventive maintenance schedule. All staff should be aware of the basic schedule the maintenance staff follows. Then they can alert the maintenance workers if their programming interferes with that regular schedule, or if there is a problem that may need addressing before the next scheduled round of maintenance. It is also important that permissions and notifications for special events like shampooing all the rugs are clearly defined to ensure that maintenance events don't conflict with major library events for patrons. If programmers have planned a library open house for National Library Week, that will not be the ideal weekend to shampoo rugs. The maintenance staff may be unaware of National Library Week when they schedule the work.

Sample Preventive Maintenance Schedule

	Responsibility	Priority
Weekly		
Emergency generator	Maintenance	Top priority
Septic pumps	Maintenance	High priority
Heating/hot water	Maintenance	Top priority
Program room kitchen	Maintenance	High priority
Staff room kitchen	Maintenance	Low priority
Alarm system	Security	High priority
Electrical outlets	Maintenance	High priority
Monthly		
Emergency lights	Security	Top priority
Fire extinguishers	Maintenance	High priority
January		
Elevator inspection	State inspector	Top priority
February		
Fire alarms	Outside vendor	Top priority
March		
Air-handling units	HVAC provider	High priority
Parking lot line painting	Maintenance	Low priority
April		
Boiler inspection	HVAC provider	High priority
Air conditioner	HVAC provider	High priority
May	Security	Top priority
Smoke detectors		
June		
Fire inspection	Fire department	Top priority

Housekeeping Checklist

Library Areas/Tasks	Daily	Done	Weekly	Done	Comments/ Supplies Needed
Restrooms					
Toilets/urinals cleaned, disinfected			▓		
Basins cleaned, disinfected			▓		
Changing tables cleaned, disinfected			▓		
Countertops cleaned, disinfected			▓		
Dispensers restocked			▓		
Mirrors cleaned			▓		
Floors wet mopped			▓		
Walls and partitions cleaned	▓		▓		
Floors					
Carpeting vacuumed			▓		
Entryway, wet mopped			▓		
Mechanical Rooms					
Floors swept	▓				
Floors damp mopped	▓				
General Building					
Wastebaskets emptied			▓		
Furniture dusted	▓				
Windowsills dusted	▓				
Drinking fountains cleaned		▓			
Front door glass cleaned		▓			
Elevators cleaned	▓				

Housekeeping expectations should also be clear, whether they are done by maintenance staff or others. The previous table demonstrates a clear way to present expectations regarding frequency and standards for cleaning. Such a checklist may be helpful in communicating between shifts which tasks are done and what still needs to be done.

Assessing ADA Compliance

Public libraries have a commitment to serve all parts of the population in their communities. The combination of the aging population in most communities and the passage of the 1990 Americans with Disabilities Act has forced libraries to become much more aware of the access to their buildings.

Note

1. Sandra Nelson and June Garcia, *Creating Policies for Results: From Chaos to Clarity* (Chicago: American Library Association, 2003), 143.

About the Author

Cheryl Bryan authored *Managing Facilities for Results* and teaches PLA's Facilities Management for CPLA certification class. Her strength is helping libraries respond to the needs of their communities and become more user-centered through long-range planning, customer service training, space-needs analysis, and a full range of staff and trustee development approaches. Cheryl brings over thirty-five years of experience working in and with libraries to her consulting. She has provided consultation and facilitation to more than a hundred libraries in long-range planning, change implementation strategies, space utilization evaluation, and building programs.

Part V

Ideas and Tips for Maintaining Open Access for All

As a library director or manager, you know that thorny intellectual freedom and rights of access issues can pop up at anytime. These short entries explore various facets of this topic and will provide you with some background information on related topics, possibly some new insights, and lots to think about. In "The Importance of Intellectual Freedom Training" from the PLA publication *Defending Access with Confidence: A Practical Workshop on Intellectual Freedom* by Catherine Lord, Lord describes, in a short essay, how training staff members allows them to support and understand the library's intellectual freedom policies, which translates to skillful handling of any issues that might arise. In the *Public Libraries* article "Intellectual Freedom in Belief and in Practice," authors Michael Harkovitch, Amanda Hirst, and Jenifer Loomis explore the differences between librarians' personal convictions and the professional code of ethics concerning intellectual freedom. Finally, James Kelly examines three significant legal cases where patrons were evicted due to appearance or hygiene and focuses on how policies should be constructed and enforced in order to avoid litigation.

Chapter 21

The Importance of Intellectual Freedom Training

Catherine Lord

If we don't believe in freedom of expression for people we despise, we don't believe in it at all.

—*Noam Chomsky*

Public libraries, a mainstay of American democracy, have a mandate to provide the people they serve with free access to information and ideas. This unfettered access, which the library community calls intellectual freedom, is not something librarians dreamed up to add drama and controversy to an otherwise inconspicuous profession. Judicial precedence tells us that as a public forum, libraries have an obligation to ensure the rights to free speech and its corollary, free access, are protected. Free access to ideas and information is as fundamentally important to democracy as wings are to flight. Without the ability to freely access and explore ideas and information, our capacity to choose our electorate, govern ourselves, or speak freely is compromised.

When I was in my mid-thirties, I made a not-so-drastic career switch from private librarian to public librarian. I had worked for almost eight years in private law firm libraries, and before that in newspaper and medical libraries. Working for the King County Library System felt like a homecoming in more ways than one. My first job, at age sixteen, had been as a page in a public library, and so I was returning to the public library environment in that sense. I also felt that I was returning to my own values. While I had enjoyed my work in private libraries, I had never felt that my work was contributing to my own value system until I became a public librarian. People who work in public libraries have the privilege of knowing that they are contributing to their communities and making big and small differences in the lives of the people they serve every day.

I joined the King County Library System during a prosperous time, just two years after the county had passed a major bond measure to build several new libraries and renovate others throughout the large county that surrounds the city of Seattle. My first three weeks on the job involved unpacking and shelving brand-new books, CDs, videos, and magazines in the newly built Federal Way Regional Library. All of us on the library staff were like kids in a candy store, giddy at the sight and feel of the shiny, pristine book covers and the fresh smell of new books. When the library finally opened its doors to the public it took no time for circulation rates to soar. The reference desk immediately had nonstop traffic, and except for a few individuals who complained that taxpayer money had been spent on art and all this wasted space (i.e. high ceilings), most people were thrilled with their new library.

The second day after the library opened, I received a phone call at the reference desk from a woman who had an edge to her voice. "Is it true that you have *Playboy* within reach of small children?" she asked me.

Trained only as a reference librarian, and not as a defender of intellectual freedom, I responded lamely with, "How small of a child?"

"Five years old."

I put her on hold, assessed the height of the magazine rack holding *Playboy,* and returned to provide the answer : "Unless the child is very small, I would say that—yes, it is within reach. Is there anything else I can help you with?" Without acknowledging the concern I heard in her voice or offering her an opportunity to fully express that concern or to speak to our manager, I allowed her to hang up and then I turned to help a customer waiting in line.

Two weeks later, when the library held its grand opening ceremony with refreshments, music, and a magician, library visitors had to cross a picket line of outraged citizens to join the festivities. Television and radio stations had picked up the story and suddenly there was a rash of parents who attested that their innocent children had received *Playboy* in the mail from the King County Library System without ever having placed such a request. (Patrons were then able to receive their holds through the mail.) It felt as if people thought it was part of the library mission to expose children to soft porn and that the library had purchased *Playboy* specifically for five-year-olds.

I was not the only staff member who received a complaint that day at Federal Way Regional Library. Other staff members received similar complaints there and at other libraries in the system. It is possible that it had become an issue in other parts of the library system before Federal Way Regional Library ever opened its doors. But I have always wondered if events would have played out differently had I responded to that phone call in a different way—if instead of skirting the issue that was raised on the phone, I had directly and courteously addressed it. Would the outcome have been different if I had said, "Yes, it is true and it sounds like you have a genuine concern for your child. I know our manager is going to want to hear what is on your mind. May I have him call you?"

Fortunately, the Federal Way Regional Library manager had a gracious demeanor and he was able to explain why the library carried this popular magazine and did not keep *Playboy* or other similar items in the collection out of public reach. While not everyone agreed with or understood the reasons, no one could deny that the library manager listened to people's concerns and that it mattered to him how they felt about the library.

Public library staff may think of censors as "outsiders"—nameless, harshly judgmental people, unconnected or disconnected with libraries—who would restrict access to materials that represent only their own narrow range of perspectives. Library staff might imagine that these people, if given half the chance, would pull books from shelves or refuse their purchase, tear down displays, or limit who may use meeting rooms and what types of programs the library may offer. But, this is not what censorship generally looks like. The organizer for the picket line at Federal Way Regional Library did not object to the library carrying *Playboy*. She wanted the magazine kept out of public reach behind the circulation desk and she did not understand why anyone would object to this. It is highly unlikely that this person would have labeled herself a censor. And in the end, she was not a censor because her proposal to restrict access to *Playboy* by keeping it behind the circulation desk was not passed by the library board. After some contentious discussion, the board voted against keeping *Playboy* behind the circulation desk because to do so would involve placing a barrier to access based on content of the item, which is clearly a form of censorship.

When we who work in libraries think about who is truly in the best position to censor materials, we have to recognize who is closest to the process of selection, display, circulation, and collection maintenance—that is, library employees. This is not to say that library employees consciously censor collections or limit access to programs and services. But unless libraries ensure that staff members act in accordance with intellectual freedom policies and have a clear understanding of the ethical guidance provided in the Library Bill of Rights, then libraries are at risk of an insidious kind of censorship. If there truly is something in every library to offend everyone, the temptation is certainly there for staff who have no guidance in the ethics of intellectual freedom to censor collections or limit access to programs and services. Perhaps more at risk, however, are materials or programs with controversial viewpoints, not only because of staff perspectives but because of the staff members' fear of what will happen when the public associates a controversial book, display, or program with the public library. How easy and convenient it would be for a library staff member to send a copy of a book that has been challenged in a neighboring library district to be weeded, based on condition, before its time. How simple it would be to deny display space to a controversial organization, explaining that the space has already been booked, and then follow up with a phone invitation to another less controversial organization for that display space. How tempting it must have been for the library board to eliminate their problem by directing staff to keep *Playboy* behind the desk, where it could no longer cause such a stir in the community.

People who are not connected with public libraries—those who do not work in them or serve on their Friends groups or board—have no reason to have heard of the Library Bill of Rights or the Children's Internet Protection Act. Or before that the Communications Decency Act, or any other issue that affects free access in libraries. And they have every reason to question what they have no reason to understand: why the library buys books that some people consider inappropriate, why libraries cannot limit children to checking out only G-rated videos, or why libraries fought mandated filtering all the way to the Supreme Court. These outsiders have no reason to understand the meaning of intellectual freedom in libraries, but people who do work in libraries or serve on their boards have every reason to understand all of it. People who work for libraries need to understand what intellectual freedom means, how it has evolved, and how it impacts library policies, services, and collections. This understanding is necessary so that staff can support policies and provide access in a fair and consistent way and help others—those outsiders who question policies, services, or collections— understand what fair, free, and equitable access means in American public libraries. If library staff do not proactively ensure and defend that access, who will?

The downside of intellectual freedom is that public libraries will have books in their collections or sites accessed on their computers that some or even a majority of people will find objectionable. It is easy to talk about providing access to information that is popular. Nobody needs training on how to do that. Difficulties arise when staff are called upon to defend access to items that are less popular—a task most public library staff hardly relish. It is a particular challenge for staff who cannot distinguish between defending access and defending the content of works. It may help to explain to these staff members another difference—the difference between unpopular and illegal. It is not a library employee's position to determine whether speech is protected or not.

Training that allows staff to understand and support intellectual freedom policies and the reasons for these policies is important even in times of tight budgets, when libraries seeking ways to cut corners may be tempted to put training on the back burner. Challenges to materials in libraries can be costly in staff and administrative time spent handling and reviewing challenges. When challenges are not handled skillfully (and sometimes even when they are), they can cost libraries public support and even legal fees. Libraries need staff members who not only understand intellectual freedom and its importance in American libraries, but who will do everything in their power to satisfy unhappy customers. When faced with a challenge, the ideal staff member listens to patron concerns without becoming defensive and finds ways to reassure or help patrons while still upholding the library's commitment to access. That kind of adeptness with customers does not happen in a vacuum; it is only through the careful selection of employees who have such an aptitude and appropriate training that staff will effectively manage challenges.

About the Author

Catherine Lord has been teaching and training on intellectual freedom in public libraries and at state and national conferences for the past ten years. She is a managing librarian with the King County (Washington) Library System, and she serves as a guest lecturer at the University of Washington I-School, teaching intellectual freedom to librarians entering into the field.

Chapter 22

Intellectual Freedom in Belief and in Practice

Michael Harkovitch, Amanda Hirst, and Jenifer Loomis

This study explores the differences between librarians' personal convictions and the professional code of ethics concerning intellectual freedom in the context of Internet pornography. A survey of librarians at Seattle Public Library finds that such a difference does exist and explores how the respondents attempt to resolve conflicts between the profession's guiding principles (as well as their particular library's mission and policies) and their own personal feelings.

While some librarians continually struggle with this issue, their attempts to reconcile the conflicts, or views about whether satisfactory reconciliation is possible, are valuable data for understanding the impact of these issues.

Believing in intellectual freedom is easy; practicing it is not. Since libraries began providing Internet access, using it as a means to view pornographic material in public libraries has been a center of controversy, eliciting the outrage of everyone from average citizens to United States congressmen. Often library patrons who innocently glance over the shoulder of someone who is surfing the Web inadvertently expose themselves to materials they find offensive. Shocked by what they have seen, patrons will commonly complain to a librarian, their neighbor, their elected officials, or all of the above.

Traditionally, the librarian's role is to champion the cause of intellectual freedom, especially with respect to controversial material. A central but understated function of libraries is maintaining an environment where all people can hold and express divergent views. Like other professional fields, librarianship has a set of ethical principles that guide its mission. Principle II of the American Library Association (ALA) Code of Ethics states, "We uphold the principles of intellectual freedom and resist all efforts to censor library resources."[1]

In practice, upholding the tenets of intellectual freedom can be challenging, though. Librarians, throughout the tumult of complaints from irate patrons and pressures from their professional organization must remain objective and respect all points of view. Suppose that the librarian, who so passionately defends library and ALA policies to patrons, personally disagrees with both. When human beings are required to go against their personal beliefs, and perhaps their instincts, conflicts arise.

In this study, we explore the differences between librarians' personal convictions and the professional code of ethics concerning intellectual freedom in the context of Internet pornography. More specifically, we investigate how great those differences are and how librarians in our study feel about them. We then ask what librarians as individuals do to reconcile defending access to material that they might personally oppose.

One hundred forty-three librarians in the Seattle Public Library (SPL) system were invited to participate in an online survey pertaining to these issues. An overwhelming majority of the 59 respondents indicated that they identify with professional ethics of upholding the principles of intellectual freedom. However, the study found that 42 out of 59 of the librarians (71%) have at some time found themselves defending access to Internet pornography in the library even though they personally find pornography offensive. Relatively few respondents reported they had developed strategies for dealing with this conflict, and the majority indicated that training or other assistance in explaining the library's Internet use policy and in dealing with ethical challenges in general would be helpful.

The goals of this research project were twofold. The first goal was to establish the degree to which a difference exists between personal views and the professional code of ethics among librarians in the SPL system regarding intellectual freedom as it pertains to pornography on the Internet. The second goal was to describe how the librarians in our sample reconcile defending access to material that they might personally oppose. To guide our study, we defined several key concepts, as shown in the sidebar in the next section.

This study aims to gain insight into how a sample of librarians attempts to resolve conflicts between their professional code of ethics (as well as the mission and policies of the institution they work for) and their personal convictions regarding access to pornography via the Internet in public libraries. We recognize that some librarians continually struggle with this and may not have reached a state that could be termed reconciliation; nevertheless, their attempts to do so, or views about whether or not it is possible to satisfactorily reconcile such conflicts, are useful data. Such information is equally valuable as seeing how a librarian *has* achieved reconciliation.

Literature Review
The library and information science literature, while vast in scope, contains few qualitative studies of librarians' feelings on the ethical challenges they face in their work. Quite a bit has been written on the subject of professional ethics in librarianship and ethical challenges librarians face, but it is framed differently

than this research study. *Ethical Challenges in Librarianship* by Robert Hauptman addresses both pornography and the Internet individually, but not together, and the impact of these issues on librarians is not addressed.[2] In *Information Ethics for Librarians*, edited by Mark Alfino and Linda Pierce, the concept of Internet pornography is referenced once, only in the notes of the article.[3] The books *Ethics and the Librarian* by F. W. Lancaster and *Ethical Dilemmas in Libraries* by Herbert S. White, both of which were published in the early 1990s, have no mention of the specific ethical challenges librarians face when confronted with issues and when their professional code of ethics is at odds with their own beliefs regarding library patrons accessing pornography via the

Definitions of Key Concepts

Pornography

Definitions of the term *pornography* differ significantly from dictionary to dictionary, but most individuals recognize pornography when they see it. The researchers recognize that the definition of pornography will vary with each respondent. Therefore, we did not provide a definition to the study participants, electing instead to allow them to apply their personal definitions while formulating their responses.

Intellectual Freedom

Within the library profession, ALA provides the primary leadership for defending intellectual freedom. Because its materials on the subject are commonly used and referred to by library professionals, we have used ALA's definition: "Intellectual freedom is the right of every individual to both seek and receive information from all points of view without restriction. It provides for free access to all expressions of ideas through which any and all sides of a question, cause, or movement may be explored. Intellectual freedom encompasses the freedom to hold, receive, and disseminate ideas."[a]

Professional Code of Ethics

Librarians' professional ethics have been embodied in the ALA Code of Ethics, supplemented by the missions and policies of individual libraries employing it, such as the SPL Mission Statement.[b] In our questionnaire, we specifically focused on the code's portions related to intellectual freedom, asking respondents whether they agreed with one sentence in particular: "We uphold the principles of intellectual freedom and resist all efforts to censor library resources."[c] A similar question specific to SPL policy examined the librarians' agreement with a portion of the library's "Public Use of the Internet" policy, which, by extension, also represents the professional code of ethics.[d]

Defense of Access

In libraries whose mission is to provide free and open access to information of all types, staff members must work to support that mission. This may include situations in which library policy must be explained, thus verbally defended, perhaps to people who are critical of that policy. In a broader sense, to "defend access" also

(continued)

parallels phrases such as "ensure access" and "defend intellectual freedom" (the latter two phrases are used in the SPL Mission Statement).[e] Both senses of the phrase *defense of access* apply to this study.

Personal and Professional Convictions

The *personal*, as opposed to the *professional*, aspect of librarians' convictions also merits definition. Personal convictions arise from values held by a person as a private individual. An individual's personal values and opinions may or may not be distinct from his or her professional values and opinions (as influenced or defined by professional associations and employers). The ALA Code of Ethics acknowledges the potential for contrasts or conflicts between librarians' personal and professional selves: "We distinguish between our personal convictions and professional duties and do not allow our personal beliefs to interfere with fair representation of the aims of our institutions or the provision of access to their information resources."

Notes

a. American Library Association, "Intellectual Freedom and Censorship Q & A." Accessed June 15, 2009, www.ala.org/Template.cfm?Section=basics&Template=/ContentManagement/ContentDisplay.cfm&ContentID=60610.

b. Seattle Public Library, "Seattle Public Library Mission Statement." Accessed June 15, 2009, www.spl.org/default.asp?pageID=about_mission.

c. American Library Association, "Code of Ethics of the American Library Association," Adopted June 28, 1995. Accessed June 15, 2009, www.ala.org/ala/aboutala/offices/oif/statementspols/codeofethics/codeethics.cfm.

d. Seattle Public Library, "Public Use of the Internet," Seattle Public Library Policies. Accessed June 15, 2009, www.spl.org/policies/internetusepolicy.html.

e. Seattle Public Library, "Seattle Public Library Mission Statement."

f. American Library Association, "Code of Ethics."

Internet.[4] An essay about the trends of library associations and ethics in the United States written by Wallace Koehler in the book *The Ethics of Librarianship: An International Survey* mentions evolving technology as one of several ethical challenges librarians have faced in recent years, but it does not elaborate further.[5]

Anecdotal evidence indicates that librarians who deal with the issue of Internet pornography in the library are faced with many challenges. For example, librarians in Minnesota filed a complaint with the U.S. Equal Employment Opportunity Commission (EEOC) against the Minneapolis Public Library System in May 2000 for experiencing third-party sexual harassment as a result of patrons accessing online pornography. Librarians were inadvertently exposed to pornography while enforcing required time limits on Internet computers. The patrons viewing this material were also verbally harassing library staff.[6] Shortly thereafter, the Minneapolis Public Library apologized publicly, expressing regret to "anyone who saw images on library computers that they found offensive."[7] As of late March 2003, the library is still suffering from the impact of this unresolved complaint.[8]

ALA, whose conferences in recent years have discussed issues related to pornography on the Internet, provides the "Libraries and the Internet Toolkit" to "assist librarians in managing the Internet and educating their public about how to use it effectively."[9] This document is aimed at librarians as professionals and, as such, their dealings with the public. It does not, however, make recommendations on how libraries as employers can ease the emotional toll of defending policies that staff might personally disagree with.

Method

This research study was conducted as part of an assignment for a research methods course at the University of Washington's Information School. The population surveyed consists of librarians working for SPL, located in Seattle, Washington, which serves a diverse urban population. In addition to a central library, SPL has twenty-two branch libraries throughout the city. At the time of our study, SPL employed 143 librarians, who have varying levels of contact with the public and with patrons who use the Internet. Both filtered and unfiltered access to the Internet are offered to patrons, while all staff computers are unfiltered. SPL's "Public Use of the Internet" policy states, "The Library makes this service available as part of its mission to provide free and open access to information of all types in a wide range of formats for library users of all ages and backgrounds . . . some sources may be offensive, disturbing, and/or illegal."[10]

With the permission and cooperation of SPL and its human resources department, the librarians were invited via the city's e-mail system to voluntarily and anonymously participate in a twenty-six-question online survey. Potential participants were informed first by Human Resources Director Lin Schnell, and then by the researchers, that data would be collected and analyzed independently of SPL, but that results would be shared with the library and possibly published at a later date. The survey was open for ten days, from May 16 to May 26, 2002.

The questions solicited responses through the use of check boxes, radio buttons, and text boxes. In order to attempt to expose the tension between the professional and personal views, we designed the survey questions to ask essentially the same thing in a variety of ways. The questions also provided the context for eliciting qualitative responses.

The survey aimed to measure several variables: the degree to which librarians identify with the professional code of ethics on both a professional and personal level; the degree to which librarians regard pornography accessed on library Internet terminals as an issue of particular significance; and the degree to which librarians feel prepared to face the challenges of enforcing a policy with which they may personally disagree. These types of questions were answered in degrees (e.g., "strongly agree," "agree," "no opinion," "somewhat disagree," "strongly disagree"). Participants were also asked a variety of questions regarding how they reconcile possible differences between their own values and those of the profession. Finally, the survey explored the strategies librarians use to deal with conflicts between personal and professional views.

Findings

The sample obtained consists of 59 respondents, roughly 41% of the 143 librarians. The librarians invited to participate consisted of three basic groups, each comprising roughly one-third of the total: 51 adult services librarians; 48 juvenile and young adult librarians; and 44 managers. Because the survey was anonymous, the sample may be more or less representative on a few counts. The differing positions and job functions may have influenced responses and participation, as might age and gender. Also, experiences and community standards particular to neighborhoods and their branches might have an influence. A final work factor influencing participation may have been personal acquaintances with the individual researchers, the information school, or the course instructor. Aside from these factors, standard limitations of questionnaire research—particularly self-selection—also apply.

Two survey questions provide further description of the sample by asking the amount of time spent at a service desk and the amount of time spent assisting patrons with Internet-related questions. The majority of respondents (62%) spent at least 4 hours per workday at a service desk. All but 19% indicated spending at least "some" of their time on Internet-related questions, with 29% spending at least half of their time doing so. (Note: results are rounded to the nearest integer percent in the narrative discussion of data provided here.)

The following sections present results from the survey questions. Categorical data is discussed first, followed by the qualitative data from the four questions that elicited written comments.

Summary of Quantitative Findings

The first two survey questions explored the respondents' degree of agreement with two statements from the ALA Code of Ethics and "Intellectual Freedom and Censorship Q & A," respectively: "We uphold the principles of intellectual freedom and resist all efforts to censor library materials" and "It is the right of every individual to both seek and receive information from all points of view without restriction."[11] A third question did the same for a statement from SPL's "Public Use of the Internet" policy: "[t]he library should 'provide free and open access to information of all types in a wide range of formats.'"[12] In all three cases, the majority of respondents indicated agreement. Responses to the first two questions were all either "somewhat agree" or "strongly agree," with more than 80% of the sample strongly agreeing to both. Responses to the SPL policy question were similar (76% strongly agreed), but 3 out of the 59 respondents indicated some degree of disagreement. Figure 22-1 shows the combined results. Personal

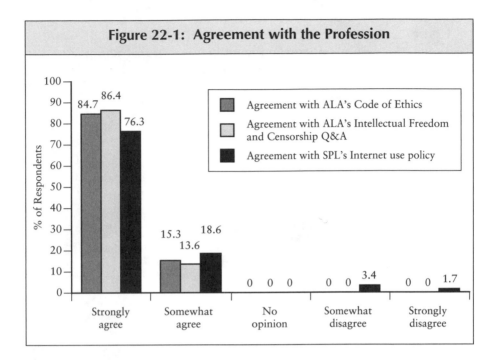

Figure 22-1: Agreement with the Profession

feelings regarding the offensiveness of pornography were mixed. The majority of respondents (60%) indicated that they generally find the concept of pornography "somewhat offensive," and equal numbers (20% each) find it "extremely" and "not at all" offensive.

As another approach to assessing personal views, one question asked whether librarians found it "difficult or easy to defend SPL's Internet use policy." Responses were mixed: 3% "extremely difficult," 31% "somewhat difficult," 29% "neither difficult nor easy," 22% "somewhat easy," and 15% "extremely easy." In sum, one-third (34%) of the respondents found defending the policy to be in some degree difficult, and slightly more than one-third (37%) found it to be in some degree easy.

To aid in assessing librarians' feelings about patrons' access to Internet pornography, one question asked respondents to distinguish between patrons having "unrestricted access to the Internet, including sites containing controversial and divergent ideas," as opposed to pornographic sites. A second question examined whether they felt differently about adult patrons and minors. For adults, all respondents indicated agreement to providing unrestricted Internet access, with 88% strongly agreeing. The respondents generally felt that minors should have this same access: 68% strongly agreed, 20% agreed somewhat, 8% disagreed somewhat, and 3% (which represents 2 respondents out of the total 59) strongly disagreed.

Two more questions explored librarians' personal views by asking about possible methods of limiting library Internet access to exclude pornographic

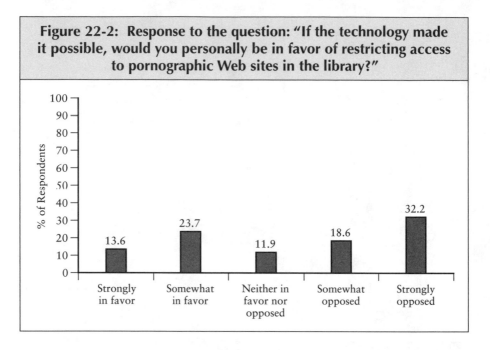

Figure 22-2: Response to the question: "If the technology made it possible, would you personally be in favor of restricting access to pornographic Web sites in the library?"

material. We first asked rhetorically, "If the technology made it possible, would you personally be in favor of restricting access to pornographic Web sites in the library?" Roughly half of respondents were opposed, with 37% in favor. Overall, however, responses were mixed: 14% strongly in favor, 24% somewhat in favor, 12% neither in favor nor opposed, 19% somewhat opposed, and 32% strongly opposed (see Figure 22-2).

The second question asked respondents if they agreed or disagreed "that library policy should prohibit access to pornographic content on the Internet." Responses leaned more heavily toward disagreement (70%); 51% strongly disagreed. The remaining 30% was split evenly between agreement and no opinion, although only 5% strongly agreed.

Following a series of questions designed to determine whether differences exist between professional protocols and personal feelings of the respondents, two questions asked point-blank about personal perceptions. The first asked, "Do you ever find yourself defending access to Internet pornography in the library even though you find pornography personally offensive?" Seventy-one percent answered "yes" (see Figure 22-3). On the other hand, only 37% felt that their "personal views about pornography contradict professional views expressed by ALA regarding patrons accessing pornography in the library" (see Figure 22-4). A lesser number, 25%, indicated having at some time found themselves "trying to reconcile this contradiction."

The final survey questions were geared toward making further recommendations to the library system. In regards to SPL developing training or an informational component around these issues, the highest-ranking responses showed the

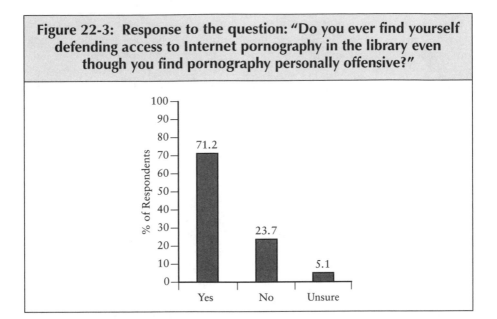

Figure 22-3: Response to the question: "Do you ever find yourself defending access to Internet pornography in the library even though you find pornography personally offensive?"

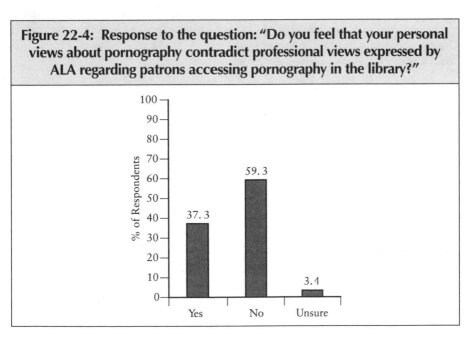

Figure 22-4: Response to the question: "Do you feel that your personal views about pornography contradict professional views expressed by ALA regarding patrons accessing pornography in the library?"

following preferences: 46% of respondents favored an informal seminar; 41% a formal training program; and 14% a written policy (for these final questions, respondents could choose all options that applied). When asked specifically about their interest in attending a formal training program addressing these issues,

56% responded yes, 29% responded no, and 14% were unsure. Furthermore, when asked "What specific issues within the context of patrons accessing pornography on the Internet would you like to see in a program or instrument?" the most popular responses were: "how to effectively explain the current Internet use policy" (71%); "dealing with ethical challenges" (59%); "dealing with difficult patrons" (59%); and "stress management" (22%).

Summary of Qualitative Findings

To explore ways of dealing with contradictions between personal views and the professional code of ethics, one question asked respondents if they had developed any strategies for doing so. While the majority of responses were "no" or "does not apply" (64%), 13 people (22%) answered "yes." Another question asked them to describe these strategies, and 17 librarians responded.

Responses for the most part discussed philosophical reconciliation and focusing on how to think about the issues relating to Internet pornography in the library. Several responses mentioned practical or active techniques beyond internal thought processes. The other dominant theme in the responses was concern over civil liberties and a desire to prevent censorship, including the importance of putting aside or not stating personal opinions in the professional role. Some respondents felt that differences between their personal views and professional obligations did not pose difficulties and that separating the personal from the professional was not a problem for them. Highlights from the responses are provided below.

Examples of philosophical reconciliation included statements regarding the distinction between professional identity and personal identity. One librarian wrote, "What I do is not who I am. It's okay that my professional obligations sometimes contradict my personal beliefs. If it gets to a point that I cannot accept that compartmentalization, then perhaps I need to consider a different type of work. . . ." Other respondents took a "lesser of all evils" approach to reconciliation: "I reconcile the contradiction by knowing ALA's policy is the least distasteful choice between censorship or porn."

Many librarians wrote passionately about the distinction between intellectual freedom as an ideal and how it plays out in libraries. One respondent articulated this distinction by stating, "I don't think the library will ever be praised for allowing porn, but if we are lucky, [we will be] praised for not allowing censorship. We can say we're defending intellectual freedom, but any observer can see that no intellect is involved in viewing porn. No great thought being advanced. For me, the gulf between this reality and the lofty ideals that allow it will never be filled, only tenuously bridged."

Other participants had strong responses against patrons viewing pornography in the library. The respondents, focusing on the library as a public space, articulated the inappropriateness of viewing pornography therein: "The issue for me is that this is a public place. It is not appropriate to view porn in a public place. I don't care what someone does in a private space. [The library] is not private."

Librarians who viewed themselves as defenders of intellectual freedom often stated that they felt it was their duty to defend access against those who seek to limit it. One respondent wrote, "As a librarian, I feel a professional obligation to be a fool for intellectual freedom, to be willing to be just as radical in promoting people's right to read and view any area of human knowledge that strikes their fancy as some other members of society are radical in attempting to restrict those rights."

Other responses indicate that while respondents might dislike pornography being viewed in the library, they do not advocate limiting access institutionally. These respondents seem to be reconciled to the disagreement between the personal and professional code of ethics. One respondent wrote, "I see no contradiction between disliking something and still supporting an institution in its ability to let everyone make their own decisions about it. Basically, it's an 'I disagree with what you say, but I will defend to the death your right to say it' kind of thing." Other librarians mentioned having learned to promote the policy despite their disagreement with it.

One respondent noted an impact of Internet pornography on researching a question for a patron: "[T]he other day I was looking for a picture of a pregnant teen for a girl's report and just about all I could get was porn! Would have been nice to have a filter that would have known the difference between porn and stuff about teen mothers!"

When asked if they had any practical, active strategies for dealing with the contradiction between their professional code of ethics and their personal feelings, respondents stated a variety of techniques. Responses included commiserating with colleagues and reviewing ALA and SPL documents.

Three questions gave the respondents an opportunity to further articulate their needs for a training program or instrument. Within the context of these questions, respondents also elaborated their needs from SPL as an employer and their view of ALA as a professional organization that represents them.

Respondents questioned ALA's approach and the effectiveness of any training programs. Many felt that training programs just repeat policy rather than offer helpful solutions to staff. One librarian highlighted the disconnect between ALA and people working in libraries, writing, "The people running ALA Intellectual Freedom Committees operate in a fog. They do not work in public libraries, and they do not have a clue about the types of patrons we deal with." The same respondent, however, recognized the need for some type of training program: "Public service staff suffers greatly from having to interact with demanding and threatening patrons. Not enough has been done to help us deal with these issues." Others requested a training program to teach them how to deal with difficult patrons, such as confronting patrons who knowingly violate SPL's current Internet use policy. Some respondents were concerned that their careers might be jeopardized if they voiced disagreement with ALA or SPL policies when deciding what type of training program they would be in favor of. A librarian responded, "I don't think it would be 'safe' for me to discuss my disagreement with SPL's and ALA's policies. Given this fact, I would rather view a written policy."

Analysis and Conclusions

Results from the survey demonstrate that the majority of respondents, as professionals, identify strongly with intellectual freedom principles as stated by ALA and SPL. However, when asked outright if their personal views conflict with their professional views, 37% of respondents agreed that a conflict exists. Further findings show that while 71% of respondents have had occasion to defend access to pornography, 79% of them personally find pornography to be generally offensive to some degree. This demonstrates that for the majority of respondents, a tension (or at least a difference of some kind) exists, in the context of patron access to Internet pornography in the library, between their personal opinions and the profession's mantra.

Despite the high degree of identification with the professional code of ethics and a positive attitude toward providing unrestricted Internet access to controversial and divergent forms of expression to patrons of all ages, more than a third of the respondents were personally in favor of limiting access to pornographic Web sites if technology were to make it possible. Therefore, it is clear that when pornography was introduced to the mix of "controversial and divergent forms of expression," respondents were more likely to support limited Web access.

Because of the small sample size and the narrowly defined population, generalizations for the entire library profession can only be speculative at this point. Further study involving other public library systems, and encompassing wider geographic samples, is recommended. Also, due to its exploratory nature, this study does not provide sufficient information for developing definitive solutions. Additional study using different research methods would be useful. Any research on this topic, however, may be difficult due to the sensitive nature of the subjects concerned: pornography, intellectual freedom, and conflict between employee and employer.

This study provides important food for thought. Librarians do make a distinction between their personal values and their professional identity. The study also underlines the fact that librarians are human and thus do not think and respond mechanically when carrying out the principles of intellectual freedom in practice, particularly when the subject is pornography. The comments of some respondents demonstrate the emotional toll that can arise from coping with this challenge. We feel that employers, in recognizing both the strengths and limitations of human beings, should pay close attention to the dilemmas facing their employees and should work to acknowledge and address those issues.

Notes

1. American Library Association, "Code of Ethics of the American Library Association," Adopted June 28, 1995. Accessed June 15, 2009, www.ala.org/ala/aboutala/offices/oif/statementspols/codeofethics/codeethics.cfm.
2. Robert Hauptman, *Ethical Challenges in Librarianship* (Phoenix, Ariz.: Oryx,1988).
3. Mark Alfino and Linda Pierce, eds., *Information Ethics for Librarians* (Jefferson, N.C.: McFarland, 1997).

4. F. W. Lancaster, ed., *Ethics and the Librarian* (Champaign, Ill.: Univ. of Illinois Pr., 1991); Herbert S. White, *Ethical Dilemmas in Libraries* (New York: G. K. Hall, 1992).
5. Wallace Koehler, "Trends of Library Associations and Ethics in the US," in *The Ethics of Librarianship: An International Survey*, Robert W. Vaagan, ed. (Munich, Germany: International Federation of Library Associations and Institutions, 2002), 325.
6. Wendy Adamson, "Sex in the City—What Happened at the Minneapolis Public Library," *NewBreed Librarian* 2, no. 2 (Apr. 2002). Accessed June 15, 2009, http://findarticles.com/p/articles/mi_qa3693/is_200209/ai_n9088077/?tag=content;col1.
7. Norman Oder, "Minneapolis PL Apologizes Publicly," *Library Journal* 125, no. 11 (June 15, 2000): 16.
8. American Libraries Online, "Twelve Staffers Sue Minneapolis PL over Hostile Workplace Environment," News for Mar. 31, 2003. Accessed June 15, 2009, at www.ala.org/ala/alonline/currentnews/newsarchive/2003/march2003/twelvestaffers.cfm.
9. American Library Association, "Libraries and the Internet Toolkit: Tips and Guidance for Managing and Communicating about the Internet," June 1, 2001 (updated Dec. 1, 2003): 2. Accessed June 15, 2009, www.ala.org/ala/aboutala/offices/oif/iftoolkits/litoolkit/default.cfm.
10. Seattle Public Library, "Public Use of the Internet."
11. American Library Association, "Code of Ethics"; American Library Association, "Intellectual Freedom and Censorship Q & A."
12. Seattle Public Library, "Public Use of the Internet."

About the Authors

Michael Harkovitch has worked in libraries all of his life. Following an eight-year stint as Library Assistant for Seattle Public Library, Michael attended the University of Washington Information School from 2001–2003. He currently works as Reference Librarian for the King County Library System, where he recently received his five-year service award.

Amanda Hirst became interested in librarianship during her first library job in Cincinnati, Ohio. From there she attended the University of Washington's Information School to obtain her MLIS degree, graduating in 2003. She has gone on to work at several nationally recognized library systems, including her current position as Teen and Reference Librarian with the King County Library System.

Jenifer Loomis is a children's librarian at the King County Library System in Washington State. She received her MLIS degree from the University of Washington.

Appendix A: The Survey

Question 1. As a librarian, to what extent do you agree with the following statement by the ALA in its Code of Ethics: "We uphold the principles of intellectual freedom and resist all efforts to censor library materials"?

__Strongly agree
__Somewhat agree
__Unsure or no opinion
__Somewhat disagree
__Strongly disagree

Question 2. As a librarian, to what extent do you agree with the following statement by the ALA on intellectual freedom: "It is the right of every individual to both seek and receive information from all points of view without restriction"?

__ Strongly agree
__ Somewhat agree
__ Unsure or no opinion
__ Somewhat disagree
__ Strongly disagree

Question 3. While working in the library, how often are you exposed to pornography on the Internet that has been accessed by a library patron?

__ At least once a day
__ 2 to 3 times a week
__ Once a week
__ 2 to 3 times a month
__ Once a month or less

Question 4. How often are you asked by patrons for computer related assistance while they are accessing pornography?

__ At least once a day
__ 2 to 3 times a week
__ Once a week
__ 2 to 3 times a month
__ Once a month or less

Question 5. How often are you asked by patrons for assistance in locating pornographic content on the Internet?

__ Never
__ 1 to 2 times a year
__ Once a month or less
__ 2 to 3 times a month
__ Once a week

Question 6. How often do you have to explain Seattle Public Library's Internet Use Policy to patrons who have observed someone viewing pornography on the Internet?

__ At least once a day
__ 2 to 3 times a week
__ Once a week
__ 2 to 3 times a month
__ Once a month or less

Question 7. Do you personally agree with the statement in Seattle Public Library's Internet Use Policy that the library should "provide free and open access to information of all types in a wide range of formats"?

___ Strongly agree
___ Somewhat agree
___ Unsure or no opinion
___ Somewhat disagree
___ Strongly disagree

Question 8. Do you personally find it difficult or easy to defend the Seattle Public Library's Internet Use Policy?

___ Extremely difficult
___ Somewhat difficult
___ Neither difficult nor easy
___ Somewhat easy
___ Extremely easy

Question 9. Apart from pornography, to what extent do you personally agree that all adult library patrons should have unrestricted access to the Internet, including sites containing controversial and divergent ideas?

___ Strongly agree
  Somewhat agree
___ Unsure or no opinion
___ Somewhat disagree
___ Strongly disagree

Question 10. Apart from pornography, to what extent do you personally agree that all library patrons under the age of 18 should have unrestricted access to the Internet, including sites containing controversial and divergent ideas?

___ Strongly agree
___ Somewhat agree
___ Unsure or no opinion
___ Somewhat disagree
___ Strongly disagree

Question 11. Almost all people are likely to be offended by certain instances of pornographic content. However, in general, to what extent do you personally find the concept of pornography offensive?

___ Extremely offensive
___ Somewhat offensive
___ Not at all offensive
___ No opinion

Question 12. If the technology made it possible, would you personally be in favor of restricting access to pornographic Web sites in the library?

___ Strongly in favor
___ Somewhat in favor
___ Neither in favor nor opposed
___ Somewhat opposed
___ Strongly opposed

Question 13. To what extent do you agree or disagree that library policy should prohibit access to pornographic content on the Internet?

__ Strongly agree
__ Somewhat agree
__ Unsure or no opinion
__ Somewhat disagree
__ Strongly disagree

Question 14. Do you ever find yourself defending access to Internet pornography in the library even though you find pornography personally offensive?

__ Yes
__ No
__ Unsure

Question 15. Do you feel that your personal views about pornography contradict professional views expressed by the ALA regarding patrons accessing pornography in the library?

__ Yes
__ No
__ Unsure

Question 16. Do you ever find yourself trying to reconcile this contradiction?

__ Yes
__ No
__ Unsure
__ Does not apply

Question 17. Have you developed any strategies for dealing with this?

__ Yes
__ No
__ Unsure
__ Does not apply

Question 18. If yes, please describe:

Question 19. If the library were to develop a program or instrument to help staff deal with the issues above, which would you find helpful? Select all that apply.

__ A formal training program
__ An informal seminar
__ A written policy
__ No opinion
__ Other

Question 20. If "other," please describe:

Question 21. Would you be interested in attending a formal training program addressing the issues discussed above?

__ Yes
__ No
__ Unsure

Question 22. Additional comments:

Question 23. What specific issues within the context of patrons accessing pornography
on the Internet would you like to see in such a program or instrument?

__ How to effectively explain the current Internet Use Policy
__ Dealing with ethical challenges
__ Stress management
__ Dealing with difficult patrons
__ Other

Question 24. If "other," please describe:

The following questions are *optional*:

Question 25. How much time do you spend per workday assisting the public at the service desk?

__ Less than 2 hours
__ 2 to 4 hours
__ 4 to 6 hours
__ More than 6 hours

Question 26. How much of your time at the service desk is spent assisting patrons with
Internet related questions?

__ Very little of my time
__ Some of my time
__ Half of my time
__ Most of my time

Appendix B: Seattle Public Library Policy

Subject: Public Use of the Internet

Seattle Public Library provides access to a broad range of information resources including those available through the Internet. The Library makes this service available as part
of its mission to provide free and open access to information of all types in a wide range
of formats for library users of all ages and backgrounds.

Choosing and Evaluating Sources

The Internet is a global electronic network of ideas, images, and commentary that may enhance resources already available in the Library. However, the Library cannot control the information available over the Internet and is not responsible for its content. Some sources provide information that is inaccurate, incomplete or dated; some sources may be offensive, disturbing, and/or illegal.

To assist our patrons in their searches, staff have identified on the Library's Selected Web Sites some links to selected information sources. Library staff review links regularly but, due to the ever-changing nature of the Internet, cannot guarantee that these links will remain valid. Similarly, the Library cannot be responsible for changes in the content of the sources to which it links, or the content of sources accessed through secondary links. As with printed information, users are encouraged to evaluate the validity of information found electronically. Library staff are available to provide assistance and to help identify appropriate sites. The Library also provides beginning, advanced, and subject-oriented classes in the use of the World Wide Web.

Access by Minors

The Library upholds the right of each individual to have access to constitutionally protected material. The Library also affirms the right and responsibility of parents and legal guardians to determine and monitor their own children's use of library materials and resources. To assist parents in their responsibility for their children's use of the Internet, the Library provides the following services:

- Specially designed Web pages for children and young adults, with links to age-appropriate Internet sites and to filtered search engines.
- Computers with commercial filtering software for public use in the children's area at each location in the Seattle Public Library system. This filtering software will block many specific sites that may be offensive to some users, but may not block all materials that may be offensive to all users. Parents should inform their children of materials they do not want them to use, and may wish to supervise their children's Internet sessions.

Rules Governing Use

In order to make the Internet available to as many people as possible and to ensure that it is used in a manner consistent with Library policies, the Library has adopted rules regarding Acceptable Use of Electronic Resources. All users are asked to respect the privacy of other users and not attempt to censor or comment upon what others are viewing. The Library's Rules of Conduct and pertinent state, federal and local laws apply to all Library users.

Policy Subject to Revision

The Seattle Public Library affirms its commitment to help patrons use the Internet effectively. The Library will continue to monitor changes and trends in Internet technology that could improve our ability to provide electronic access for library users, and will revise this policy as necessary.

Date Adopted: January 22, 2002

Supercedes Policy: Internet Use Policy adopted adopted December 14, 1999. *Source:* Seattle Public Library Web site: www.spl.org/default.asp?page10=about_policies_publicuseofinternet.

Chapter 23

Barefoot in Columbus: The Legacy of *Kreimer* and the Legality of Public Library Access Policies Concerning Appearance and Hygiene

James Kelly

Given the high cost of legal action and the growing litigiousness in American society, libraries of all types must be concerned about the possibility of a lawsuit. The American Library Association has published books on the subject, and library journal articles have discussed potential library liability at length.[1] Often, these discussions are related to professional malpractice, copyright and other intellectual property, and employment.[2] For public libraries, access to information and access to the library have become vital issues. For the last ten years, the case of *Kreimer v. Bureau of Police for the Town of Morristown* stood as a landmark case in the area of library access.[3] Richard Kreimer, now fifty-five years old, is suing the New Jersey transit system for ejecting him and other homeless people from train stations.[4] Kreimer, many librarians will recall, sued the Morristown public library and police department in 1992 for ejecting him from the library on at least five occasions. In federal district court, Kreimer prevailed.

The *Kreimer* case was overturned on appeal, but the issue of public libraries ejecting patrons on the basis of their appearance or hygiene remains, largely because of the use of these public facilities by the homeless. The San Luis Obispo County (Calif.) Library, for instance, has recently enacted a rule allowing library employees to ask malodorous patrons to leave.[5] Watchdog groups contend that these people largely have nowhere else to go and should be dealt with more compassionately. The library, however, says that people will only be asked to leave if they ruin the experience for others.[6]

This article analyzes three significant cases to examine the question of public library liability for alleged constitutional violations against patrons evicted due to their appearance or hygiene rather than for disruptive behavior. The analysis focuses on how policies should be constructed and enforced. Further, in cases where individual administrators and managers have been sued along with their libraries, the notion of qualified immunity is examined. Conclusions are reached regarding the significance of these cases and ways public libraries may be able to avoid liability and the cost of litigation entirely.

Kreimer v. Bureau of Police for Town of Morristown

While it has been discussed at length in the literature, the *Kreimer* case and its initial impact on the library profession warrant continued analysis. In 1989, the Morristown library board of trustees adopted a written policy that said that patrons not "reading, studying, or using library materials" may be asked to leave.[7] Further, the policy provided that patrons must respect the rights of, and not annoy, other patrons.[8] With regard to appearance, "patron dress and personal hygiene shall conform to the standard of community public places. This shall include the repair or cleanliness of garments."[9] Following discussion with an attorney from the American Civil Liberties Union, these policies were amended. Included in the amendments was a new provision that barred patrons from interfering with the use of the library by other patrons or the performance of library employees' duties.[10] *Kreimer* did not dispute the constitutionality of that provision.[11]

The revised language of the policy regarding appearance is significant:

> Patrons shall not be permitted to enter the building without a shirt or other covering of their upper bodies or without shoes or other footwear. Patrons whose bodily hygiene is so offensive as to constitute a nuisance to other persons shall be required to leave the building.[12]

Richard Kreimer, a homeless man, sued the public library in Morristown, New Jersey, for evicting him due to his appearance and body odor. District Judge Sarokin began his opinion with broad statements about fear and discrimination that can arise in exclusion: "The danger in excluding anyone from a public building because their appearance or hygiene is obnoxious to others is self-evident. The danger becomes insidious if the conditions complained of are borne of poverty."[13]

Sarokin goes on to idealize the public library: "The public library is one of our great symbols of democracy. It is a living embodiment of the First Amendment because it includes voices of dissent. It tolerates that which is offensive."[14] He cuts to the heart of the matter close to issues librarians have embraced: "Society has survived not banning books which it finds offensive from its libraries; it will survive not banning persons whom it likewise finds offensive from its libraries. The greatness of our country lies in tolerating speech with which we do not agree; that same toleration must extend to people, particularly where the cause of revulsion may be of our own making."[15]

Sarokin's prejudices come through before he renders any legal justification in the case. "If we wish to shield our eyes and noses from the homeless," he says, "we should revoke their condition, not their library cards."[16] He clearly sympathized with Kreimer, and found the library's policy, enacted specifically to evict Kreimer, abhorrent. His description of Kreimer as "a resident of Morristown" and "a homeless individual whose access to showers and laundry services is severely curtailed by his homeless status" implies that Kreimer is a victim of the library and society at large.[17]

The district court held that the policy violated Kreimer's constitutional rights, specifically his rights to freedom of speech, due process, and equal protection under the law.[18] First, it analyzed the First Amendment claim. The First Amendment applies because the freedom of speech and of the press includes the right to receive information. Thus, a policy "which conditions access to public reading materials" falls under the First Amendment.[19]

For First Amendment purposes, a public library is a designated public forum. Again, Sarokin seizes on this issue, which the library had already conceded, to proclaim that "a public library is not only a designated public forum, but also a 'quintessential,' 'traditional' public forum whose accessibility affects the bedrock of our democratic system."[20] The problem with the restriction here, according to the court, is that it does not serve the stated purpose and is overly broad. The stated purpose of the policy, according to its preamble, is to allow all patrons use of the library facilities to the greatest extent possible.[21] Citing U.S. Supreme Court precedent, the district court held restrictions of a public forum must only prohibit activity that "actually and materially interferes with the peaceful and orderly management of the public space."[22] The policy here, the court said, does not limit itself to actual disturbance.[23] Further, no alternative channels are left open for Kreimer under the policy.[24]

The district court's ruling stunned the library community. The *Kreimer* case seemed to disallow (or at least severely limit) public libraries from barring patrons who had not exhibited disturbing or disruptive behavior, but whose appearance or hygiene may have been disturbing to other patrons or library staff. Further, it seemed to indicate that, absent disturbing or disruptive behavior, the library could not eject someone even if the person was obviously not in the library to use library materials.

Sarokin's opinion, however, reflects some interesting ideas and distinctions. First, Sarokin portrayed the public library as more than just a traditional public forum. Thus, the standard he applied is different from that subsequently applied by the circuit court in the appeal and in other courts. Second, and perhaps more notably, is Sarokin's attributing to the library such a central role in democracy. Often the law is thought of as the application of disinterested logic and reason to societal problems. Here, it seems, Sarokin applied some personal beliefs to the opinion. Kreimer, a homeless man whose appearance and hygiene disturbed the library staff, garnered Sarokin's sympathy. The library admitted enacting this policy specifically with the aim of keeping Kreimer out.[25] Sarokin also seemed to feel the policy was a pretense: "the library patron policy at issue in this case does not limit itself to prohibitions of actual library disturbance."[26]

Following the ruling, the library appealed. Before the appeal was decided, however, the library settled with Kreimer for $230,000.[27] The appellate court decided the policy was a reasonable restriction that served a legitimate government interest.[28] The appellate court's opinion notes that, while Kreimer said he would read or sit quietly, the library claimed Kreimer would stare at patrons and talk loudly to himself and others.[29] No mention of Kreimer's alleged disruptive behavior was discussed in Sarokin's opinion. The Third Circuit found the rule regarding bodily hygiene valid; it served the government interest of having other patrons not interfered with and maintaining the library in a clean and attractive condition.[30] Further, patrons who are ejected are not barred from reentry if they comply with the rules.[31] None of the rules were held to be overbroad.

The appellate court's decision in favor of the library eased some concerns. In fact, the Third Circuit's decision in *Kreimer* has oft been cited for the notion that the First Amendment entails the right to receive information as well as speak it.[32] However, the case being settled out of court left a lot of questions unanswered. Also, the discrepancy regarding whether Kreimer's behavior or his appearance and hygiene were the cause of his ouster left the matter open.

There is no doubt that a library can eject a patron for disruptive behavior. Library policies must be able to serve their purpose, and that purpose is central to the ideals of democracy and free speech. While confirming this central purpose and the First Amendment implications of library policy, *Kreimer* seemed to raise more questions than it answered. Most importantly, can a library eject a patron solely on the basis of his appearance or body odor?

Armstrong v. District of Columbia Public Library

In 2001, the question appeared to be answered "yes," when another homeless patron sued a public library following his ejection due to his appearance and hygiene. The district court in the District of Columbia relied heavily on the decision of the Third Circuit in *Kreimer*.[33] However, it reached the opposite conclusion. The district court found that *Kreimer* applied two distinct standards for regulations concerning conduct and for those concerning hygiene.[34] A standard of "reasonableness" is applied when reviewing a regulation concerning conduct.[35] However, the hygiene regulation requires a "stricter, narrowly tailored" standard; otherwise, the First Amendment might be infringed on a whim or some other personal standard.[36]

The District of Columbia Public Library's policy allowed for warnings and, ultimately, eviction for "objectionable appearance."[37] In parentheses following this phrase, the policy listed examples, including "barefooted, bare-chested, body odor, filthy clothing, etc."[38] The district court held that, despite these examples, the policy was vague and overbroad.[39] The term "objectionable appearance" was not objective or specific enough. The policy in *Kreimer* included the term "nuisance," a clear legal standard under New Jersey law.[40] The court rejected the library's argument that "objectionable appearance" incorporated a commonsense standard.[41] "Because the regulation at issue is wholly dependent on the individual staff member's interpretation . . . its enforcement is unavoidably arbitrary."[42]

In a statement to the press after the opinion was issued, counsel for the library said the guidelines were being reviewed even before the judge had reached his decision.[43] The library policy in question in *Armstrong* had been enacted in 1979, with some revisions in 1982 and 1984. The director of the library had submitted the guidelines for review by the D.C. Office of Corporation Counsel, but the office never responded.[44]

This submission to counsel, however, did help in the judge's conclusion that the individuals named in the suit could claim qualified immunity. Qualified immunity is "immunity from civil liability for a public official who is performing a discretionary function, as long as the conduct does not violate clearly established constitutional or statutory rights."[45] In other words, this doctrine protects public officials who are performing their jobs as long as they do not clearly infringe on a person's rights. The standard for qualified immunity is not the individual person's motives, but "whether a reasonable person would have known that the . . . regulation violated a clearly established constitutional right."[46] Submission to counsel in this case demonstrated well-intentioned motives of the library officials. The library officials clearly intended to act within the law. "[T]he fact that the Director submitted the guideline at issue for review by the Office of Corporation Counsel rebuts plaintiff's claim of unconstitutional motive, even if it is not relevant to the individual defendants' claim of qualified immunity."[47]

Armstrong confirmed what many librarians already believed. Libraries could eject patrons solely on the basis of objectionable appearance or hygiene. However, the criteria for ejection must be specific. In particular, the criteria should fit within a legal standard, not the subjective opinions of library staff. Submitting the policy to legal counsel in advance of implementation serves two purposes. First, it helps to ensure the policy is objective. Second, it helps establish that the library's motives are not driven by unconstitutional objectives. The standard for qualified immunity is whether a reasonable person would have believed they were violating a person's rights. Submitting the proposed policy to counsel demonstrated positive motives on the part of the library officials. While this is not the standard by which qualified immunity is gauged, it can help a judge determine that the defense is appropriate.

Neinast v. Board of Trustees of Columbus Metropolitan Library
While he is not homeless, Robert Neinast likes to walk around barefoot. Married and a father of three, Neinast is a member of the Dirty Sole Society, an organization that promotes going barefoot. According to its Web site, the Dirty Sole Society currently has about one thousand members.[48] *The*

Columbus Dispatch interviewed him regarding his hobby of hiking barefoot.[49] He visits businesses without shoes, and he wears flip-flops to work only because of his employer's policies.[50]

On several occasions from 1997 to 2001, Neinast visited the Columbus Metropolitan Library barefoot. On these occasions, he was asked to leave under a library regulation requiring the wearing of shoes while on the library premises. In 2001, he sued the library's board of trustees; Larry D. Black, the director of the library; and Vonzell Johnson, the assistant manager of security for the library, in federal court, alleging violations of his rights under the First, Ninth, and Fourteenth Amendments to the Constitution.[51]

Neither federal law nor the laws of the state of Ohio prohibit going barefoot in public. Neinast admitted to going in many public places without wearing shoes. The Columbus library's patron regulations do not prohibit using the library without shoes. However, the library's eviction procedure does allow for eviction of patrons not wearing shoes.

Neinast sued the library and the two individuals under 42 U.S.C. § 1983.[52] The Constitution, while enumerating rights of individuals against their government, does not provide any remedy for a constitutional violation. Section 1983, in essence, provides that individuals, when acting under color of law, may be sued for violating the constitutional rights of another. Simply put, to succeed under § 1983, a claimant must show that (1) a person (2) acting under color of law (3) deprived the claimant of his or her rights secured by the U.S. Constitution or its laws.

First Amendment
In his suit, Neinast made three claims. His first claim was that the library is a public forum, and he has the right of access as well as his right of expression under the First Amendment. This claim embraces two distinct ideas—the right of access to information from the public library as a First Amendment issue and Neinast's refusal to wear shoes as a form of speech that is constitutionally protected.

Regarding the right of access to information from the public library, the Sixth Circuit recognized, as the Third Circuit did in *Kreimer,* that "the First Amendment protects the right to receive information."[53] However, this does not mean that the library must provide unlimited access. "The Library is obligated to permit the public to exercise rights that are consistent with the nature of the library and consistent with the government's intent. . . . Other activities need not be tolerated."[54] Reasonable restrictions on the time, place, and manner of speech, but not of the content, are allowed if they are narrowly tailored to serve a significant government interest, and leave open ample alternative channels of information.

The regulation in this case is not content-based. The regulation requiring shoes on the premises does not impact the content of any speech within the library. Further, the reason for the regulation serves a significant government interest—the government does have an interest in patron safety and in not getting sued for injuries from barefoot patrons. To persuade the court of this potential safety issue, the library submitted incident reports to the court of hazards that barefoot patrons might encounter. These included feces, vomit, broken ceiling tiles, splintered chair pieces, and drops of blood and urine on the floor of various areas, including the restrooms, elevators, children's area, and reading areas. Further reports documented a patron who had scraped an arm on a staple in the carpet, and a patron whose toe was caught in a door. To require shoes on library premises, the court held, is a narrow restriction designed to serve this interest.

Neinast also claimed his barefootedness served as symbolic speech. As a member of the Dirty Sole Society, Neinast believes his barefootedness conveys a message that it is not illegal under state or federal law nor is it disruptive to the library but is protected under the Constitution. For conduct to be speech protected by the First Amendment, (1) there must be "an intent to convey a particularized message"; and (2) "in the surrounding circumstances the likelihood was great that the message would be understood by those who viewed it."[55] For example, the wearing of black arm bands by students to protest the Vietnam War is protected symbolic speech.[56]

Neinast's claim fails under both prongs of this analysis. First, Neinast's going barefoot does not convey a particularized message of a political, ideological, or religious nature. Second, no one in the library is likely to ask him about his barefootedness, and there is not much likelihood that people will understand the message he intends to convey. In the library, people are unlikely to ask him about his agenda or to see the letters he carries with him from state and federal agencies stating that there are no regulations against going barefoot. The library is "a nonpolitical environment," and Neinast's arguments do not touch on matters of public concern—matters "relating to any matter of political, social, or other concern to the community."[57]

This first argument of Neinast's holds many important legal considerations for libraries. First, for constitutional purposes, the public library is a limited or designated public forum. As such, libraries may enforce reasonable time, place, and manner restrictions on library access as long as they are narrowly tailored to serve a significant government interest. One would expect the library could restrict patrons if their conduct or behavior is disruptive. Such conduct, it seems, may extend beyond the physically or verbally abusive and may entail appearance or hygiene that others may find distracting.

By implication, the court's logic indicates the library would have a difficult time removing a patron for wearing (or not wearing) an article of clothing that conveyed a legitimate message about a matter of public concern, whether or not it was disturbing to other patrons. While safety and being protected against lawsuits are legitimate concerns of the library, restricting someone based on their appearance is usually unlikely to meet those or other government objectives without running afoul of the First Amendment, as the *Kreimer* case ultimately held.

Due Process under the Fourteenth Amendment (Discrimination)

Neinast's second cause of action alleged that he has a right of personal appearance, a liberty interest protected under the due process clause of the Fourteenth Amendment. Under due process precedent, if the infringement is on a fundamental or protected right, such as the right to marry or raise a family, the court applies strict scrutiny, a rigid test that only the most narrowly tailored rule will withstand, and then only if it serves a compelling government interest. On the other hand, if the infringement does not involve a fundamental or protected right, the court applies a rational basis test. The rational basis test is a much more lenient standard. It only requires that the rules be narrowly tailored to serve a legitimate government interest.

The district court in *Neinast* found that a right of personal appearance is a liberty interest protected by the Constitution. However, the right of personal appearance is not a fundamental right. Therefore, the rational basis test applies. "Under such scrutiny, the court will not overturn the Library's regulation unless it is so unrelated to the achievement of any combination of legitimate purposes that the court can only conclude that the Library's policy was irrational."[58]

Because the library is a limited public forum, it "need not allow all modes of speech simply because it promotes some modes of speech."[59] Further, it did not matter that Neinast had been admitted to other public places, including government buildings, without footwear; "he is not guaranteed the same access at the Library if he chooses to ignore its shoe requirement."[60]

Procedural Due Process

Neinast's third cause of action alleged that the library's policies were not properly administered by the named individual defendants and thus he was denied procedural due process. In other words, the board of trustees did not have the authority to institute such a regulation because state law did not require shoes, and the trustees are not experts on health and safety. He also argued that Black and Johnson improperly used the regulation in evicting Neinast for one full day. The court found that no procedural due process rights exist in the general rulemaking of political subdivisions or agencies. Thus, Neinast's procedural due process rights have not been violated by this rule.

In this third allegation, Neinast also claimed he was denied equal protection because the shoe regulation discriminates against one group of people—those who choose to go barefoot—over another. Discrimination claims are analyzed in a manner similar to that of the due process described above. If the discrimination is based on a suspect class (for example, a class for which discrimination is unlikely to ever serve a valid purpose) such as race or alienage, the court applies strict scrutiny. On the other hand, if the discrimination does not involve a suspect class, the court again applies a rational basis test.

The regulation here does discriminate against those not wearing shoes, but they are not a suspect class. Therefore, the rational basis test applies. Again, this regulation is narrowly tailored to serve the legitimate interest of the health and safety of library patrons. It also serves to protect the library from liability.

Qualified Immunity

After dispensing with Neinast's three causes of action, the district court examined the individual defendants' claims that they were shielded from liability under the principle of qualified immunity. In the words of the court, "[t]he affirmative defense of qualified, or good faith, immunity shields 'government officials performing discretionary functions . . . from liability for civil damages insofar as their conduct does not violate clearly established statutory or constitutional rights of which a reasonable person would have known.'"[61] Claims of immunity are examined on a case-by-case basis; the standard is whether a reasonable official in a similar position could have believed his conduct was lawful. Here the defendants did not violate a "clearly established" right of Neinast. The defendants also submitted a statement from the county prosecutor's office stating their actions were lawful. The court thus held that Black and Johnson were entitled to defense of qualified immunity.

The defense of qualified immunity is very important for librarians to consider in enacting and enforcing policy. Librarians are unlikely to act unlawfully or to deliberately violate a patron's constitutional rights. Thus, the defense will likely apply to their actions. As the library here did, by consulting the county prosecutor's office, libraries should consult with counsel when creating or enforcing rules that could result in patron ejection. Unfortunately, this will not prevent the initial filing of a lawsuit and having to defend against it. However, it is available for summary judgment; a judge will decide whether the doctrine applies and, if a motion for summary judgment is successful, the case will not go through the time and expense of trial.

Neinast appealed the district court's decision, but the Sixth Circuit affirmed summary judgment in favor of the defendants.[62] The Sixth Circuit has jurisdiction over Michigan, Ohio, Kentucky, and Tennessee. The holdings of this decision thus are binding law over those states and are at least persuasive authority in other circuits. Neinast also tried to appeal to the U.S. Supreme Court, but was denied.[63] Despite its initial seemingly frivolous and silly premise, the *Neinast* case thus serves to reinforce and recognize several important legal ideas for libraries.

The first of these is that the library is a limited or designated public forum, resulting in First Amendment implications. It has been clearly established that the First Amendment embodies the right to receive information as well as transmit messages. While a public library would run into serious constitutional problems attempting to restrict the content of messages patrons wish to express, it does have authority to restrict the time, place, and manner of dispensing those messages.[64]

The second important legal idea to be drawn from the *Neinast* case is the qualified immunity for the director and manager of security. Again, this would not protect the library from being forced to defend itself against a suit, but it would prevent the time and expense of trial. In this case, the library was insured, and the insurance covered the majority of the litigation costs; however, the library was forced to expend at least $35,000 to defend itself.[65]

Conclusions

Public libraries today confront the problem of homeless people coming in and using the library as a daytime refuge from the elements and the streets rather than for its intended means. This can bring the homeless into direct conflict with library directors, staff, and other patrons. All libraries must put regulations into place that serve the library's function and ensure that all patrons are handled fairly and legally.

The cases discussed reach certain common conclusions regarding such rules. The library is a designated public forum, and the First Amendment does apply to library access as the right to receive information is as much a part of the freedom of speech as the right to convey messages. To bar someone on the basis of a political message or other matter of social concern will run afoul of the First Amendment. However, someone who wishes to speak out about matters of merely personal concern may be restricted if the restrictions are reasonable with regard to time, place, and manner; serve a significant government interest, such as health and safety; and leave open alternative channels.

Clearly, disruptive behavior may be barred. Barring someone based on personal appearance or hygiene is possible and constitutional, provided that the standards, such as those in *Kreimer* and *Neinast,* and unlike those in *Armstrong,* are clear, reasonable, and objective. Consultation with counsel regarding enacting and enforcing rules for ejection is always advisable and recommended.

Library counsel and staff must be aware of these rules when enacting and enforcing policies regarding access to patrons who, based on their appearance or hygiene, may be disturbing to other patrons or staff. While *Kreimer* was settled more than a decade ago, *Neinast* and *Armstrong* are more recent, and show that this issue is still relevant and timely. These cases reflect the litigious nature of our society, but also the growing concern over the homeless using public libraries and other public facilities. Because of the increasing cost of litigation and shrinking budgets, libraries and their staff must be aware of how to defend themselves from liability. The doctrine of qualified immunity protects against liability for individuals acting reasonably, but, unfortunately, will not protect against lawsuits being brought in the first place.

Notes

1. M. Minow and T. A. Lipinski, *The Library's Legal Answer Book* (Chicago: ALA, 2003). See also R. Rubin, *Avoiding Liability Risk: An Attorney's Advice to Library Trustees and Others* (Chicago: ALA, 1994).
2. Paul D. Healey, "Pro Se Users, Reference Liability, and the Unauthorized Practice of Law: Twenty-Five Selected Readings," *Law Library Journal* 94, no. 1 (Winter 2002): 133; Cathy Harris Helms, "Copyright Laws and Public Libraries," *Georgia*

Library Quarterly 41, no. 3 (Fall 2004): 16; Samuel T. Huang, "Library Resources on the Employment of People with Disabilities," *The Reference Librarian* no. 36 (1992): 139–52.

3. *Kreimer v. Bureau of Police for Town of Morristown,* 765 F. Supp. 181 (D. N.J. 1991), overruled by 958 F.2d 1242 (3rd Cir. 1992).

4. Wayne Parry, "Man Who Won Library Suit Sues NJ Transit," Mar. 15, 2005, www.highbeam.com/doc/1P1-106364168.html (accessed June 15, 2009).

5. Nathan Welton, "Bad B.O. Now a No-No at County Libraries," *The Tribune* (San Luis Obispo, Calif.), Feb. 22, 2005, www.nathanwelton.com/stories/generalassignment/bodyodor.html (accessed June 15, 2009).

6. Ibid.

7. *Kreimer v. Bureau of Police for Town of Morristown,* 765 F. Supp. 181, 183–84.

8. Ibid., 184.

9. Ibid.

10. Ibid.

11. Ibid., 184, fn 2.

12. Ibid., 184.

13. Ibid., 182.

14. Ibid.

15. Ibid., 183.

16. Ibid.

17. Ibid.

18. Ibid., 197–98.

19. Ibid., 185.

20. Ibid., 187.

21. Ibid. ("In order to allow all patrons of the Joint Free Public Library of Morristown and Morris Township to use its facilities to the maximum extent possible during its regularly scheduled hours, the Library Board of Trustees has adopted the following rules and regulations.")

22. Ibid., 187–88.

23. Ibid., 188.

24. Ibid., 189.

25. Ibid., 184.

26. Ibid., 188.

27. Judi Silver, "Libraries and the Homeless: Caregivers or Enforcers," *The Katharine Sharp Review* no. 2 (Winter 1996), http://mirrored.ukoln.ac.uk/lisjournals/review/review/winter1996/silver.html (accessed Mar. 22, 2005).

28. *Kreimer,* 958 F. 2d, 1264.

29. Ibid., 1247.

30. Ibid., 1264.

31. Ibid.

32. See, for example, *Miller v. Northwest Regional Lib. Bd.,* 348 F. Supp. 563 (M.D.N.C. 2004).

33. *Armstrong v. District of Columbia Public Library,* 154 F. Supp.2d 67 (D. D.C. 2001).

34. Ibid., 76.

35. Ibid.

36. Ibid.

37. Ibid., 69.

38. Ibid., 70.
39. Ibid., 79.
40. Ibid., 78.
41. Ibid., 75–76.
42. Ibid., 81 (citing *Hoffman Estates v. Flipside, Hoffman Estates*, 455 U.S. 489 [1982]).
43. "Judge Nixes DCPL Policy," *American Libraries* 32, no. 9 (Oct. 1, 2001): 31.
44. *Armstrong v. District of Columbia Public Library,*154 F. Supp. 2d., 71, fn 3.
45. "Qualified Immunity," *Black's Law Dictionary*, 8th ed. (St. Paul, Minn.: West, 2004).
46. *Armstrong v. District of Columbia Public Library*, 154 F. Supp. 2d, 71.
47. Ibid., 71, fn 3.
48. Society for Barefoot Living, www.barefooters.org (accessed Mar. 22, 2005).
49. Mark Ellis, "Toe-to-Toe with Nature: Barefoot Hikers Really Get a Feel for Trails," *The Columbus Dispatch*, June 17, 2003.
50. Joe Blundo, "Library Says No Shoes, No Service," *The Columbus Dispatch*, Apr. 12, 2001.
51. *Neinast v. Board of Trustees of Columbus Metropolitan Library*, 190 F. Supp. 2d 1040 (S.D. Ohio 2002).
52. 42 U.S.C. § 1983 (2000).
53. *Neinast v. Board of Trustess of Columbus Metro. Lib.*, 346 F. 3d 585, 591 (6th Cir. 2003).
54. Ibid.
55. *Spence v. Washington*, 418 U.S. 405, 409 (1974).
56. *Tinker v. Des Moines Indep. Sch. Dist.*, 393 U.S. 502 (1969).
57. *Neinast*, 190 F. Supp. 2d, 1045.
58. Ibid., 1047.
59. Ibid.
60. Ibid.
61. *Neinast*, 190 F. Supp. 2d, 1049 (quoting *Harlow v. Fitzgerald*, 457 U.S. 800 [1982]).
62. *Neinast v. Board of Trustees of Columbus Metro. Lib.*, 346 F. 3d 585 (6th Cir. 2003).
63. *Neinast v. Board of Trustees of Columbus Metro. Lib.*, 541 U.S. 990 (2004).
64. An interesting case in this regard is *Gay Guardian Newspaper v. Ohoopee Regional Library System*, 235 F. Supp. 2d 1362 (S.D.Ga. 2002). There, the court held that a public library could entirely discontinue its free literature table (except for government publications) when a gay rights organization wanted to place its publication there. The court held that discontinuing the table entirely was a content-neutral restriction, even if the rule was brought about by the library's discomfort with the gay paper.
65. Kevin Mayhood, "Judge Throws Out Lawsuit Challenging Library's Shoes Required Rule," *The Columbus Dispatch*, Mar. 28, 2002.

About the Author

James Kelly is a Law Reference Librarian and Assistant Professor of Librarianship at the University of Illinois at Urbana-Champaign; jpkelly@law.uiuc.edu.

Part VI

Ideas and Tips for Reference Services

Reference service is one of the most important and visible roles that a library undertakes. As you know, the reference environment has become much more complex, with Virtual Reference, 24/7 Reference Services, Google, Wikipedia, and other challenges. As your community's center for information, you'll want to ensure that your library provides a wide variety of high-quality information services and that you can provide it when patrons need it. The articles in this section will provide you with some related topics to think about. In the short essay by Susan Hildreth from *Public Libraries*, "Reference Services in a Flat World," Hildreth suggests that the 21st century reference librarian will serve as a facilitator, connecting searchers to various information sources, rather than a gatekeeper and dispenser of information. In "What Is Virtual Reference Anyway?" a PLA TechNote, written by Richard W. Boss, you'll get a concise, authoritative overview of online reference services. "Ethical Responsibilities and Legal Implications of Providing Health Information," from the PLA publication *The Public Librarian's Guide to Providing Consumer Health Information* by Barbara Casini and Andrea Kenyon illuminates a gray area in reference services. And finally, if you've been away from the reference desk for a while, Sally Decker Smith and Roberta Johnson's "The Realities of Today's Reference Desk" is a forthright account of what goes on at today's public library reference desks.

Chapter 24

Reference Services in a Flat World

Susan Hildreth

The theme of this issue of *Public Libraries* is reference services; and that is a critical issue for libraries, but I wanted to set a somewhat broader context before we begin to discuss the specifics of reference. I am busy as you all are, and when I spend time reading, it is usually to relax and be entertained. I rarely read nonfiction. My day job is the State Librarian of California and, as such, I am a member of the Chief Officers of the State Library Agencies (COSLA), an austere group to say the least. We had a thought-provoking continuing education discussion at our fall meeting that was focused on *The World is Flat: A Brief History of the Twenty-first Century* by Thomas Friedman (Farrar, 2006). It is not easy to give state librarians homework assignments, but we all had to read this book before our session. I am glad to say that I completed the assignment. I was aware of the book and had heard the author speak but had just not taken the time to read it. I would encourage any of you who have not read the book to read the 2006 edition, if possible. You can also watch a one-hour presentation by Friedman about the book available at http://mitworld.mit.edu/video/266. Friedman describes a flat world as one in which we live in a global, Web-enabled playing field that allows for multiple forms of collaboration on research and work in real time, without regard to geography, distance, or, in the near future, languages.

This flat world does not support the traditional role of the reference librarian as gatekeeper and dispenser of information. Instead, it would suggest that the reference librarian of the twenty-first century would facilitate connecting searchers to various information sources, which could be books, electronic resources, or even knowledge experts in various fields.

I have often described the current role of librarians as navigators on the sea of the Internet, but even that seems too passive in the flat world. Librarians need to help searchers navigate information sources but also to make connections between individuals or groups who may have knowledge that they can share with each other. Just think about the sharing and collaboration that occurs in creating just one Wikipedia entry!

The COSLA continuing education session was developed and presented by Julie Beth Todaro, dean of library services at Austin Community College in Texas, and a well-known and well-respected library trainer. She reflected on the difference between reference services of the recent past and those required in the flat world. I wanted to share those reflections with you.

- Librarians have provided basic reference services and may have had specialty areas but now must be able to provide many kinds of reference in a variety of subject areas and in a variety of formats.
- Customers have always needed help in finding, analyzing, and using resources. But now customers need help in discerning the validity of resources they find as well as being able to utilize the variety of equipment and modalities through which information is provided.
- Librarians have primarily assisted customers in person in one-on-one settings or in small groups. But now librarians must provide assistance in the traditional and virtual methods and settings as well as deal with a wide variety of levels and styles of learning.
- Librarians counted in-person or telephone questions, but now the question count includes faxes, e-mails, Web-based sources including chat and instant messages, and text messages.
- Reference question statistics were steady or growing. But now there is a national trend of less typical reference questions and more complex questions as well as more interaction with customers, assisting or vetting electronic information, and aiding in the manipulation, storing, or printing of that information.
- Librarians were fairly certain that the information they found was something that their customers would want to see. Now librarians are never sure what type of information or Web sites they may encounter. Although evaluating information has always been part of a librarian's job, providing customers with information literacy skills to empower them to analyze the diverse world of electronic information is an even more critical work component for librarians in the twenty-first century.

I think these reflections demonstrate that the nature of reference services in the flat world has become much more complex than in the past. Librarians providing these services must be as comfortable in evaluating Web sites and pushing them through a chat environment to a virtual customer as presenting basic computer skills and information sources to a group of new immigrants. I believe that the librarian serving as information teacher and search strategy coach is where we need to be for success in the twenty-first century.

For flat world customers to even consider the library as a source for information, access to these services must be available 365/24/7 and in a wide variety of modalities. The library world has tried to respond to this customer need with virtual reference services. I believe that virtual reference is an absolutely essential service that libraries must provide, but I also believe that virtual reference is still in its developmental stage. It is difficult to keep up with the constantly changing modalities of communication and information access. It is a tough challenge to integrate those modalities into a service that is transparent for the customer, accessible to library staff, and able to be evaluated in any way. The jury is still out on this potentially powerful service as we have not yet found protocols and systems that are as user-friendly as they could be.

Although virtual reference service has been provided in California for a number of years, I am by no means an expert on that topic. I asked one of my staff members, Rush Brandis, a library technology consultant, to review information on this topic; and I wanted to share with you a few good resources for a quick primer and evaluation of virtual reference.

- *The Virtual Reference Desk: Creating a Reference Future*, edited by R. David Lankes, New York: Neal-Schuman, 2006. This book contains great articles on many important virtual reference topics from bringing together teens and chat reference to establishing performance targets for a virtual reference service.
- Steve Coffman and Linda Arret. "To Chat or Not to Chat: Taking Another Look at Virtual Reference," *Information Today* 12, no. 7 Part 1 (July 2004); Part 2 (September 2004), www.infotoday.com/searcher/jul04/arret_coffman.shtml, www.infotoday.com/searcher/sep04/arret_coffman.shtml (accessed June 15, 2009).
- Brenda Bailey Hainer; "Virtual Reference: Alive and Well," *Library Journal* 130, no. 3 (Jan. 15, 2005), www.libraryjournal.com/article/CA491140.html (accessed June 15, 2009).
- Pascal Lupien, "Virtual Reference in the Age of Pop-Up Blockers, Firewalls, and Service Pack 2," *Information Today* 30 (July/August 2006), www.infotoday.com/online/jul06/Lupien.shtml (accessed June 15, 2009).

There are two leaders in the virtual and electronic reference field and I would recommend reading their publications: Joe Barker, librarian at the University of California–Berkeley, and Joe Janes, associate dean, at the Information School at the University of Washington Seattle. There is a lot of information and conversation on the library blogs about this topic, so if you have not visited any of them, this would be a good opportunity to do so. Check out Jessamyn West's blog (http://librarian.net), Jenny Levine's blog (http://theshiftedlibrarian.com) and Sarah Houghton's blog (http://librarianinblack.typepad.com). I think virtual reference is critical but, unlike our usual "last to adopt" position, I think libraries are serving as early adopters for this service. I hope that we will reach the nirvana of virtual reference available in all flavors and modalities in the near future!

About the Author

Susan Hildreth is City Librarian of the Seattle Public Library and oversees the operations of the renowned Central Library, 26 recently renovated and expanded branches, and the Mobile Services division. Formerly she was State Librarian of California, City Librarian of the San Francisco Public Library, and worked in other public libraries in northern California. She served as President of the Public Library Association in 2006–2007. She also served as Treasurer and President of the California Library Association.

Chapter 25

What Is Virtual Reference Anyway?

Richard W. Boss

Virtual reference is online reference service that enables library patrons to ask reference questions through a library's Web site. The user may be at home, in an office, at school, or in a library. Some virtual reference services also place answers to frequently asked questions (FAQs), selected reference tools, and access to selected databases on the Web site. The question-answering service using Internet technology is the essential component, without which the use of the name "virtual reference" is misleading.

An example of a service that uses the term "virtual reference," but is not, is the Virtual Reference Desk of the U.S. Senate (www.senate.gov/pagelayout/ reference/b_three_sections_with_teasers/virtual.htm). While it provides a great deal of useful information about the Senate and its activities, there is no opportunity to ask questions of reference librarians.

History

Virtual reference was introduced more than a decade ago. The best known of the early efforts was the Internet Public Library (www.ipl.org) a service launched in 1995 by the University of Michigan's School of Information and Library Studies. Initially an experiment, it is now a well-established service that is a collaborative effort among four schools of library and information science. As of January 1, 2007, the service host for the program changed to the Drexel University College of Information Science and Technology. The service provides a variety of online resources arranged in broad subject areas, a number of pathfinders, an extensive FAQ section, and a Web form for asking reference questions. IPL has a staff of volunteers that answers questions, usually in no more than three days. IPL can be accessed directly or through a link on a library's Web site. Despite its name, many academic libraries link to IPL.

Several public libraries initiated "ask a librarian" virtual reference in the late 1990s. Since that time, hundreds of public and academic libraries have joined them. For the first several years, the libraries provided an e mail address or a Web form for patrons to ask questions from anywhere at any time. Reference librarians, usually those already working regular hours at reference desks, would work on questions submitted when the library was closed or that could not be answered immediately as time permitted. Most libraries also added other components to their virtual reference service, especially knowledge-based online resources.

The CLEVNET consortium in Ohio launched the first 24/7 virtual reference service in June of 2001. With funding from the State Library of Ohio and the participation of many of the state's public libraries, the service went statewide in 2004. The service is called KnowItNow (www.knowitnow.org). It had answered more than a quarter of a million questions by the end of 2006. General reference is available all hours; assistance by subject specialists is available from 9:00 a.m. to 5:30 p.m. Monday through Saturday. The service is available in English or Spanish to anyone by merely entering an Ohio zip code.

New Jersey's Q and A NJ (www.qandanj.org) was launched as a statewide 24/7 virtual reference service in October of 2001. It was made possible by sharing responsibility among reference staffs at scores of public and academic libraries and at a reference center. There are two question forms, one for general users and another for college students seeking help with coursework. The service now also offers access to a number of databases. Unless connected from a library, a patron must enter a public or academic library barcode number to access the service. Q and A NJ seeks to answer most questions online within 15 minutes. It does not answer questions that involve extended research, but will get the requestor started.

Forms of Communication

Initially, the most common forms of communication between a remote library patron and a reference librarian were e-mail and online Web forms.

While ubiquitous, e-mail does not offer the instantaneous response that library patrons may seek. It is also difficult to conduct an effective reference interview using e-mail because many questions require clarification. It may take three or four exchanges just to determine what the library patron really wants.

A Web form is somewhat better than e-mail because it can be designed to elicit all of the needed information, including the all-important "needed by" information.

In the last four years, live, interactive chat was tried by many libraries to overcome the drawbacks of e-mail and Web forms. However, chat software was designed for one-on-one conversations among friends, not for high-volume question-answering services that must be able to queue and route questions. Nor do they offer a knowledge base of frequently asked questions (FAQs) with answers and electronic resources.

Increasingly, libraries are turning to Web contact center software. More than 50 companies have been supplying such software to online retailers such as L.L. Bean, Lands End, and major insurance companies. The software was designed for answering questions and providing interactive customer service.

It queues and routes Web calls to the next available staff member, allows a staff member to push Web pages to service users, supports the building and maintenance of knowledge bases, and allows questions and answers to be captured for inclusion in a FAQ file. Many of the Web call center products also include VoIP (voice over Internet Protocol) so that voice communication is possible. A particularly attractive feature of some Web contact center software is co-browsing. It enables a reference librarian and a patron to share the same Web pages, including online databases and other services that require authentication.

Among the most widely used Web contact center software packages for libraries are Ask A Librarian from Tutor.com (www.tutor.com/products/aal.aspx) and VRLplus from Docutek (www.docutek.com/products/vrlplus/index/html). Tutor.com, which has been offering homework assistance and tutoring for a number of years, purchased its virtual reference product from Library Systems & Services in 2003. Tutor not only offers software, but also back-up online reference staffing. Docutek is a subsidiary of SirsiDynix. The cost of the products varies greatly based on the size of the library and the number of reference librarians that can be online simultaneously. It may exceed $10,000 for libraries that wish to have multiple reference librarians online simultaneously.

A library that already has a virtual reference service and wishes merely to offer live chat, should consider boldchat (www.boldchat.com), a software package that leases for as little as $25 per month.

The typical hardware requirement is a small Web server costing no more than $4,000.

Knowledge Bases and Linking Tools

A library or consortium may choose to build a knowledge base as part of a virtual reference service. There are tools to facilitate the effort. The most widely used appears to be the Librarian's Index to the Internet (www.lii.org). LII has organized information into 15 broad categories and hundreds of sub-categories. A library can utilize the index as a basis for organizing its own knowledge base. It can also use the many links that LII has created to information sources.

Solo and Collaborative Reference

Virtual reference can be provided by a single library (the "solo" approach) or it can be a collaborative effort among many libraries.

The Solo Approach

When the service is provided by a single library, the service usually is available only to its own patrons. Access to online resources and a means to submit questions typically is 24/7, but responses to questions submitted after library hours are usually returned no earlier than the following day. Some libraries have found that it is more realistic to commit to two-day service. The main advantage to the solo approach is that a library determines its own policies and procedures; therefore, no compromises with other libraries are necessary.

Some libraries that have taken the solo approach accomplish 24/7 virtual reference by contracting with a commercial service that employs librarians.

The Collaborative Approach

A collaborative approach may involve as few as two libraries. When that is the case, 24/7 response is difficult to achieve, but it may be possible to extend the response hours when the libraries have different hours because of differences in budgets or because they are in different time zones. More commonly, the two-library approach involves libraries with different collection strengths and staff subject expertise. The libraries will need to agree on policies and procedures. Particularly important is agreement on the level of service because a library's reputation may suffer if the level of service extended by its partner is better or worse than its own.

The most common way to achieve 24/7 response is to participate in a consortium of libraries over a large geographic area. That spreads the burden more broadly and results in greater collection resources and staff expertise than just two libraries can achieve. It does mean that a library has to adopt the policies and procedures of the consortium even when these are not consistent with its own preferences. At least 15 state libraries were sponsoring statewide virtual reference service as of mid-2007.

In any collaborative virtual reference, the issue of access to licensed databases must be examined. Many licenses limit access to patrons of the subscribing library. Unless the participants limit access to the databases to which both/all subscribe or relicense the databases as consortium subscriptions, the patrons in the participating libraries will not have comparable resources available.

Examples of Collaborative Virtual Reference

There are a number of collaborative reference services, most coordinated by state library agencies. That of New Jersey has already been mentioned. Colorado's (www.askcolorado.org) is available in both Spanish and English. Any Colorado resident may access the service 24/7. The task of responding is shared by 43 participating libraries, including public, academic, school, and special libraries. The Colorado program was launched in 2003 with funding from the Library Services and Technology Act (LSTA) and contributions from the participating libraries. The software used is Ask A Librarian from Tutor.com (www.tutor.com/libraries). Tutor.com also provided Ask Colorado with after hours service and Spanish language service from its "Librarians by Request" service until mid-2006. At that time, the entire service was outsourced to Tutor.com.

Some virtual reference services focus on specific areas. For example, Government Information Online (http://govtinfo.org) specializes in finding government information sources of all kinds, and answers questions through chat or e-mail. It is a free service that is supported by approximately 30 public, academic, and state libraries. All of the participating libraries are official depository libraries.

There are also virtual reference services that target special audiences. Among them is a collaborative virtual reference service that serves visually handicapped persons. Known as InfoEyes (www.infoeyes.org), it is a collaborative effort among approximately 20 libraries for the blind.

The National Library of Canada coordinates a nationwide virtual reference service called Virtual Reference Canada (www.collectionscanada.ca/vrc-crv/index-e.html). There are more than 320 participating libraries.

The largest collaborative virtual reference is global in scope. It is QuestionPoint (www.oclc.org/QuestionPoint), a joint effort of OCLC and the Library of Congress that is based on the Collaborative Digital Reference Service launched by the Library of Congress and 15 partner libraries in 2000. The collaboration between OCLC and LC began in 2001. QuestionPoint is not only a virtual reference service; it is a supplier of software tools.

QuestionPoint
There are two major components to the QuestionPoint virtual reference service: Reference Management Service and 24/7 Reference Cooperative.

A library participating in the Reference Management Service receives software that enables it to offer virtual reference support directly from its Web site by e-mail, Web forms, and chat; and to create and maintain a local knowledge base. There are cooperative tools that enable a library to work collaboratively with other libraries. There is also access to a global knowledge base built by the libraries that participate in the program.

24/7 Reference is an around-the-clock reference service provided by libraries that choose to participate. A library commits a minimum number of hours of reference assistance to the service in return for access to reference groups that may be a local consortium, a statewide program, or the global network.

To join QuestionPoint, a library fills out a subscription order form on the site. There is a fee for participating. A library may join directly or as part of a statewide service or consortium. Members of statewide services and consortia pay less than individual libraries.

More than 1,800 libraries in 20 countries were participating as of mid-2007. QuestionPoint's interface is available in 14 languages. Twelve states' statewide services were linked to QuestionPoint as of mid-2007: California, Delaware, Illinois, Maine, Maryland, Montana, New Jersey, North Carolina, Oregon, Pennsylvania, Washington, and Wisconsin. In addition, there were regional consortia in Arizona, Indiana, Kentucky, New York, and Texas.

OCLC regional networks offer workshops on OCLC QuestionPoint service. They are designed to provide an understanding of how QuestionPoint works, how it can fit into a library's current reference service, and how to administer a QuestionPoint account and customize it. They usually are half-day workshops.

Outsourcing Virtual Reference

A library or consortium offering virtual reference may choose to outsource after-hours virtual reference or all virtual reference. The leading vendor is Tutor.com (www.tutor.com/libraries). It has been offering 24/7 and after-hours virtual service to individual libraries, consortia, and statewide virtual reference programs since 2003. It has been providing all 24/7 virtual reference service for Connecticut's statewide InfoAnyTime and Colorado's AskColorado since mid-2006.

Virtual Reference Guidelines

The Ad Hoc Committee on Virtual reference of ALA's Machine-Assisted Reference Section has developed a set of guidelines for implementing and maintaining virtual reference services (www.ala.org/ala/mgrps/divs/rusa/resources/guidelines/virtrefguidelines.cfm) defining the issues that must be addressed in planning virtual reference. It is unique among the many sources available on the Web in its concern for protecting the privacy of library patrons. The guidelines are based on those developed by Bernie Sloan and set forth in her article "Electronic Reference Services: Some Suggested Guidelines," *Reference & User Services Quarterly*, 38 (1): 77i-81, summer 1998.

Training Virtual Reference Librarians

Washington State has developed a unique training curriculum that addresses core competencies for library staff providing virtual reference service. Named "Anytime, Anywhere Answers," it is designed for both workshops and for delivery via the Web. Googling "Anytime, Anywhere Answers" is the fastest way to find information.

About the Author

Richard W. Boss, prior to becoming a full-time information systems consultant, was an academic library administrator. His positions have included the directorships of the University of Tennessee and Princeton University Libraries. He has written more than 30 books and hundreds of articles in the past 30 years.

Chapter 26

Ethical Responsibilities and Legal Implications of Providing Health Information

Barbara Palmer Casini and Andrea Kenyon

The ethical responsibilities and legal implications of providing health information in a public library setting deserve some discussion. Public libraries have traditionally shied away from providing medical information due to its difficult and personal nature.[1] This is no longer possible, because today the general public in its ever-increasing demand for access to health information is routinely turning to their local public library for help. Public librarians, while anxious to be responsive to the information needs of their patrons, have expressed some concerns regarding the ethical and legal aspects of providing health information. Public librarian concerns include:

- The public's inability to understand technical medical information[2]
- The fear that the patron may misinterpret the information[3]
- The legal consequences of providing incomplete, outdated, or misleading health information[4]
- Intruding on patron privacy[5]
- Worries about exceeding their professional responsibility[6]
- Patron confusion over the librarian's role[7]

What is the librarian's role and responsibility to providing health information? How can the librarian avoid overstepping the limits of his or her expertise when answering health questions? What legal liability may a librarian incur when responding to health information requests?

Ethical Responsibilities
Maintaining high standards of personal professional behavior is necessary in the delivery of health information services. The expanded roles of educator, facilitator, gatekeeper, and evaluator have generated some confusion regarding the acceptable standards of library practice and behavior. The library litera-

ture is a good source of guidance in determining library ethics. Rubin and Froehlich (1996) provide a good general overview of library ethics.[8] They identify nine major areas that concern librarians: selection and censorship, privacy, reference, intellectual property rights, administration, access, technology, loyalties, and social issues. These concerns affect the appropriate delivery of health information. Bunge (1999) states that "the reference librarian is obligated to act with competence, diligence, confidentiality, independence of judgment, honesty, and candor." All these traits affect the successful delivery of health information.[9]

Competence, diligence, and confidentiality are particularly critical in answering health information questions. Discussions on the need for patron confidentiality,[10] the patron's right to privacy,[11] and censorship and selection criteria[12] will be helpful when developing your library's ethical guidelines for providing health information services.

Code of Ethics
Ethical codes created by library professional associations are another source of guidance in the ethical provision of health information. Statements or codes of professional ethics serve as guidelines for librarians when practicing their profession. Ethical standards assist librarians in determining the appropriate action or response when faced with an ethical dilemma. Koehler and Pemberton (2000) note that codes of ethics "offer the practitioner a frame of reference to direct professional behavior. They also offer support and guidance for professionals where conflicts arise between the interests and demands of the profession and society as a whole or between their professional and corporate affiliations."[13]

The Code of Ethics of the American Library Association[14] and the Medical Library Association's (MLA) Code of Ethics for Health Sciences Librarianship[15] provide principles to guide the delivery of health information. In addition, the MLA's Consumer and Patient Health Information Section[16] has developed its own policy statement titled "The Librarian's Role in the Provision of Consumer Health Information and Patient Education." These codes and statements address collection management, knowledge and resource sharing, advocacy, access to and dissemination of information, education, and research. The essential roles of the librarian include identifying resources, evaluating resources, and showing patrons how to use the information resources.

Librarians who assume these roles in the provision of health information must take seriously the responsibility of being an advocate and conduit for health knowledge. Patrons may make critical decisions based on the health information they receive. The following ethical guidelines are particularly important for the librarian to consider when providing health information.

Freedom of Access to Health Information
The ALA Code of Ethics[17] endorse the librarian's commitment to "freedom of access to information and an obligation to ensure the free flow of

information." This statement supports the public's right to access health information. The MLA Code of Ethics for Health Sciences Librarianship[18] clearly identifies the important relationship between knowledge and decisions and the role that the librarian plays in the transfer of knowledge. The MLA Code states that "knowledge is the sine qua non of informed decisions in healthcare, education, and research, and the health sciences librarian serves society, clients, and the institution by working to ensure that informed decisions can be made." This statement is applicable to all librarians involved in providing health information.

Quality and Currency of Health Information
The ALA Code of Ethics states that "librarians provide the highest level of service to all library users through appropriate and usefully organized resources . . . and accurate, unbiased, and courteous responses to all requests."[19] The MLA Code of Ethics also declares that the "health sciences librarian ensures that the best available information is provided to the client."[20]

Health information resources will be appropriate and responses accurate only if the library has a commitment to up-to-date information that has been evaluated using policies and guidelines that address the selection of health information resources. If this is not common practice in your library, it will not only affect the quality of the services provided but it will also be in conflict with the ethical standards set forth by the library profession.

Common problems with accuracy and currency cited in the Nebraska Library Commission's STAR Reference Manual include:

- Telling a patron the information is not available when it is in your library or available through a referral.
- Providing outdated information.
- Reading information incorrectly.
- Not clearly understanding the patron's question and answering the wrong question.
- Answering the question without verifying the answer first.[21]

For example, using an outdated resource from your collection to respond to a question about current treatment options would be inappropriate and inaccurate. It would also be potentially harmful to the patron who has requested the information. The Guidelines for Medical, Legal, and Business Responses at General Reference Desks,[22] adopted by ALA's Reference and Adult Services Division (now Reference and User Services Association RUSA), addresses the issue of currency. The guidelines state that "the reference librarian should always point out publication dates to the user" and that the patron "should be advised that there may be more current information available on the topic." The guidelines also advocate the "weeding of the reference collection periodically to remove dated materials in subject areas where up-to-date information is essential." They further state that "if retention of older materials is required for historical purposes, distinctions in dates should be obvious."

It is interesting to note that studies conducted in public libraries in Ontario and Michigan report that most librarians rarely or occasionally are fearful of providing the wrong answer, nor did they express difficulty in knowing when the answer was complete.[23] It was determined that many of the problems encountered by public librarians in providing health information were related to the inadequacy of their health collections rather than lack of skills in providing accurate information. While limited or outdated collections have an impact on accurate health information responses, these studies suggest that public librarians are becoming increasingly comfortable in responding to health information questions.

The results of both studies further indicate the need for public librarians to develop resource-sharing partnerships with health sciences libraries, consumer health libraries, and multilibrary consortia. This will expand access to current, qualitative information resources, increasing the ability for public librarians to provide accurate answers to health questions.

Accuracy may further be ensured by including statements about quality and currency in your collection development policy and your reference policy guidelines. Remember to adhere to these policies. Conducting a thorough reference interview using a well-designed request form will also decrease problems and increase the probability of a more successful end result.[24]

Maintain and Enhance Knowledge and Skills in Providing Health Information

Developing and maintaining a health information service requires continual vigilance. Medicine is constantly changing, and resources addressing consumer health information needs are changing at the same pace. Professional continuing education through training classes, conferences and meetings, professional networking, participation in relevant online discussion lists, reading the professional literature, and staying attuned to the trends and issues in medicine will enhance the librarian's ability to provide quality health information services.

The ALA Code of Ethics state that "[Librarians] significantly influence or control the selection, organization, preservation, and dissemination of information."[25] It is our professional obligation to ensure that this is done in a manner that will enable us to provide credible, current information organized to facilitate consumer health education and decision making. As Mintz (1985) notes, "To ignore continuing education leads to inadequate service to clients, whether they be the general public, students, corporate staff, or fee-paying clients on retainer. Proper educational credentials and regular advance training are a means of protection against the negligence which leads to the incurrence of professional liability."[26]

Respect the Privacy of the Patron

Health issues are sensitive and personal, and they demand that the librarian "protect each library user's right to privacy and confidentiality with respect to information sought or received and resource consulted, borrowed, acquired, or transmitted."[27] The patron's privacy must be respected. Murray (1995), in a guide written for the Metropolitan Toronto Reference Library declares that "confidentiality is a key principle in a consumer health information service and must be maintained at all times."[28] The Metropolitan Toronto Reference Library has adopted the following policies and procedures with regard to privacy:

- The client's right not to give their name should be respected.
- The client's name is only used with other staff when discussing the client's information needs.
- Staff should avoid discussing requests in a public area.
- Care is given with walk-in clients to be sensitive to their need for privacy.
- When leaving a message, the service is not identified unless permission has been obtained from the client.
- The client's name is not given to any outside agency or person.
- Forms, correspondence, and other written material are not left unattended in public service areas.

In addition, when seeking assistance with a question from staff or other referral sources, the patron's name should not enter into the discussion. The focus should be on determining an accurate and satisfactory answer to the questions. Information about the patron should never be discussed outside the workplace. While it may be tempting to talk to a colleague, neighbor, or friend about a specific patron and their specific health information questions, it is not ethical to do so and violates the confidentiality of the client relationship.

Ensure Equal Access to Health Information for All Library Users

Health information must be provided regardless of an individual librarian's personal feelings about its appropriateness. This is an especially sensitive issue when the patron is a minor. The guidelines "Free Access to Libraries by Minors," adopted by the ALA Council in 1972 and amended in 1981, states that "Librarians have a responsibility to ensure that young people have access to a wide range of informational and recreational materials and services that reflect sufficient diversity to meet the young person's needs. The ALA opposes all attempts to restrict access to library services, materials, and facilities based on the age of library users."[29] Information regarding pregnancy, sexually transmitted diseases, and other health issues should be made accessible to minors when they request them.

Provide Health Information Impartially

Personal beliefs should not interfere with a librarian's professional obligation to provide information without prejudice to meet a client's information needs.[30] Biases regarding controversial topics, such as abortion, euthanasia, homosexuality, birth control, or complementary or alternative medicine, must not interfere with the impartial delivery of health information.

Legal Issues

The complicated and emotional nature of health information inquiries and the importance of responding appropriately bring into question the legal implications for the library and the librarian. The role of the librarian has evolved from one of locating and organizing information to determining the appropriateness of resources and the validity of the information. Some feel that "this has placed the librarian in a position of being held liable for disseminating incorrect or outdated information."[31] A 1992 survey of law and medical librarians found that more than half of those surveyed expressed some concern that they might be sued for malpractice.[32]

Liability "is a legal term that includes almost any obligation, responsibility, or duty that might arise as a result of a statute, contract, or tort."[33] As Rodwell (1984) notes, we live in a litigious society where people with special skills are being held accountable for their performance.[34] The proliferation of litigation against physicians and hospitals provides one example. Just how vulnerable libraries are has been debated without consensus in the library professional literature for some years. Dragich (1989) feels that "the incredible economic value of the information industry, the increase in malpractice suits against other professionals, and the suits against disseminators and producers of information in other contexts are ample evidence of the potential for liability on our part."[35] On the other hand, Gray (1988) feels that reference librarians have no contractual obligations toward their patrons and that it would be unlikely and difficult to prove negligence.[36]

In addition to malpractice, there are several areas of the law that pertain to the provision of health information:

- Practicing medicine without a license. Some librarians have expressed concern that they might be accused of practicing medicine without a license. Rees (1991) describes a common situation that librarians face at the reference desk. "Many users expect active assistance in applying information to self-diagnosis. Confronted by difficult and complex choices in terms of treatment options, users wish to engage the librarian in personal decision making."[37] Rothstein (1993) reminds librarians that "if patients ask for recommendations concerning treatment options, librarians must set the boundaries of their role properly and not risk practicing medicine without a license."[38] Allen (1982) reports that "cases of unauthorized medical practice that have been brought to trial have been cases in which the defendant has claimed to be able to cure a condition or has claimed some kind of expertise in medical matters, or has tried to persuade others to place trust or reliance on skills or knowledge that the defendant did not in fact possess."[39] Charney (1978), a physician and lawyer, reassures librarians that if they provide information and only information, not interpretations, or opinion, diagnosis or treatment, this will not be an issue.[40]

- Fraud and misrepresentation. Civil law includes intentional torts. Charney (1978) explains, "Intentional torts are acts which are done with purpose and cause damage. This is theoretically possible if an individual misunderstands information and is harmed as a result. This could also occur if you are hesitant about providing the truth and you, with all good intentions, say something misleading in an attempt to make a person happy. This person may rely on the representation that you made and for example doesn't make out a will correctly or plans a long trip when he has only three months to live. If he or his family is injured as a result of you misrepresenting the truth you could be accused of misrepresenting and committing fraud."[41]

- Defamation. A librarian who expresses an opinion about a particular physician or other healthcare professional could be guilty of defamation of character.[42]

- Refusal to provide information. Restricting or refusing to provide information that has been requested could be a violation of a person's constitutional right to know.[43] Patrons have a right to access any information in the library. Librarians are professionally obligated to guide patrons to materials that meet their information needs and cannot refuse to do this based on the feeling that they might be unsuitable or upsetting to the patron.

Malpractice and Negligence

Nasri (1987) defines malpractice as "any professional misconduct or unreasonable lack of skill in the performance of professional duties through intentional carelessness or simple ignorance."[44] Certain elements must be present before it is determined that there is a basis for litigation.[45]

- Is there a "duty of care" or obligation for the librarian to conform to a certain standard of conduct? This could occur if a librarian provides incomplete, incorrect, or outdated information or advice to a patron through personal carelessness, negligence, or ignorance. The librarian could be liable if this information or advice resulted in physical, economic, or other type of injury to the patron.[46] "Tort law seems to indicate that a medical or special librarian, implying special skill or knowledge, should be held to a higher standard of conduct than other librarians."[47]

- Was there a failure to conform to a certain standard of conduct? It must be determined that the librarian has an obligation to conform to a certain professional standard and that the librarian failed to do so. "To establish a negligent failure, one must compare the actual conduct and what is considered professional conduct. Standard professional conduct can be established by testimony from expert witnesses such as library

school faculty, published scholars, and evidence of the relevant professional code of conduct."[48] The court then decides if the librarian exer-
cised reasonable care, skill, and diligence in the provision of their
services. The plaintiff must establish that the librarian supplied faulty
(inaccurate, incomplete, out-of-date) information and that it was appropriate for the plaintiff to rely on the librarian for this information. It
must also be shown that the librarian understood that the safety of the
patron depended on the accuracy of the information that that the librarian failed to exercise reasonable care in determining the accuracy of the
information.[49] Gray (1989) makes a distinction between negligence of
the information intermediary (librarian) and a situation where the information that was faulty is attributable to the author or information pro-
ducer, such as in the case of "dirty data."[50] He does point out that the
librarian is still not "off the hook" in the latter scenario if the librarian
doubts the sources' reliability and does not communicate this concern to
the user. While there is no single code or document that lists all the ethical standards and professional responsibilities for librarians, a code of
ethics such as the ALA Code of Ethics could be determined by the courts
to serve as a measurement tool. Several authors advocate defining acceptable practice for information providers not only in terms of ethical
standards but also by establishing procedural guidelines to ensure the
quality of library services.[51]

- Is the breach of duty reasonably connected to the injury? It must be determined that the professional negligence had a causal relationship to
the injury. There must be a direct connection between the librarian's
poor performance of his or her responsibilities and the harm caused to
the plaintiff.
- Is there an actual injury? It must be proved that actual physical or
financial harm was done by the librarian's negligence. Gray (1988)
points out that the plaintiff must establish that the librarian provided
false information, that the librarian knew that the defendant's safety
depended on the information, that it was reasonable for the plaintiff to
act upon the information received, and that the librarian failed to exercise reasonable care.[52]

Some librarians feel that providing information for a fee has potential for
increased liability.[53] Cremieux (1996) states that librarian malpractice would
be difficult to prove since the "unique environment of library work makes creating a fair and universal standard difficult."[54] The lack of library malpractice
suits may be due to patron's belief that librarians try to provide accurate information and that there is no intentional attempt to mislead the patron.[55] Mika
and Shuman also suggest that litigation may be less prevalent because public
libraries generally provide services for free. It has also been noted that litigation against a librarian will reap little economic gain.[56]

However, some argue that even if librarians and information specialists
are not sued it does not mean that they should not be held accountable legally

for their actions in delivery of information.[57] General professional liability and malpractice cases have been rising, and this increases the possibility that an angry library patron may pursue legal means in order to be compensated for wrong information that resulted in injury or loss of money or opportunity. Librarians must set boundaries when patrons ask for interpretation of medical information or opinions regarding diagnosis and treatment options. Some states have addressed this issue by exempting librarians from malpractice. Some public librarians are protected under sovereign immunity. It is important to be aware of your state's stand on this issue.

Minimizing Your Risk

Libraries can minimize the risk of litigation by acting on the following points.

1. Define your role. Define your role and its limitations and the limitations of the medical information that the library provides:

    - Collect and disseminate health information based on collection development guidelines and evaluation methodology.
    - Provide access to health information.
    - Help locate information.
    - Show patrons how to use resources.
    - Advise patrons on the relative merits of sources and make recommendations regarding library materials.
    - Identify other community resources.

It is essential that the reference librarian makes a clear distinction between giving advice and interpreting information. Provide information, not advice. Medical advice should only be given by a medical professional. Be careful by applying good practice standards.

2. Ensure competence. Apply consistently high standards in the practice of your profession by:

    - Conducting a thorough reference interview.
    - Discussing the limitations of the information resources including the date of publication.
    - Avoiding errors of omission.
    - Knowing when to refer a question.
    - Adhering to established codes of ethics, policies and guidelines for acquiring, providing, and delivering health information, that have been established by professional library organizations and your institution.
    - Pursuing continuing education and training opportunities and being aware of current trends in medicine and library practice.

3. Develop written policy statements for handling health information services:

    - Collection management policy for collecting and weeding health information.

- Criteria for library Web site links to health information Web sites.
- Disclaimer statements.

4. Establish reference guidelines for handling health information requests:

- Avoid any claim or implication that you possess medical skills, training, or knowledge.
- Offer information only in response to a specific request. Do not respond to descriptions of medical symptoms.
- Do not attempt to interpret the medical information provided. Health information may be very complex and hard to understand; some materials may be written for the health professional. Patrons may ask for assistance in interpreting the information or ask the librarian how the information will affect the individual's specific situation. Beware of being put into this situation. Refer the patron to his or her physician.
- Do not recommend a method of treatment.
- Do not recommend a drug or alternative drug.
- Do not assist patrons in diagnosing themselves. A patron may ask you to confirm his or her diagnosis by providing you with a list of symptoms. You may provide information about a specific disease or a definition of the symptom but never suggest that the symptom relates to a specific disease.
- Do not recommend physicians. If a physician referral is needed, give the telephone number of the local county medical society. In many communities, HMOs and specific hospitals and health systems also offer this service.
- Maintain confidentiality and explain this to your patron.
- Always refer complex questions, specific personal questions, and questions out of scope for a librarian to a healthcare professional.

Disclaimers

No policy can cover all difficult situations. Disclaimers can be used as a caution to remind patrons of the limitations of the information provider as well as the resources they are using. Disclaimers never absolve anyone from a legal responsibility and cannot usurp the law. Many libraries display a disclaimer statement prominently on the wall. Disclaimers are also stamped on collection materials and included on forms or letters accompanying health information given to consumers. Following are examples of disclaimers that might be adapted for use in your institution:

Posted on the wall:

Attention: The purpose of the Consumer Health Library is to provide reference materials for review by the general public. While the staff will gladly assist you with locating articles or texts of a specific nature, the staff is prohibited, by library policy and public policy, from commenting on, or interpreting, information contained within these materials. If you should have a question regarding the information contained within these materials, please consult a physician.

The purpose of the Consumer Health Information Service is to provide public access to a wide range of health and medical information, not to give medical advice or interpretation. Information provided by the Consumer Health Information Service does not imply recommendation or endorsement. It is not a substitute for a consultation with a health professional.

Some information in the library may not apply to your personal situation. Please ask your physician your specific question.

The Community Health Library provides access to a wide variety of health information. When using the services and materials of the library, please remember the following points:

- All questions are kept confidential.
- The information provided may not be all that is available on a subject.
- Inclusion of material in the collection does not imply approval or recommendation by the library.
- The material and information provided by the library are not a substitute for consultation with a medical health professional.

Printed on forms:

- All questions are kept confidential.
- We do not recommend any particular treatment.
- Our material will not represent all that is available on the subject.
- The information might not apply specifically to your own condition.
- Our material should be used to formulate questions for discussion with your doctor or nurse.
- We hope that the information you find will be useful in communicating with your health professionals. If you have any questions about your unique medical condition, we strongly advise that you see your doctor.

All requests for information submitted to the library are considered to be confidential. This material is provided for informational purposes only and should not be construed as a recommendation or endorsement of any particular treatment. The information might not apply specifically to your own condition; it does not represent all that is available on the subject; and it might contain opinions of the author. Please consult your medical provider for advice relating to a medical problem or condition.

This material is intended to provide you with health information. It is not a substitute for consultation with a health professional.

Internet:

Information accessed through the Internet is of varying levels of quality and accuracy and should be discussed with your healthcare provider, NOT used as a substitute for professional healthcare.

Information provided by the Community Health Information Library does not imply medical recommendation or endorsement. The information provided should not be used as a substitute for consultation with a health provider.

Mediated literature search:

Please note that our search is by no means comprehensive or complete. The information enclosed does not necessarily reflect the views of [this institution] and is no way intended to take the place of the advice and recommendations of your personal healthcare provider.

Bibliographies:

This list does not constitute an endorsement of the information contained in the resources. It is provided for educational purposes only and is not intended for, nor engaged in, rendering medical advice or professional services. The information provided through this list and its links should not be used for diagnosing or treating a health problem or disease. It is not a substitute for professional care.

Electronic resources:

The references located through this online search are obtained from a variety of sources. No guarantees can be given that all literature pertaining to this topic has been retrieved. Further, the librarian provided information only and does not provide interpretations of such information. The material contained in the Health Reference Center is provided for informational purposes and should not be construed as medical advice or instruction. Consult your health professional for advice relating to a medical problem or condition.

Printed resources:

The purpose of X is to provide public access to a wide range of health and medical information, not to give medical advice or interpretation. Information provided by [this institution] does not imply recommendations or endorsement and is not a substitute for a consultation with a health professional.

Medical information obtained in this library should be used to begin further discussions with your healthcare provider. Although the library attempts to provide the most current medical information, it is not responsible for the information contained in the publication located in the library.

The materials in [this institution] are intended to provide general information for you. Some material may contain information that is the opinion of the author and not necessarily that of your healthcare provider. Please consult with your healthcare provider on specific medical questions.

This information is intended to provide you with health information. It is not a substitute for consultation with a health professional.

Brochures and bookmarks:

The purpose of this library is to provide public access to a wide range of health and medical information, not to give medical advice or interpretation. Information provided by the library does not imply a recommendation or endorsement. It is not a substitute for consultation with a health professional.

General disclaimers:

This information is not intended to be a substitute for medical advice or care from a physician or other healthcare professional.

The materials in [this institution] are intended to provide general information for you and do not substitute for professional medical advice. Please consult your physician on specific medical questions.

Notes

1. Beattie, Barbara C. 1998. "A Guide to Medical Reference in the Public Library." *Public Libraries* 27, no. 4 (winter): 172–75.
2. Duckworth, Paul. 1982. "Health Information for the Community." *Show-Me Libraries* (Aug): 18–20.
3. Murray, Susan. 1995. *Developing a Consumer Health Information Service: A Practical Guide.* Toronto: Metropolitan Toronto Reference Library.
4. Allen, Luella S. 1982. "Legal and Ethical Considerations in Providing Health Information." In *Developing Consumer Health Information Services*, ed. Alan M. Rees. New York: R.R. Bowker; Wood, Fred B., Becky Lyon, Mary Beth Schell, Paula Kitendaugh, Victor H. Cid, and Elliot R. Siegel. 2000. "Public Library Consumer Health Information Pilot Project: Results of a National Library of Medicine Evaluation." *Bulletin of the Medical Library Association* 88, no. 4 (Oct.): 314–22.
5. Wood and others, "Public Library Consumer Health Information Pilot Project."
6. Murray, *Developing a Consumer Health Information Service.*
7. Rees, Alan M. 1991. "Medical Consumerism: Library Roles and Initiative." In *Managing Consumer Health Information Services*, ed. Alan M. Rees. Phoenix: Oryx.
8. Rubin, R. and T. Froehlich. 1996. "Ethical Aspects of Library and Information Science." In *Encyclopedia of Library and Information Science*, ed. A. Kent and C. Hall. Volume 58, supplement 21. New York: Marcel Dekker.
9. Bunge, Charles A. 1999. "Ethics and the Reference Librarian." *The Reference Librarian* 66: 25–43, 41.
10. Huff, James. 1999. "Patron Confidentiality, Millennium Style." *American Libraries* 30, no. 6 (June/July): 86, 88; Stover, Mark. 1987. "Confidentiality and Privacy in Reference Service." *RQ* 27, no. 2 (winter): 240–44.
11. Weiner, R. 1997. "Privacy and Librarians: An Overview." *Texas Library Journal* 73, no. 1. Available online at www.txla.org.pubs.tlj-lq97/privacy.html; Garoogian, Rhoda. 1991. "Librarian/Patron Confidentiality: An Ethical Challenge." *Library Trends* 40, no. 2 (fall): 216–33.
12. Strauch, K., and B. Strauch, eds. 1990. *Legal and Ethical Issues in Acquisitions.* New York: Haworth.
13. Koehler, Wallace C., and J. Michael Pemberton. 2000. "A Search for Core Values: Toward a Model Code of Ethics for Information Professionals." *Journal of Information Ethics* 9, No. 1 (spring): 26–54, 29.
14. American Library Association. 1995. "Code of Ethics of the American Library Association." Adopted by the ALA Council June 8.
15. Medical Library Association. 1994. "Code of Ethics for Health Sciences Librarianship."
16. Medical Library Association. 1996. "The Librarian's Role in the Provision of Consumer Health Information and Patient Education." Policy statement developed by the Task Force of the Consumer and Patient Health Information Section. Approved by the Medical Library Association Board of Directors.
17. American Library Association, "Code of Ethics of the American Library Association."
18. Medical Library Association, "Code of Ethics for Health Sciences Librarianship."
19. American Library Association, "Code of Ethics of the American Library Association."
20. Medical Library Association, "Code of Ethics for Health Sciences Librarianship."
21. Nebraska Library Commission. 2001. *STAR Reference Manual*, 1994–2001. Information Services/Reference Training for Accurate Reference. "Good Reference Practice." www.nlc.state.ne.us/ref/star/star.html.

22. American Library Association. 1992. "Guidelines for Medical, Legal, and Business Responses at General Reference Desks." Adopted by the ALA Standards Committee and the Reference and Adult Services Division Board of Directors. *RQ* 31 (Summer): 554–55.

23. Dewdney, Patricia, Joanne G. Marshall, and Muta Tiamiyu. 1991. "A Comparison of Legal and Health Information Services in Public Libraries." *RQ* (winter): 185–96; Baker, Lynda M., Lothar Spang, and Christine Gogolowski, 1998. "The Provision of Consumer Health Information by Michigan Public Librarians." *Public Libraries* (July/Aug): 250–55.

24. Puckett, Marianne, Pamela Ashely, and J. Pat Craig. 1991. "Issues in Information Malpractice." *Medical Reference Services Quarterly* 10, no. 2 (summer): 33–45.

25. American Library Association, "Code of Ethics of the American Library Association."

26. Mintz, Anne P. 1985. "Information Practice and Malpractice." *Library Journal* 110, No. 15 (Sept. 15): 38–43, 40

27. American Library Association, "Code of Ethics of the American Library Association."

28. Murray, *Developing a Consumer Health Information Service.*

29. American Library Association. 1981. "Free Access to Libraries by Minors: An Interpretation of the Library Bill of Rights." Adopted by the ALA Council June 30, 1972, Amended July 1, 1981.

30. Medical Library Association, "Code of Ethics for Health Sciences Librarianship."

31. Puckett and others, "Issues in Information Malpractice."

32. Tomaiuolo, Nicholas G. and Barbara J. Frey. 1992. "Computer Database Searching and Professional Malpractice: Who Cares? *Bulletin of the Medical Library Association* 80, no. 4 (Oct.): 367–70.

33. Nasri, William A. 1987. "Professional Liability." In *Legal Issues for Library and Information Managers.* New York: Haworth Press, 141

34. Rodwell, John. 1984. "Legal Responsibilities of Special Librarians." *Australian Special Libraries News* 17, no. 3 (Sept.): 11–15.

35. Dragich, Martha J. 1989. "Information Malpractice: Some Thoughts on the Potential Liability of Information Professionals." *Information Technology and Libraries* 8 (Sept.): 265–72, 271.

36. Gray, John A. 1988. "Personal Malpractice Liability of Reference Librarians and Information Brokers." *Journal of Library Administration* 9, no 2 (summer): 71–83.

37. Rees, "Medical Consumerism," 32.

38. Rothstein, Julie A. 1993. "Ethics and the Role of the Medical Librarian: Healthcare Information and the New Consumer." *Bulletin of the Medical Library Association* 81, no. 3 (July): 253–58, 257.

39. Allen, "Legal and Ethical Considerations in Providing Health Information," 44.

40. Charney, Norman. 1978. "Ethical and Legal Questions in Providing Health Information." *California Librarian* 39 (Jan.): 25–33.

41. Charney, "Ethical and Legal Questions in Providing Health Information," 26.

42. Charney, "Ethical and Legal Questions in Providing Health Information."

43. Charney, "Ethical and Legal Questions in Providing Health Information."

44. Nasri, "Professional Liability."

45. Gray, "Personal Malpractice Liability of Reference Librarians and Information Brokers"; Puckett and others, "Issues in Information Malpractice."

46. Wan, Ronglin. 1994. "Reflections on Malpractice of Reference Librarians." *Public Libraries* 33 (Nov/Dec): 305–9.

47. Puckett and others, "Issues in Information Malpractice," 36.
48. Gray, John A. 1989. "The Health Sciences Librarian's Exposure to Malpractice Liability Because of Negligent Provision of Information." *Bulletin of the Medical Library Association* 77, no. 1 (Jan.): 33–37, 35.
49. Wan, "Reflections on Malpractice of Reference Librarians."
50. Gray, "The Health Sciences Librarian's Exposure to Malpractice Liability Because of Negligent Provision of Information."
51. Dragich, "Information Malpractice"; Puckett and others, "Issues in Information Malpractice."
52. Gray, "Personal Malpractice Liability of Reference Librarians and Information Brokers."
53. Dragich, "Information Malpractice"; Mintz, "Information Practice and Malpractice"; Pritchard, Teresa, and Michelle Quigley. 1989. "The Information Specialist: Malpractice Risk Analysis." *Online* 12, no. 3 (May) 57–62.
54. Cremieux, Karl A. 1996, "Malpractice: Is the Sky Falling?" *Special Libraries* (summer): 147–55, 152
55. Mika, Joseph J. and Bruce A. Shuman. 1988. "Legal Issues Affecting Libraries and Librarians, Lesson II: Liability Insurance, Malpractice, and Copyright." *American Libraries* 19, no. 2 (Feb.): 108–111.
56. Mika and Shuman, "Legal Issues Affecting Libraries and Librarians, Lesson II"; Nasri, "Professional Liability."
57. Nasri, "Professional Liability"; Puckett and others, "Issues in Information Malpractice."

Bibliography

American Library Association. 1980. "Library Bill of Rights." Adopted June 18, 1948; amended February 2, 1961, June 27, 1967, January 23, 1980.

American Library Association. 2000. *ALA News* 7, no. 4 (March 20).

Caywood, Carolyn. 1999. "Parents, Kids, Librarians: Can This Relationship Be Saved?" *American Libraries* 30, no. 6 (June/July): 74.

Hildebrand, Janet. 1991. "Is Privacy Reserved for Adults? Children's Rights at the Public Library." *School Library Journal* 37, no. 1 (January): 21–25.

Katz, Jon. 1996. "The Rights of Kids in the Digital Age." *Wired* (July). Available: www.wired.com/wired/archive/4.07/kids_pr.html.

About the Authors

Barbara Palmer Casini, recently retired as Director of the Memorial Library of Radnor Township in Wayne, Pennsylvania, has provided consumer health information in public and health sciences libraries for more than twenty years. She has delivered numerous presentations related to consumer health services for library professionals at regional and national associations. Among her many board positions, she served as President of the Pennsylvania Library

Association (1999) and of the Philadelphia Regional Chapter of the Medical Library Association (1992–1993).

Andrea Kenyon is Director of Public Health and Community Outreach at the College of Physicians of Philadelphia. She is Founder and Director of PhillyHealthInfo.org, a regionally focused consumer health information Web site and community outreach project serving Philadelphia and its surrounding counties. She has over twenty-eight years of experience working to improve access to and understanding of health and medical issues through information and education.

Chapter 27

The Realities of Today's Reference Desk

Sally Decker Smith and Roberta Johnson

Whether your preparation for working a public library reference desk was library school, undergraduate school, community college, or just an interest in a particular job in a particular library, we can assure you that there are many things that you haven't been taught. If you're lucky, you figure most of them out over the course of your career. If you're not, you stumble into one situation after another that either teaches them to you the hard way, or drives you out of the job you thought you'd like. And if you're really lucky, you are reading this and will get to the end as a person much better equipped to face the realities of public library reference work.

Who Are You? Who Do You Want to Be?

Are you a librarian? In some libraries, if you do not have an MLS, you are a wonderful contributor to the team, but you are not a librarian. In others, if you're not a shelver, you're a librarian. You could also be a paraprofessional, an information assistant, a member of the support staff, or a clerk. In some places, pages regularly staff a reference desk. But we will assume for the moment that you know what your job title is, whatever it may be. Are you also a Microsoft wizard, a copier fixer, shelver, freedom-of-speech advocate, teacher, or study hall monitor? There are many roles that fall under that "other duties as assigned" umbrella on your job description. Some will be assigned, all right, but some are just there, and you are the person who has to do them. Few job descriptions include requirements to help small children find missing parents, interrupt an adolescent sing-along, unjam a copier, or sharpen a pencil for a shaky senior. But if you get though a year at the reference desk without doing at least one of these, your library is truly one-of-a-kind.

You probably enjoy some of these roles and resent others, but all are a part of your job. Does the patron care? Only if your feelings about whatever role the patron needs is so blatant that they notice. And does that matter? Well, yes, because . . .

What Do You Represent to the Patrons?

Every other experience patrons have had in any library or with government officialdom of any sort colors their perception of who you are when you are at the reference desk. Are you a civil servant, an information goddess, a secretary, office supply source, Guardian of the Fortress of Knowledge, or an agent of the government? Friend, enemy, or co-conspirator? Every person who approaches the desk has a different version of you in his or her head.

And think for a moment about what it takes for a patron to approach you for the first time. They have to admit, albeit usually subconsciously, that you know something they do not, and that's very difficult for a lot of people. So they have to be brave. Or they have a problem that they have not been able to solve any other way—so even if they are not at all brave, they are desperate. Or they had such wonderful youth librarians when they were small that even though they haven't set foot in a library since eighth grade, they still think all librarians are wonderful. Or they are just accustomed to demanding what they want. But take a breath; no matter what the patron's approach is, remember that you are there to help them, and it's often much harder for them to ask for that help than it is for you to provide it.

Job Stress, Positive and Negative

Any job has positive and negative stressors, and this reference business is no exception. Even if you put aside all the issues of library philosophies, budgets, management, and everything else, the simple fact of being the person responsible for handling reference questions in a public library has plenty of plusses and minuses of its own.

Positives include:

1. Librarians are "people" people and like interacting with other humans.
2. Reference work is rarely boring.
3. You learn a lot—you can't help it!
4. You can feel good about contributing mightily to the communities you serve.
5. And there are few jobs with such immediate gratification: at least once a day—usually more often—you can be sure that someone will thank you for what you did to help them and know that they mean it.

Negatives include:

1. Some of those people are difficult.
2. You have to answer challenging and sometimes scary questions.
3. You may have to work nights and weekends.
4. You will probably work alone some, if not much, of the time.
5. You feel you're expected to know everything.

Beyond the stressors we share, everyone has personal stress points. As reference generalists, mostly we know a little about a lot, and what we know about differs widely. What one of us regards as an interesting challenge, another can easily see as something that makes us want to run and hide. Know what your personal stressors are; it makes it easier to find ways to deal with them. If genealogy, business reference, legal questions, or readers' advisory make you feel like a deer in headlights, find yourself some training or a trusty guidebook. Or find some backup. Have a list of people you can call on for help, whether they're inside your building or out. Patrons generally react positively to being told "Wow—what a great question. And it's beyond me, so if you can wait just a minute I'm going to consult an expert."

Medical and legal questions scare a lot of us, and really, they should. We are not doctors or lawyers and misunderstood information in those areas can have dire consequences, physical or financial. Know what your library's policy on answering these kinds of questions is, and follow it faithfully.

No discussion about reference desk realities is complete without a mention of disturbed—or disturbing—patrons. While part of the charm of working reference is never knowing who will approach you next with what question, part of the vulnerability is . . . never knowing who will approach you next with what question. It's important to keep in mind that while there are always members of the general public who need professional help, it's not necessarily our profession. Be nice, but be secure. Again, know your library's policies, know who and where your backup is, and know how to work the panic button (if you have one).

The USA PATRIOT Act has brought into sharp focus for us all the importance of knowing who in your building is responsible for dealing with outside authorities. If you are brand-new to the reference desk, odds are it isn't you— but at night or on weekends, it might be. Find out. And if it ever is you, be sure you know ahead of time what you are supposed to do.

Know what your library's rules and policies are, but also know how far you can go in bending them. Saying "No/We can't do that/YOU can't do that" may be easier, but using your judgment is also part of the job. You are not in the Army now.

Challenging Patrons

As well as providing technical help (absolutely expected these days), we are increasingly called on to be social workers and counselors, experts on human behavior, which is something we're not usually trained for. But if you work in a public place, the public keeps showing up. So you have to look for opportunities to improve those skills or suggest easy ways to administration to improve them. Suggest the police pay regular visits to the library, talk to staff, and reassure them about their presence. Have the city social worker or nurse come to department meetings to talk about helping people with disabilities, the elderly, the mentally ill, and the homeless. How do you feel about calling 911? The sooner you sort that question out in your head, the easier it will be to handle when it comes up.

Obviously, helping the difficult, meaning cranky, patron is something different. Also, it's very valuable to really, really understand that this isn't personal; the annoying patron will walk down the street and annoy the people at the White Hen too.

There were bullies in kindergarten, there will probably be bullies in the home for elderly library staff, and there are assuredly bullies approaching our desks. Again, know your policies and your backup, and be firm. When a patron huffs that he's going to go over your head because you tell him he can't take a nap on the couch in the high school area, help him. Giving a bullying patron your name and your boss' name and extension often takes the wind out of the sails of people whose goal was to reduce you to doing what they want out of fear that they'd tell. (We're grownups now—"I'm telling" should-n't affect you the way it did when you were eight.) In these cases, always warn your boss, just in case. Of all the things bosses don't appreciate, surprises are near the top of the list.

Reassurance
Remember: They're asking you for help (no matter how impatient or preemptory they are). You were hired because you are intelligent, flexible, and friendly (or you should be). The bottom line is that you're a library person, not a doctor or a lawyer, police officer or social worker. Better to do your job well than theirs badly.

How Are You Doing?
You can't see yourself at the desk, but there are ways to know. First, even on the busiest day, you control your behavior. Always be welcoming and approachable, at least as much as you can be without attracting more than your fair share of crazy people. Why? Because patrons deserve a positive experience, because people like being treated that way, and—the biggest reason—because that's the job you took.

Watch your body language—rolling your eyes or shaking your head at any time at a public service desk sends exactly the wrong message. Look up, smile, and greet everyone who walks by. Ask "Can I help you find anything?" as they approach and "Did you find what you needed?" as they leave. A patron who gets a negative response—or who sees you giving a negative response to another patron—will think twice about approaching the desk again.

In addition to a certain generosity of spirit, boundaries are an important part of your approach to life at the desk, too. If you share details about your personal life with patrons willy-nilly, you can be fairly sure it will eventually come back to bite you. You can be their helpful, friendly library staffer without sharing details of your surgery or listening to theirs.

Managing Traffic
A steady but manageable stream of patrons—in person, on the phone, or electronically—is the traffic pattern that most of us find enjoyable. You can make friendly eye contact with the person who approaches the desk as you're finishing up a phone call. If another call comes in while you're engaged with a

patron, you can let it go to voicemail (if you're lucky enough to have that option) or quickly answer it, get a phone number, and promise a callback. You can say things to patrons like "Would you like me to look it up for you, or show you how?" and have time to do either one. You get into the "reference zone" and time flies by in a way that feels very productive.

This traffic pattern is, of course, rare. And if you have many other things you need to accomplish while you're at the desk, this is the one that leaves you in most danger of resenting the patrons who "interrupt" whatever you're trying to get done. As soon as you notice you're feeling that way, stop whatever it is you're doing that is not directly helping patrons. Unless there's a way you can be relieved at the desk, accept the fact that that report, journal, or whatever it is, will have to wait.

Overwhelmingly busy times can be predictable (Monday and Tuesday evenings for us) or sneak up on you out of the blue for no apparent reason. The good news about them is that you have no illusion of getting anything else done, and the best way to handle them is to get your brain into triage mode as quickly as possible. A mob at the desk gets smaller quickly when you have started one person searching a database, given another three books to check the indexes of, directed two more to the copier and rest-room, told another where the audio books are, and called for backup (if you're lucky enough to have that option). And then, of course, you need to go back to the first patron, and on and on. It's like that old variety show act where someone put plates up on sticks and started them spinning and had to keep dashing from one to another to keep them all spinning. It's just what we do.

Very quiet times are a mixed blessing. Yes, you can get something done. You can also get so thoroughly engrossed in whatever it is you're doing that when a patron does approach the desk, you might not notice, and a lot of patrons are hesitant to interrupt what they see as something more important than their question. So even if there's not a single person on the floor, look up from time to time. You might see someone coming, and at the very least it's better for your eyes! You may want to think about walking the floor. People who would never dream of bothering you at the desk will often be happy to see you heading down the aisle to where they are because they can't figure out which way the numbers go. Offer to help people at the catalog—even patrons who have mastered basic searches are delighted to learn shortcuts or advanced searches that will get them to what they need faster.

Listen to Patron Responses, Verbal and Otherwise

Do patrons look pleased or doubtful of your answers? Did you ask if that was everything they needed? Did you turn the computer screen so they could see what you were doing as you searched? The reference interview is a different—and vital—part of working at the desk, but what we're talking about here is basic human interaction!

And here is as good a place as any to remind you to never, ever answer a question from your head. If you know an answer, it makes it a lot easier to look it up, but look it up we must. The longer you work reference the more you will know—and the less you will trust your own head!

Listen to Staff Responses

How often do you ask for help—and how do you feel about that? No one—it bears repeating—no one knows it all. Reference work in public libraries is about the most collegial work there is. Do you feel inadequate when you have to ask for help and avoid doing it? You may be doing your patrons a great disservice. Do you ask for help on everything because you don't trust your own knowledge? You're probably doing yourself a disservice and likely annoying your colleagues if you've been doing the job for more than a month. Acknowledge your gaps in information and fill as many of them as you can, as quickly as possible. And then remember: it's okay if someone else knows.

The Good News Sandwich

There's a helpful way to deal with having to tell a patron what would be bad news if it were delivered point blank. Sandwich it in between two positives:

> I'm sure we can answer that question (positive), but maybe not by myself, or in five minutes, or even at this library (negative). I know who to ask, or who to refer you to outside the library (ends on a positive note).

Our goal is always to end transactions on a positive note, for our sake and that of our patrons.

Do I Belong Here?

So how is your job going? Maybe you're learning that you're not such a public library person after all. Or maybe you love libraries, but your heart and soul are in cataloging. Or maybe the philosophy and public service values practiced at the library in the next town over are more in tune with yours. None of you are shackled to a job for life—and if the fit is no good, you do yourself and your patrons a favor if you make a move into something that suits you better.

Public service is not for everyone. A good rule of thumb is that if you deal with three crabby patrons in a row, it's probably not them. It's you. Your challenge is to decide whether you're having a bad day because your teenager just took the car out of town for the first time and your brain is otherwise occupied or if this is part of a larger pattern and an indication that public service is simply not for you. It's not a character flaw to admit it.

Supporting Your Library

An unwritten part of every job description in the world is "Make your boss look good." This includes making it clear by the way you do your job and your general attitude toward patrons and staff that hiring you was a great move on your boss' part. It's important to make our libraries look good, too. Never criticize policy to patrons. If you cannot support a policy or at the very least be neutral about it, unless you're in a position to change it, either keep quiet, or find a new job more in line with your values. Whoever is signing your paycheck gets the last word—it's probably not you.

Stupid Patron Stories

Because we deal with so many people and subjects, some of those interactions are going to be more entertaining than others. But does that make the patron who came to us with a question stupid? Absolutely not. Many do not know what we know—that's why they come to us, and that's pretty smart. Do you really want to think that your lawyer goes home at night laughing at her stupid client because you weren't sure whether you wanted to draft a will or a living trust? Or that your doctor entertains at dinner with the "stupid patient" story of how you didn't know why the sciatic nerve in your back could make your foot hurt? This is another example of treating people as we'd want to be treated. Further, every time you talk about "stupid patrons," you hear yourself. That's just not a concept we want in our brains. Human comedy? Sure. Stupid? Emphatically not.

Five Things to Remember
1. Tenacity is not always a virtue. (If patrons' eyes glaze over and they edge toward the door while you're enthusiastically looking at one more Web site, trust us: that question is over.)
2. Don't overexplain (the history of the DVD collection in 500 words or less . . .).
3. Don't get sucked in or take things personally. (Remember what you represent to the patron—that's who they're talking to.)
4. Don't get defensive. (It just escalates whatever situation you're in.)
5. Don't blame the computer, the city, or anyone else.

And our final piece of advice: ask what they want—maybe you can give it to them. Now go forth, head held high, welcoming smile in place, and make the library world proud to have you in it!

About the Authors

Sally Decker Smith began her library career in Circulation, as everyone should. Moving from there to her current position as Special Services Librarian involved time spent supervising pages, processing ILL, overseeing Reference, then Adult Services, then Public Services. She writes a lot, but reads more.

Roberta S. Johnson has spent two happy decades in libraries, starting in the Circulation Department, which she recommends to everyone. She had her fifteen minutes of fame for founding the fiction discussion list, Fiction_L, in 1995. She is currently Head of Adult Services at the Des Plaines Public Library in Illinois.

Part VII

A Technology Mini-Primer for Public Librarians

Technology affects all aspects of public librarianship and you and your staff members likely rely on a wide range of technologies. As library director, you need to have an understanding of the technology that affects your library on a daily basis. Whether it is to understand the benefits of different technologies in order to make budget decisions, plan services, uncover long term implications, or simply provide better, faster service, the perceptive public library director will want to keep a finger on the pulse of developments in library technology.

In this section, you'll find a variety of helpful articles. In "Virtually Seamless: Exploring the Role of Virtual Public Librarians," a *Public Libraries* article written by Janet Clapp and Angela Pfeil you'll see how traditional reference techniques can be used in virtual library service, and "Library Service Planning with GIS and Census Data" reviews the idea of using Geographic Information Systems (GIS) and census data for planning public library services. For quick, expert accounts of various library technologies, check out "eContent," "Blogs and Wikis," and "RFID Technology for Libraries." These PLA TechNotes written by Richard W. Boss will keep you up to speed.

Chapter 28

Virtually Seamless: Exploring the Role of Virtual Public Librarians

Janet Clapp and Angela Pfeil

Virtual library service is another branch of the public library, the branch that helps users where they are—online. Virtual reference librarians adapt traditional reference techniques to suit this new medium of exchange between patron and librarian.

The reference librarian in a public library expects and answers questions on a wide variety of topics, but is rarely asked, "Are you a computer?" To some users, virtual librarians are not even human. This article focuses on virtual librarianship and the public library user, using the term "virtual librarian" to include any librarian doing virtual reference. Drawing on the experiences of contract virtual librarians, this article will explore the advantages of virtual reference in a public library setting as well as describe virtual reference service and virtual users, and look at the backgrounds of current virtual reference librarians. The authors have worked as virtual reference librarians for two years with Tutor.com's Librarians by Request using the LSSI Virtual Reference toolkit, and both have previous professional experience in public libraries.

Virtual librarians bring age—and department—specific levels of experience to work, but unlike public librarians, they are unable to send a child to the children's room for help, or an adult to the circulation desk. Virtual librarians serve customers of all kinds, regardless of their previous expertise, through a relatively new medium that is becoming a common means of communication for people of all ages. They may offer reader's advisory to a young teen one minute, and bibliographic instruction to a senior citizen the next. In a virtual setting they serve everyone and try to answer every question, no matter how outlandish.

What Exactly Is Virtual Reference?

When virtual librarians tell people what they do for a living, even professionals in the library field often respond, "So, what exactly do you do?" For the purpose of this article, the term "virtual reference" is used to describe real-time, online, chat-based reference. The authors of this article use virtual reference software that utilizes chat for communication between librarian and user. It appears as a written conversation between librarian and patron, like instant messaging.

Until the mid-1990s, librarians relied on the mail, the telephone, and the fax machine to help users who were unable to come into the library for reference assistance. As the general population used the Internet more often, librarians began utilizing this new technology to deliver reference services. There are varying levels of digital or virtual reference service. The most basic technology uses only asynchronous interactions, where the user and librarian communicate in a delayed fashion, as opposed to a live one, such as in the case of e-mails sent back and forth between user and librarian. More advanced technology uses synchronous, live, real-time interaction between the librarian and the user. Some live systems allow for user and librarian to send short messages back and forth via chat software; other systems allow for the librarian to take control of the user's browser as though the librarian and user were at a reference desk looking at a single computer monitor.[1]

Virtual reference is a growing service, and it is difficult to obtain exact numbers. Many services are collaborative efforts. Bernie Sloan, senior library information systems consultant at the University of Illinois Office for Planning and Budgeting, maintains DigitalReference Services: A Bibliography (www.lis.uiuc.edu~b-sloan/digiref.html). It lists sixty-two collaborative virtual reference services, meaning two or more libraries working together to offer the service.[2] According to the Global Census of Digital Reference survey by Joseph Janes, as of November 2003 there were 162 services, 42 of which are public libraries.[3] Live Ref, a Registry of Real-Time Digital Reference Services lists sixteen public libraries.[4] Tutor.com's Spring 2004 Client List boasts more than one hundred public library clients, including statewide services, using one or more of their services, including the Virtual Reference Toolkit, Librarians by Request, Live Homework Help, and Bilingual Services.[5]

How VR Technology Works

Most of the major virtual reference service providers do not require any clientside downloads. This means that only the librarian is expected to meet certain PC requirements. The requirements for Tutor.com's Virtual Reference Toolkit include:

- administrative access to Windows (Power User is not enough)
- Pentium 200 MHz or higher
- 128 MB RAM
- Windows XP, Windows NT 4.0 with Service Pack 5 or higher, Windows 98, Windows 2000, or Windows ME
- Microsoft Internet Explorer 5.0 or higher
- 56K or better Internet connection[6]

Upon meeting these requirements, signing with a virtual reference provider, and training librarians in a new medium, libraries can deliver virtual reference to their customers. A public library may train its librarians to work virtual reference during open hours, and contract a virtual reference provider to cover their virtual reference desk when the library is closed. Some libraries use only provider librarians to handle their virtual reference desk.

The user connects to the virtual librarian by clicking the designated icon or hyperlink on the subscribing library's Web site (although it is possible for any agency to provide this service, currently all of Tutor.com's clients are library based). The user then enters some form of identifying information, such as a library barcode or zip code, and begins a session with either a remotely located virtual librarian or a public librarian monitoring the queue, the virtual equivalent of a librarian sitting at the reference desk. The user is immediately connected to a virtual librarian no matter where he or she is or what time of day it is. The virtual librarian can send information from the host library's databases or catalog, or from the Internet to help answer the customer's question. In order to respect licensing agreements, the virtual librarian only uses the resources available to patrons through their access library. The users see the information on their computer screens in the session. While specific technologies may differ by vendor (see sidebar on this page for major virtual reference service providers), the end result is the same: the patron gets online assistance from a librarian.

Major Virtual Reference Service Providers

OCLC's QuestionPoint
www.questionpoint.org

Altarama Information Systems VRL Plus
www.altarama.com/products/vrlplus.htm

Tutor.com—Ask A Librarian Express
www.tutor.com/libraries-education/products/ask-a-librarian

There are other e-commerce live chat services to choose from, not specific to libraries. For a list of real-time, chat-based services, visit www.teachinglibrarian.org/chatsoftware.htm.

Who Benefits from Virtual Reference Service?

Virtual reference offers a number of benefits to the patron. In addition to the fact that the librarian is at the user's point of need, non-native English speakers may find it easier and more effective to speak with a virtual librarian. The accent is lost in the written world, and they can use a nearby dictionary to understand the librarian's responses. Homebound people can ask questions and look at resources, receiving help that is similar to that received by those people who are able to enter the library physically. Since users can choose to remain anonymous when entering a session, either by using a fake name or by typing "anonymous" in the name field, the timid teen who wants to know about depression or pregnancy can ask a question without embarrassment. (Library administrators may also choose to have all virtual reference transactions remain anonymous.)

When public libraries use virtual librarians, the library can offer extended hours of library service without the number of staff needed to keep the physical library open. The pool of skilled librarians is no longer limited by geographical boundaries. If a bilingual or specialist librarian does not work in the local area, one might be available virtually. Perhaps the main reason public libraries offer virtual reference is to serve patrons where they want service—online.

Your future customers are online today. While some public libraries lack young adult sections altogether, homework questions comprise the majority of virtual librarians' work. Librarians only need to see the huge dip in the number of virtual reference sessions during school vacation periods to realize the importance of the students. They are on the Internet, not coming to the library. Because these patrons live in the virtual world, the real public library may not be a significant place for them. Virtual reference offers a double advantage by reaching out to school-age patrons. First, virtual reference librarians can and do suggest actual books and physical resources to these users, thereby getting them in the library door. Second, today's youth are tomorrow's taxpayers, and if the library was never a useful place to them, they will not support it in the future. Finally, librarians are educated and skilled in accessing and evaluating information for those who need it. If the patron is online looking for it, we should be there providing it.

The Virtual User

Due to privacy and anonymity issues, the virtual librarian often has no statistics or profile to define the virtual user quantitatively. There is a more amorphous understanding of who the virtual user is based solely on transactions. It seems that young adults are the largest users, and homework-related queries form the major category of questions. Most virtual reference users seem comfortable in the online world.

There is no limit to the scope of questions asked online. Patrons who walk into the physical library have a limited collection to peruse. Users at an Internet terminal in the physical library often expect a librarian to start them on a search, but not to continue until all possibilities are exhausted. In contrast, virtual users consider virtual librarians to be advanced search engines. Questions asked at the library are often library-related, such as "Where are your books on taxidermy?" Online, questions are more likely to extend beyond those related to libraries, books, and research to the Internet in general, such as "How do I download a song?" Given the misperception that all information is available on the Internet, the virtual user expects the virtual librarian to pluck the answer she wants from the vastness of cyberspace, with instantaneous efficiency. Because they have the seemingly infinite Internet at their fingertips, rather than the visibly limited resources of a library collection, virtual users expect virtual librarians to have quick access to arcane or unusual information.

The expectations of virtual users seem to be a bit higher than those of public library users. First, the latter often have enough past experiences with libraries to know what is possible. Virtual reference is a new service, and virtual users do not always equate it with libraries. They may not even be sure they are communicating with a human, never mind a librarian. Second, they expect more at a quicker pace. The virtual patron sees nobody else competing for the librarian's attention. When chatting online, the user assumes that the librarian is solely involved in that session and is not helping anybody else. There is exclusivity to the nature of the virtual session, narrowed down to the computer screen.

Customers using virtual reference sometimes expect the librarian to find the specific statistic they need and evaluate it, write their book reports, edit their papers, or design their Web sites. The virtual librarian must use the interview to educate the user about what help the librarian can and cannot provide.

The anonymity factor adds another dimension to the virtual reference transaction, both for the librarian and the user. For the user, this anonymity leads to a loss of the inhibition that usually restrains the public library user from asking rude or irrational questions. The virtual user may be more comfortable in the virtual world, and may never use the physical library. The public library is often a community center, and the physical public library user is often a return visitor, a face familiar to the librarian. The virtual librarian, in comparison, usually has no relationship with the patron, past or future. (Customers can provide a call history, which would indicate whether they are repeat customers. Patrons will also sometimes refer to a previous session in an interaction with a virtual librarian.)

Constant communication is vital between virtual librarian and user. If the virtual user does not answer reference interview questions, it can be difficult to ascertain the scope of that patron's information need. The librarian can only ask so many questions before customers feel as if they are being interrogated and refuse to talk. In the public library, the librarian can bring patrons to an area to browse on their own, and then suggest that they return for further assistance, if needed. Rather than lead customers to a collection of books, virtual librarians must send a site or source that seems the most useful, based only on their own understanding of the users' messages. Users may disconnect without indicating to the librarian whether the information answered their questions. Finally, because of anonymity, virtual patrons may log back on and repeat the question, in hopes of finding a different librarian with a different response.

Because of the nature of the virtual world, most of the time the virtual user and the virtual librarian do not share the same view. Only if certain versions of virtual reference software are used can the librarian and the user see the same search process (this still does not require a download of software on the user's part). The co-browsing feature permits patron and librarian to move together through a catalog or database. The patron can see the exact work the librarian is doing as she searches, and the librarian can see the selections the patron makes. Whether or not there is co-browsing, the librarian must explain the procedure step-by-step for doing a search.

Who Are Virtual Librarians?

A 2003 internal and informal survey of virtual librarians working for Tutor.com's Librarians by Request service shows that 58 percent of respondents have experience working in public libraries. Sixty-seven percent have worked in academic libraries, 8 percent in school libraries, 25 percent in special libraries, and 17 percent have experience in other capacities, such as IT management. Eighty-three percent of the respondents have been working as virtual librarians for less than one year. One-quarter of the respondents do virtual reference as their sole employment, while the remaining three-quarters work part-time in addition to other full-time or part-time employment. The majority of the survey respondents (59 percent) work less than sixteen hours per week in a virtual librarian capacity. All of Tutor.com's Librarians by Request employees hold MLS or MLIS degrees, work from the comfort of their home, and monitor calls during their scheduled times.[7]

Virtual librarians must be able to multitask and be comfortable in an online environment. While they do not need to be computer experts, they do need to know how to search online, and have an understanding of chat communication. Different library systems have different online resources that librarians can use for that library's clients, so virtual librarians must be familiar with numerous databases. Whether or not the client library has customer authentication software through the Web site in order to use electronic resources, license agreements and copyright rules are followed using client-driven guidelines.

Librarian training usually involves practice sessions where the trainee acts as a librarian to another librarian who plays the part of the patron. At Tutor.com, trainees then shadow an experienced librarian, joining in calls to see how the experienced librarian handles them. Finally, the trainee takes calls while an experienced librarian shadows and can offer assistance and answer questions as the trainee needs.

The Virtual Reference Interview

To many virtual librarians, public librarians seem to be at an advantage when serving customers because they can assess the person's age, state of mind, patience level, and often the purpose for the information even before starting the verbal reference interview. Library schools pride themselves on turning out librarians that understand the customer's physical signals. By beginning the reference interview with nonverbal communication, public librarians are able to avoid many intrusive, personal questions, such as "How old are you?" and "What grade is this for?"

Virtual librarians are unable to see customers, and information is usually limited to their name (which may be fictitious), the library they use, and their question. Depending on the system used, even the information the patron provides may not be verifiable. If the user logs on anonymously, there is no information at all. As a result, the reference interview conducted by virtual librarians starts with evaluating the question, as it is written on the screen, not through assessing the actual patron. The virtual librarian can make no assumptions. What might be seen as intrusive questions in a physical setting must be asked online to determine the exact information needs, the level of information required, and where the person has already searched. The virtual librarian must be precise in speech, as the only methods either the librarian or the user have for evaluating each other are language and speed of response. Because of the virtual user's expectations of rapid results, the reference interview must be quick.

One or two open questions will obtain information from the patron, but a series of closed questions will prove frustrating for user and librarian alike. If the librarian explains the reason for the interview, the user is less likely to be offended. For example, the request, "In order to find the source most helpful to you, please tell me what grade level you are in" is less abrupt than "What grade is this for?"

Virtual librarians might use prescripted messages approved by the client library. These saved messages can be accessed through a dropdown list, saving the librarian from typing commonly used phrases. For example, messages include "Where have you already looked?" and "Can you be more specific about what you need?" Without any visible signs of age or comprehension level, it is necessary for the librarian to ask sense-making questions. By knowing the purpose behind the question, as well as the customer's level of competence, they can provide appropriate authoritative information.

When a virtual librarian asks, "Where have you already looked?" the response is commonly the name of a specific search engine the patron used. Although using the virtual reference service, library users are frequently unaware of the library's electronic reference sources, such as encyclopedias, that are available to them from their home computer. The virtual librarian may introduce users to pertinent online resources, but there is a limit to the amount of demonstration that can be done through a chat medium. Bibliographic instruction requires detailed messages and continuous checking with patrons that they understand the librarian's explanation.

While serving a public library patron, a librarian can find something to get them started, and often leave them to browse those resources with a statement such as "If you need more help, come see me. I will be right over there." The physical public librarian can also return to the user, or simply look in the user's direction, to see how the user is progressing. The virtual librarian must multitask by using the keyboard for both searching and chatting with the user, while reading the user's communications and the search results. Because of the limits of technology and the human mind, a librarian cannot leave open numerous sessions while the virtual user browses online resources. If the user does not communicate satisfaction or lack thereof, the virtual librarian will be uncertain of the user's progress in understanding the information.

Finding Library Specific Information for Your Customers

Virtual reference librarians are expected to know what resources are available through the library and how to use each resource to its fullest. At Tutor.com, all Librarians by Request staff monitor all clients and must be familiar with the resources of each member library. Simply by the nature of the job, virtual librarians are adept at searching electronic databases as well as scouring the Internet to find information, and often complete many questions by simply using these resources. But there are times when they wish they could consult a book because they know a print resource would more easily answer the question. Virtual librarians who work from home do not have access to a print reference collection in order to aid the patron. Occasionally we have to refer the patron back to the home library, which may be unwelcome news to the patron, who may simply not have the time or inclination to wait. In some cases, patrons visit the virtual reference librarian because of a disappointing experience at a physical library.

Virtual librarians enter a library and see its collection in the same way the online user does, through its Web presence. Therefore, the public library collection must include its Web site. In choosing to offer online, real-time reference service, a library's Web site must be organized in such a way that any newcomer can understand it. If librarians have difficulty finding information on the library's Web site, users are even less likely to find the answers they want.

In a physical library, there are directional signs, informational signs, and staff to help direct customers to what they want. Online, even if virtual staff are available, public library Web sites often lack the signage needed for customers to feel empowered to search on their own. Information that is important to customers must be clearly visible on the library's Web site. Virtual librarians are often asked questions about the patron's account, the library's policies, and how to find articles. Answers to common questions such as "How do I renew my books?" "What is my PIN?" "How do I place a hold?" "What are the fines for overdue books?" and "What can I borrow from the library?" need to be in logical places and use nonlibrarian terms. Librarians know to look in the "About" section of any library Web site, if there is one, to find the policies and procedures common to that district. Virtual users, on the other hand, do not know this and may come to your virtual reference area to ask these questions. Others may be reluctant to ask at all and therefore never get the information they want.

If a library's Web site spells out its procedures and policies clearly, patrons are more empowered and less likely to get frustrated with the library. Even if they are baffled, a helpful site gives the virtual librarian the information to help walk the patron through the process. After all, it is the virtual librarians that are with the patron in the catalog when the library is closed. If the site offers help screens that spell out procedures step by step, with screen-print graphics, patrons might know how to help themselves next time.

Building Your Virtual Library

Through the authors' experience working in virtual reference for at least ten different public library clients, many library-related questions have been identified that are common to all clients. The library's Web site is one of the primary places that virtual librarians get information to give to library customers. The following list presents suggestions for improving library Web sites to enhance service. In addition see examples of best practices for **Cleveland Public Library** (www.cpl.org/LinksLibrary.asp?FormMode=DBNew), which uses simple terminology in classifying their electronic resources in order to provide easier access for their customers; **Ann Arbor District Library** (www.aadl.org/community), which has an entire section of their Web site devoted to community information, including local history and genealogy research tools; **Denver Public Library** (www.denverlibrary.org/card/all.html), which answers the most common customer questions in their library card resources page; and **Hennepin County Library** (www.hclib.org/pub/info/library_services.cfm), which clearly describes other services available at the library.

Information to Include

In the "About the Library" section, include the following information:

- **My card.** If patrons are on your Web site, they probably want to know how to get to their record. They want to know what items they have checked out, when they're due, what their fines are for, what is on hold, and how to renew items. Spell out how to find that information, including where to look on the screen. Explain nifty features like being able to change the location pickup of a hold, if your system offers this. Last, but not least, inform users how to get their personal identification number (PIN), if applicable.
- **Getting a card.** Include how to get a card, how much it costs, where the card can be used, who can use their card at your library, and whether items can be returned to your library from other libraries. The more information you provide the better so patrons do not walk into your library and leave dissatisfied because they did not know to bring two forms of identification. Include a picture pointing to the barcode if they need it for any reason.
- **Basics.** Include hours, directions, phone numbers and extensions, and contact information. Be specific about closed days and holidays.

- **Local history.** What kind of local history information does your library provide? The virtual librarian cannot guess what is available and may be thousands of miles away. This is also useful for the genealogy researcher who is trying to decide whether to visit you. Include local items like high school yearbooks, especially if they are not listed in your library catalog.
- **How to . . .** Outline step-by-step procedures on how to renew items and place holds, including information on what may be renewed how many times and for how long.
- **Equipment and meeting rooms.** List what equipment your library offers and what fees, if any, are charged. Include copiers (color or not), faxes, and especially computer programs that are available on the computers for public use, as well as information on reserving equipment or rooms.
- **Calendar of events.** What is happening at your library and when?
- **Policies.** If you do not want all your policies posted, at least include anything that has to do with your collection and services.
- **Donations.** Do you want somebody to drop their old *Reader's Digests* in the book drop?

In the section related to "Finding a Book, Magazine, Video, or CD," include the following information:

- **Catalog link.** The catalog link should be big and clear. Provide help, especially if you recently migrated to a new system.
- **Newspapers and magazines.** List your holdings on your Web site, or direct the customer to the online catalog if these items are listed there.
- **Booklists, new books, book clubs.** Help your users find the books they want.
- **Lists of new items.** If you provide lists on your Web site of recent acquisitions, define the time period you are using.
- **Explanation of terms.** If you tell patrons to enter "borrower ID," tell them what it is and where they can find it.

In the "Research" section, include the following items:

- **Summary of databases.** "EBSCOhost" does not mean "magazines" to a patron. Annotations and suggestions can help a patron choose which resource to try. Clearly identify which databases are accessible remotely.
- **Local links.** It is helpful to have a link to your local town or county government, as well as the state government, the local newspaper, and the local historical society.
- **Genealogy.** List what resources are available, how they are obtained, and any fees involved in this process.

Conclusion

The virtual librarian is a law librarian for every state and municipality in his or her jurisdiction. She is the academic librarian helping college students with research papers. The virtual librarian is also a computer expert, helping users find computer games or download music. He answers trivia, finds good books, and helps patrons use their library. The virtual library is another branch of the public library, the branch that helps users where they are comfortable—at home.

Notes

1. Stephen Francoeur, "Digital Reference," The Teaching Librarian. Accessed May 14, 2004, www.teachinglibrarian.org/digref.htm.
2. Bernie Sloan, "Collaborative Live Reference Services," Bernie Sloan's Digital Reference Pages. Accessed May 14, 2004, www.lis.uiuc.edu/~b-sloan/collab.htm. (Editor's Note: Resource no longer available; access attempted June 15, 2009).
3. Joseph Janes, "The Global Census of Digital Reference," Virtual Reference Desk 2003 Conference. Accessed May 14, 2004, www.vrd2003.org/proceedings/presentation.cfm?PID=162.
4. Gerry McKiernan, "Public," LiveRef(sm): A Registry of Real-Time Digital Reference Services. Accessed May 14, 2004, www.public.iastate.edu/~CYBER-STACKS/LiveRef.htm.Public.
5. Tutor.com, "Tutor.com Client List Spring 2004." Accessed May 21, 2004, www.tutor.com/company/clients.aspx. (Editor's Note: Resource no longer available; access attempted June 15, 2009).
6. Tutor.com, "Virtual Reference Toolkit Configuration Guide." Accessed May 14, 2004, www.vrtoolkit.net/vrsupport/files/VRT_Configuration_Guide.pdf. (Editor's Note: Tutor.com's Virtual Reference Toolkit is now called Ask A Librarian Express. This url is no longer available. Ask A Librarian Express can be found at www.tutor.com/libraries-education/products/ask-a-librarian.)
7. Tutor.com "Librarians By Request." Accessed Nov. 16, 2004, www.tutor.com/products/lbr.aspx. (Editor's Note: Resource no longer available; see www.tutor.com/libraries-education/products/ask-a-librarian.)

About the Authors

Janet Clapp is Virtual Reference Librarian and Mentor with Tutor.com as well as a reference librarian at Athens-Clarke County Library in Georgia. She has received the Samuel Swett Green Award for exemplary virtual reference and writes reviews for *Library Journal*.

Angela Pfeil spent ten years working in libraries and education and is currently a Project Manager with Clearwire. Her book, *Going Places with Youth Outreach: Smart Marketing Strategies for Your Library*, was published by ALA Editions in 2005.

Chapter 29

Library Service Planning with GIS and Census Data

Denice Adkins and Denyse K. Sturges

Geographic Information Systems (GIS) are popping up everywhere. The MapQuest directions you printed out for your journey, your new car with the OnStar navigational system, and your wristwatch with a Global Positioning System (GPS) chip all use GIS to orient you to the world around you. The GPS chip in your dashboard sends a signal saying that you are at a particular location. That information is combined with a road map containing latitudinal and longitudinal measurements, and as a result, your car can tell you which streets to take to reach your destination.

GIS software works by combining maps with "geocoded" information.[1] The process of geocoding information links that information with a particular place on a digitized map. The map already contains the "picture" of the information: you can see where the streets are and estimate your journey's length. The information added to that map brings more meaning to it. For instance, information can be added that gives street names, tells you which streets are one-way, where traffic jams are likely to occur, and which intersections have high accident rates. With this added information, the map is more useful to the driver. An added benefit to using a GIS system is that information can be updated relatively quickly. If an influx of winter visitors changes traffic flow in a city, that information can be added to the map for the winter months, or taken away for the summer. Although street maps and driving directions may have some applicability to public librarians who need to travel from one branch to another, or bookmobile drivers faced with new routes, the real benefit of using GIS in public libraries is in its ability to present information about the library's service community.

In this article, we review how Census 2000 information and GIS software can be used to plan library services. We'll look at real data from two branches in the Phoenix (Ariz.) Public Library system: the Ocotillo Branch in the less-developed southwestern part of the city; and the Yucca Branch in the heart of the city. Data from these two branches will be used to show how GIS software can connect the library service mission to each branch's unique demographic situation.

How Will GIS Software Improve Public Library Service?

GIS software allows you to visually represent and manipulate information about your service population. Geographically bound data, such as census demographics, can be connected to other geographically bound data. The map image can be quickly changed to present different perspectives on your information—one image could represent the number of children in your service area, while another portrays the locations of laundromats and grocery stores. Pictures and maps communicate more than tables and text, making presentations to the library board of trustees or city commissioners more memorable and meaningful.

GIS software has the potential to improve public library service by increasing libraries' awareness of the communities surrounding them. Libraries need to know who their communities really are, beyond just the small percentage who show up in the library on a regular basis. This tool allows libraries to see who lives and works in their neighborhood, what kinds of materials they need, where the library should increase outreach, and which areas remain unserved.

The Method

In addition to the decennial census, the United States Census Bureau also makes geographical information available. An easy way to learn more about your patron base is to connect that physical and demographic information to a map of your service area. The first step is to create that map of your service area. Tiger Files created by the U.S. Census Bureau allow librarians to download county road maps to their GIS program. Library locations are then geocoded into those road maps by searching for the library's address or nearest cross-streets. Then the library service area can be defined, either by creating an organic shape around the library, like a circle surrounding the library point, or a more specific shape decided upon by the library. Some libraries even use census tracts to delineate their service areas. After the library's location has been geocoded into the map, information about the library can be added to the map. Specifics about the library, including its name, size of the building, the number of staff, or the size of the collection can be added to the map at this point.

Information about the library is then combined with Census 2000 demographic information by downloading census data files and importing the data into your GIS program. You can then identify the census blocks, block groups, and tracts that intersect your library's service area, and pull results from that specific area. A census block is the smallest unit for which aggregate census data is collected. The physical size of a census block can be very small, in densely populated areas, or very large, in sparsely populated areas.[2] Tracts are designed to be relatively permanent comparison areas and are generally bounded by permanent visible features or state and county boundaries.[3] Census 2000 demographic files are available by county and are layered over the road map and library service areas already extant in the GIS program. Then the program takes demographic data from the area where the demographic layer intersects with the library service area layer. The resulting demographics from the library service area are displayed in tabular format when the user clicks on the library service area. The Census Bureau has released four Summary Files from Census 2000 data. Summary File 1 (SF1) was collected from the Census 2000 short form and contains total 2000 population, race, age, number of households, number of families, and number of housing units per census block. SF2 is grouped per census tract and contains more detailed data on United States households, including the ages and relationships between householders.[4] Detailed tables break down housing statistics by race, ethnic origin, and to a limited extent, tribal affiliation. SF3 data is collected from the Census 2000 long form, sent to one out of six households, and linked to Census block groups. SF4 information is also taken from the long form, but presented by census tract. SF3 and SF4 describe ancestry, language use, education levels, income, occupation, socioeconomic class, and data about household facilities.[5] For this demonstration article, data were taken from SF1 and SF3 files.

Connecting Library Service Areas to Demographic Information
Public libraries exist to serve the public, and to do this, they need to know who their public is and what their public wants. In 1949, Bernard Berelson maintained that public libraries were used by people living relatively close to the public library.[6] Christine M. Koontz reviewed more recent research which supports branch proximity as a factor in patron usage. However, she points out that obstacles such as raised highways or railroad tracks may serve as barriers to library use in the service area.[7] Additionally, some libraries create artificially bounded service areas for their branches in order to maintain an equitable distribution of libraries per capita. Regardless of the shape or area chosen as a library's service area, it remains important to know who you're going to be serving and how to reach them.

Even in the same city, two branches can have dramatically different service populations. In our example, the Ocotillo and Yucca branches are only nine miles apart as the crow flies. However, the service population is fundamentally different between these two locations. Materials and services appropriate for one branch may not be appropriate to meet the needs of the population at the other branch. The images produced by our GIS package have helped to make this difference visible.

Connecting Demographics to Collection Development
Once we have linked the demographic data with the maps of our service areas, we have a better idea of who our potential patrons are (see Figure 29-1). Knowing this gives us an advantage when we try to develop the collection.

Figure 29-1: Branch Library Service Areas

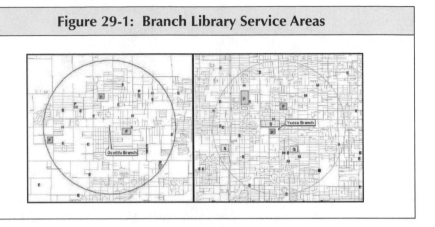

Figure 29-2: Distribution of Children, Aged Birth to Seventeen, per Census Block

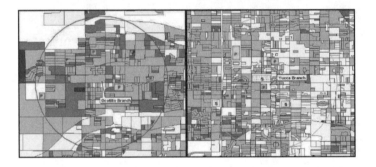

The Ocotillo Branch, for example, has a greater percentage of children in its service area than does the Yucca Branch, 37 percent compared to 27 percent (see Figure 29-2). Collection development funds for Ocotillo Branch might be adjusted to allow Ocotillo Branch to purchase more children's and school-related books.

By contrast, the Yucca Branch has a greater percentage of older adults and senior citizens than the Ocotillo Branch, 11 percent compared to 7 percent (see Figure 29-3). The Yucca Branch has an older population, and 66 percent of those who worked outside the home traveled alone in their own vehicles to their workplace. This branch might want to expend more on its large print and audiobook collection for its older patron population.

We can also see that, while the Ocotillo and Yucca branches both have significant Hispanic populations in their service area, more than 75 percent of Ocotillo's patronage is Hispanic (see Figure 29-4). More than half of the Ocotillo Branch population use Spanish in their homes. This suggests that

Figure 29-3: Distribution of People Aged Sixty-Five and Older per Census Block

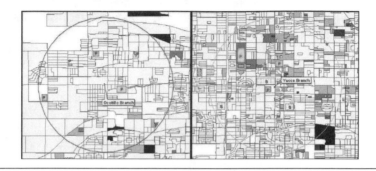

Figure 29-4: Distribution of People of Hispanic Origin per Census Block

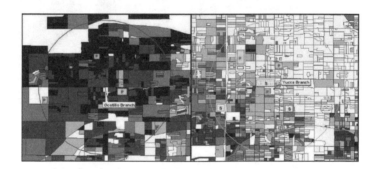

Figure 29-5: Distribution of People Who Speak Spanish As Their Home Language by Block Group

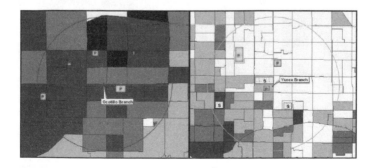

Ocotillo Branch patrons might need more materials in Spanish and more English as a Second or Other Language (ESOL) materials (see Figure 29-5).

Looking at educational attainment reveals that less than 6 percent of the service population has completed bachelor's degree programs, and only 48 percent of the population has completed high school. Materials geared toward lower reading levels might be appropriate for this community, with the understanding that patrons may request materials through system transfers at any time. By contrast, 78 percent of Yucca Branch patrons have graduated from high school and another 22 percent have completed bachelor's degree programs. The collection development plan for this library could safely include materials written for an academic audience (see Figures 29-6 and 29-7).

Further investigation of our census data shows that almost 30 percent of Yucca Branch residents have managerial and professional occupations,

Figure 29-6: Distribution of High School Graduates per Census Block Group

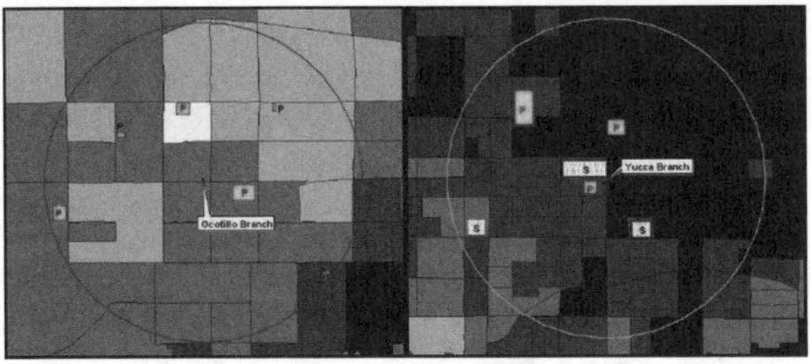

Figure 29-7: Distribution of College Graduates per Census Block Group

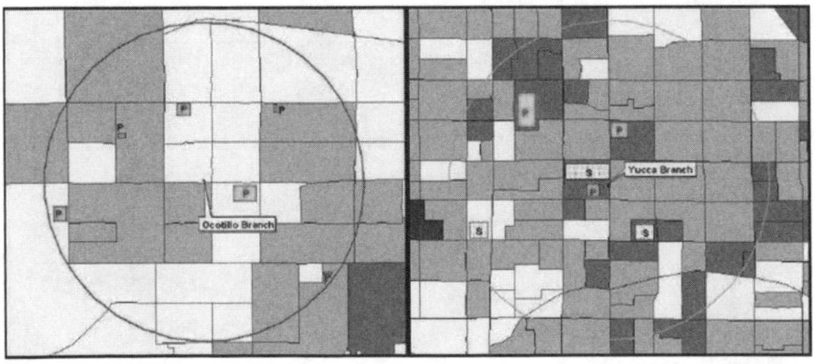

compared to 14 percent of Ocotillo Branch residents. Sales and office occupations were held by 28 percent of Yucca Branch and 25 percent of Ocotillo Branch residents.

Ocotillo Branch residents were represented in manual trades to a greater degree than Yucca Branch residents: 22 percent held positions in the production, transportation, and materials-moving occupations, 17 percent held positions in construction-related occupations, and 10 percent in groundskeeping and maintenance occupations. Yucca Branch percentages for these occupations were 12 percent, 13 percent, and 5 percent respectively. The occupational differences here suggest different work-related information needs, as well as different leisure-time pursuits, and perhaps even different leisure-time schedules. Construction workers might be employed seasonally and have more free time in the winter, compared to managers who work year-round.

Connecting Demographics to Circulation Data

Once you've developed a collection, you might be interested to know which materials are most popular at the branches, and where your collection goes after it is checked out. Researchers at Indiana University tracked the circulation of types of materials in the Indianapolis–Marion County Public Library.[8] In 1995, when this study was conducted, the researchers had to decide which census tracts most closely corresponded to branch service populations. Only after that data had been sifted through could database software connect it to circulation data. Statistics would have had to be manually added to the map of libraries and census tracts. When GIS technology became available in 1997, one of the researchers was later able to map patron usage for a particular branch, connect branch usage to census tract demographics, and correlate videotape circulation with income level.[9] These studies used 1990 census data, which was available only at the census tract level. Technological advances now make it possible for the Census Bureau to release information at the finer block-group or block level. To replicate this example today, library circulation data could be imported into a GIS system and linked with community demographic data with relative ease.

Many integrated library systems (ILS) are structured around relational databases, enabling systems personnel to save circulation data or patron addresses in formats accessible to desktop database packages such as Microsoft Access. The resulting files can be imported directly into the GIS program.

An Australian geographer took this a step further and mapped patron data to determine whether certain areas of a town were being served by the library.[10] Jones produced a map of active and inactive library users and their proximity to the library. A sample of daily circulation records could be mapped in this same fashion, connecting relevant data about the item circulated to a patron address and a branch indicator. In this way, we could estimate how many Yucca Branch residents travel to use the Ocotillo Branch facilities, or whether Ocotillo Branch patrons are making heavy use of the Economics and Finance books from the Yucca Branch. This circulation tracking mechanism would allow libraries to see exactly what types of books are popular in which neighborhoods, allowing them to develop more responsive collections. The information gathered could also help distinguish between the designated and actual library service area. As with any project in which identifying information is used, however, it is vitally important to guarantee patron confidentiality.

Connecting Demographics to Staffing

Previous research suggests that children make frequent use of the library, and adults with children are more likely to use the library than adults without.[11] As the Ocotillo Branch has a large percentage of children in its service area, the library director might want to allocate extra afterschool staff to that branch. The Yucca Branch is located in close proximity to several major retail centers. This branch may wish to keep "retail" hours, encouraging families to stop at the library on the way to or from the shopping center. The programming staff might be encouraged to offer family-oriented programs on weekend afternoons, as well as age-specific programs on weekday mornings.

Another element of staffing to be considered: the Ocotillo Branch has a very high percentage of Hispanic people in its service area, many of whom use Spanish as their home language. When a new staff position comes up, the library might be able to make Spanish fluency a priority qualification for hiring. This extra consideration would ensure better communication between patrons and their library, and this extra staff member would be in a better position to implement bilingual programming and Spanish-language collection development than an English-monolingual staff would.

The library system can also make staffing decisions based on library usage, by adding a "library visits per capita" indicator to branch data. Increased staff might be allocated to branches with higher patron counts. Nevertheless, previous studies by Christine M. Koontz and Dean K. Jue suggest that library usage cannot always be equated with circulation rates. Koontz and Jue studied "majority-minority" libraries, libraries for which the majority of the service population were racial or ethnic minorities. They found that although circulation rates for majority-minority branches were lower than those of other branches, program attendance and building use were equal to or higher than rates for those other branches.[12] People differ in their reasons for using the libraries, and libraries might want to use the most responsive usage indicators for their branches to reflect that difference in library use.

Connecting Demographics to Outreach

Not only can GIS data tell you which resources are popular and where, you can also use this data to provide customized outreach efforts to particular neighborhoods. If you have a general idea of who your service population is, it's also useful to know how to reach them—particularly if they aren't coming to the library. Ocotillo Branch demographics reveal a population that is very young and primarily Hispanic. Yucca Branch demographics suggest an older middle-class community. Even knowing this little information gives you a better idea of where to focus your outreach efforts. However, you can also add another layer to your GIS map, a layer that represents community agencies and gathering places. This layer can include schools, recreation areas, senior centers, and other gathering places, suggesting where your outreach efforts should be focused.

The Yucca Branch example demonstrates a variety of outreach possibilities. Programs could be conducted at the neighboring shopping center or park. The opportunity exists for storytime visits to elementary schools and bibliographic instruction sessions at middle and high schools. School statistics include descriptive data such as the total number of teachers, total number of students, students receiving free or reduced lunch, racial and ethnic data on students, or student-teacher ratio. Upon learning that there are 603 kindergarten students, 872 first graders, and 677 second graders attending school in their service area, Yucca Branch children's librarians might decide to do a storytelling and library card sign-up blitz during the school year. Young adult librarians can use ethnicity data to determine whether to translate Teen Read Week flyers into Spanish for a particular school. The more you know about a population, the easier it will be to design services to meet its needs.

Connecting Demographics to Branch Location and Service Hours

If your city is fortunate enough to build a new branch library, your GIS-based demographic data will help determine the best location to build that new library. Mapping new library locations can be reduced to pinpointing a prospective location for the new branch and gathering demographic data for the surrounding area. You can move your hypothetical new branch to different locations on the map, to see which location will reach the greatest number of people. In addition, knowing the languages spoken by the people in the library service area could help the library develop appropriate signage and promotional advertising for your new branch.

In addition to information on race, ethnicity, and home language, SF3 includes information about people with disabilities and types of disabilities. When constructing a new branch or remodeling an old one, this information can be shared with architects and contractors to help them understand the importance of accessible design. The population in the Ocotillo Branch service area had 1,876 sensory disabilities (impaired or disrupted sensory perception). More than 4,000 physical disabilities were tallied for this population, as were 2,532 mental disabilities.

As the population ages, the number of people with mild and serious disabilities will increase. If the library is to serve the entire community, it will be necessary to accommodate people across all ranges of ability.

Another statistic available via SF3 is workers' travel time from home to workplace, and the time they leave to arrive at their workplace. In the Yucca Branch service area, 57 percent of workers leave for work between 5 a.m. and 8 a.m. More than 80 percent of all Yucca Branch workers have a travel time of less than thirty-five minutes. Knowing this, we can estimate the best library service hours for the majority of working Yucca Branch patrons. If we assume one hour of total travel time, and nine hours of work time, we can also assume that working Yucca Branch patrons would not be able to use the library any earlier than 3 p.m. Of course, planning for workers excludes those who do not work and those who are looking for work. Another section of SF3 tells us that in 4 percent of Yucca Branch families, someone is unemployed and looking for work.

Another 43 percent of families contain someone who is unemployed and not looking for work, such as retirees and stay-at-home parents. These people are presumably able to use the library at any time, but may prefer to visit before the afternoon crowds.

Working with GIS Software

At the present time, there are several options for libraries wishing to use GIS. The first option is to do it yourself. Your library may already have a database or systems specialist working with local data, or someone who wants to experiment with new technology. GIS software is available from many vendors, and public libraries may qualify for discounted pricing. The package used for this example was ArcView 3.1, created by ESRI, Inc. ESRI (www.esri.com) is probably the best known GIS software provider, especially for the general desktop user. The software has a fairly steep learning curve, but university and vendor-sponsored classes are available to reduce that curve. Other GIS vendors and software can be located through the GIS Monitor Web site (www.gismonitor.com).

At least two kinds of data should be included in a library's GIS package: library-specific data and demographic data. The data a library chooses to include in its GIS system will vary, depending upon the problems the library is trying to solve. However, some of that data will be readily available through the library's ILS, including circulation rate, collection size, collection age, numbers and types of materials checked out, and patrons' registered addresses or birthdates. Number of staff, number of programs conducted, in-library use of materials, number of reference transactions, and building size are all factors that may affect library use by a community. This information may need to be manually collected and entered.

Demographic data can be downloaded for free from the Census Bureau (www.census.gov/census_2000/states); however, this data comes as flat ASCII files and must be converted into a form that ArcView can use. Fortunately, the Census Bureau also provides instructions and templates for some popular software packages to simplify the file conversion. Alternatively, demographic and other data can be purchased. Both ESRI and Proximity (http: //proximity-one.com) sell demographic data and offer instructions on how to use it. Combined with library related information, community demographics help the library understand its services in light of its community. It gives a visual referent, which indicates where the library specifically needs to target its efforts.

If, for instance, our Yucca Branch were to hold English as a Second Language classes, we would know that advertising those classes in the northeast quadrant of their service area would bring little return compared to advertising in the southwest quadrant.

For those who have reservations about using Census 2000 data as the decade wears on, the Census Bureau will be updating its population and housing demographics throughout the decade, via the American Community Survey.[13] The American Community Survey is an annual survey of a sample of American households, based on information normally gathered in the census long form. While this sample data will not be as comprehensive as the population demographics available from the Census Bureau's Summary File 1, it will provide an overall picture of community change.

GIS software is relatively inexpensive, and the data can be had for free. However, the library may be duplicating efforts already underway in the municipal planning department, and it may be possible to piggyback onto its service. Your library may be the only one in the community asking the planning department for help, but it is not the only agency in the community that needs information. Talk with other agencies to find out what their information needs are and what background work you might do to help the planning department meet both agencies' needs. Community data might not be immediately available in the format needed, so libraries should be prepared to work with the planning department and spell out their needs. A disadvantage to contracting through another governmental agency is the lack of control over the data. City planners may not want to spend time importing and making available library related data. An additional concern comes in when sharing sensitive data like patron addresses; will the municipal planning department treat that information as the library would wish? However, a relationship between the library and the planning department could prove useful in the long term as communities and their data change.

Some public libraries have turned to another alternative: a product called LibraryDecision (www.civictechnologies.com/library), offered by CIVIC Technologies. Billed by *American Libraries* as a "product to watch," LibraryDecision allows libraries to map their service areas and library measures to census information, then access those results via a Web browser.[14] "We wanted to provide an out-of-the-box solution for libraries that would give immediate results for decision making," said CIVIC Technologies president Marc Futterman. Using a preformatted interface, libraries provide data on library usage, facilities, holdings, and operations. LibraryDecision adds this to census and geographic data and produces a map showing library locations, demographic data, and library indicators. Libraries can access this information over the Web, so that library staff and patrons can determine how well their community is being served. While libraries are limited in the type of data that can be included in the LibraryDecision package, they have the advantage of working with a library-oriented company. An ESRI press release names several public libraries already using this service.[15] Libraries will also realize a considerable time savings using LibraryDecision over implementing their own GIS system.

You can get a taste of your library's demographic situation without purchasing software or downloading data by using the Public Library Geographic Database (PLGDB), developed at the University of South Florida.[16] This GIS map of public libraries in the United States allows librarians to look at communities surrounding their library buildings and, as demographics are included, will allow libraries to plan branch locations. Including Federal State Cooperative System public library data expands the utility of this service by allowing libraries to compare themselves to other libraries in other states. A project on this nationwide scale may make it difficult for individual libraries to include the data points that are meaningful to them, if those data are not meaningful to the thousands of other libraries in the United States. However, the PLGDB includes important national data, such as political and school district boundaries, and represents a huge step toward mapping public libraries and their communities. A similar project is available for libraries in the state of Illinois. The Illinois Public Library GIS Project (http://gis.iit.edu/instructions/project.htm) provides a GIS map of library service areas, school districts, and census demographics for the state of Illinois. This project is a joint product of the Illinois State Library and the Illinois Institute of Technology.

Another way to access demographic information comes from the American FactFinder (AFF), which accesses tract level data from the census Summary Files. These files are freely accessible at http: //factfinder.census.gov. By entering a library street address, the library can retrieve information about the census tract, block group, and block in which the library is located. Most urban libraries serve multiple blocks and block groups, making the tract the most relevant portion of data accessible from AFF. Using AFF, a basic map of the census tract area can be produced, showing the boundaries of the tract and the area served. Although library service areas may not directly correspond with census tracts, AFF is a valuable source of demographic information for your community.

What Else Can Be Done?

GIS systems provide an alternate way for public libraries to use census data and present it to their communities. Collecting demographics over time could be used to document the rate of community change; further, this information might be valuable to municipal historians as well as librarians. A library could keep track of people using Internet services to determine how far the library has reached through its provision of free Internet services.

However, once a GIS system is in place, its utility can be extended beyond just keeping track of community demographics. A librarian might map her outreach contacts and then gather the addresses of patrons attending a library program to determine which contacts were fruitful and where she needs to increase her outreach efforts. She might document classroom visits by school, using that information to predict children's demand for services. GIS systems can be used for planning services in the building as well as in the community. If she wished to keep track of in-house use of materials, a librarian might use a digital map of the library to determine where people linger, and at which times of the day. The periodicals section may get more morning use, but the computers more afternoon use. A building supervisor concerned about traffic flow in the library could use that digital map to simulate library disaster response in varying situations to determine the quickest way to control a dangerous situation.

Conclusion

GIS systems combine digital images with information. In 2000, GraceAnne A. DeCandido wrote that GIS systems "allow problem solving to happen in a new and different way, by the visual inclusion of spatial data in the analysis of spatial problems."[17] GIS provides libraries with a visual image of their service area and allows them to combine that with community-specific information. Libraries can look to GIS maps to see which neighborhoods are well served by the library and which have not been reached, where materials circulate, and where the population congregates.

A librarian's job is to be informed: to know what kind of service he or she wants to provide and how he or she will use information generated to help provide that service. Libraries may generate the same types of basic statistics, but each will have different support personnel, infrastructures, funding, and communities. The better a library knows itself and its community, the better it will be able to provide meaningful services to that community. Although GIS systems require an investment of time and money, the information they generate help create a more responsive public library.

Notes

1. United States Geographic Survey, "Geographic Information Systems." Accessed June 15, 2009, http://erg.usgs.gov/isb/pubs/gis_poster.
2. Census 2000 Geographic Terms and Concepts (Washington, D.C.: U.S. Census Bureau, 2003), A-8. Accessed June 15, 2009, www.census.gov/geo/www/tiger/glossry2.pdf.
3. Census 2000 Basics (Washington, D.C.: U. S. Census Bureau, Sept. 2002), 6. Accessed June 15, 2009, www.census.gov/mso/www/c2000basics/00Basics.pdf.
4. Summary File 2, 2000 Census of Population and Housing: Technical Documentation. (Washington, D.C.: U. S. Department of Commerce, U. S. Census Bureau, June 2002). Accessed June 15, 2009, www.census.gov/prod/cen2000/doc/sf2.pdf.
5. Summary File 4, 2000 Census of Population and Housing: Technical Documentation (Washington, D.C.: U.S. Census Bureau, July 2003), p. 1-1. Accessed June 15, 2009, www.census.gov/prod/cen2000/doc/sf4.pdf.
6. Bernard Berelson, *The Library's Public* (New York: Columbia Univ. Pr., 1949), 43–45.
7. Christine M. Koontz, *Library Facility Siting and Location Handbook* (Westport, Conn.: Greenwood, 1997), 42.
8. John R. Ottensmann, Raymond E. Gnat, and Michael E. Gleeson, "Similarities in Circulation Patterns among Public Library Branches Serving Diverse Populations," *Library Quarterly* 65, no.1 (1995): 89–118.

9. John R. Ottensmann, "Using Geographic Information Systems to Analyze Library Utilization," *Library Quarterly* 67, no. 1 (1997): 24–49.

10. Alan D. Jones, "Where Do All the Good Books Go? Geographic Information Systems and the Local Library,"*Australian Library Journal* (1993): 241–49.

11. Mary A. Collins and Kathryn Chandler, *Use of Public Library Services by Households in the United States: 1996* (Washington, D.C.: U. S. Department of Education, Office of Educational Research and Improvement, Feb. 1997), 2. Accessed June 15, 2009, http: //nces.ed.gov/pubs/97446.pdf.

12. Koontz, *Library Facility Siting,* 104.

13. U. S. Census Bureau, *American Community Survey,* June 23, 2003. Accessed June 15, 2009, www.census.gov/acs/www/index.html.

14. David C. Dorman, "GIS Provides a New Way of Seeing Service Areas," *American Libraries* 33, no. 2 (Feb. 2002): 62–63.

15. Nancy Sappington, "Check Out Library Decision at the ALA Annual Conference" (June 13, 2002). Accessed Sept. 22, 2003, www.esri.com/news/releases/ 02_2qtr/library-decision.html. (Editor's note: This resource is no longer available; access attempted June 15, 2009).

16. Christine M. Koontz, Dean K. Jue, Charles R. McClure, and John Carlo Bertot, "The Public Library Geographic Database: What Can It Do for You and Your Library?" *Public Libraries* 43, no.2 (March/April 2003).

17. GraceAnne A. DeCandido, "Geographic Information Systems (GIS): Mapping the Territory." Accessed Sept. 17, 2003, www.pla.org/PLATemplate.cfm?Section= Tech_Notes. (Editor's note: Original item no longer available. Updated April 17, 2009, www.pla.org/ala/mgrps/divs/pla/plapublications/platechnotes/GIS2009.pdf. Accessed June 15, 2009.)

About the Authors

Denice Adkins is Associate Professor at the School of Information Science & Learning Technologies, University of Missouri. She is an active member of REFORMA, the National Association for the Promotion of Library and Information Services to Latinos and the Spanish-Speaking. Denice was born and raised in Arizona and made great use of Arizona public libraries in her youth.

Denyse Sturges is Engineering and Aerospace Bibliographer and Reference Librarian at the University of North Dakota's Chester Fritz Library. She is finishing her doctoral dissertation at the University of Missouri. Denyse was raised in Carnegie Libraries across the Midwest.

eContent

Richard W. Boss

eContent—which includes electronic versions of books, journals, media, and archival materials—have become a significant part of most libraries' resources. While most eContent has been digitized from other formats, there increasingly are original electronic publications, especially eJournals.

The major advantages of eContent are integrity of the collection, availability around the clock, remote access, and multiple simultaneous users. Unlike print, media, and archival materials, eContent is unlikely to be misplaced, stolen, or vandalized. It can be made available 24/7, rather than being available only during regular library hours. Except as there are licensing restrictions, eContent is available from anywhere and to multiple simultaneous users.

History

eJournals

eJournals have existed since the mid-1970s, and have been made available by many libraries since the early 1990s, but they did not become a significant part of most libraries' collections until 2000. In the early years of eJournals, they were not routinely deposited with national libraries. In 1994, the Koninklijke Bibliotheek of the Netherlands decided to include all eContent produced in the Netherlands in its deposit collection. Elsevier Science, the large Dutch science, technology, and medicine publisher, and one of the first to produce scores of e-Journals, deposited its titles. By 1995, the depository had 315 eJournal titles. In 2002, Elsevier Science signed an agreement with the Koninklijke Bibliotheek to have it become the archival agent for its eJournals. By 2004, the collection included 2,600 eJournal titles, 4.5 million journal articles, and required 5.0 TBytes of storage. It was growing at the rate of 60,000 articles a day. As of early 2007, many national libraries were accepting deposits of eContent.

There appears to be no accurate count of the number of eJournals available. Estimates range from 25,000 to 50,000, still only a small fraction of the 900,000 ISSNs that have been issued.

One of the reasons that eJournals became popular was the existence of electronic indexes and abstracts from which links could be made to the full text. Another was that the average length of articles (8 pages) made it possible to quickly download or print them from a server. The widespread availability of PDF, a format developed by Adobe, precluded the emergence of multiple proprietary formats. It also protected publishers because it captured the image of the articles, rather than making the articles subject to revision or reformatting. In recent years, more titles have become available in other formats, including formats that allow full-text searching.

eBooks

The first major eBooks effort dates back earlier than the first eJournal effort, but has been slower to impact libraries and their users. Project Gutenberg began in 1971 when Michael Hart, its founder, was given virtually unlimited use of a Xerox Sigma V mainframe at the University of Illinois' Materials Research Lab. Rather than using his account for data processing, he decided to focus on the storage, retrieval and searching of what was stored in libraries. The focus was on having volunteers digitize books in the public domain. Despite its early start, there were just 20,000 free books in the Project Gutenberg Online Book Catalog as of early 2007. However, they were being downloaded two million times a month.

NetLibrary, now a division of OCLC, began in 1999. By the middle of 2001, it offered 11,000 titles; by early 2007 it offered more than 130,000 titles, still a small fraction of the more than 32 million titles believed to exist, more than half of them in the public domain. Carnegie Mellon launched its Million Book Project in 2001 and set as its goal the digitizing of one million books by 2007. More than 30 other research libraries also launched major digitizing initiatives between 2001 and 2005. The only public library that launched a major digitizing program during this period was the New York Public Library.

Among the reasons why eBooks were slow to be adopted was the reliance on proprietary formats and the lack of good readers. Two readers for which eBooks were produced were the Rocket eBook reader and the SoftBook Reader. They were withdrawn from the market in 2003 when their sales dropped sharply after the introduction of lighter-weight readers with more attractive displays. Unfortunately, the titles purchased to read on them could not be read on the newer readers.

Even the newer readers, which used general purpose technology configured with special software for reading eBooks, were far from popular because they sacrificed screen size in order to reduce weight. The Zire 21 from palmOne, Inc. weighed 3.2 ounces, but has a screen the size of a PDA (personal digital assistant). Hewlett Packard's iPAQ Pocket PC H4150 had a screen that is only slightly larger. One of the few exceptions was the Toshiba's Portege M2000, a tablet PC that weighed about the same as a book and has a screen that could accommodate an entire page with a font size that most people were able to read. It might well have been be the most popular unit on the market were it not priced at nearly $2,500.

Publishers of eBooks focused on the consumer market and paid little attention to libraries before 2003. Consumer sales in 2003 were under $10 million in 2003, representing just three-quarters of a million units. Barnes & Noble was so discouraged by poor sales, that it discontinued offering eBooks in the fourth quarter of 2003.

The lack of success in the consumer market was a major factor in publishers' decisions to look to libraries. They began to work with Baker & Taylor, a major distributor to public and academic libraries, and Follett, a major distributor to school libraries, in mid-2003.

It was in 2003 that libraries began to purchase eBooks in significant numbers, not only because Baker & Taylor and Follett were promoting them, but because by then many of the titles could be downloaded to a desktop machine, laptop, notebook, tablet PC, or PDA.

Initial circulation was low. One major public library tallied an average of four downloads per title in 2003. Another public library that introduced eBooks in the third quarter of 2003 estimated an average of two downloads per title over a three month period. As there was no wear and tear as with print titles, and there was no labor cost for circulation charge and discharge and reshelving, the libraries did not give up on eBooks.

By 2006, eBooks were circulating well. In part because a library offers a single source of quality titles that have been selected by professional librarians. There is no need to go to the Web sites of a score of publishers and distributors. Even more important, eBooks from a library's collection are usually free.

eMedia and eManuscripts

It was only logical that digitizing efforts would go beyond the eJournal and the eBook. By 2005, there were digitizing projects underway to offer eMedia of audios and videos, art, and maps. Increasingly, manuscripts and other unpublished documents in archives were being captured digitally to preserve them and to facilitate access.

Formats

There are literally scores of formats for eContent, but there are a few widely adopted ones. For eJournals, these are ASCII for full-text and PDF (Adobe Personal Document Format) for image files.

For eBooks, these are ASCII for full-text; Adobe eBook Reader (PDF) for PCs, tablet PCs, laptops, Macs, and Palm handhelds; MobiPocket for PCs, tablet PCs, laptops, pocket PCs, Palm handhelds, and SmartPhones; and Microsoft Reader for PCs, tablet PCs, laptops, and pocket PCs. An emerging format is ADE (Adobe Digital Editions), a variant of PDF that protects eBooks from unlawful reproduction and distribution using Adobe DRM (Digital Rights Management).

For eMedia, these are RealMedia for both audio and video; MP3, MP3 Pro (MP3 is a subset of MPEG1) and AAC (Advanced Audio Coding) for digital audio; JPEG (Joint Photographic Experts Group) and GIF (Graphic Interchange Format) for digital images; and MPEG1-4 (Moving Picture Experts Group) for videos. For eArchives, there are PDF and GIF.

Space limitations preclude discussing each of these formats in this TechNote. However, detailed information about each can be found on the Web.

In most cases, a provider of eContent will enable the download of the appropriate format. However, a library should be careful to determine that it can support a format before deciding on an acquisition. Major providers of eContent are identified in the following paragraphs, with those which provide multiple types of eContent following those that provide only a single type.

Major eJournal Providers

There are scores of eJournal providers. The two offering the largest number of titles are Dialog and Ebsco Host.

Dialog (www.dialog.com) is a for-profit company that offers access to more than 11,000 eJournals, primarily in the fields of science, technology, and medicine. It provides links to the full text of journals from its extensive indexing and abstracting databases.

Ebsco Host (http://ejournals.ebsco.com) is a for-profit company that offers access to more than 15,000 eJournals stored on its servers. It is available by subscription. It is possible to search by journal title, subject, article author, or article title. There is also an option to store searches and have an e-mail sent whenever new articles matching the criteria are added.

e-journals.org (www.e-journals.org) is not an aggregator of e-journals, but provides links to electronic journals from around the world. Access is by broad subject area or keyword.

Major eBook Providers

The major eBook providers are eBooks.com, Google, Microsoft, the Million Book Project, OverDrive, and Project Gutenberg.

eBooks.com (www.ebooks.com) is a for-profit company that offers popular fiction and non-fiction at prices averaging less than the print versions. Titles are sold only individually. Several thousand titles are available. They are searchable by author, title, keyword, or subject. Three format options are available: Adobe eBook Reader, MobiPocket Reader, and Microsoft Reader.

Google Book Search (http://books.google.com) was launched in late 2004 as the Library Book Project with a goal of digitizing as many as 15 million books from a dozen major research libraries, including Harvard, New York Public, and Oxford. The program is an expansion of the Google Print program, which offered digital excerpts of books in copyright. Searchers using Google see links to relevant books. For those in copyright, there are brief excerpts and links to libraries and booksellers that have the titles available.

For those in the public domain, there is full-text browsing and the option of downloading a PDF version. The program has been controversial because Google uses the "opt-out" approach with regard to copyrighted works. It digitizes books without seeking permission from the copyright holder. The copyright holder must specifically opt out of the program if it does not want to have its works digitized. Google argues that the brief excerpts that are available for copyrighted works actually helps sell books. As of early 2007, a number of publishers were in litigation with Google. The number of books available as of early 2007 was in excess of one million.

Microsoft's MSN Book Search (www.msn.com until it creates a URL specifically for the service) was launched in 2006 with an initial plan to digitize 150,000 books by mid-2007. It was committed to the "opt-in" approach, meaning that publishers have to specifically agree to have their titles digitized. The service was also planned to include books in the public domain.

The Million Book Project was launched by Carnegie Mellon University (www.library.cmu.edu/Libraries/MBP) in 2001. Its goal was to digitize one million books by 2007. As of early 2007, more than 750,000 were in the database. More than half were scanned in China and more than a fourth in India—countries in which there are at least 40 scanning centers with sophisticated OCR (optical character recognition) equipment to enable full-text searching. A little more than 20 percent of the books are in English, primarily contributions from Indiana University, Pennsylvania State University, University of California/Berkeley, and University of Washington. Approximately 90 percent of the titles are in the public domain. The titles are maintained on three sites: in China, India, and the United States. The URL for the U.S. site is www.ulib.org.

OverDrive. Libraries that want popular titles should consider OverDrive (www.overdrive.com). It has over 30,000 titles, including thousands of novels and general non-fiction titles. A library can purchase multiple copies of a title to accommodate simultaneous use of that title. While the titles are purchased, they remain on the vendor's server. Any PC or PDA may be used to read an eBook. The eBooks automatically expire and check themselves back into the collection. The vendor provides MARC records for inclusion in a library's patron access catalog.

Project Gutenberg. Libraries with limited resources may wish to consider Project Gutenberg, a free site with the text of approximately 20,000 titles in ASCII format. The site grows by approximately 350 titles a year. Only titles no longer protected by copyright are included. As a rule of thumb, that is books copyrighted prior to 1923. The emphasis is on classics. They are chosen by volunteers, keyboarded, and uploaded to one or more computer sites around the world known as FTP sites. The host site at www.gutenberg.net is limited to the index and links to the FTP sites. As of early 2007, Project Gutenberg planned to add eAudioBooks and other eMedia.

Major eContent Providers

The most important players in eContent are eBrary, Internet Archive, OCLC, and Questia.

eBrary (www.ebrary.com) is a for-profit company that was founded in 1999 to sell eBooks. It subsequently broadened its scope to include eJournals, and eMedia. It offers both subscriptions and outright purchase of the entire collection. It has developed its own reader software to access the eBooks on its hosted server. A library may also add its own eContent in PDF format. The company claims more than 1,000 customers, but has not provided statistics on the number of titles it has available.

The Internet Archive (www.archive.org) is a non-profit organization that was founded in 1996 to build an internet library. It relies on contributions of eJournals, eBooks, eMedia, and eArchives from the creators of the content. It includes eBooks from the Million Books Project. Other collaborators are the Library of Congress and the Smithsonian. Its Web site has links to many other eContent providers.

OCLC has two major programs, **NetLibrary and Electronic Collections Online.** Founded in 1998, NetLibrary (http://library.netlibrary.com) was purchased by OCLC in 2001. Since that time, the number of eBook titles has been increased from fewer than 40,000 to more than 130,000 scholarly and reference works in behavioral sciences, social sciences, physical sciences, management and public relations, law, and technology. A library can purchase a collection of titles tailored to its needs and budget. Only one user at a time per title can be accommodated, but the library is free to set the check-out period. It can also choose to have multiple copies of a collection. MARC records are available to enter into a patron access catalog. The titles can be read on any computer. NetLibrary offers full-text searching, a dictionary with audio pronunciation, and personalization features, including bookmarks, annotations and "my favorites."

NetLibrary also offers thousands of eAudiobooks. These may be purchased individually or as collections. These may be used on any desktop or laptop running supported media software programs. A unique subscription offering from NetLibrary is the Catalog of Art Museum Images Online (CAMIO), a collection of more than 90,000 images of art objects and photographs from major museums around the world.

OCLC's Electronic Collections Online (www.oclc.org/electronic collections) offers digital images of articles in more than 5,000 journals.

The Open Content Alliance (www.opencontentalliance.org) is a consortium of non-profit and for-profit groups committed to building a free archive of eBooks and eMedia. It was conceived in 2005 by Yahoo and the Internet Library as a response to the Google Library Project. The emphasis is on eBooks and eMedia from throughout the world. Contributions are solicited from libraries, organizations and publishers.

Contributors are required to obtain permission from copyright holders before submitting titles not in the public domain. Among the major contributors are Columbia University, the Netherlands-based European Archive, the Internet Archive, the National Archives in the United Kingdom, University of California, University of Toronto, and University of Virginia. Multiple formats are accepted, but PDF appears to be the most widely used by the contributors. There were approximately 100,000 eBooks in the archive as of early 2007 and several thousand eMedia. Yahoo provides the search engine.

Questia is a for-profit company that offers both eJournals and eBooks on a monthly or annual subscription basis, primarily to individual students, faculty, and other researchers. An institutional subscriber can provide simultaneous access to multiple users. As of early 2007, there were more than 1.5 million articles available in its eJournal service and 67,000 titles in its eBook service. Its subject matter strengths are the humanities and social sciences at the undergraduate level. Searching is by keyword, phrase, title, author, or subject.

About the Author

Richard W. Boss, prior to becoming a full-time information systems consultant, was an academic library administrator. His positions have included the directorships of the University of Tennessee and Princeton University Libraries. He has written more than 30 books and hundreds of articles in the past 30 years.

Chapter 31

Blogs and Wikis

Richard W. Boss

Blogs (short for Weblogs) and wikis (Polynesian for "quick") are proliferating everywhere, including in the library community. By early 2007, there were hundreds of library blogs and scores of library wikis.

The Differences Between Blogs and Wikis

Despite the fact that blogs and wikis have become commonplace, they are often confused with one another. A blog is an electronic broadcast by the owner of the blog. If the owner of the blog permits it, others can respond by adding comments, but they cannot edit the content. Instead, the comments are displayed in a separate area. A wiki is a collaborative content development tool. It is a Web site that allows anyone, without knowing HTML, to post content to it. Each section of a wiki has an "edit" button that makes it possible for anyone to add to or edit what is there unless some limitations are imposed. A history is maintained so that it is possible to determine what additions and changes have been made since the initial article was posted, and who was responsible. A blog typically is a single page; a wiki can consist of thousands of pages.

Libraries have been involved much more with blogs than with wikis. The author's searches using Google and several directories suggest that library blogs outnumber library wikis more than seven to one. One factor may be the degree of control over content that a library has over a blog. Others may be that wikis tend to have a much greater amount of content, more participants, and more need to monitor for possible misuse.

Blogs

The blog developed from the online journal, a way for people to keep a running account of their personal lives. In 1994, software was introduced that made it possible to create content for the Web without knowing HTML, easily update an online journal in reverse chronological order so that the latest information came first, to make it accessible with a Web browser, and to make linking to other pages much easier. The use of the term "blog" dates back only to 1999. It replaced the term "Weblog," which had been in use only since 1997. There were only a few hundred blogs before 1999, but by 2005 the number had grown to more than 400 million.

The reverse chronological order of a blog makes it easy to add information because it is posted to the top. On a wiki, it is necessary to find a place to put the post.

A blog can be personal, as it is in most cases, or for a business or organization. It can focus on a subject, product, or event. In the past few years, blogs have become increasingly more noticed for their role in breaking. shaping, and spinning news. They have become particularly important in election campaigns.

A blog is usually updated on a regular basis, but the frequency can be anything from several times a day to once a month.

Library Blogs

There are hundreds of library blogs. The most basic is a listing of library events by date, with the latest date at the top. When a page is filled, the old posts can be saved in an archive or deleted. A good example is the blog of the Adams County Library System of Pennsylvania (http://adamslibrary1. blogspot.com).

A library blog about books is somewhat more time-consuming to create and maintain. A good example is that of the Waterboro Public Library of Maine (www.waterborolibrary.org/blog.htm). It not only discusses specific books, but has commentaries on publishing. An appealing feature of this blog is images of authors and book jackets. There are also links to reviewing media.

Some of the most successful library blogs are aimed at teenagers, the group that is most familiar with blogging because of their exposure to Facebook, My-Space, and similar social Web sites. A good example of a library blog for teens is "Stuff for Teens" by the Bartlesville Public Library of Oklahoma (www.bartlesville.lib.ok.us/blog/teens). The writing style and vocabulary are designed to appeal to teens and the illustrations are colorful and appropriate.

Blog Directories

The available blog directories list a very small percentage of the existing library blogs. One of the most useful is the Blogging Libraries Wiki (Google "welcome to blogging libraries wiki" as the URL is nearly 50 characters long). The list is categorized by library type. There are more than 200 public library blogs identified as well as many academic, special, and school library blogs. There also are categories for library associations and library directors. As of early 2007, the year-old directory had already had 20,000 hits.

Blogging Software

Blogging software is required to create a blog, but only a Web browser is required to read a blog. There are many open source blogging software products available for downloading and installation. The proprietary products are available only for a fee, and are most popular with customers who want to take advantage of the hosting service that is usually made available as an option. Most of the software has features that facilitate authoring and editing of blog posts, various linking features, and the ability to publish the blog to the Web. The software usually provides many options. One critical feature for some bloggers is the ability to turn the comments feature on or off. Another option is post moderation, a feature that requires people who want to comment on a blog to be approved before the comments are posted or that require an actual review of the comment before it is posted. A very useful option for active bloggers is the automatic archiving of older posts at specific intervals.

Among the open source blogging software available are Apache Roller (http://roller.apache.org), Geeklog (www.geeklog.net), and LifeType (www.lifetype.net). Community Server (http://communityserver.org) is a popular proprietary product, as is Movable Type (www.movabletype.org).

One of the best-known hosted services is MySpace (www.myspace.com). A number of libraries have used it to promote their services because it has a membership of tens of millions of young people. Two other sites, both fee-based, target small businesses and organizations, and professionals. They are Blog.com (http://blog.com) and TypePad (www.typepad.com).

Blogging Hardware
A library choosing a hosted blogging service needs no hardware. If it's chosen to use an in-house server, its size will depend on the amount of traffic that is anticipated. In most cases, a low-end server costing just a few thousand dollars is sufficient.

Wikis
The community of collaborators in the development and maintenance of a wiki may be everyone in a business or organization, everyone in a profession, everyone participating in a conference, or everyone in a geographic area, or everyone anywhere.

Allowing a large number of people to add to or edit a wiki means that it is more easily vandalized or susceptible to misinformation. However, the more an article is viewed, the more likely that the effects of vandalism will be ameliorated and misinformation corrected. As a wiki matures and increases in size, editorial administration becomes important. Typically, a substantial majority of editors have to support the designation of a limited number of people as editorial administrators, editors who have the authority to remove articles, additions, and edits that violate the agreed upon guidelines of the wiki.

Not everything called a wiki is a wiki. A number of businesses and organizations, including libraries, have used the wiki format to create and maintain online content. When there is no collaborative content development and maintenance, the result is not a wiki. Instead, it is a Web site.

Wikipedia

The most popular wiki, and the one most emulated, is Wikipedia (www.wikipedia.org). Wikipedia is a registered trademark of the non-profit Wikimedia Foundation. The wiki was created in 2001 and has rapidly grown into the largest reference Web site on the Internet with more than 5.3 million articles, 1.64 million of them in English. The content in Wikipedia is intended to be factual, notable, verifiable with external sources, and neutrally presented, with external sources cited. There are over 75,000 active contributors. While the contributions remain the property of their creators, all of the text, and most of the images, is covered by the GNU Free Documentation License to ensure that the content remains freely distributable and reproducible.

Library Wikis

The best-known library wiki is the LISWiki (http://liswiki.org). It was launched on June 30, 2005 by John Hubbard of the University of Wisconsin-Milwaukee. It had grown to more than 1,300 articles by early 2007. Many of the articles are stubs that require considerable additional information in order to be useful, but there are several hundred useful articles that deal with such topics as cell phones in libraries, laptop checkout, and dates of upcoming conferences. While the article on wikis offers a very limited discussion of wikis, it identifies several score library wikis, including conference wikis and wikis that are library-sponsored. In its first 18 months, there were nearly 60,000 hits against the wiki.

A potentially useful library wiki is Library Success, a best practices wiki (www.libsuccess.org). It was launched in 2005 by Meredith Farkas of Norwich University. She laid out the format and identified broad categories of coverage: community, management and leadership, materials selection and collection maintenance, professional, programming, readers' advisory, reference services and information literacy, selling your library, services to specific groups, and training. Librarians who feel that they have done something at their libraries that they consider a success are invited to write about it in the wiki. Others are invited to add to or edit any article provided they have registered as editors. Many of the articles were still stubs as of early 2007, but there appeared to be active participation.

Conference wikis have become quite popular. Good examples are the ALA Annual Conference and Midwinter Meeting wikis. The most recent example can be seen at http://wikis.ala.org. Any attendee or exhibitor is able to exchange information about events, the exhibits, committee work, and more. Of particular value are the recaps of meetings. Many other library associations also have conference wikis.

A good example of a library wiki is the Butler University Libraries Reference Wiki (www.seedwiki.com/wiki/butler_wikiref). It is a collaborative review of books, databases, Web sites, etc., that are part of the Butler University Libraries' resources. Librarians, faculty, staff, and students are encouraged to add their comments about any reference resource, change text that is factually incorrect or unprofessional in deportment, or add additional reference resources.

Wiki Directories

A listing of wikis dealing with libraries and librarianship can be found at http://liswiki.org/wiki/Wikis. However, not all of the sites listed are true wikis because only one or a very few staff members are involved in content creation and maintenance. While they are organized in a format very similar to that of Wikipedia, they are not wikis because there is no opportunity for collaboration in the development of the content.

Wiki Software

Wiki software and a Web browser are necessary to create and maintain a wiki, but only a Web browser is needed to read one.

Wiki software typically allows Web pages to be created and edited using a Web browser. The principal difference between wiki software and content management software is that wiki software tends to focus on the content while content management software emphasizes control over layout.

The first wiki software was created in 1995. There are now more than a score of products, a majority available as open source software under the GNU General Public License (GPL). The most widely used open source products are MediaWiki (www.mediawiki.org) and TWiki. (http://twiki.org). The former, which was introduced in 2002, is used by Wikipedia. Twiki has been available since 1998 and has been regularly updated since that time. There are a number of proprietary wiki software programs, but they have been infrequently used by libraries except those that want not only access to the software, but also a hosting service. A comparison of a number of wiki software products is available at www.wikimatrix.org.

Most wiki software, whether free or for a fee, is available for download. A few products are also available on CD.

Wiki Hardware

Unless a hosted service is used, a library will need a server to accommodate the wiki. The number of participants and the amount of activity will need to be estimated in order to size the server. In most cases, a low-end server costing just a few thousand dollars will be enough, but it is a good idea to purchase a modular server that can be expanded, without replacing components, to at least quadruple the initial capacity.

Wiki Style Guide

The most widely used style guide for creating and maintaining a wiki is that of Wikipedia (http://en.wikipedia.org/wiki/Help: Editing#Basic_text_ formatting).

About the Author

Richard W. Boss, prior to becoming a full-time information systems consultant, was an academic library administrator. His positions have included the directorships of the University of Tennessee and Princeton University Libraries. He has written more than 30 books and hundreds of articles in the past 30 years.

Chapter 32

RFID Technology for Libraries

Richard W. Boss

R FID (Radio Frequency IDentification) is the latest technology to be used in library theft detection systems. Unlike EM (Electro-Mechanical) and RF (Radio Frequency) systems, which have been used in libraries for decades, the RFID-based systems that libraries began to install in the late 1990s not only detect the unauthorized removal of library materials, but speed staff charge and discharge, speed and simplify patron self-charge and self-discharge, support electronic inventorying, and integrate with materials handling systems. The descriptive term "tracking systems" has been applied to RFID systems, but it is not yet in widespread use. As of mid-2007, an estimated 600 libraries with as many as 850 facilities were using RFID systems.

RFID is a combination of radio-frequency-based technology and microchip technology. The information contained on microchips in the tags affixed to library materials is read using radio frequency technology. A reader (aka sensor, scanner or interrogator) looks for antennae on the tags and retrieves information from the microchips through them.

The tags used in RFID systems can replace both EM or RF theft detection barcodes and targets although the hybrid system that 3M introduced in 2000 replaced only barcodes and retained the EM strips in the belief that EM is superior to RFID for security. 3M did introduce a comprehensive RFID product that replaces both EM and barcodes in 2004.

Advantages of RFID systems

Rapid Charging/Discharging

The use of RFID reduces the amount of time required to perform circulation operations. The most significant time savings are attributable to the fact that information can be read from RFID tags much faster than from barcodes. That is due to the fact that the tags can be read regardless of item orientation or alignment (i.e., the technology does not require line-of-sight or a fixed plane to read tags as do older technologies) and that several items in a stack can be read at the same time. While initially unreliable, the anti-collision algorithm that allows an entire stack to be charged or discharged now appears to be working well. Finally, RFID tags can be read from distances of up to 24 inches—distances far greater than the use of lightpens and barcode wands used with EM technology. That is what makes RFID systems not only faster, but able to support electronic inventorying with handheld devices.

Simplified Patron Self-Charging/Discharging

For patrons using self-charging, there is a marked improvement because they do not have to carefully place materials within a designated template and they can charge several items at the same time. Patron self-discharging, which can be achieved by installing readers in bookdrops or with self-discharge stations, shifts work from staff to patrons.

High Reliability

The readers are highly reliable. Several vendors of RFID library systems claim an almost 100 percent detection rate using RFID tags. Anecdotal evidence suggests that is the case whenever a reader is within 18 inches of the tags, but there appears to be no statistical data to support the claims.

There are fewer false alarms than with older technologies once an RFID system is properly tuned. The libraries contacted by the author that have experience with both EM and RFID security systems report a 50 to 75 percent reduction in false alarms with RFID.

Some RFID systems have an interface between the exit sensors (a term often used to describe readers that are used at exits) and a circulation system to identify the items moving out of the library. Were a patron to run out of the library and not be intercepted, the library would at least know what had been stolen. If the patron card also has an RFID tag, the library will also be able to determine who removed the items without properly charging them. However, the author has not been able to identify a library that has implemented this security feature.

Other RFID systems encode the circulation status on the RFID tag. This is done by designating a bit as the "theft" bit and turning it off at time of charge and on at time of discharge. If the material that has not been properly charged is taken past the exit sensors, an immediate alarm is triggered. Another option is to use both the "theft" bit and the online interface to an integrated library system, the first to signal an immediate alarm and the second to identify what has been taken.

High-Speed Electronic Inventorying

A unique advantage of RFID systems is their ability to scan books on the shelves without tipping them out or removing them to access the barcodes. A hand-held inventory reader can be moved rapidly across a shelf of books at a distance of approximately six inches to read all of the unique identification information. Using wireless technology, it is possible not only to update the inventory, but also to identify items which are out of proper order.

Interfaces with Materials Handling Systems

Another application of RFID technology is an interface with a materials handling system, a system that consists of conveyors and sorting equipment that can move library materials and sort them mechanically by category into separate bins or onto separate carts. This significantly reduces the amount of staff time required to ready materials for reshelving. Given the high cost of the equipment, this application has not been widely used. There were approximately 100 systems in use in North America as of the second quarter of 2007.

Long Tag Life

Finally, RFID tags last longer than barcodes because nothing comes into contact with them. Most RFID vendors claim a minimum of 100,000 transactions before a tag may need to be replaced.

Disadvantages of RFID Systems

High Cost

The major disadvantage of RFID technology is its cost. While the readers used to read the information are comparable in cost to the components of a typical EM or RF theft detection system, typically $2,500 to $7,500 each, the tags are far more expensive than barcodes, EM strips, or RF targets. As of mid-2007, RFID tags were still approximately $.50 each—a price which random polling of librarians by the author has determined is the key to their serious consideration of the technology.

Vulnerability to Compromise

It is possible to compromise an RFID system by wrapping the protected material in two to three layers of ordinary household foil to block the radio signal. Clearly, bringing household foil into a library using RFID would represent premeditated theft, just as bringing a magnet into a library using EM technology would be.

It is also possible to compromise an RFID system by placing two items against one another so that one tag exactly overlays another. That may cancel out the signals. This requires knowledge of the technology and careful alignment.

Removal of Exposed Tags

3M, which recommends EM for security and RFID for tracking, argues that EM strips are concealed in the spines (30 percent of customers) or the gutters (70 percent of customers) of books and are, therefore, difficult to find and remove; while RFID tags are typically affixed to the inside back cover and are exposed for removal. The author found no evidence of removal in the libraries he visited, nor did any of the library administrators contacted by telephone report a problem. That does not mean that there won't be problems when patrons become more familiar with the role of the tags. Recently, the technology of tags has been improved to make them much thinner and more difficult to detect. The traditional manufacturing method, known as "solder and bond" created a detectable bump because the circuit on the chip attached to the antenna was raised; a latter method known as the "flip chip" fuses the chip onto the antenna, thus reducing the bump so that the tag is thin enough to conceal with a bookplate with a much less noticeable bump. A library can also imprint the RFID tags with its logo and make them appear to be bookplates.

Exit Sensor Problems

While the short-range readers used for circulation charge and discharge and inventorying appear to read the tags 100 percent of the time, the performance of the exit sensors is more problematic. They must read tags at up to twice the distance of the other readers. The author knows of no library that has done a before and after inventory to determine the loss rate when RFID is used for security. Lacking data, one can only conjecture that the performance of exit sensors is better when the antennae on the tags are larger or when the exit lanes are 36 to 42 inches, rather than the 48 inches some libraries specify.

Perceived Invasion of Patron Privacy

There is a perception among some that RFID is a threat to patron privacy. It is argued that the tags contain patron information and/or title information, and that the tags can be read from a distance after someone has taken the materials to home or office.

The vast majority of the tags installed in library materials contain only the item ID, usually the same number that previously has been stored on a barcode. The link between borrower and the borrowed material is maintained in the circulation module of the automated library system, and—unless a library takes the unusual step of retaining patron borrowing histories—is broken when the material is returned. When additional information is stored on the RFID tag, it is limited to information about the item, typically holding location and call number, but rarely author and/or title.

The RFID tags can only be read from a distance of two feet or less because the tags reflect a signal that comes from a reader or sensor and the readers that are available for the frequency range used in library tags are limited in their power to ten watts by law. It is, therefore, not possible for someone to read tags from the street or an office building hallway. In order to read tags from a distance of more than two feet, it would be necessary to greatly enlarge the tags or greatly increase the power of the readers. A library has no reason to purchase larger, more costly tags. An electrical engineer at N.V. Philips in the Netherlands told the author that it would require a high-wattage truck-mounted reader to read the tags used by libraries from a distance of more than ten feet. Such a reader would violate the maximum wattage permitted for readers on the bandwidth used for library tags.

One public library director has suggested that it would be easier to look at the book jackets on the materials a patron was carrying out of the library or down the street than to hack the automated library system to tie a patron and a book together; and very much less expensive than constructing a high-powered reader to ascertain what library patrons had borrowed.

Perceptions, even when mistaken, may have real consequences. The Intellectual Freedom Committee of the American Library Association has responded to concerns about RFID raised by privacy advocates by drafting a set of principles:

- Implement and enforce an up-to-date organizational privacy policy that gives notice and full disclosure as to the use, terms of use, and any change in the terms of use for data collection via new technologies and processes, including RFID.
- Ensure that no personal information is recorded on RFID tags which, however, may contain a variety of transactional data.
- Protect data by reasonable security safeguards against interpretation by any unauthorized third party.
- Comply with relevant federal, state, and local laws as well as industry best practices and policies.
- Ensure that the four principles outlined above must be verifiable by an independent audit.

The Council of the American Library Association adopted these principles on January 19, 2005. The Intellectual Freedom Committee has continued its work and introduced a set of guidelines for RFID use for discussion at the 2006 ALA Midwinter Meeting in San Antonio. Among them, the following are the most significant:

- Libraries should not use RFID systems to track individual library users. Libraries should remove any personally identifiable information from statistical data collected by RFID systems.
- Due to the potential for eavesdropping, libraries should use hardwire connections and not wireless connections for all communications between RFID systems and the ILS involving personally identifiable information.
- Libraries should encrypt information on RFID tags.
- Libraries using "smart cards" should use an "opt-in" system that allows library users to choose between "smart cards" and barcode-enabled cards.

What problem is being addressed? Libraries have not used RFID systems to track individual library users. Patron information is stored only in the integrated library system. The focus should be on the breaking of the link that exists within the integrated library system as soon as an item is returned. Most libraries' RFPs for integrated library systems contain that requirement. Many also specify other security requirements to protect against hacking.

Why limit the concern about wireless to RFID? A patron's need for privacy is far greater when searching the patron access catalog or the Internet.

A library that uses a local area network should require that the network in its entirety be as secure as possible. That can be done using a combination of encryption and fiber optic cable.

The area in which RFID represents the greatest potential threat to patron privacy is the use of the "smart card" as a patron ID card. A "smart card" is an RFID card with encryption. That would make it possible to have the ID card also function as a "debit" card, with value added upon pre-payment to the library and value subtracted when a patron used a photocopier, printer, or other fee-based device, or wished to pay fines or fees. Almost none of the score of RFPs the author has examined include a mandatory requirement for "smart cards." The few that do, ask for that as an option. All stipulate encryption to protect patron privacy. The quality of the encryption is the key to patron privacy.

Because of the attention that has been focused on privacy issues, it is important to educate library staff and patrons about the RFID technology used in libraries before implementing a program. The best way to do that is to emphasize that RFID technology is not one technology, but several. EZ pass is RFID that is meant to be read from a distance. It would be impractical to affix tags of that size and cost to library materials. The same is true of the tags used on pallets in warehouses. The tag type and frequency of tags used in libraries cannot be read from a distance.

Further, a library should stress that it does not store patron information on the tags in library materials, that it protects patron privacy by breaking the link between borrower and material after the material is returned, and that it subscribes to the privacy guidelines in the American Library Association's Code of Ethics.

Several states are considering legislation that would pose restrictions on the use of RFID by retailers and libraries. It is, therefore, important to monitor legislative activity and to be prepared to inform legislators about the differences between retail and library applications, and how libraries protect the privacy of their patrons. Library administrators should be sure to keep their boards informed.

Components of an RFID System

A comprehensive RFID system has two major components: (1) RFID tags that are electronically programmed with unique information; and (2) readers or sensors to interrogate the tags.

Tags

Each paper-thin tag contains an etched antenna and a microchip with a capacity of at least 64 bits. There are three types: "read only," "WORM," and "read/write." Tags are "read only" if the identification is encoded at the time of manufacture and not rewritable. This type of tag contains nothing more than item identification. It can be used for items acquired after the initial implementation of RFID and by libraries that have collections without barcodes. Such tags need not contain any more than 96 bits.

"WORM" (Write-Once-Read-Many)" tags are programmed by the using organization, but without the ability of rewriting them later. They can be used when a retrospective conversion of a collection that is already barcoded is undertaken. The main advantage over read only tags is that information in addition to the identification number can be added. However, it must be information that won't need to be changed. That could be an author and/or truncated title if the tag has enough capacity, but not library location or circulation status. The tags usually have a capacity of at least 256 bits.

"Read/write tags," which are chosen by most libraries, can have information changed or added. For example, a library might add an identification code for each branch. That information could be changed were the holding location subsequently changed. When a vendor includes a "theft" bit that can be turned on and off, the RFID tag can function much like an EM or RF tag. In library RFID, it is common to have part of the read/write tag secured against rewriting, e.g., the identification number of the item. The tags usually have a capacity of at least 1024 bits.

A minimum capacity of 1024 bits is essential if the tags are to be used in electronic inventorying and/or with a materials handling system.

All of the tags used in RFID technology for libraries are "passive." The power to read the tags comes from the reader or exit sensor, rather than from a battery within the tag. "Active" tags, which have their own power supply, are substantially larger and more expensive than the tags used in library RFID applications. It is these active tags that can be read at distances of up to ten feet.

The tags used by most vendors of library RFID are not compatible even when they conform to the same standards because the current standards only seek electronic compatibility between tags and readers. The pattern of encoding information and the software that processes the information differs from vendor to vendor; therefore, a change from one vendor's system to another would require modifying all of the software.

In mid-2007, RFID tags cost an average of $.50, with very large quantities reducing the price by 10 to 15 percent.

Tagging Materials

A library planning on doing its own tagging should consider using volunteers in addition to its regular staff. That reduces both the time and cost of tagging. Only limited training is required, typically 15 to 20 minutes. While there is little choice with regard to the placement of tags on CD/DVDs and videotapes, there are many options for tagging books. It is important to select a consistent location for book tags. The inside of the back cover is the recommended location because it is the fastest for right-handed tag installers to reach. One vendor recommends near the spine approximately three inches above the bottom. That avoids possible interference from metal shelves when inventorying.

However, a library should consider placing the tags inside the front cover under a bookplate or with a bookplate printed on the tag. That may make the tag less apparent and, therefore, improve security.

There is an argument about uniform placement of the tags. 3M suggests that three locations should be selected to reduce the possibility that the tags of two or more books will alight exactly on top of one another and cancel one another out. Other vendors and several librarians who are using RFID say that they have not encountered problems.

Most libraries are not able to tag their entire collections at one time. They must, therefore, plan a phased implementation. A common approach is to convert materials not already tagged when they are being discharged from circulation. While it might seem desirable to do the conversion at the time of charging, that may create a bottleneck during busy periods. Regardless of whether it is done after discharge or as part of the charging process, it will only be a few months before the large majority of circulating items will have RFID tags. If this approach is used, the equipment at the circulation points may have to read both barcodes and RFID tags.

Retrospective conversion requires a "programmer" or "conversion station." The purchase price is $2,500 or more; rental approximately $250 a week. The conversion of existing barcoded items, including affixing the tags to library materials, takes 15–30 seconds per item depending on the amount of information added to the tag and the skill of the person doing the tagging.

Pre-programmed tags, which are used for new acquisitions in libraries that want only identification numbers on the tags, take even less time because they do not involve scanning existing barcodes.

The speed of conversion can be increased by dividing responsibility for removing and replacing library materials, converting the barcodes, and inserting the tags among at least three people. It is essential that the tasks be rotated so that no one repeats the same motions over an extended period of time.

Almost all libraries tag new acquisitions as part of the cataloging process, however, libraries that have experienced losses of unprocessed library materials from technical services, might consider doing the tagging at the time of receipt in acquisitions. While inadvertent duplicates cannot then be returned, it should significantly reduce losses and facilitate tracking of items in technical services.

Readers

A typical system includes several different kinds of readers, also known as sensors when installed at library exits. These are radio frequency devices designed to detect and read tags to obtain the information stored thereon. The reader powers an antenna to generate an RF field. When a tag passes through the field, the information stored on the chip in the tag is decoded by the reader and stored, sent to a server, or communicated to an integrated library system when the RFID system is interfaced with it. When there is no server, most of the software is on the readers, although some may be on a docking station.

The types of readers include conversion stations, staff workstations for circulation desk charging and discharging, patron self-charging and discharging stations, book drop readers, and longer-range walk-through exit sensors to detect and read an RFID tag passage for purposes of determining whether it is a charged (authorized/no alarm) or discharged (non-authorized/alarm) event. The exit sensors are sometimes called "antennae," but that is not correct because an antenna is only one component of an exit sensor. Finally, there is a portable device that consists of a scanning gun attachment to read a group of items on the shelves for purposes of locating missing and misplaced items.

Conversion stations range in price from as little as $2,500 to as much as $3,500. Readers for use at the circulation desk typically cost $2,500 or more each. They can be placed on the circulation counter or built-in. Discharging can be done on the same units, or on one or more dedicated units away from the service counter. Check-in is particularly rapid because the materials can be moved over the unit without regard to the orientation of the material and no conversation with patrons is involved.

Patron self-charging stations are similar to those which have been available for years and are similar in cost, approximately $18,000–22,000. A number of models can support not only conventional barcoded library cards, but also magnetic strip cards and smart cards. Some models can also be used for patron self-discharging. That increases the cost of the unit by at least $3,500. A patron self-charging station can handle a minimum of 20,000 transactions per month.

RFID exit sensors at exits look much like those installed in libraries for the last several decades, however, the insides are very different. One type reads the information on the tag(s) going by and stores that information, communicates it to a server or docking station, or to the integrated library system. If there is a "theft bit," an alarm will be activated and a turnstile gate locked if one or more items have not been properly charged. If a server is used, the server, after checking against the circulation database, activates an alarm if the material is not properly checked-out. The units cost $3,500–7,000 each.

A bookdrop reader can automatically discharge library materials and re-activate security. Since they have already been checked-in, they can go directly back onto the shelves. These units can also be used with a materials handling system, including conveyors and sorters. Bookdrop readers usually are similar to circulation desk readers and cost no more than $3,000 plus the cost of installation into a desk or wall.

ATM-type patron charge/discharge stations cost at least $30,000. When combined with a conveyor and sorter with five or more bins into a materials handling system, the cost rises to a minimum of $75,000. Some large libraries have spent well in excess of $1 million for a materials handling system.

The portable scanner or inventory wand, which is priced at $2,500 or more, can be moved along the items on the shelves without touching them. The data goes to a storage unit ($2,000 or more) which can be downloaded at a docking station or a server later on, or it can go to a unit which will transmit it to the server using wireless technology ($3,000 or more).

Server/Docking Station

A server or docking station may be configured with an RFID system. It is the communications gateway among the various components. It receives the information from one or more of the readers and checks the information against its own database or exchanges information with the circulation database. If the latter, its software includes the APIs (Applications Programming Interface) necessary to interface it with the integrated library system. The server typically includes a transaction database so that reports can be produced. A server costs a minimum of $5,000, plus software. A vendor may choose not to use a server by substituting a less expensive docking station and increasing the amount of software in the readers.

Budgeting for RFID

A small library of 40,000 items should plan on a minimum budget of $46,000 for an RFID system without bookdrop readers, or patron self-charge/discharge. The shopping list would consist of:

40,000 tags @ $.55	$22,000
1 programmer/converter rental (3 weeks)	750
2 staff stations @ $2,500	5,000
2 exit sensors @ $4,000	8,000
1 wireless portable scanner	4,500
222 hours of labor @ $8.00	1,775
Carpentry and electrical	975
Installation and training	3,000

The labor cost assumes a conversion rate of three tags per minute.

A library with 100,000 items interested in patron self-charging and a book drop unit should plan on a minimum budget of $121,310 for an RFID system. The shopping list would consist of:

100,000 tags @ $.50	$50,000
2 programmer/converter rentals (2 months)	4,000
4 staff stations @ $2,500	10,000
1 patron self-charging unit	20,000
2 book drop units @$3,000	6,000
3 exit readers @ $4,000	12,000
2 wireless portable scanners @ $4,500	9,000
556 hours of labor @ $8.00	4,450
Carpentry and electrical	1,360
Installation and training	4,500

The labor cost assumes a conversion rate of three tags per minute.

A library with a collection of 250,000 items interested in patron self-charging and a book drop unit should plan on a minimum budget of $277,000 for an RFID system. The shopping list would consist of:

250,000 tags @ $.50	$137,500
5 programmer/converter rentals (2 months)	10,000
8 staff stations @ $2,500	20,000
2 patron self-charging unit	40,000
3 book drop units	9,000
4 exit readers @ $4,000	16,000
5 wireless portable scanners @ $4,500	22,500
1375 hours of labor @ $8.00	11,000
Carpentry and electrical	5,000
Installation and training	6,000

The labor cost assumes a conversion rate of three tags per minute.

Installations

While there are over 500,000 RFID systems installed in warehouses and retail establishments worldwide, RFID systems are still relatively new in libraries. Approximately 600 contracts had been signed by the middle of 2007. There were approximately 850 facilities using RFID.

Most installations are small, primarily in branch libraries. The University of Connecticut Library, University of Nevada/Las Vegas Library, the Vienna Public Library in Austria, the Catholic University of Leuven in Belgium, and the National University of Singapore Library are among the few sites that appear to have tagged more than 500,000 items each. The most ambitious RFID program is that of the Nederlandse Bibliothek Dienst (Netherlands Library Service). It envisions implementing RFID in all of the public libraries of the country, with an item able to travel among libraries that are equipped to read the tags of all of the books, not just their own. A pilot system was installed at the public library in the city of Eindhoven in 2002, and the first operational system two years later in the public library in the city of Heimlo. The vendor, Nedap N.V. of the Netherlands, uses Tagsys tags, but the equipment is also able to read the tags produced by Philips and Texas Instruments when the appropriate software is used. The deployment of RFID throughout the country is expected to take a minimum of five years. Major Dutch jobbers are now including RFID tags in all library materials purchased from them. Approximately 80 percent of recent acquisitions by Dutch public libraries arrived with RFID tags.

Vendors

There were eight major vendors of RFID systems active in the North American market as of mid-2007: Bibliotheca (www.bibliotheca-rfid.com), Checkpoint (www.checkpointlibrary.com), Information Technology Group (www.integratedtek.com), Libramation (www.libramation.com), Sentry Technology Corporation (www.sentrytechnology.com), Tech Logic (www.Tech-Logic.com), 3M (www.3M.com/us/library), and VTLS (www.vtls.com).

There are several other companies that provide products that work with RFID, including patron self-charging stations and materials handling equipment. A major supplier of patron self-charging stations used by some of the RFID vendors is Optical Solutions (www.opti-sol.com); a major supplier of book drops used by some of the RFID vendors is Birchard (www.birchard.biz); and a major supplier of materials handling products that work with the systems of all of the RFID vendors is Tech Logic (www.tech-logic.com), a company that also sells complete RFID systems.

Differentiation Among RFID Systems

While library RFID systems have a great deal in common with one another, including the use of high-frequency (13.56 MHz), passive, read-write tags, there are some significant differences:

1. An RFID system may be a comprehensive system that addresses both the security and materials tracking needs of a library by replacing both EM strips and barcodes or it may be a part of a hybrid system that uses EM strips for security and RFID for materials tracking. All of the systems currently available are comprehensive RFID systems except for the hybrid system offered by 3M.
2. An RFID system may manage security by using a "theft" bit on the tag that can be turned on or off, or it may interface with an automated library system and query that system to determine the security status.
3. The RFID system tags may contain only an identification number or they may contain considerable additional information, some of which may be permanent and some capable of being rewritten. A 74 or 95 bit tag can accommodate only identification, a 256 bit tag can accommodate a small amount of additional information such as location, and a 1024 or 2048 bit tag can accommodate limited bibliographic information for an item.
4. Some tags have a noticeable bump because they have been produced using "solder and bond" technology, while others have almost no bump because they use the "flip chip" technology that fuses the chip to the antenna.

About the Author

Richard W. Boss, prior to becoming a full-time information systems consultant, was an academic library administrator. His positions have included the directorships of the University of Tennessee and Princeton University Libraries. He has written more than 30 books and hundreds of articles in the past 30 years.

References

Part I: The Public Library Landscape

1. "Public Library Standards and PLA Planning Models," by Greta Southard, Executive Director, Public Library Association, a division of the American Library Association, Chicago, Illinois, 4/21/08.
2. "Characteristics and Trends of Public Libraries in the Public Library Data Service Statistical Report," by Mijung Yoon, Data Analyst, and Lauren Teffeau, Project Coordinator, University of Illinois Urbana-Champaign, Graduate School of Library and Information Science, Center for Informatics Research in Science and Scholarship.
3. "No Easy Targets: Six Libraries in the Economy's Dark Days," by Suzann Holland and Amanda VerPloeg, in *Public Libraries*, 48, no. 4 (July/August 2009).
4. "Forming and Funding Public Library Foundations," by Benjamin Goldberg, in *Forming and Funding Public Library Foundations*, 2nd edition (pp. 5–12). Chicago, IL: Public Library Association, a division of the American Library Association, 2004.

Part II: An Advocacy Mini-Toolkit

5. "Advocacy Basics," by Metropolitan Group with PLA @ Your Library Taskforce, in *Libraries Prosper with Passion, Purpose, and Persuasion! A PLA Toolkit for Success*, Chicago, IL: Public Library Association, a division of the American Library Association, 2007.
6. "Advocate for More: Focus on Legislative Funding," by Stephanie Gerding, in "Bringing in the Money," *Public Libraries*, 46, no. 2 (March/April, 2007): 36–39.
7. "A+ Partners in Education: Linking Libraries to Education for a Flourishing Future," by Valerie J. Gross, in *Public Libraries*, 44, no. 4 (July/August 2005): 217–222.

Part III: Ideas and Tips for Better Directorship

8. "Staffing Public Libraries," by Jeanne Goodrich and Paula M. Singer, in *Human Resources for Results* (pp. 90–112), Chicago, IL: Public Library Association, a division of the American Library Association, 2007.
9. "Leadership and Generosity," by Daniel Walters, in "From the President," *Public Libraries*, 45, no.1 (January/February 2006): 7–8.
10. "Retaining and Motivating High-Performing Employees," by Paula M. Singer and Jeanne Goodrich, in *Public Libraries*, 45, no. 1 (January/February 2006): 58–63.

11. "High-Impact Retention: Retaining the Best and the Brightest," by Jeanne Goodrich and Paula M. Singer, in *Human Resources for Results* (pp. 90–112), Chicago, IL: Public Library Association, a division of the American Library Association, 2007.
12. "Great Expectations: An Interview with Jim Collins," by Lisa Richter, in "Book Talk," *Public Libraries*, 46, no. 1 (January/February 2007): 23–27.
13. "Branch Management: An Analysis of the Minneapolis–St. Paul Area Public Libraries," by Chad Lubbers, in *Public Libraries*, 43, no. 6 (November/December 2004): 341–346.
14. "Getting Your Money's Worth: How to Hire the Right Consultants," by Paula M. Singer and Sandra Nelson, in *Public Libraries*, 43, no. 4 (July/August 2004): 223–225.
15. "The Library Balanced Scorecard," by Joe Matthews, in *Public Libraries*, 45, no. 6 (November/December 2006): 64–71.

Part IV: A Communications Primer for Public Library Directors
16. "Library Communication," by Sandra Nelson, in *Strategic Planning for Results* (pp. 240–254), Chicago, IL: Public Library Association, a division of the American Library Association, 2008.
17. "Identifying Options for Groups," by Sandra Nelson, in *Strategic Planning for Results* (pp. 221–230), Chicago, IL: Public Library Association, a division of the American Library Association, 2008.
18. "Reaching Agreement with Groups," by Sandra Nelson, in *Strategic Planning for Results* (pp. 231–239), Chicago, IL: Public Library Association, a division of the American Library Association, 2008.
19. "Presenting Data," by Sandra Nelson, in *Strategic Planning for Results* (pp. 255–265), Chicago, IL: Public Library Association, a division of the American Library Association, 2008.
20. "Assessing Your Library's Physical Message," by Cheryl Bryan, in *Managing Facilities for Results* (pp. 127–133), Chicago, IL: Public Library Association, a division of the American Library Association, 2007.

Part V. Ideas and Tips for Maintaining Open Access for All
21. "The Importance of Intellectual Freedom Training," by Catherine Lord, in *Defending Access with Confidence: A Practical Workshop on Intellectual Freedom* (p. 103), Chicago, IL: Public Library Association, a division of the American Library Association, 2005.
22. "Intellectual Freedom in Belief and in Practice," by Michael Harkovitch, Amanda Hirst, and Jenifer Loomis, in *Public Libraries*, 42, no. 6 (November/December 2003): 367–374.
23. "Barefoot in Columbus: The Legacy of *Kreimer* and the Legality of Public Library Access Policies Concerning Appearance and Hygiene," by James Kelly, in *Public Libraries*, 45, no. 3 (May/June 2006): 42–49.

Part VI: Ideas and Tips for Reference Services
24. "Reference Services in a Flat World," by Susan Hildreth, in "From the President," *Public Libraries*, 46, no. 1 (January/February 2007): 7–9.
25. "What Is Virtual Reference Anyway?" by Richard W. Boss, in *Tech Notes*, Chicago, IL: Public Library Association, a division of the American Library Association, 8/1/07. Available: www.pla.org/ala/pla/plapubs/technotes/Virtual_reference.pdf.

26. "Ethical Responsibilities and Legal Implications of Providing Health Information," by Barbara Casini and Andrea Kenyon, in *The Public Librarian's Guide to Providing Consumer Health Information* (pp. 29–42), Chicago, IL: Public Library Association, a division of the American Library Association, 2002.
27. "The Realities of Today's Reference Desk," by Sally Decker Smith and Roberta Johnson, in "Reference Desk Realities," *Public Libraries*, 46, no. 1 (January/February 2007): 69–73.

Part VII: A Technology Mini-Primer for Public Librarians
28. "Virtually Seamless: Exploring the Role of Virtual Public Librarians," by Janet Clapp and Angela Pfeil, in *Public Libraries*, 44, no. 2 (March/April 2005): 95–100.
29. "Library Service Planning with GIS and Census Data," by Denice Adkins and Denyse K. Sturges, in *Public Libraries*, 43, no. 3 (May/June 2004): 165–170.
30. "eContent," by Richard W. Boss, in *Tech Notes*, Chicago, IL: Public Library Association, a division of the American Library Association, 8/22/07. Available: www.pla.org/ala/pla/plapubs/technotes/E-content.pdf.
31. "Blogs and Wikis," by Richard W. Boss, in *Tech Notes*, Chicago, IL: Public Library Association, a division of the American Library Association, 3/8/07. Available: www.pla.org/ala/pla/plapubs/technotes/blogswikis.doc.
32. "RFID Technology for Libraries," by Richard W. Boss, in *Tech Notes*, Chicago, IL: Public Library Association, a division of the American Library Association, 8/22/07. Available: www.pla.org/ala/pla/plapubs/technotes/RFID-2007.pdf.

Index

Page numbers followed by the letter "f" indicate figures; those followed by the letter "t" indicate tables.

About the Editor

Kathleen M. Hughes is Manager, Publications, at the Public Library Association, a division of the American Library Association. She also is editor of *Public Libraries*, the journal of the Public Library Association.

About the Public Library Association

With more than 11,000 members, the Public Library Association (PLA) is one of the fastest-growing divisions of the American Library Association—the oldest and largest library association in the world. Founded in 1944, PLA is a member-driven organization that provides advocacy, communication, programming, and publication support for its members and others interested in the advancement of public library service. More information about PLA is available at www.pla.org.